D0175453

CFO Survival Guide

Plotting the Course to
Financial Leadership

CATHERINE STENZEL
&
JOE STENZEL

WILEY

John Wiley & Sons, Inc.

Library of Congress Cataloging-in-Publication Data:

ISBN 0-471-26914-X

Printed in the United States of America.

10 9 8 7 6 5 4 3 2 1

This book is dedicated to Alvaro Mutis and Maqroll the Gaviero for the resonance of their unforgettable lessons about what counts in life.

Contents

Foreword

The traditional responsibilities of the chief financial officer and the finance function—keeping the "books," safeguarding corporate assets, and meeting regulatory requirements—remain in full force. Descriptors like "compliance" and "transactions" apply to these longstanding roles. Invoices have to be paid, results consolidated, and audits performed. What has changed over time, however, is the complexity of these tasks. A burgeoning tax code, new accounting regulations, globalization, value arising from intangible versus fixed assets, and Sarbanes-Oxley are but a few of the contributing factors.

In addition to the increased complexity of the traditional roles and responsibilities, the charter of finance practitioners is expanding dramatically. The new paradigm is connectivity with the business. The strategic direction of the company needs to be set, issues and opportunities identified and acted upon, and products and services responsive to client demands provided. The finance function can play an integral role in advancing these critical requirements. Descriptors like "vision," "leadership," "strategy," and "partner" need to be added to the characterization of the finance function. In the *CFO Survival Guide,* Joe and Catherine Stenzel aptly emphasize that "the call for the CFO to transform into a strategic business partner has intensified from a suggestion to a nonnegotiable demand."

Delivering on this dramatically expanded charter remains a work in progress for most finance organizations. A survey by the Executive Board's Working Council for Chief Executive Officers found that 58 percent of finance resources are allocated to transaction processing and compliance/control. Surveyed financial executives, however, are looking to significantly redeploy resources to activities consistent with those of a strategic business partner such as growth stewardship and business unit support. By 2008, transaction processing and compliance/control activities are forecast to make up only 28 percent of finance's resource allocation.

Given that corporations' senior management and diverse clientele are providing the demand for these new roles and responsibilities, why isn't the supply keeping pace? Quite simply, the CFO and finance practitioners need to acquire and apply a new set of competencies and skill sets. Being technically proficient is still of paramount importance, but it is not nearly enough. In the *CFO Survival Guide,* the Stenzels detail the new requisites clearly.

A key theme of the *CFO Survival Guide* is the fact that businesses are social structures—an amalgam of people and personalities. The sequestered finance function of the past working in its own independent sphere of operation will no longer be successful. To facilitate change and foster strategic decision-making, the CFO and finance organization must be able to engage effectively the denizens of this corporate society: employees, investors, suppliers, customers, regulators, and so forth.

This mandate prompts the question, "How?" The *CFO Survival Guide* provides a host of practical courses of action. One area of emphasis is the criticality of "understanding the business." I am a strict adherent of this tenet. Pfizer's leadership goes through an annual exercise of identifying those areas of focus that are of the greatest import to the company and each of our lines of business. These strategic imperatives provide a key input to finance's planning process. The strategic imperatives of Pfizer Inc. are the strategic imperatives of Pfizer's finance function.

Another enabler discussed in detail in the *CFO Survival Guide* is the need for the CFO to personally develop and to sponsor the organization's development. Again, I have seen the enormous dividends that stem from this investment. By providing employees with different work experiences or views, for example, the previously cited goals of managing the social aspects of the organization and expanding the knowledge of the business are advanced. The employee's expanding of his or her skills sets and network is also personally rewarding and stimulating. Personal and colleague development is the consummate win–win. Little wonder that talent planning is another Pfizer Inc. strategic imperative.

I have cited just a few examples of the provocative framework that the *CFO Survival Guide* provides to assess and further the CFO's and his/her organization's metamorphosis to strategic business partner. Although the CFO's vantage point effectively qualifies that person to serve in this partnering role, it is not an inalienable right. Assuming or retaining this charter is predicated on execution. The effort is a daunting but highly rewarding one.

David L. Shedlarz
Chief Financial Officer
Pfizer Inc.

Preface

Remember who you are. You are an accountant. The official title you hold within the financial profession—controller, chief financial officer, financial director, finance vice president, and so on—may make you feel like more than *just* an accountant, but that's because you haven't stopped lately to appreciate what an accountant really is. Accountants have good reason to be proud. Unfortunately, corporate events in the first years of this new century have put the basis for that pride at risk. The cracked foundation of the accounting profession shifts with the aftershocks. When a profession loses its footing and understanding of itself, when the people in the profession must grapple with doubt, and when the profession's reason for being is publicly questioned, that profession travels uncharted territory. In such terrain, confusion is the natural reaction. Confusion is a healthy state because it heightens awareness and motivates the search for solutions. Yet, accountants, by nature, abhor confusion; they prefer being the ones with the answers. This, too, is good news because the profession will not rest until the air is clear and things are set right.

As financial officers reassess themselves and their profession, they must simultaneously continue to lead their organizations and carry on with the business of the day as fiduciary officers in the fullest sense of that word. Business decisions can't wait for the profession to sort itself out. Financial officers can't hesitate and second-guess themselves while accounting rules and principles slowly reshape. The CFO cannot allow inner uncertainties to impact accomplishing daily leadership responsibilities; organizations never stop needing care and direction. That's what leaders are for: to attend to sustaining the life of the organization and its people. The *CFO Survival Guide* provides fiduciary officers with methods and principles to draw clear depictions of existing and desired conditions. Within the organizational context, the *Guide* assists the financial professional in precisely identifying appropriate leadership competencies that enable organizational progress. Underlying this leadership presence, the *Guide* helps the CFO to articulate unambiguous, fundamental ethical values based on principles of human well-being, accountability, and integrity. To accomplish all this, these pages explore the answers to two root questions.

- First, *what does it mean to be a good accountant?* Most people now accept that the answer goes far beyond the mechanics of closing the books and delivering the financial statements.

- Second, *what does it take to be a great chief financial officer?* This question requires significantly more deliberation, but the "more" remains grounded in good accounting and in unwavering dedication to transparent accountability.

PEOPLE AND THE WORK THEY DO

Succinctly, the primary purpose of the *CFO Survival Guide* is to help you to become a superior financial officer through improved understanding of the web of interdependent relationships that compose any workplace. You are the one everybody else looks to for answers, but who helps you answer your own questions? You are already a technical expert in accounting, and probably finance, or you would not occupy (or be aiming for) the CFO chair. Expert voices on professional development within the accounting profession now acknowledge that technical competence is C-student work at best, and not a key professional differentiator. Therefore, these chapters refer to technical subjects only as necessary and do not intend to boost your debit-and-credit or your regression-analysis IQ. Rather, the *Guide*'s central intent is to help you better understand the most essential aspect of your work life: your *relationships* with the CEO and with your peer executives, with your staff, and with the people who make up the organization at large, its customers, suppliers, and community constituents. When all is said and done, people and the work they do together are all there is, and are therefore the priorities of the CFO.

To underscore the point about relationships, you know something new is in the air when business consultants and software developers begin offering their best attempts to fill a perceived gap in the needs of the marketplace. So, whether or not a particular method will last, we are seeing the likes of customer relationship management (CRM), business-to-business (B2B) and peer-to-peer (P2P) applications, as well as an assortment of governance consulting paradigms. Likewise, the last two decades have witnessed a groundswell of research and education in *leadership*—a word preceded by any number of adjectives, such as results-based, primal, and principle-centered. The search is on to understand—and measure—the competencies a leader must possess to assure useful contributions to the company.

Other intangibles such as brand value and customer intimacy, to name just two, are also objects of serious study. Much fine work has already been done to articulate, codify, and apply in practice these recently perceived aspects of business life. Please notice the elements not listed as pivotal: Financial Accounting Standards Board (FASB) pronouncements on stock options and special-purpose entities (more recently dubbed "variable interest entities"), the virtual close, the Securities and Exchange Commission's valiant work in defending investor interests, better budgets, or more information technology (IT) investments. Although obviously in play, these concepts and their ilk are not the essential factors in organizational well-being and longevity.

Many economists and finance theoreticians think of business organizations as one big mathematical model with norms and rules, but people like you, doing real work every day, see concerns more comprehensively based on concrete matters like worthy competitors, the loss or gain of good employees, and cash in the bank. Everything that really counts is rooted in relationships, and for that reason every CFO must become a student of human development and behavior. In their quest for more predictive mathematical models, economists and financial theorists have eschewed the study of ethics in favor of cause-effect equations, which hasn't helped. Developing "equations" for an operative ethical perspective is far more ambitious than the physical math of money and things. Perhaps the worst offenders are those people who have built shareholder maximization models outside a moral context. Quantitative models without the balance of the qualitative dimensions of human relationships get people in trouble every time. Count on it.

WHAT YOU SAY COUNTS

As a financial professional, you already have a well-developed sense of fairness and accountability, as well as keen intuitions about the business world beyond your accounting doorstep. You are concerned about the stability of business and the marketplace. You know what gives integrity to financial statements, and you know how to deal with ethical dilemmas. What you may not realize is just how much your work shapes the future and form of your organization and business in general. What you make visible through your words, your reports, and your analyses, and where you spend your time mold the very direction and routines of work, and enhances or deflates your organization's view of itself. What *you* report creates visual patterns that quantifiably display success and failure for groups and individuals. What *you* emphasize greatly influences others' perspectives and behavior. Marketing and operations may appear to garner all the attention, but *you* deliver the final accounting of their efforts. Accounting is the language of business, and the work of financial professionals manifests the very self-image and identity an organization lives by, colors the stories it tells about itself, and sustains the cultural myths it reveres.

Take, for example, the myth of growth, usually defined as increases in sales or revenue. Like oncologists, CFOs know growth is not always a good thing, for instance when growth targets drive dysfunctional behavior, glut the market, and lead to fraudulent financial reporting. What about the myth of innovation? Questioning the necessity of newer, better, faster, cheaper is practically sacrilegious. Once again, CFOs know the truth: Innovation has, at best, mixed results. CFOs know a great deal about such myths, and they readily see associations and impacts among disparate variables. Sometimes you, the CFO, know more and see more than the CEO, but this knowledge is of little value unless you have affirmative, productive answers to two questions: (1) Have you told the CEO (and appropriate others) what you see and know? and (2) What have you actually done to test your insights and to lead necessary improvements?

You are ambitious and honest, and you want to understand how to work best with your CEO and to comprehend what you are actually expected to do: by your staff, your peers, your board—and, again, your CEO. As your company's CFO or other senior finance executive, you are the person who has responsibility for the accounting and finance functions, at least, and probably more—typically, a lot more: human resources, risk management, mergers and acquisitions, and information technology, to name a few. You may also be the de facto controller and spend a great deal of time number crunching, or you may be a controller who is the de facto CFO, and who is expected to think and act beyond the constraints of financial abstractions.

Still, remember those two questions: What makes a good accountant? What makes a great CFO? Many parallel questions touch on these two: What does a CEO really want from a CFO? What do you really want out of your work? What kind of CFO are you now? Command-and-control conventional? Adept and fearless? Based on who you are now, who are you likely to become? Who will you become if you deliberately set out to continually expand and enhance yourself? What and who count the most? When do *you* count? What are the measures of value used to determine who and what count? These questions are the kinds that matter, and they are the inquiries of the *CFO Survival Guide.*

COMMON THREADS OF COMMON SENSE

Four consistent emphases run throughout the *CFO Survival Guide*: Human development, leadership, ethical behavior, and interdependent relationships. Except for leadership, these themes are not the usual fare of business books. "Development," defined in the context of scientific frameworks such as cognition, needs, moral maturity, and self-identity, rarely makes their pages.★ "Leadership," in contrast, is a frequent visitor to the business press; however, the concept is too often treated in isolation from concrete, actual workday operations. "Ethical behavior," likewise, has usually been treated separately, and of all business topics (until just lately) probably received the least attention. Recent events have pulled the whiskers of this tiger, but other events (a war, economic conditions in the doldrums) seem to have distracted the noble beast. The final thread, "interdependent relationships," simply describes the real conditions in which business—and all of us—actually exist. Financial abstractions are not the realities they seek to portray. The *CFO Survival Guide* takes these four critical aspects and places them where they belong—woven throughout the tapestry of organizational life. That's only common sense.

Consider more closely development and ethical behavior, the two perspectives that have received minimal attention in the business literature. Like so many important words—strategy, tactics, vision, system, ethics, love, in-law—the word "development" means different things to different people. "Change," "growth," "progress," "expansion," "maturation," and "evolution" are commonly used interchangeably with "development." Of these related words, only development consistently implies *value being created within a learning process* as an integral component of its meaning. The *Guide* utilizes two established human development patterns: the moral subsystem and the psychosocial subsystem. Interestingly, ethical behavior resides substantively within the moral perspective of human development. Stages of moral development have been heavily studied, yet studies of ethics principles and moral behavior have been minor players on the business stage. As this book is written, everyone agrees that we all need a refresher course in ethics. The *CFO Survival Guide* goes further and gives ethics appropriate prominence by examining ethical considerations within daily decision making, not as a separate, esoteric study.

Next reflect on leadership, a theme that has frequented the business press for some time. As the flood of management hot topics rises and recedes, leadership keeps bobbing to the surface. A sizeable body of work has been done on the subject, not the least of which is Daniel Goleman's longitudinal research and

---

★Readers interested in development may also want to read the authors' prior work, *From Cost to Performance Management* (Hoboken, N.J.: John Wiley & Sons, 2003).

modeling of emotional intelligence (EI) competencies. The four-quadrant EI model provides a platform for the *Guide*'s exploration of CFO leadership. We all instantly recognize leadership when we are in its presence, and we certainly know when it is lacking. But how does great leadership arise? To most people, this remains a mystery. This mystification is due, in part—as is the case with ethics—to the treatment of leadership as a separate subject, as if finding example bits of it and sewing the scraps together into a patchwork robe transforms the person who wears it. The big, statistically validated news is that *no separation exists between great leaders and their organizations.* They develop interdependently over time, which becomes abundantly clear in the chapters ahead and does not mesh with the modus operandi of some highly visible CFOs who change jobs more often than undecided undergraduates switch majors. These people are not leaders, but greedy executives who stay with an organization just long enough to satisfy personal career and monetary objectives.

The model of the day seems decidedly short-term, and not only in CFO careers. This outlook hardly bodes well for long-term value creation of any kind. The one thing a CFO must do is to attend to values that contribute to organizational health and longevity. Unfortunately, the word "value" has devalued in the last decade. Sad to say, too many executives believe shareholder—or even worse, personal—wealth equates to value. In truth, shareholder and executive wealth results from myriad priceless sparks of individual human energy joining forces to sustain their own and their organizations' lives. The vitality of share price—in the long term—relies on human work. A large portion of the twenty-first-century CFO's responsibility is to make this visible.

Interdependence, the fourth common thread, can be observed in the principles of ecosystems and living entities. This perspective gives a whole new meaning to short-term/long-term investments and returns. Business planning frequently suffers from the same faulty perspective as ethics. Components of a corporation are dealt with in isolation as if they were mechanical parts, separate and replaceable. Few companies have developed a perspective that allows simultaneous attention to short-term activities and long-term, sustainable conditions. Even fewer companies can articulate the short-term and long-term elements in the dynamic mix of business variables. Despite ignorance, time passes, and the elusive short-term transforms inexorably into the long-term. To ignore interdependencies makes about much sense as believing that every person is an island. Sustainable value for all stakeholders is created day after day, with a healthy sense of direction.

Development, leadership, business, and life in general are best approached via "iterative improvement." It's a lot more fun that way. Ethics, however, is not iterative by nature. Here we must err on the side of caution. Mistakes in this dimension are visible, offensive, and very hard to make right. Here cause and effect do rule, and in the short or long term, one cannot escape the consequences of one's behavior. The fact that to err is human does not exonerate anyone's unethical appropriation of real value, the unprincipled use of real resources, or the disregard for the well being of real people.

BEING THE ONE WHO COUNTS

Everyone expects accountants to have precise, accurate answers. Accountants expect this of themselves. Even so, the general public has recently been disturbed to find out how imprecise and malleable accounting actually is in practice. Only individual CFOs, one decision and action at a time, can cultivate trust, whether in the public eye or eyeball-to-eyeball with one employee. Trust is earned through information transparency, consistency, and clarity, and with a constant concern for the good of the whole.

Accountants naturally want to see, to know and to understand. They dislike saying, "This is a rough estimate." Even more unpalatable is the statement, "I don't know." As distasteful as it may be, this I-don't-know statement is an important one for accountants (and everybody else) to become facile with, because it is the entry point to exploration, discovery, and greater understanding. We can all feel comforted that no one knows for certain what to do next, in the accounting profession at large, as the financial officer for an organization, or in the next day of life as a human being. Like accounting itself, finding the right answers is a process of trial and error, whether the focus is a business decision or a career choice. Think of this iterative approach as a trial balance for repeatedly closing (i.e., integrating) the books (i.e., the experiences) on an old, valuable era, and opening the next period of life—the life of the business or your own. No doubt adjusting entries will be necessary, and mistakes found, but that too is a familiar human process.

If you are reading these words, you have already chosen the path of continuous personal and professional development. You probably have not used the word "development." Curiosity, drive, even hope, may have been the conscious motivation for you to open these pages. The *CFO Survival Guide* may have caught your eye because you are frustrated with working with financial numbers, as if they were the only reality that counts. Perhaps you are in the market for a new job or just running hard to keep the one you have. Maybe you have tried so many unsatisfactory projects and incentive schemes that you have finally understood that *relationships* and human beings—messy and unpredictable as they are—make or break a business. Whatever the reason that you have given this book some of your precious time, you did so for at least two reasons: First, you want to learn and develop, and thereby positively influence people and organizations. Second, you want to be a good—maybe even great—leader, an ethical leader, a leader who really counts. We invite you to begin.

Joe and Catherine Stenzel
Beltrami Island State Forest, Minnesota
July 2003

Acknowledgments

The authors wish to acknowledge the following people for the role they played in shaping this book:

Marjorie Kelly, author of *The Divine Right of Capital,* for her eloquence in articulating the necessary (r)evolution in corporation form, legal status, and service to the public. Her work particularly influenced the "Declaration of Interdependence" in Chapter 6.

H. Thomas Johnson, author of *Profit Beyond Measure,* for his courage in calling for, and demonstration of potential workplace transformation through use of natural systems principles.

David Shedlarz, CFO of Pfizer Inc., for being the kind of CFO and leader this book is all about.

Tim Burgard, Wiley editor and valued partner, for his belief in our work and his patience and trust as we charted this new territory.

Executive Summary

The *CFO Survival Guide* is organized in terms of the key relationships that every financial officer must navigate and understand to survive (stay in the career) and, more importantly, to thrive (find enjoyment) in chosen work. The trial-and-error path to such career fulfillment is iterative and developmental, requiring the accumulation of many small victories over technical form and over self, all in the interest of successfully collaborating with others. To profit most from the *Guide* requires openness to thinking about organizations in the context of human development and natural systems principles in addition to the current, dominant financial symbolism.

The first chapter takes stock of the accounting and finance profession through discussion of "Who We Were, Who We Are, and Who We Are Becoming." This initial chapter asks the reader to assess the persistent clarion call to become a strategic partner, and to analyze the underlying assumptions governing the work of a CFO who really counts in organizational health and longevity.

Chapter 2 puts in context the necessary technical/functional skills and the required experiential knowledge, and then begins to explore a professional's relationship to self. The chapter introduces the fundamentals of the science of human development and uses research-validated findings to shape perspective on the maturity of personal work competencies. The discussion utilizes two established human development patterns: the moral subsystem and the psychosocial subsystem. Although taken from the behavioral sciences, the discussion stays on track within the concreteness of CFO and corporate perspectives. The choice of moral development should be obvious in this Sarbanes–Oxley era; however, the *Guide* considers moral maturity well beyond the current focus on honest financial reporting to investors. The morally mature CFO attends to all organizational stake-holders, especially to the people who do the actual work of producing products and delivering services. The psychosocial developmental subsystem, with its emphasis on relationships with others, charts maturity pathways through trust, autonomy, productivity (industry), and identity, and warns of parallel pathologies: mistrust, shame/doubt, inferiority, and role confusion.

Chapter 3 puts these fundamentals to work in the only context they can be observed: the CFO in relationship to other individuals and groups. The well-known set of emotional intelligence leadership competencies, developed and validated by Daniel Goleman and others, structures the investigation of mature CFO influence and effectiveness. The discussion pinpoints the personal/professional competencies necessary for mature leadership, and guides the CFO in developing and sustaining these capacities.

With the fundamentals established for individual professional development, Chapter 4 finds the CFO on the accounting/finance home ground, working with the accounting/finance staff. This chapter details a practical assessment of the function and purpose of the office of the CFO, and carefully examines both the internal operations of the function and the practicalities of sustaining relationships throughout the company. Coverage of the internal aspects range from replacing oneself, to developing individual staff members, to forging a group identity known for its can-do energy. The chapter leaves no doubt about how to assess internal and external relationships, and includes thorough, hands-on evaluation instruments constructed around specific financial and cost accounting tasks, as well as performance measurement and process improvement. CFOs who use the assessments in practice and apply developmental findings are likely to make impressive strides in enhancing the status of the accounting/finance function.

Whereas Chapter 4 follows the CFO in day-to-day relationships with functional staff and with the operations side of the organization, Chapter 5 finds the finance chief performing the work of executive corporate governance in the interest of all major stakeholders. This chapter concretely illustrates how the CFO can strengthen the heart of executive presence by becoming a leader of leaders. The discussion provides clear guidelines for the CFO in establishing long-term working relationships with other executives and managers based on governance processes, the actual work of governance, and the development of the necessary leadership competencies. Extensive examination of five interdependent governance alliances builds a twenty-first-century governance structure with the CEO-CFO alliance as the cornerstone. The conceptual aspects of governance take on a new concreteness with three more assessments that help the CFO to discover the current state of corporate governance, and the work and leadership needed to progress beyond the status quo.

Chapter 6 extends the work, presence, and influence of the CFO into the next corporate evolution: the democratic workplace. This final chapter pulls together all the relationship competencies discussed in prior chapters and step by step puts them to work creating a meaningful and sustainable life for people and their organizations, while in parallel the chapter reestablishes the original purpose of corporate charters: serving the public good.

Chief financial officers have the opportunity to be honored as working-class heroes under the current conditions of professional crisis and corporate survival efforts. Responding to the emergency requires courage, risk-taking, and stepping into the unknown, one day, and one person at a time. The *CFO Survival Guide* travels well beyond mere survival for the CFO, and provides guidelines for an entirely new and more realistic way of seeing organizations, the people in them, and the work of stepping each day into the stream of human relationships that provide the energy to accomplish all work that really counts.

Publisher's note: Many CFOs also serve as chief information officers, oversee information technology functions, or work with a peer CIO. A partner volume, the *CIO Survival Guide* written by Dr. Karl Schubert with Joe and Catherine Stenzel, is available from John Wiley & Sons.

About the Web Site

A s a purchaser of *CFO Survival Guide: Plotting the Course to Financial Leadership,* you have access to the companion Web site to find more detailed information on many of the topics discussed in this book. Each chapter identifies additional supportive text and interactive exhibits that can be found on the Web site. Look for the www. symbol within the text and on exhibits. Specifically, text features focus on barriers and accelerators for CFO careers and on important CFO alliances within the organization and the CFO community outside the organization. Exhibits on the Internet allow readers to interact with their content so that self-assessment and diagnostic tools can be used and reused many times or simply copied for use with others in the workplace. To access the Web site, go to www.wiley.com/go/cfosurvivalguide. The password to access the files is "CFO".

FEATURES

Barriers and Accelerators: Making Room in the Fiduciary Workload★ (Chapter 1)

Alliances: Building Cross-Functional Relationships with an Emphasis on IT★ (Chapter 2)

Barriers and Accelerators: Time and Workload★ (Chapter 2)

Barriers and Accelerators: Emotional Incontinence★ (Chapter 3)

Alliances: Write the Story of your Before and After Emotional Profile★ (Chapter 3)

Barriers and Accelerators: Internal Promotions: We Know Who You Are★ (Chapter 4)

A Declaration of Interdependence (Chapter 6)

EXHIBITS AND DIAGNOSTICS

Dialogue Generated CFO Capabilities, Exhibit 2.2

Subsystems of Human Development, Exhibit 2.3

Emotional Intelligence Competency Sets, Exhibit 3.3

Domains of the Human Workplace, Exhibit 3.4

AFF Structure and CFO Responsibility, Exhibit 4.1

CFO Maturity "Quick Grid", Exhibit 4.2

CFO Roles and Professional Development, Exhibit 4.3

AFF Responsibility Diagnostic, Exhibit 4.4

AFF General Business Responsibilities Diagnostic, Exhibit 4.5

AFF Cost Management Responsibility Diagnostic, Exhibit 4.6

AFF Inventory Audit and Budget Responsibility Diagnostic, Exhibit 4.7

AFF Financial Responsibility Diagnostic, Exhibit 4.8

CEO–CFO Relationship Diagnostic, Exhibit 5.4

Executive Counsel Diagnostic, Exhibit 5.5

CFO Governance Roles Diagnostic, Exhibit 5.6

ASSESSMENT CHECKLISTS

Assessment Checklist (Chapter 2)

Emotional Intelligence Leadership Competency Assessment (Chapter 3)

AFF Assessment Checklist (Chapter 4)

GUIDELINES FOR DIAGNOSTIC USE AND CUSTOMIZATION OF EXHIBITS 5.4, 5.5, AND 5.6*

*Denotes material that appears only on the URL. All other material can be found in the text in addition to the URL.

CHAPTER 1

The Profession and the Reality

There remains the final reflection, how shallow, puny, and imperfect are efforts to sound the depths in the nature of things. In philosophical discussion, the merest hint of dogmatic certainty as to finality of statement is an exhibition of folly.

Alfred North Whitehead[1]

The use of abstract quantitative targets in the practice of "managing by results" [MBR] entails "losing touch" with the natural reality of the organizations we manage. These quantitative abstractions cause us to see the organization as a mechanistic system. We thereby believe that these abstractions can be used as tools to "amplify our grasp of the world." Unfortunately this belief ignores the reality that a human organization is a living system which can be understood and acted in only as a web of relationships, not as a mechanical collection of quantifiable parts. By ignoring that reality, MBR managers erroneously attempt to control financial results by focusing people's attention on quantitative targets. They fail to see that good results in a living system are achieved only by nurturing relationships.

H. Thomas Johnson, Anders Bröms[2]

The accounting profession has encountered the opportunity to remake itself as the result of the fall from grace of many people. After enduring grave adversity, the conditions are ripe to reshape and rebuild from what remains. The media did their part by generously publicizing the deeds of guilty executives and the unscrupulous accounting practices that enabled their performance. Congress has begun its work with passage of the 2002 Sarbanes-Oxley Act. Accounting associations, too, continue their work of repair and renewal. The profession is in a time of identity discovery, and the nature and shape of that identity remain nascent. Every accountant must ask who are we now that this has happened to us. Good news attends this time of survival. Survival often brings out the best in those who are already strong. This CFO Survival Guide intends to assist the profession in its endeavors, but the Guide's primary purpose is to serve individual chief financial officers in identifying old designs that no longer work, and new, promising patterns worth exploration.

The *Guide* depicts a healthy and positive way of looking at organizational life that reflects the good that already exists and the greater good work that is possible. Behavior without integrity, greedy people, and inadequate accounting principles are mentioned briefly and only when necessary to compare and contrast to a better way. The depiction of what may be is evolutionary and developmental, concentrating on the two fundamentals of any organization: people and the work they do together. The discussion intentionally omits such items as the squabbling over rules for financial instruments and the window-dressing of executive certification requirements. The themes and content turn toward the places where actual people make products and perform services, offering a revitalizing perspective on how organizations are created and sustained.

Appropriately, this work is seen from the perspective of the nonpartisan chief financial officer (CFO), the leader whose primary job is accountability for all facets of the organization, with particular emphasis on long life and health for the enterprise. These CFOs build what lasts. Those who are in the game for the short-term gain will, like the earnings they manipulate, dwindle and disappear soon enough.

Throw stones at this discussion if you will, but remember where you saw it, in case you need it later. The images and patterns of this prototype provide the CFO with a more complete way of seeing. The more the CFO is capable of seeing, the more certain is the well-being of the enterprise. Eventually, only CFOs who know how to see more will matter. Eventually, the rest will not survive. Not only CFO survival, but organizational sustainability depends on this kind of long-term evolutionary exploration.

Picking up this book reveals that you are consciously thinking about change and personal development. If your business card currently reads "controller" or one of a number of synonymous titles, you may be thinking about transitioning to the top finance position. If you are already a CFO, you may be considering a change because you remain restless, even now, in the profession's top position. Sitting in a meeting—subject unimportant—that nagging question shimmers into your awareness again: *Is this it?* The "it" in question takes many forms and is always intimately personal. *Is this . . . the right job for me? The right company for me? The best I can do for my family? The best I can do for my career? Good for my health? Is this where I thought I would be by now? Is this where and who I want to be for the rest of my life?*

Human beings are insatiably curious by nature. That curiosity is satisfied to some degree by the innate impermanence of the human condition that makes change continuous. That's part of being alive. The distinguishing factor between a life well lived, or not, is the degree of a person's participation in making the endless choices and extracting meaning out of the rapid, continual rush of new information. Sometimes, however, we are more acutely aware of the winds or storms of change. Recent events in corporations, in the accounting profession, and in the volatile world at large call for more acute sensitivity to what is happening, and how each of us can contribute. Conditions at this time offer each professional a good point from which to begin making personal choices and deciding how to participate in the emergent professional evolution.

AN ACCOUNT OF THE PROFESSION

Let's begin with a story about how accountants saw themselves and their peers not so very long ago. Many years ago, one of the authors served as a corporate controller overseeing seven division controllers in the United States and Canada. At one point in time, four of the seven division controller positions were open and needed to be filled with experienced people. All four division general managers stated clearly that they wanted controllers who were "operations friendly," which meant that they wanted someone who could help them solve business problems as well as keep the books straight. Soon, several hundred applications arrived, each representing a human being who wanted to be considered for one of the jobs. Several dozen interviews were conducted at various locations. The process was depressing, and at the end of the first round of interviews, only two positions were filled. Four more months and two more rounds of interviews were needed to fill the other two positions. The reason: Lack of operations friendliness in the candidate pool.

Almost every candidate had plenty of bookkeeping experience. Many had other specialized financial experience—tax, audit, budget analysis, inventory forecasting, and management. Approximately half of the applicants had over fifteen years of experience, yet were involuntarily out of work. Most did not know exactly why they had been let go. They were all good people trying to make a living with their hard-earned accounting skills. Most did not understand why month after month they were not getting a new job. All but four of the hundreds could not satisfactorily explain what it meant when a general manager used the term "operations friendly." The ones not hired made reasoned, energetic guesses: assuring accurate inventory counts, getting paychecks delivered on time, and being able to explain the transactions underlying manufacturing variances. These were honest answers from bedrock accountants, and they did not have a clue about the skills they were missing.

When a budding accountant learns about the early-thirteenth-century Italian origins of double-entry bookkeeping, there is good reason to pause for thought. Should we still be using a system *that* old? Usually, accountants prefer to see the debit-credit logic as ancient and venerable. Surely something that has been around that long has to work. These ancient roots are part of the reason that most people think that accounting has always been the way it is today, and why they believe that its reporting consistently portrays the truth. How could it be otherwise? Like ketchup and money, and all other ubiquitous cultural accessories, accounting is so much a part of life that few stop to question it or its current primacy in business.

Imagine, for a moment, a world without accounting. No annual reports, no bank statements, no paychecks, and no stock certificates—all the result of various accounting procedures. How would any of us know what we owned if not for accounting? How could any business explain its performance? How could any government tax its citizens? The reach of accounting is vast and intimidating. Most people can hardly imagine themselves without it, even though they may never understand its techniques and secrets. The monetary aspect of current civilization will not likely disappear any time soon, although its demise is already portrayed in works of fiction like *Star Trek*. Assuming that money remains the preferred method of exchange for the near future, accounting will continue to play its role: letting us all know who owns what, who earned what, and how much cash we have in our bank accounts.

So, what is accounting that it has such a pervasive influence? First and foremost, accounting is a language. The revolutionary linguist Noam Chomsky once posited that the universal presence of language in humans originates from a "language organ" that all normal people have. Of course, he was speaking of languages such as Spanish, Finnish, and Greek. In the language of accounting, the vocabulary and syntax reflect money and time concepts. Learning the lexicon of the double-entry world is essential for all business professionals, because as it is commonly said, accounting is the language of business.

The logic and emphasis of each language represents a particular view of reality, especially what is worth paying attention to. But not all languages are equal. At one time, French dominated international parlance. Now English does. Dialects are generally viewed as inferior to the mainstream speech. Why is this so? The place of a language in the linguistic hierarchy is largely determined by the power of the social group that uses it. The same holds true for the language of accounting and finance, which currently dominates business discourse.

As we shall see, other words are better suited for communicating and for understanding the work and lives of human beings. Consider the differences, if instead of monetary terms, all organizations used human and environmental linguistic frameworks to describe themselves—for instance, performance in terms of levels of pollution, deforestation rates, and employee well-being. The purpose of this alternative view is not to be *for* the environment and *against* money. Such polar thinking creates circular paradoxes. The point is to become aware of the pervasive-ness of accounting language as it is used to describe who we are and what we do when we humans band together in business organizations.

Business and commerce have always been profit-oriented. Even not-for-profits must break even to continue their good works. This is commonsense accounting. Unlike CFOs, however, many businesspeople make only marginal distinctions be-tween the two primary branches of accounting: financial and management. Per-haps not even most CFOs who are less than fifty years old know that management accounting is a relative neophyte, coming to prominence only in the 1950s. Fur-thermore, only as recently as the 1970s did the work of researchers such as H. Thomas Johnson and Alfred D. Chandler Jr. demonstrate that before World War II neither financial nor management accounting, as they exist today, were the primary management information repositories.

As accepted today, accounting may have ancient ancestors, but its current-practice roots are shallow. Before World War II, business professionals generally relied on more concrete numbers directly related to the means of production. Op-erations overhead was a small part of total cost; thus analysts focused on living la-borers and physical materials—the components of actual work. For the most part, the "analysts" were not accountants, but people experienced in operations. Many forces converged to change this situation, among them the imposition of federal income taxes, the proliferation of securities regulations, and the increasing reliance of economists on mathematical models. Arguably, this last phenomenon also caused business academics to rely more and more on abstract quantitative models to represent business practices, in contrast to viewpoints based on the phys-ical elements of work. In the midst of all this, the accounting profession flourished, for better or worse. The key point here is that the last half of the twentieth century witnessed a shift in the language that businesspeople used to describe their priori-ties and the purposes of their work—a shift from actual people and materials to mathematical models.

The Great Depression was another historical event that carved deep imprints on accounting and Western society at large. Everything seemed to be out of control. Good, hard-working people became destitute. Banks and capital markets reeled in the chaos. People were stunned at what was happening to such a promising nation. When it comes to the role of accounting in society, the psychological impacts of the traumas of the Great Depression are speculative. Yet, appreciating people's need for a sense of order and safety after the Depression experience and two world wars is not hard to do. Accounting planning and control skills became highly prized. In the second half of the century, companies grew larger and more geographically dis-persed. Corporate executives found they could not effectively manage beyond a certain scope and geographic range. Consequently, authority was delegated to di-vision- and business-unit-level managers who typically were (and are) held ac-countable for cost, profit, and sometimes investments. This approach became known as responsibility accounting, which today continues to structure organizational relationships in most large companies.

Responsibility accounting proponents had good intentions: accountability for the time people worked, the materials they used, and the profits they generated. The wrong turn came when that same accountability extended to encompass the achievement of predetermined, target financial results without due study and consideration of the operational landscape that creates those results. This situation continues today. The weakest link in the responsibility-center management chain is usually the *implication* of autonomy where in practice little exists. This situation comes about because corporate executives have their own expectations for financial results given that they too are held accountable for certain performance levels. Naturally, the executives work to align the divisions under their control to achieve these expected ends. From that point on it is a short walk to the loss of responsibility-center autonomy. The path is even shorter to financial models replacing operational realities as a way to run a business. An executive cannot substitute abstract financial numbers for an intimate understanding of the actual work performed under the business roof. Such substitutions undermine sustainable results, yet this approach remains the current *modus operandi* in most large corporations. Whether you agree or not, as a CFO, you can see where this trend is headed.

WHO WE ARE

In the 1980s and 1990s, the stock market took on a supernatural life of its own. Ephemeral stock value, boosted by greed and speculation, bloated the price/earnings ratio from historically sustainable levels of around 15 to well over 30. The inevitable correction has been swift and merciless. As the bubble burst, executives worked to prop up any sign of flagging stock price with an array of approaches that included stock option incentives for executives and a pathological cycle of mergers and acquisitions. The M&A pace became so ridiculous that even satirical cartoonists had trouble encompassing the magnitude. For example, picture a *New Yorker* cartoon depicting a newscaster announcing, "Today, in a surprising move, everything merged."

Imagine for a moment that this caption became fact. What would this say about "who we are"? Everyone knows the spirit of this cartoon is directionally correct. The names of long distance providers, electric and gas utilities, and many hospitals change so often that the average citizen stops caring. CFOs have seen up close and often painfully this rapid consolidation. Company longevity? Only for the next bigger fish whose name survives the fusion. Organizational well-being? Certainly not with endemic insecurity from executive levels on down. Accounting statements that present relevant performance data? How can they, when even segment reporting contains multiple companies. Imagine if the caption were true. What would the world gain? What would it lose? Mergers and acquisitions are the chief financial instruments that build multinational corporations. Along with their products, multinational corporations bring with a vengeance the culture of their homeland to second- and third-tier countries.

Analyses show that over 70 percent of these business combinations failed to meet their financial objectives. This result should come as no surprise, considering that for the most part the transactions were based on abstract mathematical models. The shareholders who stood to gain or lose from these massive combinations usually did so without regard for the thousands of nonequity participants affected: employees of the respective firms, and the communities that were home to dissolved companies. Culpable CFOs who masterminded these combinations may, in fact, be finally judged as substituting mathematical accounting games for the real work of management, which is attention to the longevity and health of their organizations, the deep taproot and the perennial ground of good business.

The year 2002 proved brutally debilitating for the accounting profession and for corporate respectability. However, the root causes of the affliction remain largely unexplored, and the disease is in remission, at best. As one CFO put it, "Most efforts to rectify the situation amount to washing a clod of dirt in a mud puddle." Congress has skirted the root causes of unethical corporate behavior and substituted a focus on corrective enforcement requirements with the Sarbanes-Oxley Act. The American Institute of Certified Public Accountants (AICPA), Financial Accounting Standards Board (FASB), International Accounting Standards Board (IASB) and others—so far—continue to speak about solutions from the perspective of the financial lexicon, and to concern themselves primarily with financial instruments (e.g., derivatives and stock options) as opposed to what actually matters to a business: people and work.

Almost everyone seems so preoccupied with saving face, saving clients, or saving reputation—all real or perceived survival concerns—that few are looking beyond the ruins of a business paradigm derailed and disgraced by reliance on the financial abstractions. Many of the same CFOs who built the accounting house of cards are being asked to pick up the same pieces and put the unsupportable structure back together again. If CFOs use the same financial concepts and principles as the rebuilding blocks, their efforts will surely fail over the long term.

Assessing the Call to Be a Strategic Partner

Over the past decade, the call for the CFO to transform into a strategic business partner has intensified from a suggestion to a nonnegotiable demand. To date, the strategic partner designation has stuck to the profession at large about as well as a damp Post-It Note. Consultants cleverly call themselves "business advisors" and "strategic coaches," no doubt hoping to fill the perceived gap left by the CFO. "Strategic partner." "Trusted advisor." How many seminars, courses, and articles have you seen with these words? How many actually define "strategic partner" in ways that practically apply to everyday CFO responsibilities? Can you define the term? Or are you sick and tired of it being thrown in your face? Despite this ambiguity on the part of the accounting profession, something has happened over the last ten years in the minds of most CEOs: They expect their CFOs to be strategic partners, and the CEOs have a pretty good idea of what that means.

In their 1997 book, *Reinventing the CFO: Moving from Financial Management to Strategic Management*,[3] four consultants from pre-merger Coopers and Lybrand began to summarize the difficult position of CFOs. Survey results showed only 12 percent of general managers saw their financial officers as business partners. Even more alarming, only 28 percent of financial managers thought they were. A startling discrepancy showed that 66 percent of these same financial managers considered themselves "involved in the business," but only 25 percent of their superiors thought so. (One becomes curious about the 3 percent who believed they were partners, but were not involved in the business.) The most shocking disconnect of all came in answer to the question, "What is the CFO's primary role?" Finance professionals (73 percent) said "business advocate." Their general managers (71 percent) said "policeman." Not much has changed since 1997, and subsequent surveys indicate the profile remains about the same.

Have accounting professionals really failed to make the transformation to strategic business partner? This question is tricky. The difficulty lies in a more fundamental question: What *is* a strategic business partner? The unadorned reality is that the term "strategic partner" is a disguised plea to the CFO from those living their lives amid financial abstractions. It sounds something like this: *"Please tell us what to do. When the business isn't working, we look to you to tell us why. Perhaps your numbers have failed us. If financial numbers won't help, you should give us other numbers that will."*

Because financial paradigms continue to dominate business identity, people have few other ways to communicate and understand what a business actually does. Because business people are essentially fluent only in the language of profit, financial accounting remains the *lingua franca*. On its own, that language has proven inadequate for actually running a business, as specified in such classics as *Relevance Lost*[4] (Johnson and Kaplan), *The Balanced Scorecard*[5] (Kaplan and Norton), and *The Goal*[6] (Goldratt and Cox).

In the last years of the twentieth century, thoughtful executives realized the abstract model called the "new economy" could not last, and they were nervous about what was coming. They knew that people do not wait forever for profits to blossom from promises. As seasoned leaders turned their ships of commerce back toward operations, they saw a stark reality: Capital markets, and just about every other stakeholder in the organization, wanted to see growth—big, fast growth—in financial numbers such as revenue, profit, ROI, and especially share price. In short, the well-intentioned executives discovered that over the previous four or five decades, lagging financial results had usurped all other performance indicators. Small businesses got into the act as well with IPOs, leveraged buyouts, or being acquired. When asked the purpose of his business, one Wisconsin owner/president said, "To make me rich so I can retire young." Add to this the significant influence of large, institutional investors, and the stage was set for an assault on the office of the financial messenger, the CFO.

Exceptions exist, and a few executives are in for the long haul. However, in spite of these exceptions and regardless of tremendous progress in operations methodologies, financial accounting for profit objectives remains the language of business. Thus, when performance trends downward, the rush is on to the CFO's door. The collective voice, calling for the strategic partner sounds something like this:

> "As the CFO, you have always given us all the information we needed. We have controlled our profits through the wisdom of your statements. As you suggested, we have tried to motivate our people through financial rewards. And look at these financial results! What is happening? Suddenly, we don't understand our business anymore. Profits are down. Employees are unhappy. None of us even knows for sure what the name of our company or its owners will be next week. Help us! Please be our strategic partner and help us make order out of this chaos. Advise us how to get back on track and change these numbers."

The paradox lurking here actually becomes a CFO identity crisis based on the following logic.

- Most executives have become so accustomed to speaking the financial accounting *lingua franca* that they have forgotten the native tongue of business: the one spoken by people while doing the work they do.

- Attention, study, and understanding the business, as it is and as it might become, is the work of leaders, financial or nonfinancial. Without the broader organizational information context for making decisions, the call for CFO as strategic partner is based on a simple information void. People have forgotten the importance of the operational leading indicators of performance that lead to lagging financial results.

Unfortunately, surveys frequently reveal that CFOs and controllers do not know how to meet the call or fill the void. For example, 85 percent of CFOs in one survey answered "better information" in responding to what they thought their CEOs expected of them.[7] In a work environment where everyone has learned to pay attention to financial numbers, when the financial numbers fail to give the whole story, the CFO as strategic partner is supposed to fill in the information void. It's like trying to describe an elephant in a dark room. The CFO sincerely wants to make the financial numbers "better" but struggles with a decision culture based on short-term economic priorities. Nonfinancial peers find it difficult to articulate the kind of information they feel is missing. The CFO has been encouraged to claim the title "strategic partner," so that all the responsibility for the missing information can be put neatly in one place, like it or not.

What is an accounting professional to do? The answer will not come by trying to figure out how to be a strategic partner. A better initial question for any CFO is "How can I get to know more about the business?" With this inquiry, the path is easier to see—not easier to accomplish, but at least easier to see. This is the point where understanding of and true contribution to the business begin. Other than the CEO, the CFO is the *only* executive with the consistent opportunity to exercise a holistic, 360-degree view of the company. If the nature of the CEO's duties is primarily external relations (e.g., customer contact, shareholder relationships, contract negotiations), then the CFO may be the only one in a top leadership position to appreciate the global picture as well as the internal, local detail. Everyone knows CFOs who, in essence, run their companies' internal operations. Their CEOs are continually engaged in external matters, and the CFO needs to stand as proxy, liaison, and intercessor between the CEO and the rest of the company.

So, how *does* a CFO learn more about the business? There are three key steps. More details on these steps appear in two sidebars, "Alliances Are Relationships" and "Making Room in the Fiduciary Workload." (See "Making Room in the Fiduciary Workload," in *Features* on the book's companion Web site.) For specific ways to continuously learn more about the business and to share what accounting professionals can contribute, look for these features in upcoming chapters. Here are three essential steps that lay groundwork for developing business knowledge required when a person serves in the capacity of CFO.

1. *Remove the fiduciary workload barrier.* Heavy workloads are the most frequently cited reason for staying within the CFO office walls.

2. *Consistently create opportunities to experience the work and the people* within the company. In addition to cultivating relationships, this step also unearths accounting work that can be eliminated, and points where accounting service needs shoring up.

3. *Cultivate key alliances for ongoing learning exchanges* between accounting and other functions. This is not the formal quarterly operations review because at these meetings most companies still focus almost exclusively on financial results.

ALLIANCES ARE RELATIONSHIPS

Alliance is another name for relationship, but a specific kind of relationship—one that implies affiliation, union, coalition, and most importantly, *connectivity*. Forming an alliance has nothing to do with spreading office gossip, comparing kids, or talking about sports team results. These types of "relating" might lead to bonding, but not the productive, professional alliances that create value for the organization. As a CFO, stop to think about the difference in the connection quality that exists or is being built between your staff and the rest of the company. Are interactions centered on bolstering audit procedures and internal controls or on forging a base of mutual knowledge about what the business actually does? The latter alternative is the better choice because it frequently leads to reduced auditing and fewer internal controls.

If your alliances are strong, work to keep them that way. If they are not, think about how work life could be better if they were. Forming alliances is not so difficult, but it does take time. However, time invested up front almost always diminishes efforts during the implementation of any new process or idea. The need to participate runs strong in human wiring. So does the desire to be acknowledged when one contributes to a work group. This acknowledgment involves being listened to and having a sense that one's ideas have been seriously assessed. CFOs and their staffs have at least two ways to work in this direction.

First, *consistently create opportunities to experience the work and people of the company.* Proactively take the role of both teacher and student at appropriate times, often in the same session. Invite key individuals to meet with you and your staff to discuss how accounting currently tracks and reports activities and performance in their area. Be alert for questions about why your staff requires certain information. If you don't have a good answer, the data gathering may be residual from past reporting requirements, and perhaps not relevant today. On the other hand, people at the table with little or no accounting background may benefit from learning why someone else needs the data.

Spend at least half of each session learning from your functional peers. What is important to them? What information from your office do they actually use? Are they struggling to do ad hoc analyses that really belong to your staff? If large initiatives are afoot, are accountants involved? If they are, what does the rest of the project team think of their contributions? Most importantly, deliberately remind everyone about the purpose of the meeting. It is the same for everyone: Better understanding of the business.

Second, *cultivate key alliances for ongoing learning exchanges between accounting and other functions.* Whereas the first approach centers on building relationships and business understanding overall, this second framework focuses on specific tasks. Working at critical interface points within operations, direct the accounting staff to engage their operations peers in recurring, formal dialogues about existing processes and how they may be improved. For example, have your staff deliver and explain reports and analyses in person, in operations territory, as opposed to sending them by email, or posting performance measures on intranets with no notice to those who are being measured. In short, such analyses and reporting means accountants report *on* operations *on* operations turf and *in* operations language. When a to-be-improved opportunity is identified, business partnering becomes roll-up-the-sleeves work as accounting and operations people contribute their specialist expertise to solutions. Where the best partnerships exist, accountants actually live (i.e., have their office space) right alongside the manufacturing floor.

The positive by-products of establishing relationships under these two unconventional banners cannot be exaggerated. They represent not just a way of doing business, but a way of living and working together. Even something as apparently mundane as building a cost system can bring people together. One of the authors spent considerable time on that very activity with a paramilitary aircraft manufacturer. As it happened, the cross-functional dialogues held to design the cost system were the first ever for the company. In addition to building the system, the experience turned out to be both cathartic ("I didn't know I caused your department so much rework") and instructive in constructing improved processes.

Alliances are inherently difficult for many CFOs. The generic psychological profile of the accounting/finance professional indicates that people who enter this career path (similar to engineers and information technology professionals) prefer to work alone and tend toward introversion. The good news is that just as technical skills can be learned, recent research shows that interpersonal skills can be learned as well. Daniel Goleman's work with emotional intelligence, for example, shows that the competencies of self-awareness and self-management as well as social awareness and social skills can be developed and improved. In fact, older business professionals in their forties and fifties may actually have a learning advantage over younger professionals.[8] Chapters 2 and 3 discuss interpersonal skills in more detail.

The familiar ground of financial ratios is a good place to start thinking about alliances. Ratios depict meanings between different abstract, quantitative representations: inventory to sales, cash to noncash assets, debt to equity. Viewed from a broader perspective, ratios also characterize relationships. Granted, ratio relationships are between numbers; however, the work of well-intentioned people is implicit in many of these numbers. Given that people create the conditions for such ratios, CFOs who approach ratios only as numbers take another step down the dry road of financial abstractions. Ratio analysis confined to spreadsheets and trend lines completely misses the *causes* of these numbers.

For example, consider inventory, an asset commonly subjected to intense ratio analysis. Ratios such as inventory turns and days-sales in inventory rely on the work of many people across functions. If turns are too low or days-sales are too high, a cross-functional SWAT team must be assembled to tackle the root causes such as inappropriate product mix, ignorance of declining market conditions, and reduced sales because of defective products and services. The common reactions to unfavorable ratios usually play out quite differently because many companies have chosen to manage lagging financial numbers rather than leading operational root causes. Typically, when month-end analysis shows an unfavorable ratio, a CEO or CFO holds up the bad number like a smelly, muddy street urchin who has just committed some mischief. Low, throaty murmurs around the meeting table precede the executive mandate, "Let's get on this, People." Then the meeting ends and nothing changes.

Inventory represents money tied up as idle costs when an inventory ratio turns sour. But a cost really reflects more than just a measure of money. There is no such thing as cost behavior. People behave. Costs are inert, finite representations of money on computer monitors and on paper. More specifically, people *spend* money, and *spending* could be characterized as a behavior where a *person uses* money for a *purpose* related to *work activities* based on organization *competencies* that attempt to address *customers'* needs and desires.

Here lies the real value beneath all ratio analysis. A CFO could explore the depths of ratios with a few trusty operations companions, and such a team might find that sales personnel are frightened of stockouts and therefore pad unit forecasts. A team can sink its teeth into this particular root cause and systematically improve it. Similarly, manufacturing managers may ignore unit forecasts and run higher-quantity batches in the interest of reducing performance-targeted set-up costs.

To truly understand the drivers of spending (termed "cost drivers" in some circles such as activity-based management [ABM]), the chief accountant must understand and be able to communicate relationships between people, work, competence, and customers. The valuation of inanimate objects in isolation, like inventory, may reveal problems, but such calculations provide no solutions. When objects are valued—receivables, payables, and variances to standard, to name a few—*without* connection to a responsible human being, accountability is lost. Everyone can comfortably leave that month-end meeting actually believing that someone else will attend to orphaned ratios. Most people believe they are doing the best job they can; therefore, unless accountability specifically rests on their shoulders for cleaning up the cost orphan, they continue business as usual.

Accounting is all about accountability, yet the connection has somehow been lost to how employees spend their time and to how they decide to spend the company's money. As abstractions, financial analyses are poor substitutes for deep understanding of the life of the business, which is why the CFO must continually build and work within alliances. This kind of CFO has the opportunity to achieve a 360-degree view of all organization resources, as well as the interdependencies of those resources. Very few others besides the CEO have the chance to do this.

Many CFOs already possess such a global viewpoint. The question is what they do with it. Merely reporting the monetary value of resources as they flow through the organization is not enough, so take a moment to evaluate your posture. Do you use operational insights to promote necessary process improvements or to eliminate waste, or are you more likely to say "I could have told you that" after the damage has hit the income statement? Worst of all is the CFO who gets a perverse pleasure out of delivering bad news. CFOs must be visibly involved to guide the wise use of resources and to assure accountability for resource use. This leadership cannot be done sitting on the sidelines.

The CFO who believes, or who has strongly suspected, that financial statements are an inadequate representation of business reality must step up and be counted, which means putting money in its place—a necessary utilitarian symbol for value used to exchange goods and services. People and the work they do must be elevated as the prime concerns. At the highest level, a choice must take place between enduring the constraints and compartmentalization conventionally laid out by financial models, and building connections and a workplace community with like-minded human beings. This choice is between creating connections and maintaining separation.

Point of Choice: Connectivity or Isolation

The history of human isolation parallels the history of the development of freedom. Wherever separation exists, people eventually oppose it. Slavery, women's rights, environmental activism, or any specific point where a link in the natural order of things has broken, the core of each dilemma is human separation—from each other, from other forms of life, from the planet's natural resources. Isolation and separation also breed domestication and rank ordering of roles and authority. Enforced order establishes a certain form of human control called a hierarchy. For over fifty years now, accountants have separated themselves from their nonfinancial coworkers by the very financial abstractions they design as a central part of their work.

That accountants occupy a lower rung in the organizational hierarchy somewhere within a catch-all category called "support functions" comes as no surprise. Even though the CFO sits high on the organization chart, the activities typically performed by that office rank low in the minds of people facing the demands of customers, employees, and production. Even though most companies focus most heavily on financial performance, the accounting function remains isolated and subservient simply because it serves as a universal resource to every person in the organization but seldom, if ever, to the customers who purchase products and services. Even though accountants convey fiscal results, their fate rests in the hands of others—specifically, related to what others think of the numbers they report. Accountants are eagerly sought out as oracles and prophets, and are just as quickly blamed, stoned, and dispatched when their truth-saying is not what executives want to hear. Accountants rarely resist because they are caught up in the three-part cycle of monthly accounting priorities: result prediction, result reporting, and result explaining. (For some foundational solutions to the workload barrier, refer to *Features*, "Barriers and Accelerators: Making Room in the Fiduciary Workload" on the Web site.)

Accountants working in conventional systems have plenty of company in their isolation. They may be responsible for delivering the numbers, but their peer nonfinancial executives must account for a subset of these numbers, the chief of which is profit. These executives find themselves caught up in their own cycle of prediction and explanation that keeps them from connecting with the source of their power: people and the work they do. This is like looking backward while riding a horse as you search for a horse. The financial perspective is not evil; it is just incomplete, because economic models and financial abstractions too often substitute for the actual life and work of an organization. Built on the foundations of an artificial hierarchy as a means of controlling human behavior, the working conditions of conventional accounting systems describe a freedom lost and a joy foregone. The freedom lost is the ability to work outside the constraints of predetermined monetary targets, and to work in real time with actual people. The joy lost is the pleasure of connection and achievements wrought from working together.

In such a situation, who will be the first to call for a revolution? Who will be the first to remind the others of what has been lost and can be regained? Ideally, the leader of the revolution is the CEO. Failing that, the CFO must step forward. The best alternative is a like-minded executive group lead by the CEO and CFO. Like all earnest professionals, CFOs want to contribute what is needed. Candidly, many CFOs want to carve out an identifiable niche: strategic partner, internal business advisor, project leader, anything that creates visible credibility. For those who are sincerely motivated there is a simpler, radically more effective way to proceed. Lead by understanding the deeper purposes of organization, the work of the organization, and how the work affects the people who perform it.

Please remember that the term "strategic partner" is a red herring, and a lesser goal. When CEOs and other executives say they want financial officers who are "operations friendly" and "strategic partners," they really mean they want a meaningful business relationship. They want accountants as partners who, first and foremost, understand the business; who can help make difficult, nonfinancial business decisions; and who can contribute to planning and managing the future of the company. CEOs especially want deep professional relationships with their CFOs. Good accountants find their rightful place here. They find their place by turning toward business fundamentals: good people, good products, and good relationships, that are the reality of where the accounting profession belongs. Within these contexts, ethics naturally reside with no need for enforcement or law. (For more discussion on what ethics looks and sounds like, see the "Ethical Resonance" feature.)

WHO WE ARE BECOMING

Some people may chafe at how often this chapter has referred to CFOs as accountants. Professionals who deal with accounting want to eventually become controllers and chief financial officers, not remain accountants. The title "accountant," like names for other "subservient" classes of people, has been denigrated over the last couple of decades. It goes without saying that recent events have turned slow denigration into an acute crisis, which is most unfortunate. By now, though, the cause should be obvious. Yes, somewhere along the line, those economic models and financial abstractions became much more important than good, honest accounting.

Recall a few lines from the preface: *Remember who you are. You are an accountant. The official title you hold within the financial profession—controller, chief financial officer, financial director, finance vice president, and so on—may make you feel like more than just an accountant, but that's because you haven't stopped lately to appreciate what an accountant really is. Accountants have good reason to be proud.*

Despite the recent popularized accounts of professional scandal, the reasons for professional pride do not lie in some former, better era. While the current state of affairs is untenable in many respects, there has never been a golden age of accounting. As the greatest accountants currently work to salvage what they can from the wreckage of past delusions and outright mistakes, best to look forward to what the profession may become.

A good starting point is the bedrock premise that accounting is perennially about accountability: telling the tale honestly. However, this promise begs the question: accountable for what? One might list any number of business accountabilities, but they all have a common essence. Each organization has a core purpose and a predominate measurement set designed to indicate how faithfully the organization adheres to that purpose. For many, the purpose and measure set have been about making as much money as fast as possible for a very small number of people, regardless of the consequences. Financial goals are not inherently evil, but they are incomplete, and when they have no counterbalances, they become truly dangerous. As a core purpose, financial goals will eventually prove self-destructive because they create short-lived enterprises that endure terrible relationships while they last. Stated simply, this purpose disconnects an organization from the larger human economic system.[9]

Yes, money and some degree of profit remain necessary, but few healthy, well-balanced people settle in the long run for money at the expense of pleasurable work, good relationships with coworkers, and a sense of working for a greater purpose than just making money. These aspects, in and of themselves, are organizational purposes, but they usually remain below the level of articulated consciousness.

A long-lived, healthy organization needs a conscious purpose. Executives must continuously articulate and personally demonstrate the specific ways that each person's work contributes to the purpose. Executives thereby renew the purpose as an organizational priority in all the work they perform. As an organizational rallying cry, profit cannot motivate the kind of personal involvement in work that leads to organizational health and longevity. When health and long life become an organization's primary concern and purpose, work focuses on understanding exactly how to achieve and sustain health and life. To do this, executives must understand what motivates people. Such understanding is the key to both human and financial survival.[10]

Real Work

Most of the trouble within organizations arises from misconceptions about how they actually work, evolve, and thrive or die. When people do not understand how something really works, bad decisions are inevitable. Sooner or later, bad decisions lead to bad outcomes. As human social associations based on many purposes— profit, health, education, to name a few—organizations are subject to the same influences as other biological systems. Unfortunately, the mechanical view dominates the way most organizations control workers and work activities. Exhibit 1.1 sum-

EXHIBIT 1.1   REAL WORK—HOW IT REALLY HAPPENS

Misconceptions	Corrections
as portrayed by financial models	to reflect working systems
• mechanical system with separate parts	• living, interdependent, biological
• isolated productivity components	• inter-identified groups of people
• designed for individual gain	• collective and collaborative
• demands obedience and predictability	• curious and explorative
• finite, circumcised boundaries	• generative and infinite
• control through enforcement	• self-organizing
• money-referencing	• self-referencing

LOOKS LIKE? SOUNDS LIKE?

What does ethical behavior look like? How does ethical communication sound? Wouldn't it be convenient if we had an ethics detector similar to polygraph machines designed to detect lies? You might be thinking that some executives *should* be hooked up to a lie detector. No doubt some have. But unlike a murder or an armed robbery, cooking the books does not conjure up galvanic skin responses in most people who have thought long and hard about just how to prepare a poison accounting stew.

Fortunately, the human sensory system is a far more sensitive instrument for detecting clues to unethical behavior, and trained accountants are better than most at this art because accounting is—or should be—essentially synonymous with ethics. Ethics involves accountability for choices made and actions taken. Ethical accountants do not shy away from presenting unhappy results, and they are eager to offer risk-and-reward insights into prospective activities. A very old and very bad joke about creative accounting goes like this: The boss, income statement in hand, comes to the CFO and says, "I don't like these numbers." The unethical accountant replies, "Okay. What would you like them to be?" Fortunately, no one laughs at this "joke" anymore.

An ancient Buddhist analogy states that as carefully as she tries to bury her eggs, the turtle's tail always leaves a trail from her nest. So, too, an unethical accountant—or any unscrupulous person for that matter—leaves tracks. But instead of looking for evil deeds after the fact, consider the signs of *ethical* behavior. Here are a few:

- Nonfinancial personnel without the ongoing aid of a financial professional can understand all accounting reports meant for internal consumption.
- Accountants do not always say yes. Ethics are afoot when the CFO appropriately challenges the CEO and other executives on actions that are causing or have the potential to cause harm, especially when the actions are based on greed or arrogance.
- The accounting staff spends more time with operations peers than with each other.
- The CFO assures that performance measures are balanced, fair, and accurate.
- Financial numbers are recorded because they mirror actual business performance, not because they look better fitted into some obscure interpretation of GAAP.
- The interests of employees *always* take priority over financial gain.
- The CFO is not worried about how investors and analysts view the quality of earnings reports, taking the perspective that the numbers clearly reflect current reality. This CFO knows that current reality catches up to false projections anyway.
- The CFO spends minimal time on earnings estimates, forecasts, budgets, and financial analyses, and spends the majority of the time supporting people and the work they do to produce earnings.

These are a few of the sights and sounds of ethical accounting behavior. Ethical behavior cannot be legislated, determined by a checklist, or assured by signatures on reports. Ethics cannot be enforced, for then we are not talking about ethics but rather about crime and punishment. Ethics, however, can be felt and seen in the hum of an organization going about its business—a vibration that resonates deep within us and assures us that all is well.

marizes some of the major misconceptions and their corrections. The list is just for starters. In fact, the rest of this book addresses how organizations really work when they learn, perform, and improve actual work. This understanding of authentic workplace conditions naturally carries direct and significant implications for how the CFO must work.

The first and foremost misconception is that independence can exist. The fact is that in living systems, no truly distinct points of separation exist between the parts of any whole. When does the acorn become an oak? As Lynn Margulis elegantly stated, "Independence is a political, not a scientific term."[11] As such, a CFO is not independent of or separate from the organization and its culture, or from executives or anyone else in the enterprise. No one is actually independent. Separation is one of the greatest conceptual fictions that financial abstractions promulgate about human organizations.

Separation and compartmentalization represent an incomplete picture of reality, a perceptual mistake about conditions as they actually exist. Our language-centered brain has the natural ability to conceptually break the world we experience through our senses and thoughts into separate, discrete components. While this ability works well in many analytical contexts, untold damage has been caused when people have applied it to coerce the behavior of natural systems—including the way people work together. Only mental abstractions can create an economy supported by a bubble. Only abstract mathematical models could deceive humans into thinking that a select few gigantic corporate entities can thrive without a system of checks and balances to keep them accountable to the larger systems in which they operate and depend. The majority of people work in isolation to such a degree that they have forgotten how the financial numbers—that is, targets—actually apply to their work activities with other people. The root cause of this error lies in a circular paradox:

Business purpose = financial results = the primary accounting work
= the business reality everyone believes is true
= action based on accounting results = business purpose

People frequently mistake assumptions and beliefs for immutable facts. Every culture and every person lives with a set of underlying premises that remain largely unchallenged. Human imagination, technology, and language, however, make it possible to skeptically confront any and all interpretations of actual conditions and their limits. Because almost every individual has imagination and language, everyone is capable of participating in both a personal and collective evolution. Perception is, indeed, everything. Think about how you would get to your next vacation destination if the Wright brothers had shared the common belief, "It will never fly."

Specific to this book, as the paradoxical equation depicts, most people consistently mistake financial numbers on a screen or page for reality. As an example, how else does one explain the wild swings in stock prices? Certainly, in a rare situation, a public company loses a large percent of its true value overnight. Yes, yes, it's all about the *future* value, right? Or is it really? Here are some beliefs and assumptions about accountants that some people dearly hold as immutable truths:

- An accountant's place is to support and not lead, to report the numbers rather than manage them.
- Accountants do not make good leaders because they are not people-oriented; they have no heart.
- An accountant's role must be strategic partner and leader of change.
- Only a financial professional has the big-picture perspective to run a company well.
- Financial professionals always lack sufficient grasp of the big picture; therefore, they rarely make good leaders, much less CEOs.

Conflicting assertions like these spring from differing beliefs usually based on a range of different experiences, but often only on hearsay. Each statement is true some of the time; no statement is true all of the time. "The Earth is flat" is the classic example of a strongly held "factual" belief that eventually yielded to concrete evidence to the contrary. Some people still maintain this belief despite the evidence. Things change, understanding grows, and conventions of belief eventually crumble under the weight of simple evidence. Pause for as long as it takes to distinguish your facts from your beliefs. Organizations that do not have their facts straight may not survive the decade, and certainly will not see the next century.

The CFO's Right Work

Current business climate and conditions might suggest that the CFO's "right work" is attending to concepts like earnings targets, share price, and profit. Experienced CFOs may wish it were this easy. Instead, in addition to these concerns, CFOs are also called on in both public and private companies to predict what will happen before it happens, and if they are wrong, they stand a good chance of threats, coercion, and worse. A CFO caught in this work cycle worthy of Sisyphus has reason to despair. Such pressure takes its toll. The Financial Executives International (FEI) says the average CFO now lasts just four years in the same company. There must be a better way to earn a living, and there is. This chapter has begun to lay the cornerstones for it.

In contrast, when a CFO begins a sincere inquiry into a deeper, more accurate understanding of the work an organization actually performs, and how accounting may contribute to its purpose, the straight-line targets and redundant work cycles disappear. The more a CFO participates in efforts outside the accounting discipline, the more functional lines begin to blur. The more deeply the CFO explores with people at all levels, the more the organization chart lines collapse. The greater the CFO's capacity to see more, the less the chance that CFO lives isolated between the boundary lines carved by financial statements. The inquiry itself cannot help but bring the numbers to life and reveal their relevancy or irrelevancy. In fact, a CFO working in this posture breaks down all sorts of hierarchical, discipline-based lines, opens the borders of quantitative performance information, and takes a CFO's rightful place at the center of the organization, where the best global viewpoint exists.

Humans live as physical beings in a physical world. The physical world is not abstract, even at the strange quantum level. The more one knows about the physical world, the more one sees that trying to control life is a hopeless endeavor. The more one understands how things actually work, the more one is willing to let go of control. This release into interdependent reliance can be a great relief. Although accountants dearly love to have the right answers, they are now free to say, "I don't know. Let's find out together." They can then use quantitative skills to give form and substance to the exploration.

This posture and attitude—participation in the life of work rather than the mechanics of number abstractions—requires a new, broader set of competencies. Actually, every healthy human already has these capacities as part of our genetic heritage. A few of these capacities appear in Exhibit 1.2. Each carries a pathological antithesis (in italics). This is a profile of two very different paths. The current pattern primarily manages according to the attributes of the antithesis, but human capabilities make it possible to choose differently, and to shape who and what we become.

A person whose value system aligns more with the "antithesis" statements than with the human capabilities probably would not read this far in the first chapter, much less buy the book in the first place. Those people who remain curious, and who have explored this far, may remain intrigued but skeptical. This foundational chapter lays out most of the assumptions for all other chapters. No nature–nurture debate takes place here. The argument about the basic nature of humans—peaceful/aggressive, generous/selfish, and numerous other polarities—is much like arrows meeting in the air at their tips. They stop each other at once. They remain arrows, but they get nowhere. Because the human race has already exhibited all sides of all polarities, humans, among all known creatures, are capable of choosing and shaping who and what they become. Putting the dualistic argument aside, ask yourself which set of attributes in Exhibit 1.2 is directionally valid. First answer from the intellect. Then be very still and answer from your heart. Resolve any conflicts that arise.

This book aims to challenge, annoy, provoke, and alter perception. At the very least, a CFO should be conscious and clear about personal perceptions, assumptions, and beliefs before entering the workplace. Coming from a leader, they will rub off on others. The core of the inquiry examines a person's suitability for survival and success at the top financial executive slot in an organization. If the CFO role is what you really want, the *Guide* is designed to challenge you to determine what kind of CFO you are now, and deliberately choose what kind of CFO you may become.

EXHIBIT 1.2   HUMAN CAPACITIES ABOVE AND BEYOND
THE NUMBERS

- Curiosity that leads to exploration that leads to discovery
  Antithesis: Fear of not meeting predetermined objectives retards new thinking and action
- Sensing what is happening in each encounter as it happens
  Antithesis: Coming to each encounter with preset biases and beliefs
- Patience with the pace of unfolding processes
  Antithesis: No matter the speed, it is never fast enough
- Ingenuity and adaptation in the face of barriers to objectives
  Antithesis: Fear and paralysis-by-analysis when obstacles appear
- Trust of and release into the natural strengths and variety available through collaboration
  Antithesis: Mistrust, hoarding information, power plays, political intrigue
- Reliance on and interdependence with other human beings, with their specific abilities, to create a 2+2=5 synergy
  Antithesis: Rugged individualism

Professional Redemption

Even as the accounting profession is under its worst stress in history, everyone from Congress, to the standards-makers at FASB and IASB, to financial giants like Paul Volcker continue to stew over financial instruments and concepts—derivatives, stock options, and proper earnings guidance to name a few. Unfortunately, these well-intentioned people labor within the constraints of their worldviews, which are predominantly financial and legislative. They may have not created the problem, but their abstraction-based beliefs and assumptions constrain their work in devising lasting solutions. The hope for a lasting resolution to what troubles business and accounting must come from within the accounting profession itself. Most people say this is improbable, but it is less likely to come from those who identify themselves as financial professionals. They still rely on the same economic and mathematical models that created and perpetuate the problem, maintaining an unproductive separation from actual business purposes and conditions.

The chief reform accomplishments to date have been setting directions. Accountability and transparency are now front and center. Enforcement of punishment for the most grievous offenses is in place. Organizations, especially global corporations, remain vulnerable to their own strength. Corporations operate largely outside human law and morality. Only good people within corporations and other large institutions can provide moral leadership to balance the sheer power and size these organizations possess.

Some say the accounting profession does not have the stomach to heal its own wounds. The stereotypical accountant may be shy, retiring, and slow to anger, but once aroused, there is no greater ally. Accountants are engineers at heart. They want to know how things work, and when things are not working, why they are not. Accountants want to build visible structures to exhibit how and why things perform or not. At heart, they are uncomfortable with mysteries, and they have excellent intuitions to ferret out secrets others do not want told. Good accountants keep things grounded and real when marketing talks blue sky or the CEO has a flight of fantasy.

CEOs and other executives may lead the way, or it may take a new generation of leaders to make the necessary adaptations. In the current context, the one who has the best shot at guiding organizational purpose, work, and integrity is the chief financial officer. Banded together within industries, geography, and professional affiliations, these chief accountants can stop the financial shell games; call to task those who act out of fear, greed, or ego-arrogance; and begin to assure longevity and health for their workplaces. Accountants are the ones who can create professional self-redemption. One CFO at a time, and small groups of accountants together, can flap butterfly wings in the current corporate chaos and raise up a righteous storm to clear the air.

BEING THE ONE WHO COUNTS: UNDERLYING ASSUMPTIONS

This book is about new beginnings, and about a profession that *counts* in all meanings of that word. The word "finance" has roots in the word "final" that conveys the end of something, and the common etymological thread of both "finance" and "final" is the French, *finer,* to make an end, and the Latin, *fin,* an end. Synonyms for "final" include "last," "ultimate," and "definitive." The set of equivalents for the word "end" include "cessation," "die," "closure," and "termination." From a financial perspective, this survey of original meanings begins to sound like settlements complete, payments made, taxes charged, and period-end statements issued—some of the conventional tasks of accounting. This characterization portrays a tidy business, with few, if any, loose ends, where debits equal credits, and assets equal liabilities plus owners' equity. Indisputably certain and undeniably finished. Unmistakably mechanical and predictable, without a hint of life, much less a "new beginning."

While every other aspect of life seems uncertain, somehow accounting is supposed to gift its reporting with assurance and certainty. The profession has found that even reporting of the highest integrity cannot provide these attributes if consumers of the information cannot understand what they are looking at. Obviously, something more is needed. If CFOs and other accounting professionals are to successfully generate new beginnings and continue improvements already in progress, a particular set of revolutionary new assumptions becomes necessary. If conventional accounting provides only a partial answer, where is the rest? The premises put forth in the following sections lay a foundation for the answer. In addition, they align with the human capabilities in Exhibit 1.2, and with scientifically validated models of human development.[12]

ACCOUNTABILITY REQUIRES MATURITY

The *CFO Survival Guide* assumes that accountability based on organizational purpose is the primary concern of financial officers. The first job of the CFO is to consistently lead all other executives in cultivating awareness of accountability linked to purpose. The sense a person has of accountability is a matter of maturity. Developing a sense of accountability means the continual practice of seeing more, and of widening the circle of productive working relationships. As a person—or an organization—sees more, interdependencies and connections emerge, as does a sense of answerability and responsibility. These fresh insights lead to new possibilities and opportunities. In the least mature people, no sense of accountability is present beyond one's own immediate needs and desires.

Normal human development in the context of societal values encourages an ever-widening circle of accountability—to family, to schools and churches, to nations, and later to jobs, friends, and extended family. The same development sequence holds for the sense of accountability that CFOs and businesses must maintain as they actually mature, survive, and flourish. As recent events demonstrate, the least mature CFOs conspire with other immature executives to satisfy their personal interests at the expense of others, while they hold themselves aloof from accountability. Many degrees of accountability exist between these immature behaviors and the CFO/executive group that practices consistent ethical conduct in its business dealings with all constituents. Beyond this high level of maturity lies an even more mature demonstration of leadership whose concern and integrity expand to caring acts for communities where they operate, to preservation of planetary resources, and to the health of the global collective.

For the CFO, as with everyone, accountability matures along a predictable sequence of stages. The good conventional CFO deals with accountability through delivery of truthful financial statements based on extant accounting principles. This highly aggregated static type of accountability reporting focuses on depicting the final monetary results for a specific time period in the life of a company. The CFO at a stage of greater maturity does what the conventional fiscal officer does and more. The accountability work of this CFO goes beyond traditional financial reporting, into the day-to-day work of the business. This CFO is concerned with every aspect of the organization: all its processes, employees, suppliers, and customers.

The most mature chief financial officers take a holistic perspective. Such a CFO considers the company's impacts on stakeholders external to the firm's inner circle, including those elements that cannot directly speak for themselves. For example, they carefully weigh the impact of the firm's marketing on children, the repercussions of operating offshore plants with poverty-burdened employees, and the damage to those with no voice at all—forests, animals, water, and air. They see how these attitudes and values connect to good business sense in ways that less mature fiscal officers cannot. They understand that bad press over marketing and manufacturing practices may lead to reduced sales or even boycotts. They know that human lives have unquantifiable worth. They accept energy expenditure limitations as a necessary definition of all naturally occurring resources.

The practice of cultivating a sense of accountability, in itself, generates the ability to see more. The practice begins with the question, To *whom* am I accountable? The second question is for *what* am I accountable? The third through fifth queries naturally follow. *When* and *where* am I accountable? *How* can I be accountable? The final question tests the moral maturity of individuals and organizations: *Why am I accountable?* This last query is the most comprehensive, and if answered correctly, supports the answers of all the preceding queries.

TRANSPARENCY, LEARNING, AND MEANING

Transparency receives a lot of press now. In the context of accounting, the word means that when information is visible, understandable, and accessible, consumers of that information have a better chance of learning something from it. At the moment, most people mean financial information when they speak of transparency issues. In the *Guide*, transparency refers to considerably more than finance.

First and foremost, meaningful information by nature requires broad *participation*. When a person or group relies on information to make decisions, those same people should participate in determining information type, scope, and format. When an organization asks people to make decisions—as opposed to the "uneducated worker" assumption of scientific management—the organization does so because those people have valuable perspectives and insights to contribute to the common knowledge pool. In fact, the information consumer has *the most intimate* knowledge of the local decision context. When combined with a transparent global picture from executives and managers, overall information quality and locally made decisions improve. When decisions improve, the company is more likely to achieve its purpose.

Another key element of meaningful information is transparency of *association*. A person may have exactly the kind and amount of information needed to perform locally, but if the interlocking impacts on other workers remain unrecognized, organization performance suffers. A critical part of real information transparency is knowledge of sequence, linkages, timing, and potential work redundancies.

Secret information is the least transparent knowledge of all. Some physicists claim that "information" is all that really exists, and when its flow is impeded, disorder emerges. The transparent information in question here is not legally required reporting or unavailable data such as exists in employee personnel files. Transparency moves the focus to data concerning the company's health and well-being, delivered in language suitable to the audience. A large percentage of organizations, by policy, restrict employee access to financial information. Performance measurement and management methods such as the balanced scorecard attempt to correct the transparency problem by linking and openly reporting critical measures and accountabilities throughout the organization.

NUMERICAL REALITIES AND OTHER OXYMORONS

Alfred North Whitehead's words in this chapter's epigraph apply directly to the work of the accounting profession. During the last fifty years, the profession has done more than merely "hint" at "dogmatic certainty." At the very least, the profession has allowed a misperception to persist, namely that financial statements and analyses are certain, immutable representations of business realities. Permitting this misapprehension to continue may have been the profession's greatest "exhibition of folly." An extreme example of an inappropriate reliance on numbers and calculations is active in the highest levels of U.S. government.

John D. Graham, the current head of the Office of Information and Regulatory Affairs, makes decisions based on sophisticated cost/benefit and risk analyses, which are his management specialties. He applies these methods universally. "Every economically significant regulation drafted by every executive branch agency to carry out the laws of Congress—on power plants or forest conservation, on meat inspection or dioxin—must cross Graham's desk before it goes into force. He decides whether the protection is worth the price." The purpose of cost/benefit analyses "is to quantify in dollars, every cost and every benefit of a possible course of action. Because Graham has spent his entire professional life working to enshrine [cost/benefit analysis] (and its near cousin, risk analysis) at the center of public policy, his nomination process was highly contentious. He got thirty-seven 'No' votes in the Senate—second only to Attorney General John Ashcroft."[13]

In responding to Graham's process of pricing both costs and benefits, Harvard-trained economist Frank Ackerman points out the endemic biases of cost-benefit analysis: "The process of reducing life, health, and the natural world to monetary values is inherently flawed. . . . The idea of assigning a price to human life is very troubling, morally and ethically."[14]

While the financial perspective is not inherently evil, used alone to manage an organization—or a country—it produces unhappy ends. The finance/accounting perspective is useful, but incomplete. Although accounting-career surveys entreat accountants to affiliate with operations, the work of accountants (also verified in the same surveys) continues to focus on fiduciary transactions, internal control efforts, and standard reporting. None of these is the purpose of the organization. No matter how often professional CPE courses and professional publications (e.g., *CFO Magazine, Strategic Finance*) exhort accountants to gain better knowledge of the business, lead planning efforts, and communicate clearly, not much seems to change. Why not? Once again the root cause lies in that paradoxical equation containing more than one false circular reference:

> **Business purpose** = financial results = the primary accounting work
> = the business reality everyone believes is true
> = action based on accounting results = business purpose

Cosmological mathematics aside, numbers are not reality. They are quantitative symbols for close-ended, snapshot-points of matter, space, and time. Artificial constructs produce conditions of labor and life that humans do not long tolerate. So, if financial models are useful but incomplete, what better displays conditions as they actually are? To find out, go where the living members of the company are working. Organizations are not doomed by nature to short lives and entropy. Rather, because organizations are made up of people, they are alive and evolving. Most of what lives and evolves within the organization goes on in the heart of operations. Almost everything else is a reflection of this centrality.

Accountants typically have highly developed observational skills. They see the details, and the best accountants remember the details for later meaningful associations. The kinds of activities described in the "Alliances Are Relationships" feature in this chapter put those powers of observation to work for the good of the company as opposed to watch-dogging travel and expense reports, and calculating deferred taxes every month-end. When a CFO is out and about the company, participating in cross-functional efforts, the facts of existing relationships, animosities, trouble spots, and islands of excellence appear as part of the process. People are an organization's only real assets, and the only means by which anything happens. They are the assets a CFO must safeguard, but typically monetary, material, and machine assets receive all the attention.

A notable exception to the numbers obsession is the operational process focus of a well-run hospital emergency department. By virtue of its healing mission, health care focuses on operations first because its point of reference is actual people with actual illnesses and injuries. Corporations who value inert products, amorphous market segments, and absentee shareholders more than proximate, living people can learn much from watching good hospital operations.

COST, SPENDING, AND OTHER INEQUALITIES

Managerial/cost accountants really want to believe that their talents are used for more than balancing books. However, conventional cost accountants often accomplish little more than very fancy bank account reconciliation. Where management accountants can be worthwhile contributors is in *spending* management. If people's spending behaviors are the actual source of cost behaviors, understanding human spending patterns and causes becomes vital information. In contrast, mechanical work on isolated cost-reduction efforts or directing departments to cut an arbitrary percent of their costs creates collateral damage.

"Spending" is an archaic and simple word. It does not sound very sophisticated to say, "This is what we spent on such and such a product or customer relations effort." However, in another context, spending is a principal organizational focus. Businesses strive to provide customer-preferred products and services. To do so, the people in those businesses decide when, where, and how to spend time, money, and resources. Significantly, not paying attention to spending can have adverse affects.

"If no one can tell me how much I use (spend), I won't pay attention to how much I use or spend."

Spending relevance was lost with the rise of the economies-of-scale concept with its focus on pushing supply into the market rather than responding to demand. Economies of scale actually promote increased spending, and the spending variance in standard accounting helps track faults in such a system. As every intermediate accounting student knows, the spending variance is part of overhead and absorption accounting. Why do you suppose such accounting had to be developed? Right. The margin for error in economies-of-scale thinking is so great that standards and variances are required to track the variations and outright mistakes. This brand of accounting is also a core breach in fiscal integrity. Unless an organization spends even more on advanced methods (e.g., activity-based costing) to dissect overhead, cost cannot be linked to an individual or group and accountability is lost. Just as important, whenever accounting systems aggregate spending data too highly (e.g., overhead, cost of goods sold), they lose important information critical to operational and strategic decision making.

Logically, unless accounting systems link personal accountability to spending, spending spins out of control. Enter higher spending on travel-and-expense mavens and the internal control experts. Accountants must make the causes of spending visible, and that means knowing who did the spending and their reasons for doing so. As a result, that simple word, "spending," turns out to be vital to the organization's well-being. If and when an accounting system can reveal how much people spend, who makes the spending decisions, and how those spending decisions contribute to the good of the whole, then accounting begins to be worth something. Simply by following meaningful spending patterns, an accounting system can transform from a backroom general ledger nerd to a robust operations system—what it should be in the first place.

VALUE ANYONE?

Value is in the eyes of the beholder . . . and the beholden. This twist on an old truism sums up the general failure of a trend called "value management" to make much headway beyond supporting share price management. Value is a relatively popular word about town: value propositions, economic value, and value chains, to name a few. The value craze began with efforts to increase shareholder wealth— one objective among many for organizations. Shareholder value is easy to define: stock sells for more than its purchase price. Corporate executives are beholden to shareholders for investing their money, but value management is no way to show gratitude. Value cannot be managed. Isolated attempts to manage value to shareholders exact a price later. Any other struggles to manage value of other kinds—

employee- and customer-value propositions, for example—are far more compli-cated. Outside of short-term shareholder wealth, value concepts have no place in accounting, and short-term shareholder wealth objectives almost never have a place in organizational health and longevity.

Value is a perception. In a society where goods and services cost money, gold, gems, cash, and equity certificates are valuable. In a wilderness survival scenario, a blanket may be the most valuable thing in the world. Anyone who has ever had the wind knocked out of their lungs from a harsh impact knows the value of a simple breath. Value depends on changing contexts, on immediate needs, and on individual beliefs about the relative worth of one thing to another. Remember the sale of Manhattan Island? Any company that has tried to determine what employees value quickly discovers that individual opinions vary widely. Then add the annoying fact that people change their minds about what they value. Daycare at work means nothing to an employee, until that employee becomes a parent. Customers, being people, also vary widely in what they value. They, too, have been known to change their minds.

If it saves cost, it's valuable—the inverse, false logic of putting a value on objects and people. Cost saving has been a problem child for a very long time. Primarily because of lack of information transparency and the subsequent impacts of removing resources, cost reduction efforts, more often than not, do more harm than good. A classic example is cutting costs in research and development work, the source of future revenue. Unless done with full knowledge of impacts, this game is a dangerous one.

This discussion all adds up to one thing: value is arbitrary and impermanent. Share price, while easy to calculate, changes from minute to minute. The circumstances and conditions for customers and employees change, as does what they value. When it comes to people, identifying what they value and satisfying their desire for it is a one-by-one process. Thus value management becomes a contradiction in terms.

NOTES

1. Alfred North Whitehead, *Process and Reality: An Essay in Cosmology*, corrected ed., ed. David Ray Griffin and Donald W. Sherburne (New York: The Free Press, 1978), xiv.

2. H. Thomas Johnson and Anders Bröms, *Profit beyond Measure: Extraordinary Results Through Attention to Work and People* (New York: The Free Press, 2000), 50.

3. Thomas Walther, Henry Johansson, John Dunleavy, and Elizabeth Hjelm, *Reinventing the CFO: Moving from Financial Management to Strategic Management* (New York: McGraw-Hill, 1997), 19.

4. H. Thomas Johnson and Robert S. Kaplan, *Relevance Lost: The Rise and Fall of Management Accounting* (Boston: Harvard Business School Press, 1991).

5. Robert S. Kaplan and David P. Norton, *The Balanced Scorecard: Translating Strategy into Action* (Boston: Harvard Business School Press, 1996).

6. Eliyahu Goldratt and Jeff Cox, *The Goal: A Process of Ongoing Improvement,* 2d rev. ed. (Great Barrington, Mass.: North River Press Publishing Corporation, 1992).

7. Editorial survey: "Key Career Benchmarks," *Controller Magazine,* July 1998, 26. The next two most frequent responses were "efficient accounting processes" (78 percent) and "planning for the future" (62 percent).

8. Daniel Goleman, *Emotional Intelligence* (New York: Bantam Books, 1997), and Daniel Goleman, Richard Boyatzis, and Annie McKee, *Primal Leadership: Realizing the Power of Emotional Intelligence* (Boston: Harvard Business School Press, 2002).

9. The term "human economic system" is credited to H. Thomas Johnson and Anders Bröms, *Profit beyond Measure,* 195.

10. For a more detailed discussion of "conscious purpose," see for example, Gregory Bateson, *CoEvolutionary Quarterly,* Winter 1982, 62–67.

11. Lynn Margulis and Dorion Sagan, *What Is Life?* (New York: Simon & Schuster, 1995), 26.

12. See Chapter 1 in Catherine Stenzel and Joe Stenzel, *From Cost to Performance: A Blueprint for Organizational Development* (Hoboken, N.J.: John Wiley & Sons, 2003).

13. Steve Weinber, "Mr. Bottom Line," *OnEarth,* Spring 2003, 34.

14. Ibid., 36.

Development

THE SCIENCE OF BECOMING

He who is skilled at traveling
  leaves neither tracks nor traces;
He who is skilled at speaking
  is flawless in his delivery;
He who is skilled in computation
  uses neither tallies nor counters;
He who is skilled at closing things tightly
  has neither lock nor key,
    but what he closes cannot be opened;
He who is good at binding
  has neither cord nor string,
    but what he binds cannot be untied.

For these reasons,
  The sage
    is always skilled at saving others
      and does not abandon them,
        nor does he abandon resources.
  This is called "inner intelligence."

Lao Tzu[1]

As an accountant, I believed firmly in my early years that numbers shape reality and that quantitative abstractions explain what matters in the business world. Today, some forty years later, I see the world quite differently. I now believe that businesses cannot use financial data either to perceive or to achieve what really matters.

H. Thomas Johnson[2]

Y ou have seen the lists—the ones that catalogue all the skills that a marketable financial chief needs. You know what the lists include: the same skills listed under qualities of a strategic partner. You know how much the list is worth when applied to actual work: marginal at best. Fortunately, the lists have nothing to do with being a good, honest accountant and a great CFO. Have you stopped to think who creates most of these lists? The largest professional associations (e.g., the American Institute of Certified Public Accountants [AICPA], the Institute of Management Accountants [IMA]) generate the majority of these accounting/finance skill-set descriptions, and this is as it should be. However, these descriptions are only the beginning, and the lists seem to miss something. You may even have an intuition what it is. This chapter explores the two most critical missing elements of professional competence: *intentional development* and *conscientious competence integration*.

The words "intentional" and "conscientious" add important characteristics to the development and integration work they characterize. Human beings—and all life forms—cannot help but develop and integrate when living balanced lives. People also possess the unique ability to mentally compare events from the past, the present, and the future. Partnered with our linguistic capacity to explore a number of alternative actions and choose among them, we find ourselves less constrained by the instincts, drives, and urges that configure bird, insect, and other mammal behaviors. People mature biologically, and they also mature in their capability to form clear intentions and act consciously on them. Of course, the degree of conscientious intention varies widely across the human race.

Two parallel forms of growth occur the longer any person conscientiously practices new skills within the context of professional development. People become more *capable* of successfully performing specific skills as practice continues;[3] they also become more professionally *competent*. They integrate many skills into a set of capabilities that qualify them to apply what they know to a broad range of work situations. This chapter addresses necessary capabilities in terms of the technical skills and the experience expected of the CFO.

The ubiquitous list of expectations for CFOs usually appears in two columns. One column refers to traditional accounting, conventional practice, scorekeepers, and the like. The other column heading typically reads Strategic Partner, the New Controller/CFO, What Executives Want, and so forth. This chapter's exploration begins with a representative list of capabilities that CEOs and CFOs say are important CFO attributes. In addition to the expectations in Exhibit 2.1, others frequently reported include personal chemistry with the CFO, personal trustworthiness and integrity, process improvement skills, and teamwork abilities.

Pushed to select just one quality they want in their CFOs beyond accounting and financial competence, CEOs most often choose "understanding the business." Specifically, this phrase means industry and line experience, and underscores in

EXHIBIT 2.1   TWO VIEWS OF THE MOST IMPORTANT
CFO CAPABILITIES

CEOs say:[4]		CFOs say:[5]	
Strategic planner	75%	Better information	85%
Leader	51%	Efficient accounting work	78%
Objective	38%	Planning for the future	62%
Creative	27%	Quality staff	38%
Good communicator	26%	Global perspectives	10%
Business partner	19%	New business development	10%
People developer	10%	Risk manager	5%

plain English the perennial plea for strategic partners who can help resolve business concerns and plan the future of the organization. Each of the professional expectations in Exhibit 2.1 is significant; nevertheless, they still do not directly address the nemesis of the accounting profession: how to acquire and master both personal and leadership intelligence.

To better characterize this central challenge in professional development, reconsider the demand that CFOs perform as strategic partners in terms of how well they resolve business concerns and plan the future of the organization. Resolving business concerns cannot be done in functional isolation, the preferred work mode of the average accountant. Such performance requires people to work together in relationship for the purpose of addressing the identified concern. Similarly, collaborating with other executives and managers to plan the future of the organization requires that the CFO enter directly into the fabric of the organization's most important social/business relationships.

So, the lists, demands, and priorities probably look familiar. Weary eyes glaze over just thinking about how to approach, much less master, all these items of expertise. At this point, old accountant jokes may even begin to arise—the ones that ridicule accounting practitioners under a thin veneer of civility. At this point, pause and remember that most people choose a profession based at least in part on natural aptitude and disposition. The challenging part of professional life that captures a person's interest over the years comes on two levels: the personal and the professional. Each of us enters the game with high skills in some areas and low skills in others. Meeting the challenge of filling in personal competency gaps brings a sense of mastery. Similarly, most people also look forward to participating in the ways the entire profession evolves and innovates.

In addition, conventional skill and capability expectation lists are pointillist and unintegrated; they offer no guidance on how to acquire the items they list. To the authors' knowledge, no one has formalized a curriculum for CFO experience and education. MBA programs definitely do not count, although they are excellent for broad exposure and entry points to the range of business disciplines. Executive education, especially when concentrated in a multiweek format, comes closer. A degree in accounting, finance, or taxation greatly helps an accountant in learning technical skills, but remains incomplete. The missing element is a coordinated, balanced, lifelong approach to professional learning that integrates the technical CFO skills and capabilities with personal maturity and leadership intelligence.

When professional organizations try to address the gaps in this long-term view, they usually end up listing another level or two of pointillist courses and seminars under several of the items in Exhibit 2.1. Nothing wrong here, but these more detailed lists often neglect coherency and correct developmental sequences because professional associations operate with insufficient resources to incorporate these more sophisticated aspects. Their curricula are rarely coordinated by forces other than marketability and unscientific surveys. This information becomes outdated and only randomly addresses the individual CFO's needs. Furthermore, research on complex skill acquisition and retention indicates that unless a skill is immediately and frequently used, expertise wanes at a rapid pace. Everyone knows the frustration of comprehending a software application only to discover a few weeks later that very little learning has been remembered.

The investigation of the CFO profile continues by examining another list, from a very different source and context. As will become apparent shortly, accounting professionals usually already know what they need. They can even articulate the specifics of their nemesis, personal leadership intelligence. In 1998, the authors designed and developed a course for the Institute of Management Accountants. The course title: *CFO/Controller: Strategic Business Partner and Internal Advisor.* (Okay, chortle if you must at the use of the term "strategic business partner." Consider it the authors' willingness to learn and have no ego about it.)

Subsequently, the authors served as instructors a number of times, including instruction for a group of more than one hundred CFOs and controllers at an IMA national conference. Each time the seminar was delivered, the authors spent time with participants coming up with their own profiles of the "ideal" CFO/controller. Exhibit 2.2 displays a composite of the dialogue-generated responses in all sessions between 1999 and 2003. The responses in this exhibit have a richer character than survey-generated lists. The categories used in Exhibit 2.2 mirror those used in the detailed discussions later in this chapter. Notice that financial and accounting skills barely merit a nod. Hundreds of participants agreed that these skills are simply entry tickets just to get into the game. The majority even hold this opinion about specialty, technical skills such as mergers and acquisitions, SEC savvy, and IPO skills.

The ability of a CFO to execute objectives lies deep in established relationships far more than in technical expertise. People help other people do things, and people are more likely to collaborate with someone they know and trust, and who has exhibited consistent follow-through in the best interests of both the organization

www.

EXHIBIT 2.2   DIALOGUE-GENERATED CFO CAPABILITIES
AND COMPETENCIES

CFO Position	+	**CFO Posture**	=	**Presence**
CFO Stance	+	*CFO Attitude*	=	*CFO Impact on Others*
Proactive		Confident		Inspires trust/has integrity
Committed		Risk taker		Respected by peers
Challenges the status quo		Passionate		Radiates calming confidence
Sees the big picture		Implementer		Known for follow-through

Skills	**Personal Maturity and Leadership Intelligence**	
Team facilitation	Intuitive	Communicator
Selling ideas inside the organization	Adaptable	Mentor
Understands human capital	Candid	Good listener
Finance and accounting expertise	Accountable	Visionary
Negotiation	Responsible	Facilitator
Strategic in all activities	Innovative	Motivator
	Follow through	
Experiential Knowledge	Selflessness	
Educational scars	Genuine	
Operations experience	Consistent	
Industry commitment	Controlled impatience	
Entrepreneurial spirit	"Just says no" when necessary	
Cool under fire	Personal chemistry with others	
Excellent with people	Courage to back up convictions	
	Balance of personal and family values	

and the individuals in it. The elements that constitute the mysterious aura called "executive presence" used to be only a matter of opinion and debate, but this is no longer the case. Chapter 3 provides substantive support for this statement.

One of the most comprehensive ways to appreciate executive presence is to see it as a result of many integrated qualities, not unlike financial results as the outcome of multiple predecessor activities. The interaction equation at the top of Exhibit 2.2 is written two ways. The first is merely descriptive, whereas the second shows the first's *position, posture,* and *presence* in active relationship.

$$\text{CFO Position} + \text{CFO Posture} = \text{CFO Presence}$$

$$\text{CFO Stance} + \text{CFO Attitude} = \text{CFO Impact on Others}$$

Position and *stance* characterize the CFO's predictable, consistent values and expectations for both personal and organizational behavior. When the CFO's behavior is steady, dependable, and based on known values, everyone understands the ground where the CFO stands. This is a good beginning. However, when someone takes an intellectual stand or position but will not take action, strong principles count for little. *Posture* and *attitude* provide the visible evidence that one can make good on one's principles. Being *intellectually* confident or passionate is not possible. Confidence and passion are energies of the heart.

The question remains: How does one develop qualities like these if they are missing from one's natural gifts? Recent research fortunately provides a relatively simple answer: *Leadership attributes can be learned.* The learning is hard. Many educational paths are available. None hold guarantees. All possess risks. Most cost money. Only the individual CFO's deliberate, intentional, *guided* practice of leadership competencies guarantees positive outcomes while minimizing risk. Whether it is a person or a method, the "teacher" is a requirement.

Exhibit 2.2's *experiential knowledge* category equates to *understanding the business*, which in turn facilitates contributions to the resolution of business concerns and permits participation in planning the future of the organization. Significantly, most of the ideal CFO attributes chosen by the seminar participants fell in the final category of *Personal Maturity and Leadership Intelligence.* The seminar discussions with the participants during the construction of the profile clearly indicated that most people had no doubts when identifying the desirable qualities. The participants had equal certainty that CFOs and controllers have some serious work to do.

The good news is that the CFO who is keen on personal and professional development has no lack of resources. The bad news is that except in expensive, personally customized offerings, the resources are poorly coordinated and often dated. Every CFO clearly needs to take personal responsibility for formulating clear intentions, executing personal development plans, and conscientiously integrating new technical skills and experiential knowledge—a far cry from warming a chair at a few CPE-credit courses. Whether recently promoted or a seasoned professional, for a CFO this discussion all sums to the following maxim: After the promotion or to keep the promotion, you still have to do your own laundry. If all your linen is clean, help your staff members with a little spot removal. "Give me a fish, I eat for a day. Teach me how to do the laundry, and I will always look spiffy."

THE SCIENCE OF BECOMING

At this point in the discussion, "development" requires a more precise definition. The word is often used interchangeably with "growth" and "change." Even if confined to the topic of human development, the range of scientific information on this process is significant. But within that last statement lies a word of good news for people who want some hard information on the subject: the word "scientific." If you have a degree in business, particularly an MBA, pause for a moment to examine how "scientific" your training and education have been. Business acumen worth its salt does not typically come from an academic or scientific context. It comes from practical experience combined with refined instinct and intuition that become business intelligence—the human kind.

One of the first questions for any intentional and conscientious developmental expedition is: What can be improved and what cannot? Developmental science rigorously explores this essential question. Because the entire physical world and everything in it is subject to constant change, categorical "change management" stands as one of the most absurd management notions ever concocted. Change in the physical universe generally takes two patterns: 1) *entropy*—the gradual loss of order and increase of randomness in any closed system as occurs in the life cycle of a solar system; and 2) *autopoiesis*—a network of processes of production (transformation and destruction) which (a) maintain their defining organization throughout a history of environmental perturbation and structural change and (b) regenerate their own components in the course of their operation.[6] Autopoietic systems characterize change as it occurs in living systems. Entropic systems characterize change as it occurs in mechanical systems.

A specific definition of "human development" applies, whether the context is individual, group, or organizational:

> **Human development:** *Integrating new and more comprehensive **capacities** to **see** relationships between the self and the environment.*

Within this definition, "integration" means that the new capacity becomes a permanent ability or competence; "capacity" infers a new faculty for potential growth, development, or accomplishment; "see" literally means that perspectives on relationship broaden; and "new" has several shades of explicit meaning. A new capacity to see means seeing something never seen before, not just more of what has always been there. A new capacity to see adds more comprehensive perspectives that do not negate the previous simpler perspectives but rather add meaning to and complement them. For example, CFOs (and other executives) who use performance management often claim that using a set of strategic financial and nonfinancial measures increases the successful execution of strategic priorities. Specifically, a more comprehensive set of performance measures encourages *seeing* new opportunities for connectivity and efficiency.

Everything changes, but not everything develops. Three conditions characterize the ability to initially see the point of personal/professional change, and then engage the development process:

1. Threat to survival
2. Incentive
3. Readiness

People and their organizations most often realize their goals when guided by a well-tested method that invites, or even creates, a noncoerced readiness to embrace change. At this point, the science of human development becomes a blueprint for professional development, because the only "change" that counts as development is the learning experience wherein a person develops *new capacities within a learning context* because the person has become *ready* to do so. Beyond the relatively simple parameters of an individual's personal preferences or willingness, readiness in a developmental context means the *capacity* to engage and use a new way of seeing. Personal preferences and willingness change from day to day based on many individual factors. In contrast, the capacity to see in new ways is a permanent acquisition.

Children need to learn basic arithmetic and algebra before they can learn calculus. Likewise, developmental sciences provide a map for assessing and creating a person's readiness to acquire new capacities. Giving a tome on an advanced strategic method to someone without practical business experience is just as futile as giving an eight-year-old a calculus book. Developmental patterns do not guarantee successful change; they characterize the sequence in which healthy positive change occurs. The hard work lies *between developmental milestones* where learning and practice take place, and where readiness naturally evolves. That said, some essential principles of human development help characterize the processes and dynamics behind the definition.

DEVELOPMENT ESSENTIALS

Most of the many schools of human psychology have created a specific perspective on human development and behavior; therefore each school represents a subsystem with a specific focus within a yet-to-be-defined complete set of the steps normal people move through as they achieve greater levels of maturity. Some of the more meticulously characterized subsystems of human development include cognitive, moral, needs, self-identity, and psychosocial shown in Exhibit 2.3.

Despite this wide range of focus, the subsystems of human development demonstrate four essential consistencies that apply to the capacity of a person, a group, or an organization to successfully navigate developmental milestones.

1. All developmental processes follow a fixed sequence of stages, and all individuals must master the stages in the same order.
2. While some may learn more quickly, *no one skips any stage*, and the lessons

www.

EXHIBIT 2.3 SUBSYSTEMS OF HUMAN DEVELOPMENT—STAGES

Cognitive[7]	Moral[8]	Needs[9]	Self-Identity[10]	Psychosocial[11]
sensorimotor	punishment and obedience	survival	symbiotic	trust vs. mistrust
preoperational	instrumental hedonism	safety	self-protection	autonomy vs. doubt and shame
concrete operational	law and order	membership	conformity	industry vs. inferiority
formal	universalism	self-esteem	conscientious	identity vs. role confusion

learned in all earlier stages are retained. Early stages contain lessons that are necessary for mastery of the stages that follow.

3. Consequently, developmental learning is truly an integrative process. Developing beings experience lasting change as they move to more mature stages. Unlike the lessons of an MBA statistics course, *developmental lessons become a permanent part* of one's outlook.

4, In the normal process of developmental integration, *subsystems coevolve*. Individuals are as mature as their *least* mature subsystem. The idiot savant who calculates π to 150,000 digits but cannot tie his own shoe is less mature than the five-year-old girl who knows 2+2=4 and dresses herself.

While milestones mark the completion of a stage of developmental work, the real work of each stage of development lies in the day-to-day active learning and integration processes that fall between milestones. A mathematics teacher cannot simply hold up an algebra book, describe the general theory, and expect the students to become "algebratized."

What can one expect while working between the milestones? Simply put, the experience feels like learning, which may be pleasant, frustrating, or downright painful depending on personal history. Learning has no beginning or end points once in motion. Ideally, people within executive leadership groups work together to identify developmental needs, and then set the learning pace for themselves, critical groups, and the organization as a whole. Of course, this is not the common experience. Typically, only CEOs select training for themselves because they have the budget authority to do so. Beyond that, the rest of the executives and their staff must fend for themselves.

In contrast, the CFO, more often than not, must carve out a career-specific development path alone. In practice, most CFOs need to clear a number of roadblocks to personal development before they can set foot on the path. Some people lack the energy or resolve to clear these barriers. CEOs should know that the alternatives to encouraging developmental work are either to fall back on "the way it has always been done," or worse, to lose a good financial chief to some other lucky employer. The most common developmental roadblocks impede positive transformation and progress when:

- The CEO places unrealistic workload and leadership demands on an unprepared and/or inadequately supported CFO and/or management group.

- The CEO cannot or will not see the wisdom of the CFO's recommendations for personal/professional development.

- The CFO may recommend changes unsuited, or too advanced, for organizational needs, or that support parochial interests at the expense of the larger organizational community.

- CFOs, because they are people, have been known to hold too closely to familiar (i.e., comfortable) suboptimal approaches, systems, and behaviors.

- CFOs aggressively step out of the scope of their usual activities, with incomplete knowledge of the global picture, pushing for inappropriate changes.

All barriers occur at the executive level and can potentially be resolved there. These and many other similar behavior patterns boil down to one of three basic dysfunctions in personal or organizational development scenarios:

1. A more mature person or group sees beyond the abilities of the others but does not know how to communicate their perspective.

2. One person, group, or the entire organization is stuck in a developmental delay that even with intense communication and modification efforts seems insurmountable.

3. People at all levels are reluctant to see beyond their own local set of responsibilities.

Scenario 1 represents a *temporary* developmental imbalance. Scenario 2 represents an *identifiable pathology*. Scenario 3 describes an *invisible pathology*—like an undiagnosed malignancy.

Although all human development subsystems are relevant to certain aspects of the duties of the CFO, the *Guide* concentrates on two: *moral* and *psychosocial* as key elements of professional development. The common core of both the moral and psychosocial subsystems is, as you might expect, relationship. The cognitive subsystem describes how humans receive and process information, create systems, and how, when, and why they learn. This subsystem is of substantial interest and is described in detail in the authors' previous book, *From Cost to Performance,* in reference to the sequence of maturity that guides the way organizations develop their management information systems.[12] Abraham Maslow's needs hierarchy is probably the most well known subsystem and is regularly covered in academic coursework. The self-identity subsystem is quite important to this discussion; however, development in its realm is usually of an intimately personal and unique nature. Work in self-identity development falls within "scenario 2" parameters.

In the context of the work of a CFO, development is accountability. The following logic stream supports this concept. *Who am I?* I am the CFO. *What do I do?* I assure accountability. *When must I assure accountability?* It depends on my moral values and psychosocial maturity. *To whom am I accountable?* This answer, too, depends on my moral and psychosocial maturity, as well as my self-identity. Perhaps most important, *Why am I accountable?* A person at an early maturity stage might answer, "Because no one trusts me" or "Because I will be punished if I don't obey." A person at the highest level of maturity, who has widened the relationship circle beyond self and significant others, would answer the same question, "Because I know who I am, and I am not independent. Our actual condition is one of interdependence. Recognizing this, accountability within interdependent living is the only realistic way to conduct myself." The next two sections clarify and expand on this progression in the human development moral and psychosocial subsystems.

MORAL DEVELOPMENT

The ethical aspects of moral development have recently become an area of intense interest to a lot of people, and this is a very good thing. Pause here, and consider the amount of training and practice in ethics and moral development you received in your formal education. How much have you sought out after-degree programs? (Mandatory diversity training and Sarbanes-Oxley education do not count.) If you have taken more than one course, or have been fortunate enough to encounter any instructor who naturally taught from a moral/ethical foundation, consider yourself advantaged. If you root your decisions and actions in ethics and moral maturity, either consider yourself enlightened or thank your parents.

In many company cultures, funding interpersonal learning faces heavy resistance. Morality and ethics have been practically off limits—too personal, too close to religion, too soft, not actionable. Now every organization, no matter the size, that has more than one or a handful of shareholders must seriously evaluate business practices in light of these very paradigms. (See the "Ethical Resonance" sidebar later in this chapter for a discussion of the 2002 Sarbanes-Oxley Act.) Corporations are receiving a required crash course in ethics and morality, like it or not. Unfortunately, this enforced tutelage will have little or no effect on the underlying developmental arrests responsible for personal and organizational malfeasance and criminal conduct.

These statements are intended to be descriptive, not judgmental. If they sound critical, perhaps the corporation is old enough, grown up enough, and certainly powerful enough that it rightly should be held accountable by the highest ethical and moral developmental standards. So should its executives. At the risk of giving an inert entity a voice, Exhibit 2.4 articulates questions and answers a corporation might ask along its moral development path.

Moving into more detail on each stage of moral development clarifies the progression in relationship perspectives. The descriptions characterize a behavior profile for each level of moral maturity, as validated by scientific study and research on human development. Undesirable behaviors at any level of maturity should not trigger blame; they should stimulate guided self-examination and a search for appropriate behaviors and responsibilities consistent with the maturity level. Similarly, a high level of moral maturity is not cause for arrogance. First of all, moral arrogance is inconsistent with greater maturity. A morally mature person takes no

EXHIBIT 2.4   MORAL/ETHICAL DEVELOPMENT STAGES

Development Stage	Inquiry	Discovery Milestone
Punishment and obedience	Do I have to?	Yes, I will be hurt if I don't.
Instrumental hedonism	What can I get away with?	Anything, just don't get caught.
Law and order	What *should* I do?	Follow the rules.
Universalism	Whose way is best?	Dictated by the circumstances.

time to gloat, but rather seeks actions that do no harm. Remember, these are scientific characterizations, not moral judgments.

Punishment and Obedience Stage

In the punishment and obedience stage, the individual, group, or corporation readily accepts the mandates and injunctions of a higher authority, often without question. At the organization level, the higher authority takes the form of budgetary compliance and growth and profit imperatives. Groups and individuals line up to support this higher authority, often simply because they do not know (or fear finding out) how else to earn their livelihood. They are dependent, just as a young child is dependent on guardians. In this stage of moral development, people relinquish personal authority to another person or entity.

Organizational authority figures often behave unpredictably. Good examples are the patriarch or matriarch in a family business, Norman Bates's mother, and CEO management styles modeled after "Chainsaw" Al Dunlap. The authority answers the question, "Why do I have to?" with the predictable "Because I said so."

At less mature stages of moral development, people recognize the consequences of resistance, and usually protect themselves from harm and pain. The corporations for whom recent accountability legislation is intended are at this extremely early stage of moral development. The overall maturity of any executive team represents an average of the mix of individual moral maturity levels of the entire team. Some executives have developed a more responsive, highly tuned moral code than others. However, individual behavior can change according to the overall moral fabric of the entire team. A CFO who has performed at a higher level may revert to the moral behavior of the first stage under the pressure of an unscrupulous CEO who uses punishment as a means of "motivation." Likewise, a CEO may fall under the influence of an unethical CFO. A mature person not only *knows* better but also *behaves* accordingly in all circumstances.

Instrumental Hedonism Stage

In the instrumental hedonism stage of moral development, a person chooses personal fulfillment, generally in terms of things that give pleasure, even if one must manipulate others to get it. Conveniently, in this level of moral maturity the end often justifies the means. In a corporation, hedonistic behaviors take the form of an obsessive focus on growth, profit, and shareholder wealth—at any cost. Executive behavior at this maturity level typically includes ego gratification through the cultivation of personal power and prestige. Before 2002, when legal constraints on corporations were comparatively loose, some unethical accountants (and CFOs) aided and abetted unscrupulous corporate executive aims by playing "How much can we get away with?" and "How can I manipulate this situation?" and "How far can we stretch this interpretation of GAAP?" These immature games are played by immature people.

Law and Order Stage

In the law and order stage of moral development, conduct is codified across roles, not arbitrarily from person to person. Those mature enough to understand and follow the code do so, for they see it as a reasonable way to protect the rights of self and others. People at this stage of moral development for the first time begin to generalize codes of behavior that include the rights and safety of others beside themselves. In other words, how can we get everyone to behave consistently in terms of the needs of both the individual and society? Notice that this approach represents a more mature viewpoint trying to deal with a less mature viewpoint. Consequently, monitoring systems are typical of this stage. When they work as designed, the three branches of U.S. government represent a more mature set of checks and balances on behavior. Corporate governance boards, when they are mature enough, provide moral checks on corporate executives and others. A CFO of this maturity level interprets GAAP more by intent and spirit than by the extrapolated letter of the law.

Universalism Stage

In the universalism stage, a person, group, or organization has reached a level of moral maturity that does not rely on any conventional source for guidance on proper conduct in any circumstance. Entities who have developed this far see themselves as part of a widened circle of relationships. Because persons, groups, and organizations in this stage can see impacts of interdependent action, they simply do not engage in any activity that would harm anyone or anything. This stage, more than the previous three, has a wide range of progressively more mature behaviors. A CFO this mature does the right thing because it is the legally mandated or societal convention to do so, but the primary driver of action proceeds from a sense of interconnection with and accountability to the many others in the relationship circle. This CFO would find it very difficult to follow a mandate to enforce a 10 percent across-the-board cost-cutting frenzy without studying holistic impacts. The CFO would leave an employer who asked for dubious or fraudulent practices.

PSYCHOSOCIAL DEVELOPMENT

Relationship is the intersection of all human development subsystems, and this is most evident at the nexus of the moral and psychosocial subsystems. The cognitive, needs hierarchy, and self-identity subsystem milestones evolve interdependently with the moral and psychosocial; however, moral and psychosocial dynamics bring a person, group, or organization into the most intimate contact with others—other individuals, other groups, other organizations. Naturally, these dynamics apply to nations as well as all other human social structures. Relationships are the fundamental units of biological life. They are what matter most. People are the only real wealth an organization has.

Refer again to Exhibit 2.3 and note the stages of moral and psychosocial development. Among other aspects, psychosocial maturity characterizes the beliefs about responsibility from which the individual acts in relationship with others. These beliefs are based on assumptions about self-worth and one's place in society in relationship to one's beliefs about the worth and roles of others. This complex web of assumptions is grounded in prior experiences and learning opportunities. Psychosocial maturity stems from proximity to, relationships with, and the significance attached to other persons, groups, and organizations.

A relationship requires communication mechanisms. Humans use language—verbal and written—to such a degree that other available devices have atrophied from disuse. However, although most people remain unconscious of nonverbal skills, these options remain available and operative—for example, eye contact and listening posture. Placing more emphasis on the full range of human communication and perception expands a person's intelligence about relationships.

Other modes of understanding ourselves in relationship to others include aural (vibration, tone), tactile (energy, actual touch), and olfactory (pheromone detection, body odors). Cultures have varying rules for physical proximity and for touching, and these rules differ by gender and social class in some places. Eastern spiritual leaders regularly express a sense of compassionate shock when they first encounter the low self-esteem that exists in so many first-world Westerners. "What do you mean when you say that you do not think highly of your self?"[13] One way or another, individual capacities for relationship to self and others mature along a well-defined series of psychosocial milestones (see Exhibit 2.5).

The interdependencies between subsystems of human development should be obvious by now. Consider that all these subsystems function actively in every human being, at varying levels of maturity, and that the complex of the subsystems works together to impact every single human action, word, and encounter, and this alone justifies study of the science of development. To demonstrate the importance of the psychosocial subsystem in the context of leadership skill development, each psychosocial stage can be identified by a specific set of relationship behaviors.

Trust versus Mistrust Stage   The trust versus mistrust stage of psychosocial development is foundational to all aspects of and all progress in human development because we are, by definition, social beings, and relationships cannot mature unless all involved parties establish a baseline level of trust. People begin to test and learn about trust in relationships from the moment of birth. The presence of the word "trust" in the human language implies that all humans cannot be trusted all the time. Because trustworthy behavior is unpredictable from person to person, people who experience predominantly untrustworthy relationships develop an automatic posture of mistrust based on the degree and number of personal experiences where trust has been violated—especially in childhood. A very important corollary runs deep within the dynamics of this stage of psychosocial development: People who have not learned to trust others rarely learn to trust or esteem themselves.

The classic organizational example should be popping into view about now. The profile is one of a founder/CEO/chairman who has given a large chunk of life and energy to create The Business. Such people often develop a pathology so severe that they really cannot tell the difference between themselves and the busi-

EXHIBIT 2.5   PSYCHOSOCIAL/RELATIONSHIP
DEVELOPMENT STAGES

Development Stage	Inquiry	Discovery Milestone
Trust vs. mistrust	Who can I trust?	Depends on the person
Autonomy vs. shame/doubt	Can I trust myself?	Depends on my experience
Industry vs. inferiority	What can I do?	Depends on how much I trust myself
Identity vs. role confusion	Who am I?	Depends on my relationship with myself and others

ness. They believe that taking care of business is taking care of themselves. All manner of difficulties ensue. Managers cannot critique the business without the founder taking personal offense. Because the founder sees no end to the business, no need arises for succession planning. The founder's every waking hour is willingly given to the business. Anyone who has ever been intimate with a dysfunctional family business should recognize the symptoms. For a nonfamily CFO, this set of conditions can be a nightmare of rivalries and anguish.

At the opposite pole are leaders who, although they have taken their lumps in the trust category, have not generalized or personalized the experiences. These individuals enjoy their work life but keep it in balance with the rest of who they are. According to plan, at the end of their work career, they turn the business over to the next generation. A CFO can serve long and happily in this situation and find satisfaction in helping to assure business continuity through mentoring incoming family members and guiding succession periods.

Autonomy versus Doubt and Shame Stage

The first trust/mistrust stage of psychosocial development occurs early in life, so it is one of the most common places for people to hit developmental setbacks. If the stage is negotiated without too much damage, people eventually discover that self-protection is a simple and effective way to respond when too many incidents of violated trust arise in any give relationship. In a logical, healthy progression beyond the trust/mistrust stage, people develop a sense of personal autonomy. When a person has learned to engage in trusting relationships (trust and be trusted), a trustworthy person begins to feel a sense of self-worth, and as a result, the freedom and ability to act independently. On the other hand, when people repeatedly experience violations of trust, they begin to act from a posture of doubt, or in the worst cases, shame.

In the organizational context, this maturity stage is vividly evident in healthy companies that find themselves the targets of hostile takeovers. The target company rightfully fears that its autonomy will be snuffed out under the dominance of the acquiring firm. Thus they do everything they can to protect themselves. This scenario is not exclusive to publicly traded firms. In their practice, the authors have seen examples of large companies (always misbehaving within the first or second stages of psychosocial maturity) forcing smaller, private companies to sell under duress. A hostile takeover, by definition, indicates moral immaturity.

A different type of psychosocial arrest occurs in individuals—many in the declining years of their careers—who hold implicit trust in their employers, the Willy Lomans of corporate life. They can be identified from their naïve beliefs: "The company would never lay me off. I just have to work harder and be *worth* more.

The company will take care of me." These unfortunate people have all the trust in the world, all the way up to the firing when they discover they do not know how to protect themselves, and that they have no identity outside of work. Like the first-stage founder/CEO, this employee's identity is symbiotic with the business.

A more positive developmental vignette describes a worker, at any level of organizational status, who works well and happily while autonomously keeping a self-protective eye out for signals that something is amiss (a good practice for anyone in these insecure times). Many people discover this aspect of their maturity during mergers and acquisitions. They do not take for granted that the senior player or the acquirer can or will make good on the "no layoffs" promise. Very mature workers often protect themselves proactively by leaving.

Executives take note: People who are mature enough to take autonomous self-protective action may be among the better and more mature employees. If the less mature stay on with an undercurrent of mistrust in their hearts, they may take the moral low road and steal time, goods, and intellectual capital from the company in self-righteous acts of compensation for the betrayal. Developmental choices are only predictable one person at a time.

Industry versus Inferiority Stage

The behavior of people in the third psychosocial development bifurcation point, industry versus inferiority, depends on their achievements during the first two stages. Follow the logic with the "moral low road" example just mentioned: This employee has learned not to trust employers. But she also has low self-esteem and dependency issues so common to this developmental profile, and so, if allowed, she stays on at your company. Shame and self-doubt undermine the sense of personal industry that trustworthy, autonomous people bring to their work as a manifestation of personal pride and self-respect. People who approach their work relationships with a sense of industry stand out in the work force; people subject to feelings of inferiority work under a cloak of virtual invisibility. People who work with a sense of personal inferiority censure the expression of their innovative ideas—too risky if they're wrong. They withhold their opinions because they might rock the boat. Such people, however, expertly offer opinions to peers and subordinates with similar development profiles. This personal dynamic becomes a group dynamic that sometimes engulfs an entire function.

Of course, the opposite happens when more mature people can autonomously discern when and when not to trust while they keep doing good work because it is *their* work. They think enough of their own ideas and experience that they do offer opinions and contribute innovations. In short, because of a positive sense of self and a moral compass magnetized to law, order, and rules, these people are industrious and productive.

Identity versus Role Confusion Stage

The final psychosocial stage describes a self-actualized, unique, self-defined, personal identity functioning in all relationships. At this stage of development, a person defines identity in relationships more by "who I am" than by "how I do things." Beyond the trust/mistrust stage, people progressively define themselves in relationship by their working autonomy and their work quality as judged by others. In the final stage of psychosocial development, people learn to value their own specific contribution—their own unique identity—as an integral part of the relationships they conduct. In this stage, the person still behaves trustfully, autonomously, and industriously, and now the person's identity in terms of personal relationships is rooted in a sense of a unique self rather than a role to play out or perform.

When all goes well, a person emerges at a stage-4 level in all five developmental subsystems, someone who sees more in themselves and the world than do less mature people—someone with an immensely widened circle of confident relationships that generate better information for making decisions. Most importantly, this person has no confusion about role and identity. In fact, this human being is a composite of many identities capable of serving many roles, as appropriate to the situation at hand.

When people see from the perspective of moral universalism, they see many perspectives at once. A straightforward example is an executive who lives comfortably in the United States, but who can actually *see* what it is like to live in Beijing or rural India. Demographic, cultural, social, climatic, and economic information may be incomplete, but far more important, this executive understands the human experience of others, and therefore can make better long-term decisions.

When one sees, one cannot unsee. When one knows, one cannot unknow. Successful development is permanent. There is no going back. Development is a one-way path, and its construction determines all behaviors. So, from a self-identity perspective, this stage-4 executive cannot be anything but conscientious, and cannot do anything that harms others. To act in any less mature manner causes personal pain and anguish. At humanity's best, there is no doubt when high levels of maturity are operative. We remember those moments best in words.

> We hold these truths to be self-evident . . .
> . . . inalienable rights . . . life, liberty and the pursuit of happiness.[14]

All of this discussion describes what really matters in organizations and in life—what makes or eventually breaks individuals and corporations. This short explanation of human development is also what CFOs and executives, on average, never consciously manage. If a person in a leadership position is mature enough to recognize this knowledge gap, the accountability for acquiring an understanding of developmental science essentials becomes obvious. The logic is simple: Corporations and all organizations are social structures created by human beings; therefore the maturity of these structures depends on the composite maturity of the people who have created them.

Likewise, behavior is based on maturity; therefore, individuals, groups, and organizations that have grown unconsciously and not attended to achieving appropriate developmental milestones are bound to harbor pathologies of varying degrees. Pathologies can be treated and corrected, but only if the healthy state of being is desired and clearly defined. Fostering healthy development is the right thing to do for many reasons, including for business common sense because people are the only real wealth an organization has.

THE NATURAL HUMAN MATURITY SEQUENCE: LEARN, EXPERIENCE, DEVELOP

Professional education seminars frequently portray a dual profile for the accountant. To the left of the palpable great divide, the column lists the traits of the "conventional" or "traditional" professional, while the right column depicts "the new controller" or the "strategic partner" or some other label for the evolving paradigm. This either-or picture betrays the tendency of accountants to see polarities and linearity where, in fact, a more accurate portrayal involves a nonlinear, multivariable complex of professional responsibilities. In practice this shows up as waxing or waning profits, favorable or unfavorable variances, and of course, the ubiquitous debit or credit. Few accounting professionals realize just how extensively this flat, two-dimensional perspective pervades their thinking.

The purpose of the following sections is to remind people, who just happen to be accountants, about their native capacities that come with being human. In the context of human development already outlined, this section uses a natural human maturity sequence that accountants working to become better leaders can use to support their professional development. Just as human development unfolds in ways that simultaneously combine cognitive, moral, psychosocial, and the other developmental subsystems, so too, professional maturation simultaneously unfolds by working three parallel discovery processes. First, people begin by learning specific technical information. Next, people then apply lessons in actual working context and accrue experiential knowledge. Finally, those people who aspire to positions of leadership integrate their learning and experiential knowledge with emotional intelligence to develop personal competencies and leadership intelligence.

The distinction between learning and knowledge may seem trivial at first. The difference is significant. Learning technical skills is the first step. Knowledge entails the application of what has been learned. In this context, people engage and practically test what they learn as they apply the lessons to actual life experience and thereby accumulate knowledge about what works—when, where, why, and how. Over time, a composite professional intelligence emerges from accumulated skills and experience. The term "intelligence" can now be incorporated into the definition of general human development given earlier in the chapter.

> **Professional development:** *The intelligent integration of the capacity to see relationships between the self and the workplace environment in new ways.*

Intelligent professional development is an order of magnitude more complex than learning and knowledge. Intelligence encompasses the capacity for awareness by means of learning from experience, the ability to acquire and retain knowledge, the ability to respond quickly and successfully to new situations, and the use of reason in solving problems and directing conduct. Clearly, intelligence is the discerning application of learning and knowledge. The first two columns in Exhibit 2.6 provide a quick synopsis of the three elements of the natural professional maturity sequence and their most tangible results.

Each of the three elements of the natural maturity sequence has a very different operating mode. Just think about the two ends of the spectrum. The lowest meaningful level in the learning continuum is acquiring data. Every CFO knows that even when data can be wrestled into a form that yields information, neither learning nor knowledge, much less intelligence is guaranteed to follow. Intelligence is the creative force in the workplace: organizing, directing, changing, assessing, and innovating.

In all three maturity elements, the genetic wiring a person is born with determines a baseline set of capabilities, tendencies, and preferences. More and more qualities once thought to be genetically determined are turning out to actually be quite mutable—leadership qualities, for example. Research now shows that a person who is not a "born leader" might now become one. The research also shows that a person's motivation to develop intelligently determines what new

EXHIBIT 2.6   NATURAL PROFESSIONAL MATURITY SEQUENCE

Element	Practice	Result
Learning	Information acquisition	Skill
Experience	Knowledge application	Capability
Development	Emotional intelligence	Competence

capabilities people can actually develop. Someone else cannot mandate lasting development. A person must participate voluntarily, and the growth experience must be personally meaningful to be motivating.

LEARN SKILLS

An accounting professional just has to go out and learn disciplinary skills just like learning to tune up a motorcycle engine or cook ethnic food. For our purposes, the distinguishing feature between a skill and a capability is that a "skill" is a body of information intended for a specific purpose (e.g., standard cost theory), and a "capability" is the personal capacity to apply the skill (e.g., using standard cost theory to calculate variances) in the context of knowledge that comes with experience. For instance, a theoretical genius in standard costing cannot necessarily design and implement a useful standard cost system for a given company.

Expertise, Functions, Specialties

A skill is a particular technical expertise. For a financial officer, expertise includes discipline-related baseline facility with double-entry bookkeeping, financial statement preparation, and cost accounting, and budget construction, investment decision analyses, cash management, and information technology. Pick up any beginning or intermediate accounting textbook in financial or managerial accounting for a ready list of skills.

When a CFO or controller supervises specific accounting functions, more than technical expertise is needed. Function examples include fixed asset management, accounts payable, accounts receivable, credit and collection, and payroll. If a financial officer has missed hands-on work in such areas, filling in the blank spots from a wide variety of resources is not hard.[15] In addition to baseline and functional skills, many CFOs choose to develop specialized expertise in technical areas: tax preparation, audit, internal control design, treasury, investment, merger and acquisition techniques, operations divestitures, pension and benefit management, and international currency management, to name a few. For publicly held companies, and for companies that wish to make a public offering, an additional set of specialized skills is required. Established and recent legislation adds regulatory demands to CFO shoulders, including everything from government cost accounting to the 2002 Sarbanes-Oxley Act. Still, all this remains within the accounting/finance discipline. (A feature on Sarbanes-Oxley, or Sarbox as it is known among CFOs, appears in the sidebar.)

Adding to this broad range, top-notch CFOs are expected to possess cross-

THE 2002 SARBANES-OXLEY ACT

"Honor among thieves" is an apt phrase to begin this section because it refers to a code of conduct that evolves outside societal and cultural norms. Such codes usually arise within marginalized groups of people, among those who choose to operate outside the law, and in extreme survival situations. Only the second category applies to those corporate executives and their accountants whose behavior engendered the congressional passage of the Sarbanes-Oxley Act. The critical qualifier is that thieves know they are operating outside the letter and spirit of the law while unethical executives have a very clear understanding of legal details as the context for their choices. In the most egregious cases, executives carefully plot and design their criminal activities. How can this be so? Strong testimonial evidence might lead one to believe that many of these people convinced themselves that they were acting within the letter of the law and not doing anything worse than practicing some aggressive accounting. This may sound implausible until one considers just how many letters make up the accounting "law," Generally Accepted Accounting Principles (GAAP), which continues to provide enough wiggle room for criminal creativity and innovation.

Accounting currently remains the language of business, and GAAP provides extensive and complex rules for speaking that language. The 2002 John Wiley & Sons edition of GAAP is over two inches thick and runs over eleven hundred pages. Separate GAAP guides are published for particular uses such as not-for-profit accounting, government accounting, and employee benefit plans. Add to these the International Accounting Standards that are rapidly increasing in influence especially for multinational corporations.

Skip the fine print. No wonder business people need specialists and CPAs, as well as specialists within specialists to interpret especially thorny GAAP items. Such bloated codes of practice are sure signs of special-interest influences, the belief that more detail equals better accounting, and at the very least, rules suffocation that obscures what truly matters: safeguarding the integrity of actual people and their work as the primary source of wealth generation.

At the risk of setting too high a standard, if the Judeo-Christian God found a ten-item moral code sufficient, and the Buddha was content with only four noble truths, accountants ought to be able to condense their principles just a bit. They can and should, but until that happens, it seems we are stuck with legislative mandates as a substitute for clear, self-determined principles and the common sense of doing the right thing. But there is the rub. "Doing the right thing" is subject to almost as many interpretations as GAAP. Enter moral and psychosocial development. The underlying conditions are facts, not excuses for immoral behavior. Maturity is about not yielding to temptation that does harm to others.

The Sarbanes-Oxley Act of 2002 (SOA) explicitly targets corporate and accounting wrongdoing. Examining the provisions of the SOA reveals just how immature are (or were, in the case of those that no longer exist) the corporations and their accountants that SOA has in mind. The most important guiding principles in the SOA appear to be *disclosure*, *controls*, *audits*, and *certification*. The need to legislate these important principles is a clear-cut case of people with a law-and-order level of maturity attempting to contain the unbridled exuberance of other people at an instrumental hedonism (or lower) maturity stage. The need for the structure of rules usually reserved for preadolescent children applies to immature adults as well. Let us see how the four law-and-order-based SOA principles address the maturity stages of the moral developmental subsystem.

The 2002 Sarbanes-Oxley Act

Focuses	Universalism	Punishment and Obedience
Disclosure (Sec. 409)	Transparency	Mandate truth-in-reporting
Controls (Sec. 404)	Accountability	Sanction disobedience
Audits (Sec. 404, 806)	Trust	Monitor and enforce compliance
Certification (Sec. 302)	Integrity	Authenticate responsibility

Every parent will recognize the set of behaviors and responses listed under the punishment-and-obedience stage of moral maturity. Healthy children, and some developmentally delayed young adults, go through the same sequence in the practice, testing, and cultivation of moral standards.

Next, let us take apart the SOA and examine how appropriately Congress has deployed a law-and-order level of moral maturity compared to the characteristics of a more mature, universal stage of moral behavior. Intriguingly SOA sections 409 and 404 most closely parallel the transparency and accountability attributes of the universalism stage of moral development. Note that neither section had mandated specific compliance deadlines at the time this book was written. Section 409 requires real-time disclosure of any material change in financial condition. Section 404 requires management to state in annual reports how it has addressed a range of internal controls and financial reporting procedures.

Disclosure parallels transparency, and controls parallel accountability. If and when Congress sets compliance deadlines, it remains interesting that the two leading indicators of integrity, disclosure and controls, received deadlines *after* the lagging indicators, audits and certification, suggesting that the law-and-order focuses of congressional leadership center more on punishment for after-the-fact deeds by means of audit and certification, than on obedience to real-time disclosure, and the impact of current control requirements on future outcomes.

Moving on to the ways audits and certification parallel trust and integrity provides further insight into the workings of development in SOA. Section 806 requires that the CEO and other appropriate company officers personally sign financial reports attesting to their validity. The connection with *integrity* is obvious. A subtler developmental dynamic is how close the signatures and certifications come to the old-school practice of writing-on-the-blackboard over and over, "I will not steal from the school lunch money box again." Punishment? No doubt! Based on mistrust? Count on it! Of course, the side benefit exists of a binding legal statement for use in future punishment.

Finally, a second look at Section 404 shows that a company's external auditors must show due diligence and perform attestations to management's assessment of internal controls, suggesting the psychosocial developmental question, "Who can I trust?" From a congressional point of view, the answer obviously is not corporate management. So, even though management is punished with certification, Congress does not trust that executives will suddenly mature and "never do it again." Congress clearly expects that corporations need monitoring requirements (external auditors) to enforce compliance. Profound mistrust finds expression in Section 806, which provides accommodation and protection for whistle blowers. This combination says, "We *really, really* don't trust them." Deserved by some? Yes. Deserved by most? To be determined.

All this analysis is meant to make absolutely clear the incredible depth to which developmental catalysts go—so deep that almost no one sees them. Like the air we breathe and the culture we live in, we are so intimate, interdependent, and symbiotic with our own personal development that it is essentially invisible to us without deliberate examination. None of this is intended to be a criticism of SOA. Congress took on its public protection responsibilities with gusto, as it should. One can hope that our lawmakers are truly as interested in the small investor (e.g., those who lost their retirement funds) as they are with influential institutional investors. Good, honest financial chiefs and their CEOs, and a large number of other people, will spend countless hours and precious resources answering the charge of "guilty until proven innocent," all because of personal immaturity at corporate levels where none of us can afford it. Scott Leibs, editor of *CFO-IT* magazine, in interpreting remarks made by Cynthia Glassman of the Securities and Exchange Commission (SEC), quipped in the Spring 2003 issue, ". . . an unexamined corporate life may ultimately be lived in jail."[16] This extreme consequence may await developmentally impaired individuals in high places.

disciplinary skills. Frequently listed items in professional education curricula include strategic cost management, supply chain expertise, strategic competitor analyses, strategic performance measurement and management, and process improvement methodologies. Then also include the ever-evolving array of specialized cross-disciplinary tools that are largely based in accounting, such as activity-based costing and management, resource consumption accounting, and target costing. These lists are intended to represent categories and are not exhaustive. Every CFO must consciously build a skill set that is needed by the organization served, and of course, those skills that a CFO enjoys. This process is one of lifetime accumulation of degree programs, executive education, Internet study, and hands-on practice.

A mature learner does not just attend a seminar or take a course, but quickly seeks ways to apply new expertise to test its usefulness. A skill does not become capability until one becomes facile with its application. A mature learner also takes every chance to integrate education and training to gain more knowledge and experience. A mature learner does not isolate skill education and hoard new information from others. A mature learner's primary concerns are self-improvement in the interest of becoming a more valuable contributor in organization life, and of experiencing self-fulfillment.

Application in Context

Any skill on the laundry list is best learned in contextual application, and this goes back to the point about the predictable decline in applicable memory when learning (but not using) new software. New learning must be applied immediately and consistently first to consolidate the lesson and then to gain proficiency. Practice problems help, but nothing substitutes for applying the new skill in an actual work context.

Watch one, do one, teach one. For example, when taking a new course of study, be creative and design a project that requires use of the new skills. Another excellent way to cement learning is to teach to others what you have learned. As a simple illustration, say you have just finished a course or seminar in inventory management techniques. Most likely, you will want to implement some of what you have learned. An excellent way to retain what you have learned is to teach it to your staff, and perhaps to personnel from other functions who may benefit. Two important things happen in this teaching approach beyond building staff expertise. First, you create a venue for deepening relationships with your staff and others; second, you can teach discernment and evaluation skills by explaining why you intend to implement some facets, and why others are not appropriate for your firm, and inviting discussion and debate. Too many times, professionals come away excited from an educational experience only to have their enthusiasm wither for want of application or sharing what has been learned. This apply-it-now dynamic is, in fact, the bridge between learning and experiential knowledge.

A new skill usually has a range of possible applications. As an example, a CFO decides to learn about strategic performance measurement and management, and chooses the well-known balanced scorecard (BSC) model developed by Robert S. Kaplan and David Norton in the 1990s. The CFO purchases *The Balanced Scorecard*, Kaplan and Norton's first book, and studies it, taking notes about how the BSC might be implemented locally. In this CFO's context, the BSC is a technical, mechanical process: Start with the company's strategic plan, use the four measurement perspectives (financial, customer, internal process, and learning and growth), identify measures for each perspective, and then manage by the measures.

The CFO only glances over the second half of the book concerned with four "management processes." Armed with a new skill (i.e., building a set of balanced measures), our eager CFO sets out to craft a scorecard for the company—all alone. A few weeks and much hard work later, the CFO presents a BSC to the CEO and executives. The proposal falls flat and is not even considered for implementation. You already know the two reasons. First, the CFO concentrated on technical measurement, barely glancing at the second half of the BSC paradigm devoted to implementation and management. Second, no one else participated in the CFO's learning and discovery. In other words, no one else got the tire-kicking experience.

This approach exemplifies immature use of new skills and brings us to the subject of mature application.

The BSC example demonstrates the critical difference between learning and experience. People can learn technical information through private study. People accrue experience only in a relationship context, applying new learning in workplace activities with other people. (See the Web site for a discussion of "Building Cross-functional Relationships with an Emphasis on IT.")

EXPERIENTIAL KNOWLEDGE

Just as a professional has to just go out and learn technical skills, so too, one must find a way to bring it all back and capably apply new skills in the workplace. Application is the bridge to experiential knowledge. Knowledge accrues when specific learning activities translate into cumulative experience through the application of what has been learned. More directly, the learning process can, but does not always, result in accumulated knowledge. The capabilities discussed in this section assume proficiency in the three learning categories of the last section: discipline-related baseline facilities, functional skills, and appropriate specialized expertise. Fundamental skills are analogous to the materials needed to build a house or a hydroelectric dam. They are necessary, but unorganized until properly assembled. The capability to build a house or a dam or a business is no ordinary academic exercise. Here are examples of five tasks that require both skills and experiential knowledge.

1. Competitor analysis and business intelligence
2. Actionable business plan development
3. Aligning resource allocation
4. Business structuring such as divestment, mergers, and acquisitions
5. New business generation

On the surface, these capabilities might look like technical skills, but compare them with basic technical skills like pension plan administration, 1120 tax preparation, and payroll. The difference is stark. The basic learning domain of professional accounting skills includes performance of routines, attention to detail, and keeping up with laws and regulations relevant to the tasks. The five items in the list require skills and something more: the experiential knowledge necessary to apply them in a variety of contexts. Two examples offer more clarification.

Aligning resource allocation with special projects, business plans, and strategic priorities requires budget and forecast skills, as well as general ledger familiarity. But is this enough? Any experienced CFO can quickly answer that it is not. A CFO who designs resource alignment draws on accumulated knowledge of business priorities, current and long-term strategic objectives, a coherent picture of existing resources, and many more complex information sets. The CFO does not view these complex information sources in isolation but rather as pieces of the big picture. Sure, a brand-spanking-new MBA who has specialized in accounting can perform the task called "resource alignment," but does so from a zero-level experience base. The seasoned CFO works from a base of many events and encounters that constitute a distinctive knowledge base. The freshly minted MBA has theory and practice problems, but little else. Such comparisons explain why so many recruitment ads say, "Experience a must."

Experiential Knowledge: A Scarce Resource

Experiential knowledge is a scarce resource because receiving cross-functional exposure is not always easy, particularly for accountants, and because accountants are not always eager to seek that exposure. Lifetime careers with the same company are no longer the norm. Similarly, a long time has passed since accountants were just bookkeepers. Both of these facts are good news for the accounting professional seeking accrual of experiential knowledge. Although some CFOs make job-hopping a nasty habit for their own reasons, the mid-career CFO with multiple companies on a résumé may be in just as strong a position as a financial chief with twenty years service to the same company.

Because accountants are now far more than bookkeepers, mature CEOs look for broad experience with other functions, within and between industries, and in various job titles. So, the career doors are now open to multiple jobs as long as transitions show progress. Likewise, experiential knowledge is now easier to accrue during one's career. Still, professionals with strong accounting/finance vitae commonly have little to show outside their home discipline. The bottom line is that understanding the business, that cherished CEO expectation, means more than a strong accounting-based résumé.

What keeps an accounting expert from garnering new professional capabilities and experiential knowledge that applies to "understanding the business"? Fear of moving out of a personal comfort zone, fear of starting over in a new firm, fear of family and personal impacts of a new job or hefty extra assignment. In short, it is developmentally interesting that synonyms for fear are *anxiety* and *mistrust*. Not one of these fears is unreasonable, especially for a person who, by training, if not native disposition, is risk averse.

But a distinction needs to be made between professional fundamentals and behavioral preferences. The *CFO Survival Guide* is full of information on development and maturity, so this section examines other factors blocking accrual of new professional capabilities and experiential knowledge. The exact focus of the experiential knowledge a CFO needs is unique to every individual and changes with every organization; therefore, the discussion offers no silver-bullet list of sure-to-please résumé items. Instead, this section examines the major obstacles that impede the process of accruing new capabilities. Removing the obstacles strips off unnecessary restraints. With a lightened mental/emotional load, the CFO (or aspiring CFO) adds more degrees of freedom of choice.

Time, as a perceived obstacle to development, is a good place to start. Accountants at all levels consistently cite "lack of time" as a chief reason that they cannot seek broader experience or learn to better understand the business. Do you know *anyone* over eight years old who has enough time? The time obstacle is hardly unique to the accounting profession. When anyone says, "I don't have time," the translation can range from, "That other thing I could be doing doesn't fit my sense of priorities" or "I don't like new things; they frighten me." Well, these same people should be more and more prepared for this response: "Grow up."

Yes, fiduciary transaction work, budgets, forecasts, and financial analyses are full of details that take time, but here lies a circular paradox. Yes, this kind of work is time-consuming, but who creates and maintains these time-consuming procedures and routines? Right. Accountants. Put simply, each professional needs to rationalize transaction-based work, ruthlessly critiquing which parts of one's work are necessary or of value to others.

Many accountants and CFOs are not willing to personally shoulder this responsibility. They eschew spring cleaning the reporting-and-analysis house because, well, someone might *need* that information—some time. So-and-so *did* ask for it—once—two years ago. More information is better; more information is safer.[17] Even CFOs exempt from any of these descriptions might think about the mind-set of staff members toward their recurring work. Consider how many resource-hours may be taken up by unnecessary and redundant work. (See the "Barriers and Accelerators: Time and Workload" feature on the Web site.)

Another problem can really get in the way of gaining cross-functional, experiential knowledge: an organizational culture that is anti-accounting/finance. These companies are usually run by executives who came up through the marketing, production, and engineering ranks. This nut is truly a hard one for accountants to crack. Still, even accounting bigots need accounting, so plenty of people in the profession end up in this climate. The story of a never-say-die controller is instructive here.

As a division controller, Jeff was one of the best accountants around. He knew the nuances of both financial and managerial accounting, and he was extremely operations friendly. He had youthful energy in the bargain. His supervisor, the division general manager, was pleased with Jeff's work. There was only one problem. After working in financial services for several years, Jeff had come to this multidivision manufacturer and quickly realized he wanted to make his career in production. He spent as much time as he could on the shop floor, made a point of striking up professional friendships with the production staff, and went back to school for his MBA with an emphasis in operations and management science.

Every time a supervisor or manager opening came up in production, Jeff applied. He never even received an interview. Having a good relationship with his GM, Jeff sought some answers after four attempts to make the transition. "You're an accountant!" his GM stated the obvious. "We don't hire accountants in production." "Why not?" Jeff asked. "Now don't take this personally, Jeff, but accountants don't make good ops people. They can't take the political heat of the shop, and well, frankly, accountants aren't leadership material." The GM believed every word he said, and while reassuring Jeff of his value to the team, essentially said, "Forget it." The end of the story is that Jeff left the company within the year to become the COO of a smaller company, and the GM lost a good person in two areas. Ways to heal the breach between operations and accounting are available. For an excellent, but brief, map to this territory, see the work of Brian Maskell, experienced in both operations and accounting.[18]

The easiest entry point for accruing cross-functional, experiential knowledge is through participation on multifunction project teams and leadership of such teams. Often other team members are more than happy to cede leadership and the work that goes with it to a willing volunteer. If you are not asked to be part of such teams, proactively seek them out. Do not be embarrassed to request a seat as an observer. As experience grows, make yourself available for initiatives in performance measurement, quality, customer relationship management, and the like. A CFO can stay fresh and quickly build experience and credibility by continually leading efforts with distinctly nonfinancial purposes. Respect for such accountants rises swiftly.

Common Threads

In the big picture of most corporations, financial and accounting skills are like the dial tone on a telephone line. When you go to use the phone or the modem, it better be there. Routine reports, functional accounting operations, and dial tones are all taken for granted. People only notice their absence. Think about it. When is the last time your payroll supervisor heard a genuine thank-you for delivering pay on time? In contrast, stand ready if someone misses a paycheck. The same alert status goes for accounts payable getting checks to suppliers. The reverse goes for accounts receivable and credit and collection, where customers want to hear the dial tone, and not you, when they pick up the phone. *Baseline, functional, and special-expertise accounting skills are nothing special.* This first common thread pertains to an accountant's profile.

If the first common-thread assumption is true, some other commonality *must be* considered special in CFO performance. Yes, the phrase *understanding the business* emerges again. Only imagination limits a CFO in ways to demonstrate this understanding: for example, contributions to planning the future of the business, that is, strategic and business plans, effective and efficient budget systems, ideas for new business, sensitivity to resource needs, to name a few. Perhaps most important is weaving together the profile that makes the CEO think of the financial chief as the right- *and* left-hand person. If the CEO holds this view, a CFO truly understands the business, at least the CEO's version of it.

The third common thread is *stand up and lighten up*. Be seen. Be heard. Appropriately challenge the CEO and other executives. Most of all be a person who is known for moral courage and ethical conduct. That's the "stand up" part. "Lighten up" means work on that stereotype accountant personality. Auditor and accountant jokes do not come from nowhere. Get out of your office and into other people's areas—with respect, of course. Get out of the details and into the big picture. Get out of your head and into your heart. The mature CFO has already practiced these behaviors and attitudes so long that any other way seems awkward.

A visible path begins to emerge: Learn skills, practice them until they become automatic, and then apply those capabilities to expand experiential knowledge. These skills make a "good accountant" as discussed in the preface. And the "develop" portion of the natural maturity sequence that appears in the title of this section? Great CFOs emerge only with the addition of personal maturity and leadership intelligence. The rest of the chapters in this book explain how people acquire them.

CFO TECHNICAL SKILL AND MANAGEMENT EXPERIENCE ASSESSMENT

The *CFO Survival Guide* works to make professional learning and development more accessible and practical by offering self-assessment tools so that the CFO can gauge current skills, experience, and leadership competency in terms of personal strengths and weaknesses. This section provides you with the opportunity to assess your professional technical skills and management experience based on a range of some of the increasingly common responsibilities for the CFO. A similar section in Chapter 3 assesses general leadership competencies, and in Chapter 4, accounting and finance function leadership responsibilities.

Move through each of the assessments item by item and answer the following question: Is this one of my strengths or one of my weakness? Use a scale of one-to-five, or the like, if a more numerical assessment helps. After completing each of the assessments in this book, you can focus on which areas need maintenance and which areas require new learning, experience and development.

ASSESSMENT CHECKLIST

See the last few paragraphs of Chapter 2 for this assessment's context.
Circle **S** if this is a strength or **W** if this is a weakness.

Accounting Technical Skills
S   W   Financial reporting
S   W   Compliance/government/regulatory reporting
S   W   Internal controls
S   W   Internal audits
S   W   Fixed asset and inventory management
S   W   Treasury management
S   W   Cash management
S   W   Taxation
S   W   International currencies, taxation, etc.

General Business Skills and Management Experience
S   W   Budgeting
S   W   Capital budgeting
S   W   Quality systems
S   W   Line and nonfinancial experience
S   W   Outsourcing
S   W   Strategic cost management
S   W   Performance measurement and incentives
S   W   Customer and product profitability
S   W   Mergers, acquisitions, divestitures
S   W   Industry-specific experience
S   W   Appreciation of significance of differing economic and cultural environments

Information Technology Expertise
S   W   *Ability to use standard business applications*—spreadsheet, database, and presentation software: I am familiar with these applications, and I am technically proficient at their use.
S   W   *Internet:* The Internet is a regular resource for my tasks as a financial professional.
S   W   *Enterprise-wide/client-server systems:* I know how to use these information technology platforms to widely distribute financial information and reports within my organization's strategic focuses and contexts.

Business Analysis/Information Interpretation
S   W   *Ability to use appropriate decision-making techniques* such as regression analysis, learning curves, sensitivity analysis, spreadsheet analysis, probability concepts, decision trees, and simulation: I am technically proficient in using these techniques as I characterize my organization's business and financial profile.
S   W   *Ability to provide counsel on general business matters:* After the dust settles from my financially focused report, I can put the financial information that I just presented into the context of my organization's strategic focuses.

S   W   *Ability to develop frameworks for guiding decision making:* Rather than following my financially based job description to the letter of the law, I supplement the financial frameworks with strategic oversight when creating models for decision-making within my area.

S   W   *Competitor analysis:* Using my organization's strategic plan, I look for information about my organization's competitors when analyzing our business position.

S   W   *Interorganizational cost management:* I support the work of our value chain, including suppliers, internal processes, pricing, customer cost structure, and life cycle management in terms of interorganizational cost management responsibilities for the finance function.

S   W   *Human and intellectual capital management:* I work with peer executives to understand and manage this new area of executive responsibility.

S   W   *Customer profitability analysis:* I am able to use activity-based and other technical models to report customer profitability, and then work with sales, marketing, and operations to analyze customer management, and then work with customers to improve cost structures.

S   W   *Enhance customer revenue:* I work with peer executives to strategize ways to increase customer revenue while serving the customer better.

S   W   *Customer relationship management (CRM):* Whether or not my company has CRM software, I consistently work with sales and marketing to smooth customer relationships.

Process Improvement

S   W   *Benchmarking:* When asked to consider benchmarking initiatives for my organization, I know when this tool is appropriate as well as what and who to benchmark.

S   W   *Total quality methods:* I have had experience with the nonfinancial considerations behind total quality methods. I am always careful to ask the question, "Quality of what?"

S   W   *Reengineering and other process change methods:* When faced with reengineering or any other process change instrument, I ask why this specific instrument was chosen in the context of my organization's strategic choices.

S   W   *Activity analysis and management:* When engaged in activity analysis, I can look beyond process efficiency and effectiveness parameters to also include an analysis of how well activities align with my organization's strategy.

S   W   *Activity-based costing (ABC):* Any ABC work I am involved with is directly linked to operations processes. I make certain that operations employees are equal partners in designing and using ABC models.

Strategic Planning

S   W   *Vision creation:* I can see beyond accounting and finance functions in terms of what my organization might become in the future.

S   W   *Mission statement creation:* I am aware of what my organization as a whole must do well to fulfill its vision.

S   W   *Environmental scanning:* I have specific practices that I regularly use to keep myself up-to-date on the business environment surrounding my organization.

S   W   *Business plan goal/target setting:* When I am given a strategic plan, I can translate the strategies into business plan goals with targets that will align my area's efforts with the whole organization.

S   **W**   *Detailed action-plan development:* After establishing strategically aligned business plans with appropriate targets, I can see and implement supportive detailed action plans and specific initiatives.

S   **W**   *Performance monitoring and adaptation:* I am comfortable and familiar with creating performance measurements for my action plans and initiatives, and I routinely use the performance measurement information to guide my management decisions.

NOTES

1. Lao Tzu, *Tao Te Ching*, trans. Victor H. Mair (New York: Bantam Books, 1990), 23.
2. H. Thomas Johnson, "A Recovering Cost Accountant Reminisces," *Journal of Innovative Management,* Fall 2002, 43.
3. George Leonard, *Mastery: The Keys to Success and Long-Term Fulfillment* (New York: Plume, 1992).
4. Based on information published in *CMA Management*, February 1999, 8, as summarized from a *Financial Executive* survey of Fortune 1000 CEOs published in November-December 1998.
5. See "Key Career Benchmarks," *Controller Magazine,* July 1998, 26.
6. Francisco J. Varela, *Principles of Biological Autonomy* (New York: Elsevier North Holland, 1979).
7. Jean Piaget, *The Essential Piaget*, ed. H. Gruber and J. Vonech (New York: Basic Books, 1977).
8. Lawrence Kohlberg, *Essays on Moral Development* (San Francisco: Harper, 1981).
9. Abraham Maslow, *Toward a Psychology of Being* (New York: Van Nostrand Reinhold, 1968).
10. Jane Loevinger, *Ego Development* (San Francisco: Jossey-Bass, 1977).
11. Erik Erikson, *Childhood and Society* (New York: Norton, 1963).
12. Catherine Stenzel and Joe Stenzel, *From Cost to Performance* (Hoboken, N.J.: John Wiley & Sons, 2003).
13. The Dalai Lama expressed such sentiments when he first encountered Western lifestyles in *Stages of Meditation,* (Ithaca: Snow Lion Publications, 2001) 14.
14. The Declaration of Independence.
15. Example sources include John Wiley & Sons' recent "Essential Series" covering a range of functional topics. For a textbook reference, the authors are particularly fond of the multiple editions of Sidney Davidson, *Intermediate Accounting: Concepts, Methods, and Uses* (Hinsdale, Illinois: CBS College Publishing/The Dryden Press, 1982).
16. Russ Banham, "The Power of 3," *CFO-IT,* Spring (2003, 4).
17. The authors wish to credit Dr. James Wetherbe for this information principle.
18. Specifically see Brian Maskell, "The Reconciliation of Finance and Operations," *Journal of Strategic Performance Measurement* 3, no. 5 (1999) 23, and his book *Making the Numbers Count: The Accountant as Change Agent on the World Class Team* (Portland: Productivity Press, 1996).

In the Company of the CFO

MATURITY, LEADERSHIP COMPETENCY DEVELOPMENT, AND WORKPLACE APPLICATIONS

This chapter completes the characterization of CFO development tasks by focusing on what it takes to become not only a good accountant but a great CFO. Successful leadership competency development and application depends on two contexts: (1) personal and professional maturity and (2) the needs of the organization, its people, and the work environment. Chapter 2 defined professional development as the intelligent integration of new and more comprehensive capacities to see relationships between the self and the workplace environment. The first section of this chapter examines how CFOs develop their own unique expression of maturity through integrated workplace perspectives within a specific set of role-related responsibilities.

From the context of personal and professional maturity, this chapter's second major section indexes a full set of leadership competencies for CFO professional development, just as key technical skills and experiential knowledge were catalogued in Chapter 2. The final major section in this chapter characterizes the application of CFO leadership competencies in the context of the workplace by articulating the dynamic interdependent relationships between the organization, its people, and their work environment.

As human beings, CFOs are subject to all the developmental principles discussed in this book. Adults easily forget that development does not stop at age eighteen. Development has no end point as long as there is a desire to learn. In this fact lies the untapped energy and resources latent in the human beings within organizations; people of all ages feel more fulfilled when they learn in a positive environment. For a CFO helping to properly utilize these energies and resources, professional development becomes a set of continuously expanding personal and professional accountabilities: to oneself, to shareholders, to peer executives, to the CEO, to the rest of the company, to the community, to the planet, and full circle back to self again. In this context, CFO maturity can be assessed in terms of the essence and function of that role.

CFO MATURITY—ESSENCE AND FUNCTION

A CFO's stance and attitude reflect the degree of self-development, consciously and unconsciously. Regrettably, too many people accept a notion of self that is complete, finished, and immutable upon reaching adulthood. "That's just the way I am"; "I'll never change"; and "You'll just have to accept me the way I am" are all signs of a person who considers development complete.

One of the very first tasks of a person who wishes to correct this mistaken perception, CFO or not, is to form an opinion on this subject of when a human being is complete and has stopped developing and then take action accordingly. From the perspective of a person with lifelong development goals, the answer becomes obvious. Investment in self-development reflects not only a high degree of maturity but also a fundamental appreciation of learning as one of life's great joys. People differ in the degree to which they intentionally participate in their own development. Questions and doubts arise. *Can I change if I want to? Can I expect others to change too? What kind of changes will improve my life or cause me difficulties?* Unchallenged by these healthy questions, patterns become familiar, even comfortable, and a predictable sense of self remains the same, for good or ill.

The second step on the road to professional development self-discovery and improvement focuses on the results of the first step: ruthlessly ferret out and modify unhealthy aspects of self. This work is like weeding the garden and tilling the soil before planting—remove obstacles to personal growth and happiness before piling on new skills. On the most practical level, a person cannot develop healthy leadership competencies if the relationship with one's self is ailing. Once unhealthy obstructions have been cleared, the cultivation of strengths and competencies for an ever-stronger presence can begin.

Leaders and their organizations are interdependent; they develop together. Although leadership capacities are now being taught based on statistically validated models, sincere use of such methods remains the exception. Unlike balanced scorecards and total quality programs, there is no widely accepted leadership curriculum, much less a tested human development course of study. In contrast, functional skills constitute the bulk of professional training and education. Most professionals are inundated with paper and electronic advertisements on functional topics. Recall that the CFO function refers to purpose, capacity, utility, and role. This translates loosely to answering three questions: (1) *Why* is the CFO here? (2) *What and how much* can the CFO do? and (3) *What meaning* does the CFO's presence have in the organization?

Ask anyone why the company needs the CFO. The majority of answers typically run like these: to do the books, to get me my paycheck, to make sure the company does not go broke, to do the taxes and other government-required work. With few exceptions, CFOs know this is true. Financial and accounting departments go to great lengths to garner acknowledgment for higher purposes than these routine tasks. CFOs are pulled in three directions—essential, routine accounting tasks, unpredictable ad hoc priorities, and major initiatives mandated by the executive team. The executive group expects the CFO to provide decision-quality financial and operational information. Employees expect dial-tone financial services—pick up the phone and it's always there (payroll, expense checks), and they ultimately hold the CFO responsible. Everybody expects the CFO and staff to drop everything and work on *their* priorities. Executives expect the CFO to make new mandates a top priority. From a time perspective, this professional trifecta means that the CFO must work simultaneously on historical data, current work pressures, and initiatives designed to build the company's future. The CFO exists to link all this as a distribution node for the practical information and services that employee and executive groups need from one another to accomplish their local and holistic intentions.

As seen by nonfinancial employees, answers to the second question—*What and how much* can the CFO do?—usually flow directly from the first question. Their answers change to the degree that the CFO aligns finance and accounting work behind defined and executive-validated purposes. This positioning is nothing more than executing the responsibilities of the finance/accounting department according to the mandates of the mission, strategic plan, and business plan. Yet, when the balance between executive and employee priorities teeters, CFOs more often than not find themselves changing priorities as often as underwear, and eating pizza or Chinese take-out with staff members as they all work past marketing's quitting time.

Because accounting is the language of business for most organizations, everyone wants accounting to solve their business problems by coming up with some magical numerical formula to make their numbers look better. In contrast, when a CFO runs the accounting shop with the following seven principles in mind, order can be wrought out of chaos and the function and priorities of both the CFO and the accounting/finance department become clearer for all stakeholders.

1. Establish the *explicit functional purposes* for the office of the CFO and have directives formally validated by the CEO and executive team.

2. Based on those functional purposes, *design staff competencies* and their work

descriptions. Assign routine tasks and ongoing designated priorities that are specifically connected to major company objectives.

3. The executive team is likely to forget (or intentionally ignore) the two items just mentioned. Therefore, with the CEO, *develop selection criteria for ad hoc work* and requests. Keep a running log of all work in the office, and review workload priorities with the CEO at appropriate intervals.

4. Make sure the CEO and anyone else who controls your department resources *clearly understands what you and your people are doing* and where priorities are placed. This information can be presented numerically, for ease of communication in terms of percent of time devoted to recurring work. Next, layer on current staff commitments to projects, in terms of weekly or monthly staff hours and total time to finish projects. Finally list active ad hoc assignments and the estimated time to completion.

5. *Do not accept significant new, long-term assignments* if all of the above show that staff resources are already stressed and may become exhausted in the near term. Establish reasonable plans for how the new requirements can be addressed.

6. Insist on *quarterly performance reviews with the CEO* or equivalent supervisor. You can do all the work so that all the CEO needs to do is spend an hour or two with you. Your preparation also gives you the advantage of setting the discussion agenda. Reiterate previously agreed-upon objectives and priorities, show progress on each; for completions, show results against preset performance targets and work-in-process status.

7. Don't set yourself and your staff up for failure. *Do not always just say yes.*

The third query—*What meaning* does the CFO's presence have in the organization?— depends entirely on the work entailed and on the results related to the first two questions. Of course, the answer also depends on developing the personal maturity and leadership competencies characterized throughout the entire *CFO Survival Guide.* At this point, however, having characterized the CFO's role in terms of essence and function, the next section characterizes the CFO in terms of the CFO's primary accountabilities from a high-level perspective.

The CFO's Primary Accountabilities

This section is not a catalogue of technical skills, nor a checklist of reporting responsibilities, and certainly not a list of obvious accountabilities such as closing the books and paying taxes. The CEO should not need to check up on the CFO's dial-tone functions like timely payment of quarterly payroll taxes, whether or not SEC filings are complete. These silent housekeeping tasks are no different from the ways that a production manager must see that products are made, a salesperson must sell, and an engineer must design.

For many decades, the function of the CFO has been to report and archive the past. Financial statements report results, payroll compensates for work already done, and so on. Recently, one of the primary shifts in the CFO's functional perspective is a focus on the present and future. In terms of specific expertise, this new outlook on functions may include

- Involvement/leadership in cross-functional continuous (and discontinuous) process improvement
- Performance measurement and management
- Coordination of diverse improvement initiatives
- Partnership with IT for design and construction of IT services
- Contributions to planning for the organization's future through market intelligence, demand analyses, and capability assessments, to name a few

Each of these activities requires complex competencies, interpersonal adeptness, and a sense for legitimate shifting of high-level organizational priorities. Four ethical principles guide the transformation of the CFO to work more maturely and responsibly.

1. The first responsibility of CFO leadership is to *tell the truth* in order to establish consistent credibility, and thereby earn trust in all encounters. All other leadership responsibilities depend on this primary obligation.

2. Represent work and business conditions *in concrete, human-accessible terms,* (not financial and mathematical abstractions) so that they are meaningful to the widest possible circle of relationships. As much as possible, weed out numerical representations that do not address people and the work they do.

3. Lead all other executives and managers in cultivating *awareness of accountability* in light of their purposes in the organization.

4. All of these ethical principles attend to the *care and direction* that organizations need. That's what leaders are for: to fearlessly attend to sustaining the life of the organization and its people.

Now listen to actual CFOs tell how they want to contribute concretely to their organizations:[1]

- "Drive out waste. Better yet, don't let it get built in the first place."
- "Communicate often and schedule regular meetings with all units—a marketing call—to showcase accounting/finance services."
- "Become consultants/facilitators to our companies (and get the skills to do so)."

- "Be a guinea pig for the 'new try' where top management is supportive."
- "Run some classes to teach accounting to nonfinancial employees."
- "Develop a human capital model for future investment in people."
- "Rationalize financial reporting and transaction load."
- "Share knowledge with colleagues."
- "Assist top management in making their decisions clear to the whole organization."
- "Temper CEOs who indulge in 'word of the week' notions because they have attended too many seminars."

In these practical ways, among others, CFOs see themselves making good on their ethical responsibilities—to assure accountability for the care and direction of their organizations. To accomplish this, financial professionals must overcome some serious stereotypes and establish a new presence for themselves.

CFO Presence

> *He wore gold-rimmed glasses and had those rather automatic but slow gestures typical of men who live with numbers and accounting books. He carried a dark brown briefcase with his initials in gold—no doubt a gift from his company for some recent anniversary. "Your first twenty-five years with us, my dear Peñalosa": the rote phrases of a manager who, for those same twenty-five years, must have kept the poor man in a perpetual hell of uncertainty and humiliation.*[2]
>
> Alvaro Mutis

Consider this epigraph as the antithesis of the desired CFO presence. This quote is the stuff of an accountant's nightmares. Accounting and finance professionals know the stereotypes only too well. In spite of them, most of these professionals feel a genuine dedication to their work and sincerely wish that their profession could find its way to a more elevated status in the eyes of their coworkers. Many CFOs and controllers work hard to identify the next steps in their professional development. On a personal level, professional development and learning to see more is exciting work, but putting those insights into practice is a bit harder. Read the following words spoken by CFOs and controllers as they remind themselves that mature conduct shapes other people's perceptions of the profession:[3]

- "Remember, financial professionals must stick their necks out; we won't be asked to be a business partner; we must take initiative and constantly be learning to fill that capacity."
- "We need to spend more time to integrate our information with operations information so that it means something to everybody."

- "We have to learn the language and terminology of other functions and disciplines so we can become multilingual translators."
- "It's important to reach out to other parts of the company and be ready for initial skepticism about this outreach. We have stereotypes to overcome."
- "If we really want to learn certain skills, we have to arrange to teach them to others."

The CFO who desires something better, something more than survival, for oneself and career must go deep into the developmental dynamics that drive the behavior of people and the work they do. This assignment is not easy for people trained primarily in a technical discipline. Technical skills and abilities are second nature to a person who has the talents to be a good accountant; however, everyone's first nature is to be a continually developing human being. Fulfilling this primary nature is what makes a great CFO. Most people still believe that leaders are born, not made. Companies hire mature leaders more by random luck than by any reliable procedure. Leadership and interpersonal competencies *can* be developed. They are based on seeing oneself in relationship to others, an inherent human capacity that operates whether one guides such development or not.

DEVELOPING PROFESSIONAL MATURITY AND LEADERSHIP COMPETENCIES

[W]e learn the deepest things in unknown territory. Often it is when we feel most confused inwardly and in the midst of our greatest difficulties that something new will open. We awaken most easily to the mystery of life through our weakest side. The areas of our strength, where we are most competent and clearest, tend to keep us away from the mystery.

Jack Kornfield[4]

Chapter 2 detailed CFO maturity in terms of learning skills and experiential knowledge but ended abruptly (and for good reason) before characterizing the most important element of CFO survival: the development of professional maturity and leadership competency. Why did Chapter 2 stop where it did? Characterizing the development of professional maturity and leadership competency takes the rest of the book. A CFO must be rich in technical skills and experiential knowledge, but these are entry- to intermediate-level requirements. In addition, a person in this position must model self-discipline, act calmly and steadily, and skillfully draw out the best in others. While aligning with executive priorities, the CFO also demonstrates a uniform commitment across all employee levels to help everyone understand the business.

The time has come to integrate the notions of leadership intelligence competencies and professional development maturity. As previous chapters have suggested, the apparent key to leadership intelligence competencies lies in the practice and mastery of emotional intelligence, as fully defined in this section. Emotions and cognition are interdependent elements of our daily awareness of our social environment and ourselves. Try to imagine a workplace where decision making is free of any emotional context. Maybe that could happen in a world without birth, sickness, old age, death, taxes, competition for limited resources, war, poverty, or personal computers. In this world, the workplace and its relationships present an endless stream of changing emotional contexts that inform cognitive decision making. Therefore, intelligent decisions and behavior depend upon more than intellectual horsepower, as in high IQ. Intelligent leadership is an alloy of cognitive and emotional awareness tempered by discipline.

One framework comprehensively addresses the practical ways that CFOs must work to develop and apply the highest professional levels of cognitive, ethical, and relationship milestones. Daniel Goleman, author of *Emotional Intelligence*,[5] and the people working with the Consortium for Research on Emotional Intelligence in Organizations have developed a statistically validated framework of leadership competencies based on four areas of emotional intelligence from more than twenty-five years of longitudinal research. A representation of the emotional intelligence framework[6] appears in Exhibit 3.1. The rest of this chapter discusses how the different dimensions in Exhibit 3.1 apply to CFO maturity and leadership competencies. Chapters 4, 5, and 6 discuss the application of emotional intelligence and leadership competencies in the context of a CFO's work with the accounting and financial function, with executive peers, and with the organization as a living system within the larger workplace environment.

Emotional Intelligence

The emotional intelligence (EI) framework and research claims to encompass 85 percent of the competencies that distinguish adequate leaders from great leaders.[7] Scientifically, EI is defined as "a set of competencies that derive from a neural circuitry emanating in the limbic system."[8] The EI framework terminology has become more and more precise since it was first introduced in the 1990s. This *CFO Survival Guide* interprets the EI framework and its evolving terminology to make it congruent with the historical and cultural focuses of the accounting profession and therefore more accessible as a guide for CFO professional development. The EI framework gives a working context to the maturity models of personal development already presented.

Rest assured that this discussion is not just a rehash of Goleman's work. First, the moral and psychosocial development models provide a tight focus for grounding

EXHIBIT 3.1 EMOTIONAL INTELLIGENCE COMPETENCY SETS

Self-Awareness	Social Awareness
Emotional self-assessment	Empathy
Accurate self-awareness	Organizational awareness
Self-confidence	Service
Self-Management	**Relationship Management**
Self-control	Inspiration
Transparency	Influence
Adaptability	Developing others
Achievement	Change catalyst
Initiative	Conflict management
Optimism	Teamwork and collaboration

the EI competencies in some of the most important responsibilities the CFO carries out in practice as functional and organizational leader: assuring accountability and facilitating interrelationships. Second, this discussion uses examples of how actual CFOs have applied the EI framework in actual working conditions.

When reading this material, keep in mind some good news and two clarifications: The good news is that EI research and practice show that EI competencies can be learned at any time in a person's life. The two important caveats: First, the framework considers measurable intelligence (IQ) and technical skills as developmental entry points, and makes no claim to assess technical or cognitive skills because they are secondary in terms of leadership requirements. Second, as Goleman stated: "People should be rewarded for excellent performance. They should be promoted, however, for specific competencies."[9]

The first section below addresses self-awareness and social awareness competencies followed by a section discussing self-management and relationship management competencies. "Awareness" means conscious, deliberate attentiveness, like the mind-set required during the performance review of a problem employee compared to that of a long daily commute. Broader levels of personal self-awareness support social awareness. Self- and social awareness-competencies support people in their insights about self-management. Relationship management competencies clearly depend on how well one knows oneself, knows the social system, and can manage oneself within the forces of that social context. The steps of this awareness sequence all work in the context of personal maturity and professional development; the person is the vehicle through which the wealth of all skills, abilities, and knowledge are or are not transmitted to others and transformed into valuable contributions for the organization.

More than most disciplines, accounting is a team-based practice of sharing information. A CFO must be deeply conversant with personal strengths and weaknesses, remembering that the reverberations of a significant leadership competency shortcoming cascade throughout the organization. For example, if a CFO lacks self-confidence and dissects every transaction, large or small, the staff follows that lead, usually making a lot of work for themselves and everyone else. The more leadership competencies a person has consciously developed, the better their technical and interpersonal performance. For a "how-not-to" discussion on emotional intelligence, see the Web site Barriers and Accelerators feature, "Emotional Incontinence."

Four Sets of Core Leadership Competencies

Awareness   The *Self-Awareness* set of emotional intelligence competencies listed in Exhibit 3.1 is the cornerstone of all further leadership competency development. The first competency on the list is *emotional self-assessment*. Think of the number of times in a typical workday that impatience (an emotion) leads to anger (another emotion) that interferes with your ability to listen carefully or consider all the options you need to make a rational decision. The road to broader leadership competencies begins with greater self-awareness of emotional strengths and weaknesses, where a person is able to acknowledge some key insights about emotions: *I have them (nope, not me); I can recognize them (or not); and their recognition guides my choices by revealing a larger context of opportunities (or not).*

Accurate self-assessment comes next. Leaders use some of the frameworks in Chapter 2 to candidly assess the technical skills and experiential knowledge that support their work. Accurate and candid go hand-in-hand. A sense of humor goes a long way in providing the openness required for such candor. Accuracy? Self-assessment is not entirely a matter of personal opinion. Look for an objective means to assess professional experience sets against peers. Once a person has rigorously assessed emotional awareness and professional capacities in terms of strengths and weakness, leaders can act with greater *self-confidence* by leveraging their strengths and beginning to address their weaknesses.

The second set of awareness-related EI competencies relates to *social awareness*. The common sense of a self-aware CFO argues for cultivation of an awareness of the social structure of the workplace. Once again, the EI framework recognizes three supportive competencies. Based on their own emotional awareness, CFOs with *empathy* use their emotional insights to recognize important messages in the behavior of fellow employees. Empathy gives the CFO the ability to see through the eyes of others—a critical skill when working to bridge organizational designs that feature silo functions working in isolation.

Aristotle wrote an entire book on politics, and the *organizational awareness* competency in the social awareness set of the EI framework acknowledges the leadership importance of monitoring the political fabric of the organization. Organizational awareness tunes in on official and unofficial sources of information. Leaders use all resources to gauge the intent and influence of the organization's power brokers. Working from insights generated by practicing empathy and organizational awareness competencies, the CFO moves into action with a sense of *service* to understand the needs of a very important member of the CFO's social network: the customer. CFOs who demonstrate the importance of empathy within customer relationships thereby model service competency values to accounting and finance function staff members.

Management   The two management sets of EI leadership competencies parallel the two awareness sets. *Self-management* competencies come first and support the application of *relationship management* competencies in the social arena. Interestingly, the EI researchers have established twice as many competencies for each of the management sets. Moving through this section, recall concrete examples from your own experience when you and other leaders you respect have demonstrated each of the competencies. Try to recall your emotions and the emotional context of the people around you.

Just as emotional self-awareness establishes the foundation for the self-awareness set of leadership competencies, *self-control* is the foundation of the self-management competencies. The workplace seems designed to overwhelm people with an endless set of performance expectations. Budgets, targets, strategy, incentives, and holiday parties are but a few of the common organizational activities that create very high performance expectations. The emotional consequences? How many expectations do you and your business exceed to the degree that your success results in widespread satisfaction, joy, or elation? Unmet expectations generate disturbing emotions, and disturbing emotions influence cognitive choices unless a person has learned to channel such energy in useful ways. Emotionally competent leaders remain calm and focused when faced with unexpected outcomes. In fact, an emotionally competent leader might be defined as a person who can retain self-control during an emergency. Such leaders are easy to spot; everyone else is panicking.

Self-control opens the door to the five other self-management competencies. *Transparency* is one of the most important leadership competencies for a CFO. CFOs who practice transparency lead openly; they openly discuss what they believe and value, why they do what they do, and yes, how they feel. If intelligent leadership depends upon emotional awareness, leaders should appropriately express emotional transparency tempered by disciplined self-control. In the early versions of the EI framework, *trustworthiness* and *conscientiousness* appeared in the place currently occupied by transparency. Because trustworthy and conscientious competencies support transparent leadership, the change in terminology makes good sense. However, given the specific responsibilities of the CFO function, this discussion treats trustworthiness and conscientiousness on the same level of emphasis as transparency.

Adaptability is a leadership capacity with two important elements. First, adaptable people openly engage with grace and ease the inevitable and unexpected "changes in plans," even when the change in plans is someone else's better idea. Second, the adaptable leader can go with the flow of ever-changing priorities, remain focused, and perform effectively as each new priority emerges.

CFOs who demonstrate the *achievement* self-management competency live according to high personal standards and look for ways to improve themselves at every turn. In doing so, such a leader applies the same approach to people in the workplace by setting practical, challenging goals and measuring progress at reasonable intervals along the way. This learning CFO cultivates the same learning values in the organization.

What kind of a leader would a person make without a good dose of *initiative*? Specifically, leaders demonstrate initiative by taking it whenever they can. Within the constraints of their high personal standards, a leader will ask for forgiveness rather than permission when important opportunities arise. Initiative clearly draws support from a foundation of self-confidence because leaders take chances to create better futures.

Optimism is another self-management competency with clear ties to the emotional dynamics of the high-expectation workplace. Things often go differently than expected and sometimes go terribly wrong. When a person who is perceived as a leader throws in the towel, everyone else follows. Sometimes this action is appropriate, but when a leader can model ways to see something positive in all outcomes, other people will follow as well.

Relationship management competencies (the fourth set) flow from social awareness competencies. CFOs who become aware of the social dynamics of the organization can apply that awareness to the ways they manage different relationships by practicing the EI relationship management competencies. As with so many other aspects of the EI framework, the relationship management competencies support one another in a highly interdependent fashion. *Inspiration* tops the list. Leaders have to create some kind of influential energy that moves people to follow. To inspire, a leader needs to be able to recognize and articulate a common vision and purpose of the collective work that makes such work meaningful for each person who contributes to that vision.

Influence is a relationship management competency closely linked with the dynamics of inspiration. While forging and maintaining relationships with individuals and groups with a wide spectrum of dispositions, emotionally intelligent CFOs sense and deliver a persuasive argument with just the right appeal to match the disposition of the listeners—dozens of times every day.

Developing others draws heavily on empathy and awareness of how people can actually be helped. Drawing from personal work from the accurate self-assessment competency in the self-awareness set, emotionally intelligent CFOs apply their own experiences of assessing strengths and weaknesses to those around them. Enforcing new skills and experiential opportunities is not enough. Leaders can see what a person needs and when they are ready to develop a new ability. Importantly, emotionally intelligent CFOs stay involved when they begin to develop others by giving appropriate feedback in the form of coaching and mentoring.

Functioning as a *change catalyst* is hard work. Enzymes work as catalysts by bringing parts of vital chemical reactions into close proximity so that the reaction occurs more quickly and with greater yield. In terms of facilitating change, the CFO sits right in the middle of all the barriers to change and persuasively articulates reasons to move forward. This work depends upon being able to see that business as usual is not enough anymore. Being a change catalyst also depends upon the ability to quickly solve a multitude of small and large problems as representatives of the old order try to obstruct implementation of the new vision.

On the heels of working as a change catalyst, *conflict management* competency makes perfect sense. Organizations depend upon affable, productive, long-term relationships, and authentic consensus is one of the best resolutions of any conflict in a working collection of people. Reaching consensus depends on the abilities of someone to draw out into the open the most important goals of each party. Because strong emotional stands usually create the context for each side of the dispute, an empathetic leader uses personal awareness of the strength of disturbing emotions to help people in conflict move beyond the postures and back to the best course of action for the common good. Empathetic leaders watch for openings in the dialogue to approach the actual source of a person's disturbance.

Teamwork and collaboration are the natural outcomes of all these applied relationship management competencies. Or are they? Leading a team is one thing; being a part of a team is an entirely different matter. Emotionally intelligent CFOs know when to simply blend and occasionally join in performing activities beyond those that go with the office. In the process, such CFOs model collaborative work behaviors for others.

EI Awareness in the Context of Moral and Psychosocial Professional Development

An exploration of self-awareness must be direct, concrete, and tolerate no euphemisms. Individual accountants and the accounting profession too often ignore, make excuses, or beat around the bush when it comes to accountants' interpersonal skills. Most businesspeople—including CFOs—see the to-be-improved aspects of the majority of engineers, technology professionals, and accountants who all fall into the same personality profile: introverted, detail-sensing, judgmental, averse to working in teams, cautious about change, and the like. These professionals are not known for their sense of humor or for their ability to quickly assimilate new information or situations. They are known to speak specialized, opaque languages (accounting, finance, mechanics, chemistry) that very few nonspecialists understand; they are not known for making their information easily accessible.

That stereotyped negative profile is a very long way from the ideal profile created by several hundred CFOs in Exhibit 2.2 in Chapter 2. The ideal profile includes characteristics such as *intuitive, works with instinct, candor, sees the big picture,* and *sense of humor,* as well as *accountable* and *responsible*—two positive qualities for which accountants are well known. Most people appear to accept, or at least tolerate, the shortcomings because they see them as part of the personality package—a package also expected to contain honesty, responsibility, reliability, and so on. For that reason, the recent wounds inflicted by unethical accountants, accounting consultants, and CFOs run deep in the public psyche. "We were certain we could count on you," the collective voice seems to say to the profession. "We never thought *you* would betray us." Thus the interpersonal skills needed to restore faith in the profession are more urgently required than ever.

Thus we reach the attribute at the epicenter of the accountant identity, the one that has been shattered in the eyes of the public: *Tells the truth.* That is the core attribute of an accountant's identity. Truth sayer, deliverer of hard news, messenger of the organization's strengths and weaknesses. Such a job is not an easy one. Telling the truth requires a person of integrity, one who is ethical, credible, and trustworthy. This approach means a specific kind of truth on a technical level (e.g., stock option transactions) and truth on the interpersonal and relationship level. The technical level is easy (or should be); the interpersonal level is more difficult. The reason for the difference is that interpersonal truth depends on a person's maturity, which in turn depends on self- and social awareness and self-management competencies. Developmental models like the moral and psychosocial subsystems give people in leadership positions formal structures for assessing their maturity in terms of their ability to tell the truth both technically and interpersonally.

The work of the CFO emphasizes moral and psychosocial maturity because these characteristics provide a context for ethical maturity that is grounded in relationships. This context is specifically applicable to the relationships that a CFO faces in the organization community where empathy and the desire to serve make all the difference. The EI model characterizes self-awareness in terms of accuracy, emotions, and confidence. When a person attentively recognizes these competencies and works toward proven developmental milestones, personal growth is accelerated. Consider, for example, a CFO who has difficulties standing up to skepticism about accounting results. Under this kind of often accusatory probing by the CEO and nonfinancial executive peers, a CFO might naturally feel anxious and unable to think clearly. This CFO sincerely wishes for more self-confidence, yet has no idea why the competency eludes him. Herein lies a key feature of the EI framework as a system of personal and professional development. A person might be born with stunning eyes or flaxen hair, but competency development takes practice.

A person may be introverted by nature and, given a choice, prefer to work alone. Those characteristics are personal preferences, but they are not immutable. So, our model CFO must look for ways to improve self-confidence through a thorough exploration of emotional self-awareness to recognize patterns of the way feelings affect performance and an accurate self-assessment to identify strengths and weaknesses to focus self-improvement activities.

Where a solid relationship based on mutual respect exists between the CFO and the CEO, CFOs ask their CEOs for feedback and mentoring for professional competency development issues. Such concrete steps are the beginning of self-management competency practice that affect the relationship management activity that started the sequence: this CFO's fear and anxiety about having financial results questioned.

Now consider an introverted CFO. In this case, the CEO and the vice presidents of marketing and operations are the only ones who receive bonus incentives. These executives are not brazen enough to come right out and say, "Change the numbers!" However, together the threesome takes advantage of GAAP complexity to conceive alternate accounting scenarios that meet the letter, but not the spirit of the rules. The CFO knows the difference and has experience with this dilemma. Based on a firm commitment to tell the truth, the CFO anticipates and thoroughly prepares analyses and answers to undermine the inevitable maneuvers of the executive trio. Despite all the preparation, the CFO lacks the self-confidence to carry it off. None of the careful preparation is used; the senior executives tell him what to do, and he does it.

This CFO has a triple dilemma. First, respect for one another's values does not even enter into the relationship dynamics of this executive group. Second, the unethical agenda of the other executives compromises the CFO's personal and professional values. Third, the CFO seems to have no options for developing and practicing new, more mature emotional intelligence competencies that could confront and rectify the first two dilemmas. Or does he?

Falling back on technical skills and data preparation to articulate a successful response to suggestions of unethical conduct is not enough. This example shows how the development and practice of emotionally intelligent leadership competencies is far more difficult than the practice of technical skills. Competent leaders learn to overcome the barriers of disturbing emotions when making ethically correct but unpopular decisions. Emotional intelligence competencies stabilize a person during difficult tasks and confrontations. The stabilization clears the way for clear articulation of ethical considerations. Once the CFO pointedly raises others' awareness of unfair, deceitful, immoral, or illegal considerations relevant to a course of action, for others to carry off unethical behavior becomes problematic.

Ethical Behavior and Emotional Intelligence   Looking at the moral developmental subsystem, a CFO can assess truth-telling self-awareness by asking a simple question: *What is the most important barrier that prevents me from telling the truth?* Accurate self-assessment is crucial in this foundational exploration. Be conscientious in your scrutiny. You can ask the question on both the technical and interpersonal levels. One by one, consider your executive peers, your staff, and other key relationships to see if different people affect your truth-saying ability. For example, are you concerned about punishment, failure, or disapproval in the dynamics of obedience when you receive a tough assignment from a superior or as you give a hard assignment to a staff member? Do any of these concerns arise when you report unexpectedly poor performance to the CEO? Do you ever avoid the risk of being looked upon as an outsider by reporting disappointing truths that you could just as well camouflage under the wide berth that GAAP allows? Do you often find yourself in a position where inflexible, rigid rules and mandates carry more importance than simple truth?

An actual example of instrumental hedonism at the executive level involves the behavior of a large minority shareholder at the third-quarter board meeting of a multidivision milling company. The general manager of the division that had outperformed every other division in the first two quarters—as it had consistently done in the two previous years—was chastised by the shareholder for missing his third-quarter profit goals by 7 percent. Only perfect or better profit achievement pleased this shareholder. His behavior severely demoralized the general manager and his direct reports who were also at the meeting. If you are lucky, you do not work in an immature ethical environment, but rather within an organization where both you and your coworkers trust and respect one another, work autonomously and industriously, with natural ease, while being able to clearly see the boundaries between where one person's work stops and another's begins. If you are lucky, you work in a mature ethical environment where people and functions are encouraged to easily see and honor one another's points of view.

Clearly, organizational culture influences the ethical behavior of the people working within it. No leader ventures into the difficult territories of awareness, self-management, and relationship management competency development in a cultural void. To reach desired developmental and EI competency milestones, a leader needs to be able to contrast personal and professional development within the context of current organizational moral and psychosocial behaviors and expectations. That is, even if other executives behave at low ethical maturity levels, the CFO's fundamental accountability is to continue to tell the truth openly. The developmental maturity to do so involves a level of awareness and self-management competency such that the CFO can convey truth in ways that people who do not, cannot, or do not want to see it can still receive it.

The organization's current moral and psychosocial maturity is an important variable. Conformity is a relatively mature stage of self-identity. In a business environment, this stage may be, in fact, the middle of the bell curve for the population of company employees. A person in this kind of conformity culture behaves according to ethical standards guided by law and order—that is, rules (see Exhibit 3.2). People in the conformity stage can be overtly encouraged to follow a more mature pattern; however, demonstration by personal example is more likely to influence people's behavior. For a flavor of these interrelationships, ask yourself, *From the perspective of a moral developmental sequence, do I ever find myself afraid to act with integrity or tell the truth, or am I tempted to follow the appetites for growth and profit of those around me?* (Of course, the CFO's own appetite for money, power, and other trappings also needs to be questioned.) Think about all those people at Enron who did not come forward, who were "just following orders" (i.e., conforming) or "didn't see anything wrong" (i.e., rationalization, perhaps based on a need for safety).

Relationship Maturity and Emotional Intelligence   If telling the truth is the most important EI self-management competency for the CFO, relationship maturity provides context for the CFO's application of EI social awareness and relationship management competencies. Turning to the psychosocial subsystem depiction of relationship maturity milestones, you can assess relationship maturity by asking questions that compare your status to the maturity of the organization's cultural values. Psychosocial development poses its own emotional awareness milestones. The difference between the moral and the psychosocial is that the moral framework focuses on personal behavior, whereas the psychosocial framework focuses on personal performance expectations.

EXHIBIT 3.2   SUBSYSTEMS OF HUMAN DEVELOPMENT— STAGES

Moral	Self-Identity	Psychosocial	
Punishment and obedience	Symbiotic	Trust	Mistrust
Instrumental hedonism	Self-protection	Autonomy	Doubt and shame
Law and order	Conformity	Industry	Inferiority
Universalism	Conscientious	Identity	Role confusion

Referring again to Exhibit 3.2, an important distinction exists between the right and left columns that separate relationship outcomes for each of the psychosocial milestones (e.g., trust versus mistrust). The left-hand column—trust, autonomy, industry, and identity—represents outcomes when one successfully negotiates each relationship milestone. The right-hand column—mistrust, doubt/shame, inferiority, and role confusion—represents outcomes that prevent a person from moving forward in relationship development. As such, the psychosocial subsystem provides richer but more complex examples of applied self- and social awareness for developing relationship management competencies.

Try these assessment questions. Depending upon the maturity of your reports and your peers, are you able to openly trust both groups? Accountants are detail-oriented. Some CFOs and controllers have an obsession with rechecking others' work. Do you? Conversely, are you trusted? How do you know you are or are not? Building upon a foundation of trust, can you work autonomously? Can you expect those around you to do the same? Do other executives of less mature psychosocial or moral development pressure you to alter reports, and do you begin to doubt yourself if they do?

When doubt undermines a sense of personal autonomy, work performance suffers. Many accountants contract the emotional disease called "perfectionism" because they identify so strongly with their work. Such a person believes, *If my work is wrong,* I *am wrong.* Everyone needs to be encouraged to see personal identity and livelihood activities as related but not indistinguishable.

This ability to separate personal worth from work results is another example of how developmental subsystems demonstrate the most important focuses of emotional intelligence work for any given CFO. Successful initiatives depend upon leadership presence; leadership presence depends upon a balanced set of awareness and self-management competencies. Working with development in conjunction with a mature set of emotional intelligence competencies gives a person the means to first identify and then correct technical and professional shortcomings and missteps, track competency development, and visibly acknowledge the significance, substance, and worth of a growing personal competency profile.

In addition to perfectionism and other unique personality traits, cultural influences can create a sense of self-doubt coupled with a strong conformist self-identity and thus put a damper on industriousness and productivity. A Minnesota tax accountant worked for almost twenty years in an unappreciative culture before she sought a new position. Only two months into the new work, her new supervisor terminated her employment saying that she "just didn't do things our way." No issues arose with her technical work; the best she could interpret from the little he said was that her termination had to do with her lack of self-confidence and her mild-mannered demeanor with clients. She was also told that she "checked in with the boss" too often.

She felt ashamed about the termination and doubted her abilities. Then she did some astounding work from a developmental perspective. Working with people she trusted, she performed an accurate self-assessment, deciding that she was in good technical shape but acknowledging that her interpersonal competencies indeed needed serious attention. The cultural performance expectations of her prior job set the context for her developmental delay. She had been required to check *everything* with the boss for almost twenty years! Checking in made her a good employee in that immature culture. While deciding what to do next, this new self-awareness made her more self-confident in all her interactions.

Her expanded self-awareness competencies almost immediately enhanced her relationship management competencies. Although the situation may seem counterintuitive, when her former employer called to ask her to return, she accepted his offer. Why? First, she wanted to practice her newfound self-confidence in a familiar work environment. Second, she enjoyed the client relationships she had established while working at her former employer; she just did not like the many different ways she lost her autonomy at work. This developmentally enhanced, more emotionally intelligent tax accountant used her new competencies to clarify future working relationships as soon as she returned to the employer, and they signed a letter of understanding as a social contract between them. In the interest of fair disclosure, the employer had good reason to be so flexible. He lost about a third of his clients because they had followed the accountant when she left his firm.

Moving forward beyond the foundations of the trust and autonomy relationship milestones in Exhibit 3.2, do you and others within your organization have the self-awareness, social awareness, self-management, and relationship management competencies to work with a natural industriousness—that is, an ease and earnest engagement with your work? In conventional language, this trait is called "productivity," but common usage of that term misses the human energy and emotional connotations. In contrast, is human work performance always judged as inferior or superior from person to person? Comparative judgment almost always breeds conflict. One midwestern Fortune 500 company implemented an extensive Six Sigma/black-belt initiative. The technical model was sound, but the human dynamics proved disastrous. Intracompany competition to reach performance goals severely damaged research and development productivity because of conflicting objectives. In this case, while a group appeared to be working industriously per the Six Sigma measures, they were actually doing so at the expense of downstream functions.

How many times do you or your coworkers feel inferior and act accordingly? If autonomy and strong self-identity are not present, perceived or actual failure to perform up to expectations leads to another common accountancy disease: the inferiority complex. Giving high-quality service to the organization is difficult when one constantly feels doubtful and inferior. Feelings of worthlessness and low self-esteem may arise even though circumstances, such as inhumane workloads, are beyond individual or group control. Emotional awareness of self and others strongly impacts all these situations, and the amplified importance of a leader's awareness of self and others' emotional states quickly becomes obvious. Social awareness depends on accurate self-assessment and self-awareness. Assessing personal and professional development milestones points the way to important emotional intelligence competence priorities.

Accounting is a profession based on truth telling. CFOs, until recently, were trusted truth sayers. Most still are. Whenever telling the truth feels like a matter of negotiation or reaching a compromise, unethical behavior choices are sure to follow. Unless a CFO has personally prepared for this kind of encounter, the economic, social, and cultural influences can be overwhelming. That instrument of knowing called the human heart does not and cannot lie, and when the ethical choice is made, the heart feels a rush of relief and deep joy even if hard events are to come. One of the greatest kinds of work a CFO can do is to simply cultivate the confidence and the courage that it takes to tell the truth when faced with people, cultures, and environments that make decisions based on other standards. Developmentally structured work on emotional intelligence is the best way to prepare.

Truly brilliant CFOs can translate new ways of seeing ethical and relationship challenges so that people at all points on the maturity spectrum can understand and accept the information. Anyone who cannot at least aspire to this kind of CFO presence might want to look for another line of work. When a CFO reaches this stage of maturity, no confusion endures about identity in the psychosocial sense, and the truth-teller role is the center of that identity.

Similarly, a CFO with a secure sense of personal identity and role more easily sees from a moral perspective of universalism and performs better work with more lasting and positive impacts. People in the conformist identity stage know clearly what the rules are. From a universalism perspective, though, the CFO hears and sees more than the conformist line of behavior, relies on information gathered from empathetic listening to diverse points of view, and then acts on all facts and advice to the benefit of most people. At this level of professional maturity and leadership competence, the linkage between the moral, self-identity, and psychosocial subsystems and the EI competencies becomes almost unshakable. The CFO has worked to integrate awareness and competency into a unified understanding of self and personal work responsibilities—all because of the commitment to tell the truth, to everyone all the time.

Amidst all the positive aspects that come with working on professional maturity and emotional intelligence competencies, everyone should be prepared for some turbulence along the way.

APPLYING AWARENESS: SELF-MANAGEMENT AND RELATIONSHIP MANAGEMENT

Successful application of relationship management competencies in business associations depends on a solid self-management foundation. Using self- and social awareness competencies as a developmental context for personal growth, this section focuses on CFO self-management and relationship management milestones. Exhibit 3.3 suggests a sequence of EI competencies that self- and socially aware CFOs can use to prioritize their professional development practices. The sequences are ranked according to the self-management and relationship management competencies demanded of the CFO. This prioritization is not part of the original EI framework. In fact, Exhibit 3.3 uses some terms (identified by asterisks) from earlier versions of the EI framework because they more precisely characterize the specific competency accountabilities of the CFO.

Self-Management Applications for the CFO

The following sections present opportunities to identify gaps in self-management and relationship management competencies by using specific questions and scenarios to demonstrate how mature CFOs respond to specific professional challenges unique to that office.

WWW.

EXHIBIT 3.3   CFO MANAGEMENT COMPETENCY SEQUENCE

Self-Management	Relationship Management
1. Trustworthiness*	1. Building bonds*
2. Conscientiousness*	2. Teamwork and collaboration
3. Self-control	3. Communication*
4. Transparency	4. Change catalyst
5. Adaptability	5. Developing others
6. Initiative	6. Conflict management
7. Achievement	7. Inspiration
8. Optimism	8. Influence

Trustworthiness   Acknowledging that self-control is the foundation of all self-management competencies, the CFO carries out trustworthy stewardship of all organization resources—financial, human, and information. Because much of the CFO's work depends upon record keeping, a CFO's trustworthiness depends upon the ability to act and communicate transparently—working openly, hiding nothing. Two principles run throughout the *CFO Survival Guide: (1) Accountability equals maturity, and (2) transparency demonstrates competency.* If, after this application section, any doubt remains about what obstacles persist to telling the truth, then stop. Work through a month or quarter of events and cycles, paying attention to your own trustworthiness and that of others. Go back to the self and social awareness work of the prior section, identify the obstacles, and begin to address self- and social awareness competencies that create a readiness to tell the truth. Most accountants pride themselves on being highly trustworthy as part of their professional identity; others in the organization depend on it. While all self-management competencies are closely interrelated, transparency and trustworthiness are the foundations of the CFO's relationship with others.

Conscientiousness   One of the best ways to explore the maturity of one's professional trustworthiness is to assess conscientiousness, which brings us back to the importance of personal conscience and following one's heart. Trustworthiness implies honesty. Conscientiousness implies consistency; outside pressures will not alter the steadfast application of personal beliefs. Such pressures range from requests to withhold information and threats of reprisal, to direct attempts at coercion. While a conscientious CFO experiences the full force of the emotional impact of such pressures, the emotional self-awareness competencies support the self-control competencies that the CFO needs to resist the pressures and act according to conscience. Likewise, a conscientious person has the discernment to know what information is appropriate to reveal under varying circumstances. For instance, in private companies, nonunion payroll is usually confidential, but if one manager chooses to tell another the difference in their salaries, and the second manager feels slighted by the difference, a CFO must be able to explain the variance. As such, trustworthiness and conscientiousness each demonstrate leadership transparency.

Salary/wage rates and benefit-level information are excellent places to deepen the practice of conscientiousness. Do so by being prepared to explain any inappropriately divulged information that has already caused harm. Can you explain why two managers of the same gender, education, experience, and responsibility receive significantly different salaries? Salary discrepancies often create problems for employees with company longevity. New hires come in at current market prices while good, loyal, longtime people fall behind. Are you prepared to explain why? Would you rather address inequities before or after they become public knowledge? Can you explain why two supervisors—one male, one female, with the same level of experience, education, and responsibility—receive differing rates of pay? Are you aware of the potential for legal troubles under wage and hourly laws? If executive pay and benefits becomes an issue, can you sort out the rationale? Test yourself with various scenarios, and remedy those that cause you to lose sleep.

Self-Control Even though self-control appears third in this ranking of CFO self-management competencies, it remains the cornerstone of all the others in this section, and leadership self-control depends on a deliberate, honest emotional self-assessment. One of the greatest obstacles to self-control is reflexive emotional behavior. Just as a knee autonomously reacts when a doctor taps it, most people experience spontaneous emotionally triggered cascades of habitual behaviors. For that reason, the influence of the self-awareness competencies spans the other three competency sets. These automatic responses come in many forms: verbal, postures, gestures, and tone.

For example, consider a CFO who has made the choice not to have children in favor of career objectives, and in the process has developed a bias against pregnancy leaves and childcare benefits. While everyone is entitled to an opinion, prevailing cultural and legal values favor such benefits. Recognizing this, the CFO resolves to keep her personal opinions personal. Her self-control censors the expression of thoughts related to childbearing choices appropriate to her business responsibilities. She simply avoids speaking about such choices in the workplace and faithfully administers the company's policies. Soon, she is able to keep her personal beliefs in a personal context. At work, she conscientiously complies with benefit norms, and takes her discussions about disturbing emotions to close personal friends outside the workplace.

Each person's unique life experiences create preferences and expectations. Professional development responsibilities include learning self-control when those preferences are not met and channeling the energy to productive solutions. Identify your worst—as in least controlled—emotional triggers. What situations, conditions, places, settings, people, words, and behaviors light your fast fuse to emotional meltdown? For example, do you have a habit of displaying annoyance or anger when someone interrupts your work? Are you vulnerable to displays of temper and an endless string of apologies? The order and method of self-control development are important. A skeleton outline of the EI framework suggests that the first step involves identifying the emotional triggers that cause the most trouble. Second, practice strategies for changing your outward reactions to the trigger. This approach may involve private counseling, or something as simple as tying a string on your finger to remind you of your intentions.

Adaptability The developmental sequence is especially important in learning to be adaptable. Imagine trying to be adaptable without competence in self-control. Similarly, the wisdom to choose specific, appropriate adaptations depends on the competence to accurately assess organizational conditions and needs, and the readiness of people involved in the adaptation. The adaptable leader can go with the flow of ever-changing priorities, remain focused, and perform effectively as each new priority emerges. Adaptable people openly engage the inevitable and unexpected change in plans with grace and ease, even when the change in plans is someone else's better idea. For example, an enterprise resource planning (ERP) installation requires that the accounting/finance function adapt as much as—sometimes more than—other company business activity centers. The adaptive CFO proactively helps choose the ERP vendor, involves appropriate staff members in planning the implementation, keeps internal and external customers informed of what to expect from the function during the transition, and generally observes how all module implementations are progressing, because almost every module impacts the accounting system.

One CFO who actually argued against an ERP installation not only accepted the CEO's "go" decision, but took every opportunity to do two things concurrently: project a positive attitude toward the project while simultaneously working hard to avert the downside factors he had predicted, such as a decline in the quality of inventory control. Before the installation, inventory was very well managed by a close-knit group of manufacturing and sales personnel who had developed a unique communication protocol that relied on their trust for one another's judgments and their ability to quickly process a number of interdependent variables for making production decisions. The CFO understood their unorthodox method and knew no computer in the world could duplicate or outperform them. The ERP did not, but not for lack of effort on the part of the CFO who did everything he could to help make the system work better than the old team's system. About a year later, the company reverted to the unconventional method while tracking inventory on the ERP for book purposes.

Adaptable people always have a strong and confident sense of self because they practice self-control and the ability to see beyond ego-identity concerns. Because they have learned to identify and actually guide their responses to both common and unexpected situations, such people feel more free to spontaneously explore options as they occur. Their maturity allows them to patiently take more time to accurately determine causes, as opposed to rushing into action with an immutable game plan, or formulating an entirely self-serving agenda before any encounter with the actual facts behind the situation.

Initiative   Based on the word "initial," initiative is the characteristic that allows a person to be the first to see or suggest a new or better way. This ability to be the "first to see" depends on readiness to adapt to more information and changing conditions. Initiative can only be exercised when one is self-confident, because initiative, by definition, takes place with some degree of risk. People about to take initiative do better or worse depending on the accuracy of their social and organizational assessments.

Identifying single leadership competencies becomes more and more difficult at the more mature levels of self-management, where excellent leaders simultaneously integrate and apply several competencies to form a composite synergy. More mature people simply have learned to use more behavioral options. Recall a principle of development: *Developmental achievements are permanent and become part of one's outlook.* Consider the following example of how one CFO recently took initiative under very uncertain conditions, adapted like a great football running back, and drew on some experiences acquired very early in life.

In the wake of corporate scandals, Janet, CFO of a Fortune 1000 retailer (not Wal-Mart), was not about to run any risk of doing the "perp walk." Among the many activities and changes she launched, she determined to strike at the heart of the beast: earnings per share (EPS). As a public firm, the retailer had historically published financial forecasts, including the much-watched EPS. Janet was not only tired of spending what she considered to be non-value-added time with investor analysts, but more importantly she wanted absolutely no suspicions about her financial integrity. She reasoned that even though the company ran on explicit ethical standards, and though her accounting/finance shop was squeaky clean, her forecast analyst's uncanny ability to deliver extraordinarily accurate forecasts (average variance-to-actual on key measures ran less than 2 percent) would certainly draw skepticism. In short, she was not about to fight accusations of "managing earnings" just because she happened to have a wizard for a financial forecaster.

Janet had the trust and respect of everyone in the circle of top executives, but when she proposed that the company stop issuing forecasts, they thought she had lost her mind. She could see the fear in their eyes and hear it in their voices as they said, "Institutional investors won't hold our shares if they have to rely on actual results; they *need* our forecast to do their own forecasts," exclaimed the vice president of public relations. Even the marketing vice president was concerned, "Our franchise managers may think we're in financial trouble and begin to look for other associations." And so on. The CEO, as usual, mostly listened as the executives freely spoke their minds. Janet listened too. She could see that she had proposed too much. The executives were not ready, and she made a commitment to rethinking her proposal and reporting back at the next general meeting. She did.

She was hesitant to take her next approach, but it had always worked with her younger brother. He was afraid of the dark and refused to go down into the basement to help fold the wash. She would take him into the heart of what he feared, but with comforts and assurances he could use to support himself. For example, she would carry him piggyback down the stairs, promise they could go back whenever he wanted, and entice him with the promise of a sweet when they finished their chores. Janet definitely did not think of her fellow executives as little brothers and sisters, but she did want to address their fears using similar tactics. Here is the approach Janet used to sell her innovation.

Principles:

- If we decide to stop forecasts, we can return to doing them any time this group sees reason to do so. That's a promise.

- Make this change a proactive, positive move. Only a few others have decided to go this route, but that may change soon. Now, we can publicize this change as a very positive move, showing how we are leading the way toward more rational relationships with analysts and investors. (At this, the public relations vice president jumped in with several ideas of how this strategy might be accomplished, and how to make it a sweet piece of public relations.)

Approach:

1. The first step is to put this concept in front of the analysts during the upcoming round of talks. Present them with the pros and cons, and let them have a say in the decision. (The public relations vice president loved this one too, but this approach worried another executive, so Janet adjusted and committed to running the idea past the company's most trusted board advisors first, to toe-test the intention.)

2. Naturally, we will want to clear this with the board, so based on reactions to the selective toe-testing, we will take it to all members via our electronic meeting method.

3. For two to three quarters, Jack (the forecast wizard) will continue to calculate the pro forma numbers, as always. I'll share them with Mike (the CEO), and if he sees a problem, we'll all huddle and decide the appropriate response.

4. Keep tabs on reactions, including a regression analysis and other research to correlate this move with share price changes. (Janet knew there were too many variables affecting share price to link changes to the decision to stop forecasting, but she also appreciated that the studies would give her additional insight into price movements. She had been meaning to enhance that work anyway, and Jack would be just the one to spearhead the effort.)

Janet finished her proposal with a lead-in to her next intention. "Financial measures like EPS will always be important to us, but lately, I think we've all had our noses too far into my accounting books. We should think seriously about how balanced our perspective is in the measure sets we use. But I'll bring that up at another meeting in the near future."

The package convinced the executives to give Janet's idea a try. She had particularly reached them with her closing comment. Everyone knew, and informally many had discussed, how far into the numbers they had gone during the dot-com era. They knew the time had come to revisit their guiding measures. Thus Janet deftly moved forward with a sensitive change and planted the seeds for the next development.

Achievement   While this milestone may seem like a throwaway, too many people possess all the prior competencies but are known to have trouble with follow-through and implementation. These people are usually brilliant visionaries with truly great ideas. However, they are poor implementers and usually have difficulty organizing others to do the necessary work. CFOs who demonstrate the achievement leadership competency live according to high personal standards and look for ways to improve themselves at every turn. In doing so, such leaders apply the same approach to people in the workplace by setting practical, challenging goals and measuring progress at reasonable intervals along the way.

Randy, a real CFO whose name has been changed to protect the innocent, accepted the offer of a small hospital to be its finance chief: he had grown tired of the politics and the extremely long hours he had put up with for many years at a regional HMO. He took a cut in pay, but he and his family moved from an expensive metropolitan area to a town of ten thousand in another state with a more modest cost of living. Randy spent a great deal of time with his small staff during the first month. More than any other request, they emphasized that they did not want Randy coming in with any fancy city-consultant methods and projects. They had been through eight major initiatives during the two-year tenure of Randy's predecessor, a charismatic young CFO full of good ideas—"too full of good ideas," the staff reported. Apparently, the staff had regularly put in sixty- to seventy-hour weeks to accommodate their superior's voracious appetite for something new. When Randy questioned them about results from three of the projects—a hospital scorecard, reengineering the finance function, and studying process capacity constraints in hospital operations—at first no one answered. Then the controller reported that not one project had borne fruit because they never had the chance to finish one before they were hustled onto another.

Randy, too, had some good ideas that he hoped to rapidly implement. Staff disposition caused him to reconsider. With this tired and disillusioned group, Randy radically adapted his original intentions. Early on, he asked them which of all the unfinished projects had the most potential. Randy was surprised to hear that it was the capacity study. (He had an incorrect, preconceived notion that this staff would not be sophisticated enough to handle an operations-oriented project. As it turned out, three of the eight on his staff had more than adequate backgrounds for the task. Randy gave himself a mental slap on the wrist for his bias.) He promised the staff that when they all decided the getting-to-know-you period was about finished, the capacity study would be up first—the one and only initiative they would explore until it was finished. Two months later, the staff asked Randy when they could restart the capacity project.

Randy personally led the project, carefully assigning team roles and duties, and setting up a timeline and project performance measures posted on a long piece of paper taped to the wall. He encouraged—and sometimes insisted—that staff members record ideas, concerns, and feelings about the project. He checked every day for new comments and highlighted them in blue so he could spot any new additions the next day. This simple method proved one of the most important vehicles for driving project achievements because the staff observed and wrote down details that turned out to be critical to the overall process, asked questions that helped them work more efficiently, and in addition to a few emotional comments, took to writing project-related humor on the sheet.

Randy shelved most of his original other "good ideas," for the time being. While easily running routine processes and actively leading the capacity project, he took time to do something he had always wanted to do: observe actual medical and surgical procedures in the interest of better understanding the real business of health.

Relationship Management Applications for the CFO

The final set of leadership competencies is *relationship management*. Exhibit 3.3 also ranks these competencies for the CFO. In self-management there is only one person to consider. Obviously, social skills are used in different combinations with various individuals and groups.

Building Bonds   Truth-in-relationship is the other side of the accurate self-assessment coin. Just as truthfulness is the foundation of CFO self-management, applied social skills depend on consistent practice of building bonds to foster trust throughout the organization. Politics and diplomacy are the surest signs of a work environment lacking foundational trust. Without trust, people spend an immense amount of time engaging in political rumor mills, checking and rechecking the work of those they do not trust, and building personal empires rather than bonds. The ability to build bonds depends on one's adeptness at teamwork and collaboration, as well as communication competencies.

Teamwork and Collaboration   This competency is an excellent example of how self-management skills support building bonds in a CFO's professional relationships. Because teamwork and collaboration are participative activities, leaders cannot build an effective team or form successful collaborative relationships without the solid personal foundation of self-confidence and adaptability. With mature facilitation, empathetic listening, and careful feedback, participation yields more ways of seeing and more potential expertise contributions. Humans are participators by nature. Watch for a few days. When you receive an assignment from the CEO, you can't help but tweak the perspective to insert a bit of your own creativity or add a flourish of your own expertise. Likewise, when you assign analysis tasks to your staff, try to recall the last time they did not add a single new idea or make an observation about a discrepancy. When people participate, they simultaneously become part owners and creators of the idea, the task, or the project. This action appears to be an innate result of participation.

A classic example comes from the headquarters of a $500 million engine manufacturer. In the early 1990s, a team of six accountants, including the headquarters controller, decided to launch a cost management initiative—an activity-based costing (ABC) model—in response to CEO and CFO demands for more accurate product cost information. This U.S. company had experienced a steady loss of market share to Japanese engine manufacturers who delivered high quality at lower costs. Without consulting anyone outside the team, the controller and his people decided to "get the ABC design right" on their own and fine-tune the model later based on manufacturing and production support feedback. As the result of a multiyear unit volume analysis by model, the team narrowed the scope of the ABC work to four engines that made up almost 80 percent of unit volume. Much discussion underlay this decision because three team members felt strongly about accounting for 100 percent of production cost; in other words, reconciling ABC cost to general ledger cost. The controller, Mark, and the other two members disagreed based on the case studies they had read in the professional literature.

This team had worked together several times before (e.g., implementing a J.D. Edwards general ledger system) and had developed a habit of paying careful attention to strong differences of opinion. They had learned that collaborative "debate" always yielded a higher-quality decision. Over time, Mark noticed that discussions centered on strong, at-odds viewpoints actually built strong ties between team members. This approach was counterintuitive for Mark; he had always assumed that conflict and arguments create enemies. Somehow the chemistry of the team bubbled up a strange dynamic that Mark had not experienced before. Members debated passionately for their points of view, while at the same time, they kept drawing out points (and noting them on a white board) when they all agreed. Meetings that sometimes went on long beyond five o'clock always resulted in genuine consensus and stronger team bonds. Mark was relying on this dynamic to design a solid ABC model. He had read about the importance of cross-functional ABC teams, but he judged that his people had enough intellectual horsepower to do the job. He also reasoned that this work would save time for production managers.

Meanwhile the rumor mill began to turn in production. A brief segment of conversation displays the flavor of the scuttlebutt. The production supervisor of the engine line with the highest unit volume and his production manager exchanged these words.

Supervisor: I hear Mark has rounded up a bunch of his number-crunchers to do some sort of cost study on engine lines. What do you know about it?

Manager: I heard about that from my brother who is a peon in accounting. He overheard some talk about something called cost-based activities. That's really all I know. My brother is going to snoop around a bit and see what's up.

Supervisor: Keep me posted, will you? I sure hope they aren't going to lower the axe on costs. We've cut to the bone already.

A few weeks later, the same pair:

Manager: Well, I got the skinny from my brother. Looks like we better get ready for the pencil jockeys upstairs to tell us how to run our shop again. This activity cost stuff is all about getting rid of waste to cut costs. Waste! What do they think we're doing down here?!

Supervisor: I knew it! Here we go again. Another round of "cut your costs without sacrificing quality." We just can't cut much more.

Neither of the two production people chose to approach the controller. About three months later, Mark invited these two and six other production managers and supervisors to have a look at their work. They had a look, all right. The production people marched into the meeting room like a string of linebackers glaring at the opposing team. Mark caught the scent immediately and instantly broke out in a nervous sweat that persisted through the entire presentation of the ABC model. When he was finished and asked for questions, silence hung heavy in the room. The meeting was a complete bust, and the two teams parted ways, barely holding back their anger (production) and anxiety (accounting). The model lay in shreds, and the accountants wondered where they went wrong on such good work.

Then one member who had actually worked in production before returning to school to get an accounting degree said, "I think they're bent out of shape because we designed this thing without them, like we knew everything about their shops. I'm pretty sure that's what made them mad." The group commiserated for a short time; two people were really angry about what they considered production's ingratitude. Soon, they moved into their "debate" mode, and by the end of a long impromptu meeting they knew what to do: Start over again, this time with a cross-functional team at the table. They did so, and six months later, with the support of production, they implemented a stand-alone ABC model that over the next two years supported waste reduction and process improvement to the tune of 17 percent cost savings, revealing quality improvements in the process.

In summary, the lessons learned, other than the importance of cross-functionality included:

- Do not ever give the impression you know everything about another function's work, even if you think you do.

- If you have made that mistake, go hat in hand, apologize, and ask for a second chance. (This attitude and Mark's explicit acknowledgment of mistakes were major factors in persuading the production people to participate in the second team.)

- If you haven't participated in the work, you don't own it and probably won't use it. You may even sabotage it.

- If you try to build something for another function without their presence, you simultaneously build really bad rumors and feelings.

The results of the second ABC model work, other than a good costing alternative, were as follows:

- Much greater communication and camaraderie between accounting and production.

- The start of an increasing stream of process improvement work between the two functions.

- Promotions for four members of the cross-functional team because of their cost management and process improvement contributions.

- A long "chat" between Mark and the helpful accountant-brother about the damage caused by conveying opinions without intelligence.

Communication   For some strange reason, communication remains the Holy Grail on the quest for the rarified levels of professional leadership competency development. Equally strange is that communication usually places first on professional education "soft skills" curricula. Several years ago, a large accounting professional association responded to a membership survey indicating that communication skills was their number-one topic of interest. The association spent a great deal of money developing a series of communication courses. Though they answered a need, almost nobody came. The attendance at these very reasonably priced communication seminars was so low that it did not even cover expenses.

When you think about it, blaming the absence of communication skills on any person who grew up with the television as one of their primary caregivers is dubious. Whether we listen to the media or attend any level of public education (K–12 and college level), we are talked to. Executives have a tendency to talk to (or talk at) people when they share strategic plans, explain a major procedural change, and deliver performance results. CFOs, too, are not known for participative styles of public speaking. The opportunity to exchange ideas and information is simply rare. So, after years in the workplace telling people what to do and repeatedly watching them fail to do it, one begins to doubt all communication skills. Hardly anyone communicates well because few people are taught how to do it. Fewer still have a native talent for communication. Secondary school courses in communication topics are usually electives, and university-level communications majors tend to become wound up in technology where their wires are miserably crossed.

Communication is a give-and-take process. When encountering other people for purposes of debate, conversation, or an exchange of information, you should make a point to stop and practice listening at regular intervals. Check yourself when another is speaking. Are you taking in what the person is saying, or are you rehearsing for your turn to talk? You know what that level of participation and listening means: Any effort at communication takes three to four times as long. The alternative pathologies of pretending to listen are most often token expressions of communication (e.g., quarterly "chats," or periodic satisfaction surveys but no follow-up feedback or action) and executives who demonstrate listening postures and then do exactly what they were going to do in the first place.

Yes, communication takes time. The research behind the emotional intelligence framework boils it all down to a simple practice: Spend extra time on the front end listening well to make sure everyone understands, and when appropriate follow up with written documentation. Periodic communication check-ins can proceed from that solid base. The silver lining in the extra front-end work is that you rest easier, parry fewer problems over time, and build bonds with people who do the work.

Change Catalyst   This attribute is very tricky. The word "change" and the appellation "change agent" have both become seriously tainted, stemming largely from a lack of focus on relationship with people about the work they do. Executives regularly announce directives for change, but very few people in these ranks know how to facilitate transformation gracefully. Part of the problem is a lack of articulate vocabulary. Executives tend to rely on the terminology in the abstract financial models discussed earlier. The lexicon is not particularly thrilling, especially if only someone else's paycheck or stock price gets the benefit of change. Another part of the dilemma is that many top managers are can-do, on-task sorts of people. They are highly motivated high achievers, and they find annoying the task of having to motivate other people.

Staying true to the emphasis on people in relationship, a change catalyst is not someone who brandishes financial targets or crusades for alphabet-soup solutions: ABC, BSC, TQM, or TOC. CFOs who get work done through other people do not bombard them with silver-bullet acronyms or bludgeon them with oversized technology systems. A change catalyst in this context is someone who knows how to apply self-managed, mature personal identity in relationships with others so that work becomes naturally smoother and more fruitful.

Developing Others   Value management. How often we focus on the numbers instead of the people and the work they do. In almost every circumstance the best way to make the numbers better is to make the people better. As a leadership position with a broad perspective on the organization, the CFO can have a first-hand effect not only on the financial staff, but also on peers and other functions. If, for example, a CFO explicitly practices developmental disciplines with staff members, these accountants may begin to take initiative when they see more interdependencies and potential for efficiency. As people from the office of the CFO begin to exhibit greater understanding and take action on that understanding, their behavior is bound to rub off on other functions. A very simple place to start is setting aside a staff budget for education, whether or not company policy does so, and then guiding staff in appropriate, sequential educational activities. Developmental guidance is the key to the success of this approach. Otherwise, educational efforts degrade into just another day away from the office. Also, recognize that people do not limit their friendships to their functional coworkers. And what do people from the same organization talk about when they socialize? Of course: work! A natural communication conduit arises. So, from working with the microcosm of the accounting staff, the CFO can have immense impact throughout the company.

One of the greatest challenges when working to develop others is to achieve balance between what must be done today and what might be improved if done tomorrow because the employees have been prepared and developed. The train of thought that proves a good rule of thumb is, "Today we have x amount of energy, time, and attention. What will we use it for? What is the most important service we can offer *today*?" This leadership tradeoff is natural, and it works far better than the to-do list from hell that remains intimidating and unprioritized. Some of the best financial chiefs spend time two or three mornings a week meeting with staff and asking these very questions.

Choices depend on whether or not the organization is operating in crisis/survival mode where the work of today is vital and takes precedence. Crisis mode happens to the best of companies. The difference in immature companies is that fire fighting becomes a way of life. Any time survival or crisis is not the order of the day, a primary commitment should be to make an investment in developing others. Some CFOs make a habit of meeting with each direct-report manager once a week to discuss work priorities and personal workload balances, as well as previously agreed-on developmental objectives and progress. Seasonal businesses and organizations (such as schools) that have after-hours time available have excellent, built-in opportunities for learning.

Conflict Management   Blessed are the peacemakers, for if they are really good they spread peace of mind—one of the necessities of sustainable human productivity. Conflict management, in this context, is not the kind of thing you ordinarily see in a typical daycare center where small, immature, emotionally driven little people engage in a battle of wits with each other and with adults. That's how immature beings act: pushing on things until they break. While this approach may sound like the typical scenario in most workplaces, a person in a position of leadership will learn to see conflict as a *resource* to be managed.

Specifically, while many episodes of conflict in the workplace may be of the daycare variety, more often than not they represent two poorly articulated, but reasonable, alternatives. In the first, people quickly become frustrated and emotional if their ideas are either dismissed or misunderstood. Consequently, opposing parties take up postures, bury any value that might exist between them, and require mediation or arbitration from someone who can listen to both sides and uncover the buried value. This scenario arises frequently between functions that speak different languages while actually talking about the same thing: accounting talking variances and operations talking waste, sales talking satisfied customers and production talking quality products.

The second scenario is the opposite. Drawing on self-management capacities as the foundation for this kind of arbitration, a self-confident person can withstand the inevitable personal attacks often experienced during arbitration, and patiently listen for common interests. Finding the good, even if it is only one small shred of commonality and working from there, is much more productive and less stressful than focusing on differences and charged emotional states. An information technology staff often needs translators so that other functions can understand them. Some savvy CFOs who manage information technology (IT) or management information systems (MIS) functions create a formal liaison position by hiring a person with the unusual combination of fluency in both computerese and English, which saves wear and tear on all concerned.

Inspiring, Influential Leadership   In the early versions of the EI framework, "leadership" appeared as a relationship management emotional intelligence competency. However, "inspiration" and "influence" have replaced the term "leadership" as the EI framework has matured. Leadership is the result of all other competencies described in this section. Most people approach leadership development in a reversed order. Think of all the books and courses on leadership that start with descriptions of how to behave like a leader. These descriptions are akin to working for more sales by starting with the profit/loss line on the income statement! Note that this reversal dynamic highlights the inappropriate nature of all performance target setting without leading activities. A target alone is at high risk of not being met if precursor milestones are missed.

That's why leadership is so mysterious. It is a composite of many complex competencies—some that come naturally and some that are learned. If an essential component is missing, or a developmental step skipped, the leader is out of balance: extraordinary in some aspects and dismal in others. The good news is that development is how leaders can be made. They don't have to rely on being born right from the beginning.

Inspiration and influence remain essential leadership competencies, perhaps two of the most important. However, this section has highlighted some specific ways that CFOs can learn and apply those EI competencies most important to the responsibilities of that office. Unlike some of the competency examples given above, each and every CFO needs to personally identify and define inspirational and influential leadership competencies according to the unique mix of readiness expressed by fellow employees, the organization, and the environment that supports their work.

Three points of leverage and influence exist in all human social and economic structures, including the workplace: (1) individual human lives, (2) varying forms of human organization, and (3) contingent[10] environmental conditions that impact individual and corporate lives. These three primary domains are where mature leaders intentionally work—a *triple helix*[11] of interdependent human work domains, the sources of all energy and raw materials where all work is performed. Exhibit 3.4 details some of the most important interrelationships between CFO leadership competencies and people, their organizations, and their work environment, and the "Ethical Resonance" sidebar discusses some living-system correlates for the organization as triple helix.

In other words, executives can only modify, adapt, improve, and correct their organizations through leadership competencies that influence people, enhance organizational design, and improve the environment. Notice the absence of a financial

WWW.

EXHIBIT 3.4 DOMAINS OF THE HUMAN WORKPLACE

Work Domains	Basic Resources	Living Systems Parallel	
People	Skills Experience Competence	DNA	
Organizational Form	Structure Control/guidance	Organism	
Work Environment	Raw materials Productive space	Ecosystem	

perspective in any of the three domains. Financial concepts are abstract representations of actual people, organized work, and conditions. Look for unique opportunities to practice inspirational and influential leadership competencies in your own organization in the context of the workplace discussion in the next section. But first, take the Emotional Intelligence Leadership Competency Assessment and find out where you need to focus your practice in terms of your activities in each of these three domains.

www.

Circle **S** if this is a strength or **W** if this is a weakness.

Self-Awareness

S   W   I am usually *aware of what I am feeling* and can clearly identify the emotions as they arise. I am rarely confused about emotions I experience in my workplace.

S   W   I *see my strengths and weaknesses for what they are,* and I am rarely surprised at the perceptions supervisors, peers, or reports have of me.

S   W   I *can confidently say* that I am comfortable with *all* my workplace relationships and responsibilities.

Self-Management

S   W   Emotional expression is a matter of choice for me. I seldom find myself wishing I hadn't acted in certain manners. *(self-control)*

S   W   I am *trustworthy*. I have a reputation for being as good as my word throughout all levels of my workplace.

S   W   I am *conscientiousness*. I cannot be persuaded by authority to act against my sense of right and wrong.

S   W   I am *adaptable,* can react well to unplanned events, and adjust smoothly to the agendas of supervisors, peers, or reports when they make good management sense.

S   W   I am *achievement oriented*. I organize my time each day around the most important results we need as a team rather than the routine tasks falling under my job description.

S   W   I am known for taking *initiative* and being action-oriented. Coworkers don't have to wait for me to step up to the plate and take a swing at new and spontaneous opportunities.

Social Awareness

S   W   I am known for my ability to *empathize* with others—especially peers and reports. I often find myself in conversations with coworkers who have sought me out because they know I will understand them.

S   W   I am aware and objective about the big picture in my organization. I not only take an interest in company-wide matters, I regularly look for strategic information and look for opportunities to incorporate strategic awareness into my daily activities. *(organizational awareness)*

S   W   It is important to me that I am able to be of service to others in my organization. *(service orientation)*

Relationship Management

S   W   I regularly look for opportunities to bring out the best in others. *(sharing skills according to the developmental readiness of others)*

S   W   If projects or initiatives are in need of direction, I am usually the person my coworkers look to for *inspiration*.

S   W   When I strongly believe in a specific management choice, I am much more likely to try to *persuade and influence* coworkers of my opinion than be directive and impose my will over theirs.

S   W   Whether I need to communicate
- Something routine or critical,
- To supervisors, peers, or reports,
- To a single person or to a large group,

I almost never find myself wishing I had used a different format or wishing that communication tasks like speaking, writing, or presentation weren't so stressful. *(communication skills)*

S   W   I am a *catalyst for change.* When I am involved with teams working on challenging management issues, I can see and express creative alternatives to the status quo that lead to significant organizational change.

S   W   I *manage conflict* well. If a confrontation has been brewing or a tricky negotiation is needed, I am usually called upon to resolve the conflict. When faced with conflict, I do not try to avoid it.

S   W   *Building bonds* with people is important to me. Rather than treating my coworkers as temporary fixes to my management issues as they arise, I work to build lasting relationships for the long run.

S   W   *Teamwork and collaboration* are strengths for me. Depending upon the task, I am equally comfortable working on a team as I am working alone.

Other CFO Leadership Attributes

S   W   I am considered to be a *risk-taker.* I'm not known for trying to talk someone out of a new practice, especially by saying, "We just don't do things that way around here."

S   W   I have good *personal chemistry with the CEO.*

S   W   I regularly seek business *relationships outside my functional circle.* People at work are often surprised by how many people I know in all areas of my organization. They also turn to me when they want to discuss cross-functional management issues.

S   W   I am known for *asking a lot of questions.*

S   W   I regularly *share knowledge and information*, and I am not protective of it.

S   W   I have a *sense of humor* (and I'm not the only one who thinks so).

S   W   I *quickly absorb and assimilate new knowledge.* I don't go home wondering how all the information I just heard will affect me and my area. I can see how big-picture decisions concretely affect my day-to-day activities.

TRIPLE HELIX ETHICAL CONTEXT

If a business really does operate as a triple helix of people, cohesive organizational form, and workplace environment conditions, certain ethical relationship implications between these three strands naturally follow.

Interdependence

Factors that influence any member of the organization, the organization form, or the workplace's supportive environment can be felt throughout the helix, for good or ill. Internally, harming one person or group without harming the entire organization is very difficult. This harm may take some time to manifest, but its spread is predictable. This living-system perspective explicitly acknowledges the interconnectivity of the parts and the whole. No room is available for parochial excuses. Misconduct eventually affects other people, how they work together, and the environment in which they work. It is simply a matter of time.

Collective Mind-Set Convergence or Drift

When a group of people works together day after day, they develop common attitudes and beliefs—for better or worse. Some individuals are able to resist merging with negative group-thinking patterns, but most people do not resist because they are unconscious of the power of the group dynamic on personal thinking. As a steward of organizational interests across all functions, departments, and units, one of the CFO's most important responsibilities is to regularly check in on the pulse of the organization and to attend to any negative group-think disharmony as it arises. Group-thinking pressures work to undermine personal ethical standards. When groupthink is inappropriate, executives need to correct employee misperceptions before they begin to act out unethically, usually in the form of passive or active defiance.

Power

Every member of an organization directly or indirectly influences all others as a part of the interdependence dynamic, but some members influence more directly and quickly than others because they have been granted authority by the organizational design structure. The average organization contains a number of people who are immature from a leadership perspective. These people have not consciously developed their leadership competencies and integrated them with their work identity. When people exercise leadership authority that is granted but not learned and earned, authority becomes an arbitrary form of personal and organizational power that is easily abused. Professionally mature, emotionally competent leaders act from the authority of their own personal standards rather than leaning on the imprimatur of the organization chart. Naturally, hierarchical structures magnify both artificial forms of authority and ethical misuse of that authority, particularly for executives. Therefore, every executive needs to be aware that every action and every word has the potential to reverberate and amplify throughout the company. Genuine leadership authority flows from actions that demonstrate transparent competency. In the hands of genuine leaders, power becomes less a function of force and manifests in the form of influence and inspiration.

Defining the Scope of Professional Development

Don't think that a small group of awakened individuals cannot change the world. Indeed, it is the only thing that ever has.

Margaret Mead[12]

As a consequence, all the van Brandens in the world verified his ineluctable solitude, his impregnable skepticism when faced with the intractable vanity of all human enterprise, of everything undertaken by those unfortunate blind creatures who come to death without ever having suspected the marvel of the world or felt the miraculous passion which fires our knowledge that we are alive and that death, without beginning or end, a pure, limitless present, is a part of that life. He gave himself over to pleasure in the countryside, but he was aware that the various sensations piercing the numbness of his fatigue with wondrous, endless celebration were coming to him eroded by a torpid memory that the years had worn away.[13]

Alvaro Mutis

What kind of company surrounds you at your workplace? What kind of company do you provide there—that is, company in the sense of associates, companions, and coworker friends. Do you have the kind of company marked by solitude, skepticism, numbness, fatigue, and sensation eroded by the years? Or the kind imprinted with miracles, passion, pleasure, and wondrous, endless celebration?

In the midst of relative luxury and economic success, the typical American workplace harbors a disproportionate number of angry, depressed, and exhausted people. Not all, but too many. Studies show that a large percentage of Americans are chronically sleep-deprived and becoming steadily more dissatisfied. At the same time, despite the most recent economic downturn, productivity measures like sales dollars per employee remained steady. More and more people leave corporate jobs to start their own businesses, citing unhealthy corporate conditions, confusion caused by mergers and acquisitions, and the need to straighten out their priorities. While the average vacation time in many Western European countries is four to six weeks, in the United States it is two to three weeks. Some Europeans say that Americans are *all* workaholics.

Indeed, many people first come to a twelve-step group called Workaholics Anonymous because they have literally worked themselves nearly to death and suffered strokes, heart attacks, and emotional breakdowns related to their work-dominated lifestyles. These people have seen the other side of life and don't wish to return there any time soon. Recovering workaholics say they struggle with two major difficulties. First, just as people who eat too much still have to eat something, people suffering from work-addictive behaviors still have to make a living. Their second difficulty is a greater challenge: working within a culture that rewards work obsession with its highest titles and the most money. Working-yourself-to-death behaviors are prized, approved, and encouraged. The Hopi Indian language has a word meaning "life out of balance": *Koyaanisqatsi*.

In this context, leaning more toward the somber than the joyful descriptions that started this section would come as no surprise. No one can afford solitude and impregnable skepticism for very long, perhaps least of all leaders, because even in the land of rugged individualism, leaders still set the tone for life in the organization. "Where there is no vision, the people perish" (Prov. 29:18, KJV). While Americans pride themselves on individualism, self-reliance, and the hardworking, explorer spirit, their desire for inspiring visions, leaders, and heroes endures, perhaps now more than ever because everyone is so tired.

LEADERSHIP COMPETENCIES—FINDING THEM AND KEEPING THEM

Unfortunately, genuine leadership is a scarce commodity almost everywhere. Not everyone, however, wants to be a leader, and not everyone who wants to can meet the requirements to do the job. Of those who possess leadership qualities, some choose more solitary paths, others grow bitter with harsh experiences, and more than a few of the best people care about their work and coworkers so much that they burn out in a few years. The last leadership profile describes the kind of person who organizations can least afford to lose. These leaders are people of committed heart. They engage their work with high energy and passion, but they neglect their own needs because they have never learned how to balance their work and personal lives. Their level of intensity, fervor, and commitment comes with a corresponding measure of the attendant risk that those conditions bring. If anyone reading these words experiences a jolt of recognition that *I am losing my interest, my passion, or my endurance,* the time has come for sober introspection.

Gnothi seauton. Don't worry, it's Greek to everyone: "know thyself," inscribed on the Oracle of Delphi. Or as Polonius urged Laertes in Shakespeare's *Hamlet:* "To thine own self be true."[14] The first obligation of a true leader is to oneself. A person in the CFO position who desires something more than mere survival in the workplace must begin with an accurate assessment of personal and professional well-being before turning to assessing others. Before one can be present for others, one must be present for oneself. This presence may be especially true for a CFO because of the intense analytical nature of accounting/finance work, as well as the typically introverted, hard-working personality profile. In terms of professional leadership development, an essential part of knowing oneself means knowing how the workplace works. To know the workplace means to know how workers work. Knowing the different dimensions of human work gives a leader the necessary perspectives for leading others while taking care of oneself. This chapter connects personal capabilities, self-knowledge, organizational knowledge, and the intelligent perception of ambient work environments, thereby widening the circumference of the work-life self of the CFO. To do so, the CFO focuses on the personal maturity and leadership competencies essential to shouldering the job's responsibilities.

Many business professionals hold the opinion that accountants, including CFOs, are rigid, unmalleable people. Conventional accountants may, at times, deserve this reputation. On the other hand, an interesting paradox underlies the general accounting personality profile. A person who fits this profile can be unbending, rule-fixated, and uncommunicative. Just as likely, however, the same person's detail orientation, broad view, and sincere desire to provide accurate answers are qualities of an invaluable advisor. Similarly, these same propensities may make accounting professionals more capable of developing professional leadership competencies, but this is not to imply that such changes are easy. They take dedicated and persistent practice, until they become an integrated mode of behavior. They also require a well-tested means for developing such competencies. The next section begins to lay out the details of how to travel that road.

PEOPLE, THEIR ORGANIZATIONS, AND THEIR WORK ENVIRONMENTS

These three strands form a triple helix that characterizes all the myriad shapes and surrounding conditions of human organizations. This trio of interdependent domains establishes the patterns of work routines, ethical behavior, relationships, resources, and all other traits of human groups from families, to religions, to nations, and of course, in places of work. Individual human lives are the elemental particles—the genetic code—strung together in myriad organizational formations to serve a wide range of purposes. In turn, the organized formations of individuals—family, church, work, social, economic, spiritual—are interdependent within the prevailing environmental conditions that support them.

Each domain brings its own basic resources to the workplace mix. People bring their personal skills and experience. The design of organizational forms provides varying collections of individuals with a work structure, and work design itself exercises some measure of control or guidance that aligns the individual skills and experiences toward a common, practical outcome. The work environment supplies people and their organizations with the raw materials for their work and a place in which to work safely. Although all organizations work within these three domains, the predominant way to see them is by means of an abstract representation of their resources, the accounting and finance language—financial targets for operations performance, return on investment (ROI) capital project performance, and unfortunately, earnings per share (EPS) as the prime measure of the entire enterprise.

The perspective on each domain varies with leadership maturity and competency development. For example, a less mature CFO cannot see the work environment beyond the four walls that enclose the building that houses the business. A more mature CFO understands that the work environment includes commercial, technological, economic, social, and ecological resources. Importantly, the triple helix work domains are interdependent; the resources of one are meaningless without the resources of the other two.

As a representation of human work as a living system, the three work domains are so intimately interwoven that leaders cannot abstractly separate them and make practical decisions about applications that fall across domains. The three domains of the helix are separated only for the purposes of discussion; they cannot and do not exist separately. As a representation of the scope of a living system of work, the helix intuitively suggests the unpredictability of workplace management and leadership. Let economists build as many formulaic abstractions as they like; none of them reliably predicts anything. Too many contingent conditions are ignored or are simply unknowable. Economic model building may be the most effective means ever devised to divert an entire society's organizational attention away from the way work is actually accomplished.

In contrast to economic models, the way that the three domains characterize the workplace has decidedly different implications. A CFO must expose and interpret the actual domain resources that are the facts behind abstract financial representations. Wider perspective requires a highly mature composite of interactive skills, experience, and leadership competencies. In placing the CFO at the center of the domain interrelationships, one can visualize the concentric waves of influence like ripples in glassy water after a stone drops. Moving outward, the waves influence immediate staff; the CEO, peer executives, and the rest of the people in the organization; the community and culture that is home to the firm and its people; the network of suppliers, bank creditors, and other resource providers; on out to industry and competitors, to all industries and sectors; and at the widest points, all nations and cultures on the planet. All these ripples form the increasingly broader context for the work life of a mature CFO, and a lot of other people. While a CFO can limit the role's sphere of leadership influence to staff and peer executives, such a CFO works with incomplete information.

Likewise, the myriad web of relationships within and outside the organization cross, diverge, intersect again, loop back, and leap forward, in a constant unchoreographed dance of human associations creating something larger than any individual and certainly beyond the generation of financial wealth alone.

The working environment and shifting conditions have enormous influence on the development of organizations and the individuals within them. Consider the example of a CFO in a firm that has succumbed to the myopia of precisely meeting the quarterly earnings number. This finance chief sits within a dominant cultural condition: short-term earnings. Now imagine circumstances converging over time that result in a worldview where nobody pays attention to the quarterly forecast or actual EPS calculation. Such a condition is unthinkable now for many reasons, not the least of which is Securities and Exchange Commission (SEC) mandates. However, foreseeing a time when contingent conditions make the measures irrelevant is not unthinkable. It may take time, but individuals and their organizational practices reciprocally influence ambient work environment conditions. For instance, what if political-social winds blew in changes that demanded, first, socialized medicine like the Canadian health care system, and then state-run transportation systems (not so unthinkable at all considering the plight of the airline and train sectors), followed by nationalization of industry? Each of these examples of changing conditions has a long history into the present environment. The U.S. airline industry was regulated for part of the twentieth century, then deregulated, and has recently received government bailouts, the first step toward reinstatement of the former regulatory environment.

Here are a few more actual contingently evolving environmental situations.

Situation 1: A European chief of state unexpectedly decides to divest assets in the form of a huge tract of troublesome, undeveloped land because of the overhead involved for simple maintenance and stewardship activities, thus opening territory for a relatively new junior business player.

Situation 2: Trade competitors solicit and spend large sums of money from investors eager to discover a channel for faster trading that will connect them with important suppliers. After more than fifteen years of expensive failures, they give up.

The first scenario is Napoleon's decision to sell over half a million acres of land, culminating in what eventually became known as the Louisiana Purchase. A modern corollary of large geographic areas opening to trade is, of course, the North American Free Trade Agreement (NAFTA) and its international trading implications.

The second scenario is the search for the Northwest Passage. Internet equivalents include the prospectuses of more than one dot-com company that attracted venture capitalists interested in finding a faster route to consumer pockets. In the modern case, the channel was there but the boat often went missing.

Human Lives

[N]ot understanding your own mind is a very grievous fault.[15]

Padmasambhava

Individual human lives are the logical place to begin digging for intelligent leadership competencies because, in an organizational context, people are the elemental units of work. The first life a CFO must attend to is his/her own. When a company loses a CFO or any significant figure to lack of self-care, others tumble behind in a downward spiral. In contrast, an inspiring CFO can lead not only the immediate staff, but also a whole organization, including the CEO, to success and well-being.

People who think that they are nothing special are mistaken. In complexity theory, a scientific discipline that seeks to understand more about how living systems work, individuals are the greatest source of systemic differentiation, divergence, and transformation. Napoleon, Hitler, Disney, Gandhi, Christ, and the Buddha each demonstrate the impact one human being can have on the entire planet. With that dynamic in mind, the discussion turns to the basic care and feeding of the first integrated element of the workplace, the individual human being now reading these words.

All the major traditions on the planet, from scientific to spiritual, acknowledge three dimensions of the human being: physical, emotional/cognitive, and numinous. People generally agree on the characteristics of the physical and emotional/cognitive dimensions, probably because they are so observable. Although different cultures characterize the numinous in different ways, even the atheist acknowledges that there is more to the human being than meets the eye. This third constituent goes by many names: soul, human spirit, vitalizing force, and morphogenic field, to name a few. In the context of a CFO's professional development, the most important manifestation of the numinous is conscience—as in the conscientious performance of all required duties. The atheist too feels pangs of conscience. While a Mark Twain protagonist lived gleefully after killing his own conscience, no one has since been able to duplicate this feat.[16]

Organizations, too, exhibit these three integrated but identifiable dimensions. Truly successful organizations demonstrate capacities beyond their concrete assets, people, and emotional profiles. Arie de Geus calls the interdependence of these three dynamics "The Living Company."[17]

Physical Presence—Up Close and Personal   Healthy physical presence is a core requisite for almost all meaningful relationships. Communication helps sustain relationships, and where connections are cursory—a bank transaction, an Internet order, booking a hotel reservation—physical presence is not necessary. When it comes to people working in the same organization, however, physical proximity is vital. One illustrative example concerns the founder-CEO of a young, prosperous company who was known for being everywhere at once. Everyone in the company knew they could get the CEO's ear just about any time, and there would be help and answers. The decision to venture an initial public offering required more and more of the CEO's time and energy. The CEO, assuming the people could manage on their own, soon was hardly ever on site. The IPO took some time to organize—about six months, in fact—time enough for an entire CEO image to disintegrate, along with productivity and financial results. The cause: Employees who were used to the CEO's presence, encouragement, and guidance felt a true loss.

Other points related to the importance of positive, encouraging physical presence include:

- The physical presence of leadership has a primary and lasting impact.

- In a multidivision company, frequent supportive visits by the CEO and other executives can break down barriers about "what's going on at corporate."

- With rare exceptions, direct reports should have a permanently open door to their supervising executive. This condition applies to all supervisor-subordinate relationships at all levels of the company.

- People rarely believe an executive or manager is "working at home," unless (a) a trusting relationship is well established, (b) work results are occasionally shared to maintain that trust, and (c) wherever possible, all staff have the same privilege for appropriate assignments.

- The continuous presence of executive participants (and project leaders) for major initiatives is the number-one factor determining project success.

- When it comes to the people one works with, executive quarterly meetings are an insult if they are the only means of direct relationship, but an annual visit from a high-ranking executive many layers up is like a presidential visit to troops in the field. The effect can be for good and forever—of course, both in the positive and the negative sense.

Emotions and Cognition—A Functional Composite   Importantly, humans and organizations learn both intellectually and emotionally. Although emotions can be a nuisance at times, they are a rich source of information and can be deep wells of wisdom when they are acknowledged. Unlike strictly cognitive information, humans can acquire emotional learning just by observing or hearing. Partly solids, partly water, meaningful discussions of the human body cannot separate these two vital, interdependent components. Emotions and cognition work together in the same interdependent fashion.

Individuals—and as we shall see, whole organizations—learn through the interplay of emotional and cognitive intelligence. Test this for yourself. Without pausing, spontaneously come up with a word or phrase from the right column of Exhibit 3.5 that most closely matches your emotional state of mind at the time or place (on average) described in the left column. Don't "think." Just choose.

Review your responses. Tally the number of lines where you picked a disturbed, unhappy state of mind. Tally the number of uplifting/happy emotional states. What do you see? This exercise creates an emotional snapshot of current cognitively

EXHIBIT 3.5 WORKING EMOTIONAL PROFILE

1. Monday morning or first day of your workweek	(a) exhilarated; (b) indifferent; (c) numb
2. Friday nights or the end of your workweek	(a) exhilarated; (b) indifferent; (c) numb
3. Doing a performance review—satisfactory employee	(a) alert; (b) anxious; (c) annoyed
4. The days you are paid your salary	(a) gratified; (b) indifferent; (c) resentful
5. Meetings with your staff as a group	(a) alert; (b) anxious; (c) annoyed
6. Meetings with your boss	(a) eager; (b) nervous; (c) irritated
7. Travelling with your boss	(a) adventurous; (b) edgy; (c) claustrophobic
8. Coming home at the end of a typical workday	(a) relaxed; (b) irritable; (c) depressed

based work activities and the emotional context in which they are performed. Practicing cognitive activities with greater emotional intelligence integrates a CFO's technical skills, experiential knowledge, and personal maturity and leadership competencies into a presence that can address the working needs of fellow employees, their work units, the entire organization, and the environmental contingencies that support all work.

Humans are susceptible to disturbing emotions. "Disturbing" here does not mean negative, but it does mean unpleasant. Everyone has experienced an event of such intensity that disturbing emotions dominate all aspects of day-to-day life—death of a loved one, loss of a job, demotion, to name but a few. The ability to think symbolically means that people can live not only in the present moment, but also abide quite completely in a time past or a time imagined in the future, which is not always such a good thing. For example, a traumatic event of enough severity can freeze-frame a person to continually focus on that one event. Disturbing emotions impair cognitive function.

The Numinous Dimension and Conscience in the Workplace Conscience and most other aspects of the numinous human dimension occupy a very private place for most people—so private that the subject rarely makes its way into a business-related book. However, as a survival guide, this book draws on all the available resources that CFOs can use to help themselves, because this very separation of conscience from physical presence, emotions, and cognition cuts off the roots of ethical behavior in organizations. Conscientious performance carries no obligations beyond being true to oneself, but the presence of an ethical conscience in an organization is easy to notice. The absence of such spirit is even more noticeable. In the conscientious company, people are vital; in a company dominated by emotional and cognitive control, a cloud seems to hang over everyone's activities.

Why is the numinous dimension usually ignored in the workplace? What is the root of the fear beneath this taboo? Why until recently was personal conscience usually omitted from workplace discussions? The answer lies in the same reasons that conscientious objection became one of the cultural turning points for the United States during the Vietnam War. The business community may currently be evolving a more conscientious approach to general ethical business conduct, but then again, maybe not. As offshoots of the scientific management paradigm, modern corporations use mechanical models of control and reward rather than living models of production and learning. A strong, healthy conscience resists attempts at control even against overwhelming odds. An equally ineffable word, "spirit," comes from the root "inspire," which in turn, is related to the word "breath," and therefore directly related to living systems of work. Acknowledging all the central operative conditions of a living organization brings the proper perspective to management.

Organizational Form

The second strand of the triple helix is the design and structure of the organization itself. People generally think of businesses as economic structures. The business is also a social structure, but thinking of a business as a social structure is uncommon. If it were more common, perspectives on the company would be quite different. Hope for new perspectives brings up a second taboo word: community. Speaking of the business as a community requires thinking about relationships and what they mean to the organization. You know the feeling of being with close family and stalwart friends, knowing that these people will support you in your life choices. Most people do not feel this way at work. Part of this disconnect has to do with how the organization is built. Functions and departments that seldom interact undermine the sense of relationship, much less community.

What does a company look like? How do we usually depict it? Nice, linear, hierarchical reporting lines on the organization chart. But is this the way a company actually works? If it were, organizational charts would not become so frequently irrelevant, and executives would not endure with marginal results round after round of shuffling the boxes on the chart and the living people behind them. Put simply, people usually design their companies in answer to the question, "Why are we here?" If the answer is constrained to financial numbers, people sooner or later become dispirited because their work becomes just another input to the numbers. If the answer is only to lower defects to a Six Sigma level, the nearly perfect products may lose their market share in the process. If the answer is only about bottlenecks/

constraints or activity-based perspectives or a window-dressing performance scorecard, the organization suffers from identity confusion each time management designs the organization around a new method. The answer includes some portion of all these tactics applied, balanced, and executed in the right amounts, at the right times, and in the right places.

Building on mature relationships between employees and departments, how would organizational form look different if designers recognized the importance of social structure and community in the workplace? First of all, organizational form would place greater emphasis on supporting the health and longevity of the organization, rather than the economic profits that can be wrested from it in the short-term. Ironically, this shift of focus often results in both short- and long-term economic success. Second, a design emphasis on building relationship bonds would ameliorate counterproductive internal competition, secrecy, and power plays.

Creating an organization design that integrates community and social structure seems idealistic without firsthand experience of mature organizations that have learned to do so. People are used to thinking of business as a hierarchy. This organizational structure has served humanity well in its early stages. However, as a form of organizational design, hierarchy depends upon developmentally immature leadership notions like superior/inferior, dominance/submission, and obedience/punishment. The first step in designing a more responsive kind of organization is simpler when recalling that an organization is a community of people.

One way to begin the maturity transformation of an organization away from hierarchy involves replacing the isolated functional and hierarchical views with perspectives that demonstrate the organization's interdependent processes and relationships. The ability to see processes and relationships enables a company to re-align resources, adapt and train personnel, and engage in continuous process improvement. If these characteristics appear to represent an entrepreneurial firm, they do. Agile, flexible relationship interdependencies characterize some of the more mature design qualities that new companies must have in order to survive.

To demonstrate that this kind of organizational design can be practically applied, consider a type of organization that exhibits most of these qualities. Surprisingly, large consulting firms stand as good examples. These firms depend on adaptable special expertise, relationships of all kinds, and the ability to quickly reshape teams to meet client needs. To be fair, these firms have their closeted skeletons and close-up warts just like other types of companies. However, they excel at organizational design dynamics that a hierarchy could not tolerate. Let's look at the capabilities of these consulting firms one by one.

Adaptable. Consultants never know for sure what their next client will want, but the client's wishes determine the work the consultants will do. Consultants must be multiskilled, quick on their feet, and most importantly, not attached to any ego agendas. This description does not fit the typical large corporation, but it could.

Special expertise. Every consultant is hired for depth of experience in one or two particular areas, but in addition, these people must be quick learners. Like a skilled emergency medical team, they must be able to react and adapt to situations as they occur. These abilities are in stark contrast to departmentalized companies where chains of command, approval routings, and death-by-committee rule.

Consulting firms live and die on the health of their relationships. Internally, the consultants themselves must adapt by networking in ever-shifting teams according to clients' needs. Of late, corporations have attempted to become customer responsive, but usually in the form of gathering customer information passively or surreptitiously. This activity includes surveys, bar code analyses, and interactive product option programs. As a rule, only a small percentage of employees in large companies ever come face-to-face with external customers, which is diametrically opposed to the consultant position where day-to-day contact with clients is the norm. When you see someone every day and your livelihood depends on him or her, relationship becomes imperative.

So, although imperfect in so many ways, consulting firms make a reasonable prototype for rethinking organizational structure. After all, doesn't every organization exist to serve someone? Whether focusing on the needs of customers, clients, or patients, a productive service relationship must exist for the association to continue. The trouble with most organizations is that they seem to fear getting too close to the customer, perhaps because the customer may ask for something the company cannot do. Such a request is actually good information for the organization. Consulting firms take all the information they can get about their clients.

Companies use many images to express their identities. REI, a high-end sporting goods company, uses a cooperative approach and emphasizes attributes like customers sharing in year-end rebates that look a lot like modest dividends. Vanguard, a financial services firm, uses nautical terms to create the feeling of a ship's crew. Whatever the image, analogy, or touchstone, all organizations have only three helix-related turning points, three resource elements that are amenable to transformation efforts: people, organization form, and sometimes environmental conditions.

People. Organizational redesign depends on the readiness of employees to test new ways to work together. The ways organizations can prepare and motivate their people to receive more efficient, humane organizational designs include new skills training and new work experiences that begin to bridge the artificial boundaries between departments and functions. Human beings never lose the capacity for further development; therefore, with guidance no limit exists to the potential competence and design configurations of a human collective.

Organizational form. The physical environment and infrastructures that house and support workers influence performance for better or worse. These forms include both working spaces and information systems. Unfriendly, information system design can be as difficult to navigate as a haphazard plant layout, and just as dangerous. Physical layout, workspaces, proximity to work partners, and adequate resources are some of the physical infrastructural details of organizational design. Information, process, and procedural systems are the cognitive infrastructural design details that are analogous to the human nervous system passing information and coordinating activities to specific ends.

A more subtle but important influence on organizational form is the culture or management philosophy that influences decisions, determines relationships, and ultimately drives an organization's success or failure. For example, a founder/president who knows that she is not immortal and has concerns for her company when she is gone puts serious attention on transferring her knowledge and sets up a succession plan. The underlying cultural energy of this company encourages a broad base of employee confidence, emphasis on employee development, and sense of optimism about the future.

Workplace Environment

In its broadest sense, the workplace environment is a web of systems whose working conditions are contingent upon one another. What are "contingent conditions"? Examples for living organisms include weather, temperature, and food availability. For business organizations, some common contingent conditions include geographic climate, war zones, politics, macroeconomic trends, availability of skilled workers, market sector innovations, and competitor strength.

Environmental factors exert an enormous influence on the development and form of organisms and organizations. Significantly, the consequences of these external factors are not predictable, and the jobs of the CFO and other organizational leaders become guiding organizational design adaptation to the workplace environment. Just as different environmental conditions select the genetic survival trait that best suits survival of any life form, people running a business who remember that the organization is also subject to the complex interplay of environmental factors monitor the workplace environment for organizational threats and respond to adaptive opportunities. Meteors, earthquakes, and hurricanes aside, an organization that can adapt its form to meet changes at all levels of the workplace environment stands a much better chance of surviving and prospering than a mechanically rigid counterpart.

IN THE HEART OF THE HELIX

This chapter has provided a very brief look at how organizations actually work. Companies have long tried to connect the dots between materials, facilities, people, and organization charts, all in the constant flux of contingent environmental workplace conditions.

The discussion now turns back to the CFO standing at the center of the triple helix and moving out into an expanding circle of information, relationships, and awareness. Living and leading in the heart of the helix—people, their organization, and the workplace environment—is exciting business, and the CFO has more opportunity to experience this than most. When a CFO becomes aware that personal upgrades and improvements would make life better and easier, one question dominates all others, "Can I change?" In a practical sense, the answer is always yes—it's guaranteed. Change happens to everyone whether they want it or not. Can I develop the leadership competencies that a CFO needs? The biggest variables are personal motivation and open-mindedness. If a CFO is satisfied with the role constrained to finance and accounting, requirements are minimal. Recall, however, that this profile does not appear to be what CEOs and organizations want to hire. Take the maturity and emotional intelligence frameworks and begin to develop your own profile. Writing the story of your emotional profile as is, and after you put your mind to improving is an excellent way to see even more deeply. The "Alliances" feature for this chapter on the Web site shows you how to write your before-and-after story.

To make progress, the fundamental elements must change in both the organization and its leadership. The mechanistic perspective that views people and companies as isolated parts and components can open to a new mind-set. Many groups speak about relationship webs: scientific community, social activists, and even some business writers and consultants. While the human community struggles to *make* a living, new ways of making work *part* of living are emerging. People and the work they do replace the deluge of strategic and economic models as the focus of new organizational form and design.

NOTES

1. The authors received permission to record and compile these quotations from CFOs and controllers who participated in IMA-sponsored seminars under the title, "CFO/Controller: Strategic Business Advisor," at four different locations across the United States in 2000 and 2001.
2. Alvaro Mutis, "Illona Comes with the Rain," in *Maqroll: Three Novellas,* trans. Edith Grossman (New York: HarperCollins Publishers, English trans. 1992), 147.
3. "CFO/Controller" seminar.
4. Jack Kornfield, *A Path with Heart* (New York: Bantam Books, 1993), 229.
5. Daniel Goleman, *Emotional Intelligence* (New York: Bantam Books, 1997), and Daniel Goleman, Richard Boyatzis, and Annie McKee, *Primal Leadership: Realizing the Power of Emotional Intelligence* (Boston: Harvard Business School Press, 2002).

6. From resources posted by the Consortium for Research on Emotional Intelligence in Organizations at www.eiconsortium.org/.

7. Joe Stenzel and Catherine Stenzel, "Measuring Leadership Attributes That Matter: A Conversation with Daniel Goleman," *Journal of Strategic Performance Measurement* Vol. 4, Jan.-Feb. no. 1: 7.

8. Richard E. Boyatzis and Ellen Van Oosten, "Developing Emotionally Intelligent Organizations," in *International Executive Development Programmes*, 7th ed., ed. Roderick Millar (London: Kogan Page Publishers, 2002), page 4. Available at www.eiconsortium.org/.

9. Stenzel and Stenzel, "Measuring Leadership Attributes That Matter," 6.

10. In this context, contingency recognizes the uncertainty implicit in the complex set of interdependent processes that make up natural living systems.

11. Although the authors independently arrived at the descriptive term "triple helix," while performing due diligence research, they discovered a book by Richard Lewontin called *The Triple Helix: Gene, Organism, Environment* (Boston: Harvard University Press, 2001). This book explores the complex interdependencies of gene, organism, and environment in the context of DNA sequencing for purposes of genetic engineering.

12. Margaret Mead, *And Keep Your Powder Dry: An Anthropologist Looks at America*, ed. Herve Varenne (New York: Berghahn Books, 2000) 105.

13. Mutis, "Un Bel Morir," in *Maqroll*, 207.

14. William Shakespeare, *Hamlet*, 1.3.78.

15. Padmasambhava, *Self-Liberation Through Seeing with Naked Awareness*, trans. John M. Reynolds (Ithaca, N.Y.: Snow Lion Publications, 2000), 10.

16. Mark Twain, "The Facts Concerning the Recent Carnival of Crime in Connecticut," in *Mark Twain: Collected Tales, Sketches, Speeches & Essays, 1852–1890, Vol. 2*, (New York: Library of America, No. 60, 1992) 898.

17. Arie de Geus, *The Living Company* (Boston: Harvard Business School Press, 1997).

Working with the Accounting/ Finance Function

Preeminent is one whose subjects barely know he exists;
The next is one to whom they feel close and praise;
The next is one whom they fear;
The lowest is one whom they despise.

When the ruler's trust is wanting
    there will be no trust in him.
Cautious,
    he values his words.
When his work is complete and his affairs finished,
    the common people say,
    "We are like this by ourselves."

Lao Tzu[1]

[T]he wise leader does not push to make things happen, but allows process to unfold on its own." . . . *[T]he leader does not insist that things turn out a certain way.*

John Heider[2]

Т he first three chapters sketch out some of the requirements and guiding principles of leading the accounting and finance function. From this point on, the *Survival Guide* fills in the details and devotes the remaining pages to continuous practice toward mastery. Specifically, "mastery" means practicing skills, applying them to actual situations to gain experiential knowledge, and from this platform of skills and experiential knowledge interweaving the sounds, sights, and feelings of maturity and leadership competencies, like a concert maestro interpreting and coordinating the streams of musical sound according to the notes of a great classical symphony. "Rehearsal" is exactly the right word because practicing various aspects of unfamiliar competencies can initially feel quite awkward. The alternative is to move backward because conditions change whether a person chooses to or not.

Chapter 4 talks about leading the accounting and finance function staff. The executive circle is the locus of Chapter 5, and Chapter 6 expands to the organization as a whole. Together, Chapters 4, 5, and 6 provide a set of CFO practice parameters designed to impart greater health and longevity for people that apply them. Each focus gets its own chapter to parallel how executives commonly manage these three organizational components: the accounting and financial function staff, the executive circle, and the organization as a whole. However, in the context of the CFO's daily work, thinking of these three strands of the interdependent triple helix is abstract and unrealistic. Consequently, each chapter also associates its central focus with some of the most important internal relationships to the other two parts of the helix. For the CFO, these internal relationships include the board of directors, the executive circle, most managers and supervisors, and by extension, the rest of the people in the organization. That's before the CFO's external relationships with major suppliers, financial creditors, absentee shareholders, constituents from the cities, towns, and countries that are home to the company, members of the social and investment communities, and so on, until it seems the CFO manages relationships with just about everyone. To one degree or another, this statement is true. In each of the next three chapters, the *Guide* takes the conventional notion of customer relationship management (CRM) and creates a constituent relationship matrix for the CFO and for the accounting and financial function.

After all, for optimal finance function health, some person or group must connect with all of these constituents and communicate pertinent information as specified by their needs. Equipped with this array of constituent intelligence, the CFO and staff members become a precious organizational resource. The purpose of this chapter is to explain how to build and enhance such a constituent relationship intelligence repository, and how to connect it to the organizational requirements for a tightly patterned accounting and financial function structure that aligns with constituent needs. "Tightly patterned" is a version of the three-bears formula: not too hot, not too cold, but just right. The CFO version translates as just the right kind and amount of data, information, analyses, and reporting.

The CFO provides a self-referencing perspective that structures accounting and finance services and functionality for these many constituents. Virtually every natural system in the universe is a self-referencing system—a system that references all new designs and applications based on a repeatable organizing structure that can be replicated and regenerated in an endless variety of new forms. Think of atoms on the microscopic scale, DNA on a mid-range scale, and solar systems on a macroscopic scale. Each of these systems has a self-referencing pattern that instructs and guides new work within system parameters. Specifically, the CFO becomes a self-referencing organizational resource by using financial accounting, managerial accounting, and operational and strategic information to help people throughout the organization make appropriate decisions that balance local interests with holistic concerns.

This kind of self-referencing assistance and guidance must be capable of treating both routine and exceptional circumstances. People have very local perspectives even though their work always aggregates to holistic objectives. A local focus is normal because local stimuli are immediate and tangible. Examples include a phone call from a supplier wondering where payment is, irate or extremely satisfied customers, an Internal Revenue Service (IRS) or Securities and Exchange Commission (SEC) visitation, or an appointment with the Occupational Safety and Health Administration (OSHA). Because people's day-to-day work lives are dominated by local concerns, the CFO can use the entire set of organizational information to create a pattern that all employees can use to reference their own work to the big picture. The CFO, as chief ambassador and advisor, establishes a pattern for balancing the good of the whole and the desires of the few.

For a more accurate picture of how this job looks, think of an organization (the company) as the living organism it actually is. Within every organism, many organ systems (e.g., heart, brain, financial staff, executive group) coordinate for the best health of the entire organism. Each organ system contains specialized cells; blood cells cannot band together to pull bones across joints any better than muscle cells can distribute and share oxygen; analogies within the financial function include tax specialists, cost accountants, and payroll supervisors. Specialists within the executive group include functional and business unit representatives such as top managers responsible for sales and marketing, finance and accounting, and business units. Importantly, when specialists, whether they are cells or people, serve their intended purposes, they perform simultaneously at both the local and the holistic level.

Unless pathologies are present, an organ system never fights the organism within which it resides, and the specialized cells within the organ system continue to do their jobs for the good of the whole. Likewise, in a healthy company, individuals serve their functional purposes, and functions serve holistically. Unfortunately, this experience is not common because people hold the illusion that they are separate from, better than, or at least different from (as in more important than) others with whom they work.

FORGING FUNCTIONAL IDENTITY

This chapter begins rehearsal practice within the inner circle of the CFO: the immediate staff members of the accounting and finance function. Part of any leader's job is functional identity management. For the CFO, this work begins deep within home territory with a relatively small, but consequential, group of people: the staff members of the accounting and finance function (hereafter referred to as "Function" or "AFF"). Although the executive circle may generate deeper intimacy over time, the AFF is the most immediate relationship for the CFO. All staff members reporting to the CFO must know their exact responsibilities and how they contribute to their Function and to the rest of the company. Equally important, the CFO must discover what the rest of the organization thinks about the AFF—in other words, how the Function's identity is faring with other groups. To lead a group of any size in coordinated fashion, the CFO must understand not only the technical aspects of accounting and finance responsibilities, but also understand the business. In the specific context of this discussion, "understanding the business" means understanding the maturity of the organization itself and knowing the contingent environmental conditions most likely to affect the enterprise. The first expression of the CFO's influence becomes apparent through the members of the AFF. Work here is the first expression of maturity and development of the CFO and the Function.

To get a feel for the locus of the AFF in terms of the CFO's leadership relationships, picture the CFO standing in a central position between local Function matters and holistic organizational concerns (see the diagram with directional arrows representing the flow of relationship.). To the CFO's figurative right, the counsel of executives and the rest of the organization form the greater part of the relationships in the work life of the CFO. To the left stand the individuals who serve within the AFF. The AFF group stands central with the CFO as everyone in the Function works to serve the people on the right. The CFO must attend to the details within the AFF where activities are most nested and local. Concurrently, attention resides with high-level perspectives, balancing priorities amid shifting conditions.

AFF individual staff members ↔ CFO/AFF group ↔ Organization/executives

The job of the CFO is to skillfully lead the individuals who embody the AFF to continually better understand and adapt to these shifts so that they can more usefully serve the company. In parallel, the AFF members know they have an advocate in the CFO who constantly works to connect the needs of the organization with the set of staff abilities and their potential contributions. Visualizing or even mapping out exact CFO and AFF service relationships and their positions in the cross-organization activity flow greatly enhances AFF staff intelligence and its ability to guide and serve.

The left-hand column in Exhibit 4.1 lists the CFO responsibilities in which the CFO and the AFF serve, followed horizontally by the particular CFO work focus and primary CFO responsibilities required in each dimension. Primary CFO responsibilities identify the specific developmental competencies required for each service relationship. Notice that the CFO responsibilities in the exhibit parallel the triple helix structure of the organization discussed in Chapter 3: individual human beings, organizational form, and environment. Every group of human beings and organizational relationships converges along these lines. Notice that in this exhibit, the dimensions run from largest to smallest. Much like systems design, the sequence acknowledges that the AFF members and group cannot organize their work unless they know their work space, each other, and both their organization and the external environment.

REPLACE YOURSELF

Upon arrival, the first job of any CFO or controller is to find and begin to groom a replacement, or eliminate the finance chief position altogether. This approach is about as intimate and personal as it gets. An actual elimination example concerns a general accounting manager for a $50 million manufacturing firm who worked to eliminate her own position for two reasons. First, she believed that the company did not need *both* her position and a cost accounting manager with a separate staff,

www.

EXHIBIT 4.1 AFF STRUCTURE AND CFO RESPONSIBILITY

CFO Responsibilities	Work Focus	Primary Responsibilities
Environment	Work space	Scan/align physical space and resources
AFF responsibilities	Actual work	Coordinate/align services to organization
AFF staff	Composite team profile	Assure attraction and retention of best staff
Individual members	Learning, experience, development	Plan and execute staff growth opportunities

and that paying two moderately high salaries was a waste. Second, being a consistent achiever, she intended to move up within the company, or if necessary leave for a more responsible position. She considered self-elimination a career cap feather, with attendant demonstration of her skills in delegating authority and fostering staff autonomy. By the time she voluntarily left the company because of a lack of advancement opportunity, she had delegated, cross-trained, and groomed supervisors to such an extent that, in essence, they worked autonomously. In her exit interview with the CFO, the departing general accounting manager made a strong case for not replacing her position, and suggested combining the entire accounting staff under one manager. The incumbent cost accounting manager got the job. Job elimination is not always possible or desirable, especially in the case of the CFO position. More commonly, the CFO's job is to groom a replacement. If no one in the current staff seems a likely candidate, this situation does not speak well for the bench strength of the team. In this case, the CFO has training and development or recruiting work to do.

The importance of the CFO position cannot be overstated. Likewise, the importance of the staff structure reporting to the CFO should have clear lines of authority, and should not have redundant or conflicting management positions. In many organizations, the CFO is second only to the CEO and frequently stands in for the top executive position. In addition, the CFO is usually the only other executive who has a holistic view of the company because of the nature of the responsibilities of a finance chief. In some cases, when a CEO has heavy external responsibilities, the CFO may actually know more about the internal workings of the company than does the chief executive. If a CFO never steps into the top leadership role, events remain that call for immediate backup. The CFO may be injured, need to attend to a family member for a long time, or depart suddenly for other reasons. Because the company cannot last long with a severe impairment to its information circulatory system, it is essential to ensure that people in AFF are ready to step in and perform CFO activities with backup skills, experience, and competencies. A short leap of logic suggests that backup and succession processes are important in all functions with specialized skills. Backup planning should be part of emergency preparedness. What could be more worth protecting than the valuable, mobile resources represented by the people in the most critical positions?

Succession planning for a CEO is common; however, this statement is not true for the CFO position. Robert Half Management Resources surveyed fourteen hundred CFOs in 2002 regarding their processes for selecting and developing a successor. Eighty percent said that such efforts were "very valuable." However, 58 percent of those surveyed said they did not have a formal process in place, despite the fact that 72 percent said they were currently working to develop a successor.[3] Such statistics beg the question of the training methods of the 58 percent who have no plan, and whether or not the 72 percent are actually doing enough to assure succession stability. Promotion and succession work must be handled case by case; however, the feature "Barriers and Accelerators: Internal Promotions: We Know Who You Are" on the Web site discusses one of the more difficult scenarios: the promotion of someone who was a peer.

ASSESSING CURRENT CONDITIONS

Exhibit 4.1 outlines the internal functional terrain that the CFO manages: environmental *conditions*, the composite AFF *group*, and individual staff *members*. These dimensions of the home territory each have a specific work focus and related primary responsibilities for the CFO. This view of AFF is high-level and in the aggregate. The rest of this chapter assesses internal AFF dimensions in detail, using concrete accounting and finance tasks and functional responsibilities. Emotional intelligence competencies necessary to lead the Function take center stage, because they enable smooth, effective execution. Explicit measurable attributes like the EI leadership competencies are usually missing from the accounting and finance function and its responsibility maps. Categories such as strategy, process, performance measurement, and cost management often find their way to lists of expectations and desired CFO attributes, but the personal and interpersonal competencies required to execute and sustain mature methodologies of this kind are usually missing.

A term that comes up repeatedly in the discussion is "identity." The term encompasses individual AFF employees' sense of themselves, their role, and how they are viewed in the rest of the organization. Naturally, the composite CFO identity has tremendous impact on these identity aspects of the AFF and the company. The critical point is that these perceptions of self, group, and organization influence the behavior of all concerned. Repeated behaviors become behavioral patterns that become habitual ways of seeing and acting. Forging a strong and positive functional identity must begin with a careful assessment of the current state of the AFF office and its chief officer.

Current Status: Assessing the Office and the Officer

After starting the process of personal replacement, the next order of business for a finance chief is to assess the functional status of the entire AFF, including the skills and competencies the CFO brings to the table. Based on the emotional intelligence competency structure from Exhibit 3.1, a CFO can begin the assessment process by establishing the AFF's current profile and identifying obvious skill and competency gaps. After quickly gathering first impressions, the CFO can then use an *AFF Development Diagnostic* (introduced in the next section) to detail the gaps and to begin planning for improvements in terms of required development, technical upgrades, and staff reassignments, to name a few. Naturally, this discussion centers on the maturity and leadership competencies necessary to execute any particular activity, but it never forgets the actual context in which they operate.

A caution is in order: CFOs typically assess the AFF and its staff members from an inside-looking-out perspective. When scrutinizing activities that are strictly internal to AFF, e.g., tax preparation and accounts receivable collection methods, an internal-only dialogue is acceptable. In all other cases, the CFO must facilitate a two-way communication channel; that is to say, input about the Function's service relationships is equally critical to any evaluation. As a case in point, recall from Chapter 2 the dearth of technical skills on the CFO profile created by hundreds of CFO seminar participants. Learning functional skills remains a baseline expectation. From the same chapter, remember the discrepancies between what CEOs said they expected of their CFOs and what CFOs thought their CEOs expected of them—a definite case of too much AFF inner vision. A diagnosis compiled from critical organization viewpoints—executive and operations, to name two—indicates where the CFO has work to do with AFF members.

Many good models attempt to create a matrix that demonstrates "the excellent finance function" and "what it takes to be a CFO in the twenty-first century." While most fail, a 1997 effort established a good starting point. Partners and managers from Coopers & Lybrand (as the firm was then known) wrote a book called *Reinventing the CFO: Moving from Financial Management to Strategic Management* that does a fine job of presenting a structure of important aspects of the CFO's responsibilities that rub off on the AFF.[4]

Reinventing the CFO goes to considerable effort to link the financial and accounting function to executive and operational requirements. The discussion is organized under major headings such as business partner, strategy, processes, and systems. Specifically recommended skills for all CFOs include strategic performance measurement and strategic cost management. The authors must have intuitively recognized that professional development is a vital focus because they created evaluation charts from "lagging" to "leading" CFO performance that included "behind, median, and ahead" categories for all the book's major CFO management topic areas. They illustrated in a series of grids critical CFO skills within this lagging-to-leading maturity scale, which is an excellent beginning. See Exhibit 4.2 for a summary of the Coopers & Lybrand work.

However, like many efforts of this kind, little to no mention is made of the personal and interpersonal competencies needed to bring these requirements to life. The emotional intelligence competencies discussed in Chapter 3 supply the energy, insight, and developmental intelligence behind every aspect of the CFO profile represented in the Coopers & Lybrand book. Similarly, certain standards of

EXHIBIT 4.2 CFO MATURITY "QUICK GRID"

Maturity Level	Lagging	Behind	Median	Ahead	Leading
Business	Conformist	Reactor	Controller	Team player	Team leader
Strategy	Reviewer	Supporter	Analyst	Marketer	Strategist
Strategic cost management	Bad cop	Historian	Hit man	Analyst	Primary director
Strategic performance measurement	Police officer	Gatekeeper	Analyst	Advocate	Director
Process management	Silos	Controls	ABC	Value maps	Architect
IT Structures	Old data	Rigid legacy	Mainframe, PC	Strategic	Flexible, responsive

moral and psychosocial maturity must be manifest in the work of a CFO. Without maturity and leadership competencies, the model CFO everyone is looking for remains elusive. Therefore, for purposes of this book and its focus on professional development, an enhancement has been added to the Coopers & Lybrand work in Exhibit 4.3: a CFO maturity range in terms of a time perspective. The Coopers & Lybrand categories present a good high-level view, but for a more comprehensive picture of professional development, more detail is needed to explicitly demonstrate how the AFF represents itself as a group of individuals working to support one another and the organization.

Current Status: Determining Organization Expectations and Information Focus

Before beginning to evaluate the CFO and AFF diagnostically, we should acknowledge that an accounting and finance structure must align with the overall maturity of the organization to minimize development squabbles. Within ethical boundaries, the CFO is responsible for carrying out executive mandates and for addressing the needs of the rest of the employees who use the AFF services as a resource for executing their own central mandates. If work mandates or requirements are impossible, ethical, or unwise, the CFO serves as liaison and arbitrator of resource distribution in terms of ethics and policy dilemmas. In short, the CFO becomes the development champion by pacing and leading the organization according to its readiness.

For example, if the CFO ascertains that the organization is a rigidly structured hierarchy, the CFO's organizational development work has two focuses. First, the CFO must align with the organization's maturity level and stand ready to introduce more mature ways to use accounting and financial information as the people in the organization become ready to listen. As opportunities arise, the CFO coordinates the introduction of more mature levels and methods of management.

Different functions within the organization become ready for more mature accounting and finance insights at different times. The more complex the organization, the more challenging this readiness surveillance becomes for the CFO. Performance management theory suggests one way that the CFO can create a system for monitoring the organization's readiness for change: the diagnostic. In a sense, all performance measurement activities perform diagnostic tests on different aspects of the organization—people, processes, machines, and even strategy itself. A well-designed set of measurements serves as a testing structure or diagnostic for performing a critical analysis of a problem and suggesting appropriate remedies. Exhibit 4.4 shows significant portions of an organization-wide diagnostic that a CFO can use to lead the AFF. This AFF Readiness Diagnostic per-

www.
EXHIBIT 4.3 CFO ROLES AND PROFESSIONAL DEVELOPMENT

PROFESSIONAL STATUS:	In Trouble		Good Accountant		Great CFO
TIME PERSPECTIVE:	Short-term only				Short-term serves long-term →
Changing Roles					
Business partner	Conformist	Reactor	Controller	Team player	Team leader
Strategy	Reviewer	Supporter	Analyst	Marketer	Strategist
Performance management	Police officer	Gatekeeper	Analyst	Advocate	Director
Cost management	Bad cop	Historian	Hit man	Analyst	Primary director
MATURITY LEVEL:	Lagging				Leading →

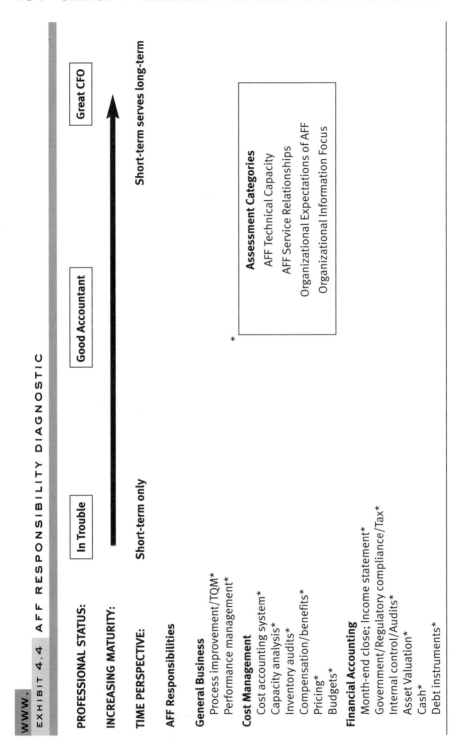

WWW.

EXHIBIT 4.4   AFF RESPONSIBILITY DIAGNOSTIC

PROFESSIONAL STATUS: | In Trouble | | Good Accountant | | Great CFO |

INCREASING MATURITY:

TIME PERSPECTIVE: Short-term only   Short-term serves long-term

AFF Responsibilities

General Business
Process improvement/TQM*
Performance management*

Cost Management
Cost accounting system*
Capacity analysis*
Inventory audits*
Compensation/benefits*
Pricing*
Budgets*

Financial Accounting
Month-end close; Income statement*
Government/Regulatory compliance/Tax*
Internal control/Audits*
Asset Valuation*
Cash*
Debt instruments*

Assessment Categories
AFF Technical Capacity
AFF Service Relationships
Organizational Expectations of AFF
Organizational Information Focus

*

forms a critical analysis of the AFF's *general business, cost management*, and *financial management* responsibilities in terms of organizational readiness at different levels of company and AFF maturity. Each line item is assessed in terms of four key AFF responsibilities:

- Technical capacity
- Service relationships
- Organizational expectations of AFF
- Organizational information focus

CFOs can tailor this kind of diagnostic to include any other important AFF responsibilities in their own organizations. Of course, to ensure the appropriate alignment of the development of the AFF and the organization, it becomes necessary to assess current maturity profiles of both. The objective of this diagnostic is to determine the "as is" status of the Function as well as the organization in terms of AFF responsibilities and to identify maturity gaps that indicate where work needs to be done. The ongoing work of the CFO, in this context, amounts to preparing the organization for an ever more mature accounting and finance function, as well as a more mature way to conduct business. Refer to the Web site for the AFF Responsibility Diagnostic in its complete, printable form. The guide to the Diagnostic in the next section is more easily understood when the entire Diagnostic form is visible on screen or in hardcopy.

A GUIDE TO THE AFF RESPONSIBILITY DIAGNOSTIC

The AFF Readiness Diagnostic (Exhibits 4.4–4.8) is not meant to be all-inclusive, but rather representative of many typical AFF responsibilities. Any CFO using the grid is encouraged to customize it to better represent the particulars of actual conditions. Adjustments may include more accurate responsibility items in the far-left vertical column, added responsibility categories, and other recurring duties. Attempt to stay within work responsibilities that are about actual people and the work they do, and resist the temptation to start listing sophisticated, but abstract, financial methods. A rule of thumb for selecting AFF responsibilities for diagnostic assessment comes from the answer to the following question: Will nonfinancial professionals know enough to evaluate AFF performance on this item? Make other adjustments as necessary to bring the diagnostic as close as possible to actual conditions. No fancy terms are necessary. The AFF Readiness Diagnostic carries one important caveat: Results are qualitative, not quantitative. Evaluations of maturity do not add up to a numeric score. Such an approach would be not only incorrect but arrogant and/or harmful. The alternative to numerical abstractions will become obvious. Some other features of the diagnostic deserve careful attention.

Time Perspective

No other duality plagues American businesses as much as the apparent choice between short-term and long-term priorities. In a business context, "short term" refers to financial objective performance within a timeframe of less than a year, most commonly quarterly. The most common financial measures are return-on-investment, share price, profit, and earnings per share. Many influences reinforce a short-term perspective, including the rapid growth of institutional investors and their focus on the rapid returns that reflect well in their own quarterly performance. Only in the last few decades have large institutional investors, such as pension funds, been able to control share price in the marketplace.[5] Nothing is inherently wrong with short-term priorities. In fact, attention to immediate tasks is necessary to create long-term results. A manufacturing operation by nature has a predominantly short-term focus, because workers must attend to material components passing through processes in real time. The trouble arises when two conditions exist in regard to the short term: (1) *only* short-term objectives receive management attention and (2) the objectives are all financial.

Myopia is the core of the short-term perspective pathology that meets the two conditions cited. In other words, executives who focus only on the short term also are interested only in local results—very local, as in personal. *How will my stock options be affected by quarterly numbers? How will my bonus be affected by this period's profit?* In contrast, long-term objectives in balance with short-term goals make a healthy combination. Within this context, "long term" means organizational health and long life.

The AFF Readiness Diagnostic includes a *time dimension* to expose imbalances in management focus. For example, a company may have a very sophisticated accounting system and advanced measurement paradigm such as a performance scorecard. But if executives focus almost exclusively on short-term financial measures, the power of the accounting system and the contribution of the scorecard are hamstrung. So, for example, the diagnostic may show a virtual close for month-end (a technically sophisticated method), but the *organizational information focus* remains riveted on EPS and share price. The equivalent in private firms is an overemphasis on short-term profit.

Note that the balance of short-term and long-term focuses falls on a continuum; finer degrees may be added at the discretion of the CFO. Another informative analysis using the time perspective aspect of the diagnostic lists the most important company performance measures and describes each one in terms of the time continuum. Notice the balance between long-term and short-term measures, as well as the symmetry between financial and nonfinancial.

Maturity Spectrum

Levels and stages of maturity should be familiar by now. In the diagnostic, however, "maturity" takes on added performance-related meaning. So far, this discussion has covered three subsystems of maturity: the moral and psychosocial development subsystems and the emotional intelligence leadership competencies. The AFF Readiness Diagnostic addresses concrete AFF responsibilities. Maturity in this context means the level of professional practice within the Function. For example, a virtual close is far more advanced and technically sophisticated because a conventional month-end close takes, at minimum, one week to accomplish. As one might expect, the success of methods and technology depends primarily on the maturity of the people operating and using them.

Enterprise resource planning (ERP) systems are good examples of the importance of maturity and leadership attributes. ERP is a tremendously complex and powerful technology, but if the processes it automates are immature or if the people operating the ERP system cannot see the holistic flow of information and materials portrayed in the system's modules, a company ends up with nothing but a very fancy and expensive hardware/software implementation. Based on such discrepancies, the detailed discussion of each line in the diagnostic centers on maturity and leadership attributes necessary to *execute* methods and technologies. AFF maturity follows CFO professional maturity as they increase together, moving across the diagnostic from left to right.

Professional Status

Before moving on, take a moment to notice that this category and the two just previously discussed form a three-sided mirror, like the ones in apparel shops. Examining the professional status row in Exhibit 4.4, a "great CFO" is, of course, the most mature and is able to address short-term concerns while keeping a perspective on long-term objectives. Hardly any CFO sits neatly in just one of the three columns: accountants in trouble, good accountants, and great CFOs. The CFO who ends up predominantly in the first category probably doesn't read books like this one. At the other extreme, great CFOs are rare.

The AFF diagnostic reflects CFO leadership, and as such, it directs the CFO to her or his own professional leadership competencies that require improvement attention. This approach can be especially helpful for incumbent CFOs. Specifically, if the diagnostic demonstrates that one of the AFF's responsibilities—say, cost man-agement—is poorly developed, the CFO may also need to work on the same pro-fessional focus. In short, the three categories in the "professional status" row provide a simple way for the individual CFO to examine both a Function and per-sonal developmental status.

AFF Responsibility/Assessment Categories

The time, maturity, and professional status perspectives in the diagnostic pro-vide important context for the detailed diagnosis that comes next. This part of the diagnostic examines specific AFF responsibilities. Remember that the categories and items under this heading are illustrative and must be customized to the CFO's particular situation. Similarly, the three descriptions for every row item should be modified to express the CFO's and the organization's priorities. Each item is ex-amined from four diagnostic points of view. The first two perspectives characterize AFF staff technical and relationship capabilities. The third and fourth viewpoints focus on the entire organization, its expectations of the AFF staff, and the most im-portant points of information focus. Each of these four diagnostic perspectives is described briefly in the next sections.

Notice the AFF responsibility items are first characterized as a high-level cate-gory (e.g., General Business), and second as several specific examples of the general category (e.g., Strategy and Process Management). In other words, the heading AFF Responsibility indicates the general area of performance. The tasks listed be-neath the general headings are concrete examples of AFF responsibility. These con-crete examples (e.g., Process improvement/TQM) are evaluated from four perspectives listed below each item identified in the box next to the asterisk in summary Exhibit 4.4:

- AFF Technical Capacity
- AFF Service Relationships
- Organizational Expectations of AFF
- Organizational Information Focus

For example, the diagnostic guides the CFO to assess AFF performance meas-urement and management responsibilities according to the Function's develop-mental readiness in each of these four assessment categories. A CFO using this instrument may use this general templates (Exhibits 4.5–4.8) as a first pass, or pro-ceed directly to a customized version.

As stated earlier, one of the most important pieces of information coming from this diagnostic is the gaps that exist between AFF maturity and the organization's maturity and expectations of AFF. To reiterate, when the CFO finds a significant gap, the AFF must adjust to the organization's needs. Only when appropriate levels of service have been established can the CFO proceed to cultivate more mature management methods and leadership competencies within the organization.

Perspective 1: AFF Technical Capacity   This first perspective is straightforward, referring to the maturity of the systems, methods, and processes that the AFF uses to perform its duties. Exhibit 4.5 shows a full version of the General Business portion of the diagnostic. Moving left to right, the descriptions characterize technical practices from different levels of AFF maturity. For example, looking at "Process improvement/TQM," an AFF at the least mature end of the developmental spectrum would not participate in these initiatives because they have not become familiar with the methodology. The organization expects this AFF to stick to its department and perform conventional accounting and financial tasks. In contrast, at the far right end of the maturity spectrum, the AFF has learned to become familiar with several different process improvement and quality management techniques so that certain staff members can actually manage some of these projects with other functional owners.

Perspective 2: AFF Service Relationships   Some finance and accounting functions do a great job of getting routine reports out on time with a high degree of accuracy, based on conventional standards. They do so, however, at the expense of many others around them. This second AFF diagnostic perspective balances the technical in terms of its relationship impacts. Here, the EI competencies pay off in a big way, with the CFO beginning to find out how well the staff is doing outside the Function and what kind of identity and reputation they have.

This profile can be performed two ways. The recommended way is for the CFO to meet face-to-face with internal associates who depend heavily on the AFF. The CFO should make a list of the services provided to each associate and discuss how well needs are being served. If particular staff members devote a large portion of their time to particular functions or individuals, the CFO should seek maturity and development information about such members. In the best case, appropriate staff members should accompany the CFO to the associate meetings. The finance chief must use discretion if any staff member is not ready for such an encounter and would be unduly intimidated by it.

Service surveys are not recommended because people often see them as a burden (if they fill them out at all), and because a valid survey design is difficult to construct and keep current. When the CFO simply does not have time to gather information face-to-face and instead uses a survey, the finance chief should follow up on surveys not completed, and thank those who have submitted them.

Based on the maturity of AFF practices, the CFO can create a functional relationship profile from this perspective. Customize this section to your own needs by

www.

EXHIBIT 4.5 AFF GENERAL BUSINESS RESPONSIBILITIES DIAGNOSTIC

Professional Maturity Status	In Trouble	Good Accountant	Great CFO
AFF General Business Responsibilities:			
Process Improvement/TQM	Does not participate	Cost analysis, e.g., cost of quality	Identify research-based improvement opportunities
AFF Technical Capacity	Methods unfamiliar	Understands improvement method theory	Selects among methods; assists implementation
AFF Service Relationships	Not their role	AFF provides quantitative skills; ABCM	AFF as equal partners
Organizational Expectations of AFF	Nothing	Quantify improvements; know processes	Identify, help select, and execute improvements
Organizational Information Focus	Financial measures	Explore financial/ops measure links	Coordinate process and financial interactions
Performance Measurement & Management	Only financial measures/controls	Implement and run technical system	Lead projects, link measure sets and business plans
AFF Technical Capacity	Only financial measures/controls	Understands improvement method theory	Selects among methods; manages project
AFF Service Relationships	Enforcer, snitch, naysayer	AFF provides quantitative skills	AFF as equal partners
Organizational Expectations of AFF	None outside of control function	Support project; accuracy validation	Champion, team expert, design/coordinate project
Organizational Information Focus	Financial measures only	Manages by financial; explores ops linkage	Holistic, interdependence, sees causes and effects

selecting time-consuming, high-priority tasks that involve many workers outside the Function. Cost accounting tasks are a good example, specifically inventory audits. Record the names of individual people outside the Function who are most affected, that is, the ones who do the most work during inventory audits. The CFO or designated staff members contact non-AFF workers to determine where their disposition falls on the range of responses. Often, coworkers have ideas as to how to make the job easier. Of course, the ideal is to move to more mature practices in inventory management.

At the least mature end of current practices, an inventory audit is a huge event. An organization that manages its inventory conventionally often has a lot of it. Inventory obsolescence is probably also high. Audits are cumbersome and time consuming. Many people outside the AFF are involved: purchasers, stock clerks, fabrication and assembly supervisors, and many more. Obviously, the AFF-driven audit does nothing for the popularity of accountants. In contrast, the most mature organizations rarely conduct inventory audits, because they have inventory levels that are immaterial. The question of whether accounting is serving operations or the reverse never comes up, because collaboration exists between functions.

A note of caution is warranted. An accounting and finance function should resist the temptation to survey all its relationships. Because the Function usually does payroll, the absurd extreme would be to view every employee as an AFF relationship. Common sense dictates that the CFO only evaluates significant relationships: the nonfinancial people with whom AFF spends a great deal of time. When pricing is problematic, AFF may have to spend some time with sales and marketing. The rule of thumb is to create relationship profiles with those who have significant experience with the Function. If a worker gauges AFF value based on paycheck delivery alone, time can be better spent elsewhere. The CFO's concern should be to manage the Function's identity and the professional reputations of AFF staff members.

Perspective 3: Organizational Expectations of AFF   The third perspective assesses organizational expectations of the Function. In contrast to the specific service relationships of Perspective 2, this viewpoint speaks to overall cultural beliefs and general attitudes toward finance and accounting. In other words, this perspective helps the CFO determine the perceived role of AFF within the organization. Using the example of the income statement, a company that has a general anti-accounting bias expects timely and accurate reports, but does not expect any interpretation or analysis. Under such conditions, the AFF is considered a bookkeeping center. On the other hand, a company within "the norm" probably expects analysis to go along with the statement. In this case, the function is appreciated for the analytic expertise it brings to the table.

The emotional intelligence social awareness competencies are critical in this perspective for correctly gauging the expected responsibilities of AFF in the current culture. When the CFO finds that expectations are quite low, he or she can respond by intensifying the practice of the service competency and then pace and lead key decision makers to appreciate the additional contributions the AFF can make. A CFO must be proactive in such a situation, watching for opportunities to contribute intellectual capital.

Perspective 4: Organizational Information Focus   Once again, the CFO must be aware of what information the organization considers important—in other words, which reports and analysis are actually used and which special projects are acknowledged for their cross-functional contributions. Another developmental subsystem plays an important role in this perspective. The *cognitive* subsystem addresses what units of information people of different maturity levels are capable of understanding, and how these same people cognitively process that information. For example, executives who are focused on the income statement and short-term financial measures have a hard time seeing the value of an activity-based system, even though it may actually improve some of the decisions that they make based on a short-term, financial perspective. As in all developmental subsystems, cognitive maturity allows a person to see more, appreciate expanded circles of relationship, and apply a more complete set of information points. Using specific examples, this fourth AFF diagnostic perspective focuses on the units of information that the organization prizes.

The CFO Professional Development Perspective   The information from the four AFF diagnostic perspectives is of little use if the CFO lacks sufficient experience to make use of them, which does not mean that only great CFOs have the necessary capacity to utilize the diagnostic. Good accountants can make a valuable use of this instrument for professional developmental purposes, especially as the diagnostic points out the need for new leadership competencies. They can also encourage their troubled professional associates to explore more mature ways of conducting business and relationships.

An extremely important part of the maturity application equation is that organizations are set up and structured to build expectations. When we are deep within companies we cannot see this dynamic, but what are budgets, forecasts, performance targets, and incentives, if not performance expectations? Planning strategy and setting strategic objectives create the biggest expectations of all. Crafting unrealistic targets when the goal is far away is so easy.

Expectations have a nasty habit of setting people up for disappointment, and where there is disappointment, disturbing and sometimes destructive emotions arise at every turn. The job of the CFO and the AFF is to help manage the process of expectations by providing decision-quality information, guiding the systems that concretize expectations (e.g., incentives), and when actual results and expectations do not match, helping the organization and individual workers to clearly understand what causes and forces led to the mismatch. Likewise, the CFO and AFF staff must vigilantly observe when things go right, and expectations are exceeded. Under these conditions, the AFF points out the forces and causes of success.

Using diagnostics like this one begins to uncover actual work conditions, but only if those CFOs who use such instruments remain more open to new ways of seeing the responsibilities of the Function, less reliant on numerical representations, and have a sincere desire to improve themselves along with their Functions and the organization. Humans are very good at spotting patterns, parts that don't fit, and discrepancies of all kinds. We don't get away with very much with one another, at least in the long term. Patterns, misfits, and discrepancies are the constructs most useful in this kind of endeavor. Equipped with an analytical mind, once the CFO sees broken processes and what breaks them, it is a short road to process improvement, one of the most prized capacities for financial professionals. Once a CFO knows that staff members spend countless hours on reports that no one is using, the finance chief has incentive to eliminate the wasted hours. Diagnostics provide actual information that finance and accounting functions can use to determine what role they should play, what the organization expects of them, and what information contributions are valuable to others. A sincere practitioner who uses this or any other valid diagnostic moves rapidly in the direction of the "great CFO" camp.

USING THE DIAGNOSTIC

The overarching categories of time, maturity, and professional status keep the diagnostic in scope. The objective of assessing current status keeps the boundaries of the study focused on the "as is." The four perspectives—two each for the AFF and the organization—assure that the diagnostic points to the correct objects of study. Some readers may be thinking that this effort presents a great deal of trouble, only to establish "current status." Much more is to come. Return on investment (ROI) and earnings per share (EPS) look like child's play compared to the work involved with such a diagnostic. Yes, ROI and EPS are easier, but they are highly aggregated lagging financial abstractions. Any concrete truth they carry is a snapshot of a moment in time already passed, and their numerical value is based on dozens of predecessor assumptions and calculations (not unlike last Monday's weather report), which in turn are based on one thousand pages of generally accepted accounting principles (GAAP).

Financial measures are not without value, but people should recognize them for what they are: numerical representations of physical reality that provide high-level indicators of the company's past health and performance. Financial measures are important guideposts that serve as a common language between businesses, investors, and creditors. Sophisticated as they are, they remain symbols. Behind the monetary calculations stand what really counts: people and the work they do. So, this diagnostic is the first step for a CFO and staff who are serious enough about their professional work contribution to begin to work where it counts. Use of the diagnostic begins with principles and definitions that apply for the entire instrument.

Refer to Exhibit 4.4 for the diagnostic's general structure and to Exhibit 4.5 through Exhibit 4.8 for examples of detailed application. Later in this chapter, Exhibit 4.8 details six financial accounting responsibilities for the AFF. The four detailed exhibits (4.5-4.8) are also available on the Web site. Using a common format, the following exposition for using the diagnostic focuses on five example tasks within AFF responsibility areas. The diagnostic process logic can be applied to the explication of any other AFF responsibility analysis.

1. General Business: Process Improvement (Exhibit 4.5)
2. General Business: Performance Measurement and Management (Exhibit 4.5)
3. Cost Management: Cost Accounting System (Exhibit 4.6)
4. Cost Management: Inventory Audits (Exhibit 4.7)
5. Cost Management: Budgets (Exhibit 4.7)

For each of these examples, the discussion addresses diagnostic application according to the following headings:

- *Attend to EI competencies*

  Leadership competency application in a CFO/AFF context

  Identify service relationships

  Leadership competency application in an AFF/Organizational Context

- *AFF Technical requirements & GAAP/GAAS (generally accepted auditing standards) vulnerabilities*

- *Ethical Resonance*

As the first heading indicates, the focus of the discussion is on the emotional intelligence leadership competencies most important for each of the five AFF responsibilities discussed. Most accounting professionals already possess a high-level of domain skills and expertly administer accounting and finance functions. As covered in Chapter 2, good accountants must just go out and learn skills and special expertise. Likewise, professionals must just go out and work to accrue experiential knowledge. Skills and experience are the rudiments of any profession. Excellence in these two makes a good accountant who fits well within professional norms. A balanced set of leadership competencies is needed to be a great CFO, as they emerge from a unique composite of each CFO's self-awareness, self-management, social awareness, and relationship management work. In these competencies, every person is unique and original. The three headings under EI competencies discuss leadership competency application contexts.

Leadership competency application in a CFO/AFF context (CFO ↔ AFF): Before a CFO attempts to serve the organization, some degree of certainty must exist that the AFF staff and the CFO have the expertise to meet the needs expressed. This subheading addresses relationships between the CFO and the AFF. Notice that the information flow is two-way.

Identify service relationships: No doubt can exist about who is being served. With CFO guidance, the AFF staff clarifies who the customer is and what their requirements are. Because the CFO separately explores the maturity of other functions besides the AFF, guidance on interpersonal competencies required in specific work relationships supports smooth connections. Importantly, this activity is what links the AFF to the rest of the organization. During this part of the dynamic the CFO must identify and explicitly acknowledge the organizational level of maturity. The CFO does not need to discuss service and relationships in terms of maturity—such an approach could be quite harmful—but rather uses the assessment to appropriately guide staff, assigning or suggesting concrete approaches and tasks.

Leadership competency application in an AFF/organizational context (AFF ↔ ORG): Again here the information flow is two-way. The CFO and staff move into the organization with confidence based on leadership competencies identified by the CFO that characterize the service relationship responsibilities for the AFF staff members. They do so with appreciation for the human beings they work with, a knowledge of the organization form, and an understanding of the present environmental conditions.

AFF technical requirements and GAAP/GAAS vulnerabilities: Each AFF responsibility requires a specific set of technical skills, which will be briefly cataloged as a reference point that complements the emotional intelligence competencies. Where applicable, the discussion covers vulnerabilities related to accounting and audit principles that may be encountered below the most mature level. Vulnerabilities are good reason to mature faster.

Ethical resonance: This section has a particular focus in this discussion by dealing with only the most mature AFF practices. Acknowledging that few organizations consistently practice at the "most mature" level for all AFF responsibilities, this section starts with a brief description of the conventional organizational practice of the task being discussed, and then discusses the first concerns and developmental tasks that arise when moving to the next level of maturity. The diagnostic is a template, meant to be customized, expanded, or tightly focused as actual circumstances dictate to reflect actual conditions.

Working with Maturity Gaps

Becoming a CFO who really counts is largely about aligning AFF functional services to the current needs of the company. The professional literature seems to suggest that, unlike operations, the AFF usually falls behind the performance curve, begging the question of whether or not the accounting and finance function are actually behind, or if their thinking is ahead, yet they have failed to communicate more mature ideas to other functions. One of the reasons that the *Survival Guide* emphasizes maturity and leadership competencies rests on the belief that the accounting and finance profession is no farther behind than any other discipline. The gap problem is a silence problem. Whether the root cause is lack of communication skills, poor self-confidence, unskilled team participation, a propensity to land in the middle of conflicts, or some other undeveloped EI competence, this book stands by the accounting profession's intellectual capacity and encourages accounting professionals to develop the competencies necessary to visibly contribute to the organization.

In this context, the work of the CFO is to determine the maturity of the AFF function and the development level of the organization. Gap analysis is a good way to think about applying the results of any diagnostic. First, the CFO selects a service where work is needed—for example, the cost accounting system. With that concrete focus, the CFO can evaluate where the AFF sits on the development curve, and whether that position is significantly different from the general organization's cost accounting needs; in other words, identifying any gap. For instance, the CFO and AFF staff may have thoroughly studied activity-based concepts and now wish to conduct a pilot proof of concept. This kind of work falls in the mid-range of maturity in Exhibit 4.5 and begins to explore the effects of short-term activities on long-term success.

In an actual case where such conditions existed, the CFO wisely put out informational feelers to determine whether or not nonfinancial professionals were familiar with activity-based concepts. Discovering that they were not, the CFO gave a brief tutorial to the division manager, and with his blessing, expanded the education effort to all key personnel. The result was a successful pilot and subsequent implementation of a much-improved cost and price quotation system based on activity principles. This example demonstrates five specific steps that a CFO can use in maturity gap analysis:

1. Identify a more mature and appropriate method than is currently in use.

2. Conduct a gap analysis between the AFF and the rest of the company.

3. Begin a deliberate education effort to build support for the more mature method.

4. Lead a successful pilot.

5. Ultimately implement an alternate cost accounting system that gives the company better ways to compete on price and better ways to see its costs.

Once again, the responsibility of the CFO is to determine maturity levels and align the AFF with the organization's current needs while pacing and leading more mature approaches. This process separates many good accountants from great CFOs.

GENERAL BUSINESS: PROCESS IMPROVEMENT

Let's move into a detailed discussion of how the AFF Responsibility Diagnostic works. Of the three major categories in the diagnostic, nonfinancial employees rarely complain about accountants shirking their financial statement and financial accounting duties. Cost management and general business responsibilities commonly have a different story; the last twenty years contain many chapters of the profession's attempt to create better cost systems: activity-based, resource-focused, quality-based, to name a few. When nonfinancial executives complain about financial professionals not understanding the business, they usually do not refer to either financial accounting or cost accounting. The two areas most consistently mentioned are process improvement capabilities and performance measurement and management expertise. Consequently, this explication begins with these two general business focuses, proceeds through cost accounting and management, and omits financial accounting examples altogether. Once again, keep in mind that the objective is to assess the current level of maturity in AFF and in the organization. For ease of identification, EI competencies are italicized. Refer to Exhibits 3.1 and 4.4 as often as necessary throughout this subsection.

Attend to EI Process Improvement–Related Competencies

Developing skill and accumulating experience in process improvement is relatively straightforward from a technical point of view. Learning about total quality methods or about the theory of constraints is within the capacity of almost all business professionals. Implementing improvements through these or any other methods is seldom a technical problem. Difficulties arise when people discuss general business activities under headings such as change management, cultural paradigm shifts, leadership commitment, and other equally nebulous terms. What is going on here? By now it is probably obvious. People managing general business process improvement methods lack an articulate vocabulary for discussing human development, leadership competencies, and gaps in maturity in practical ways. So, what EI competencies must a CFO possess to get the office and the AFF in the process improvement game?

The first requirement is *organizational awareness*. When it comes to processes, this characteristic includes knowledge about primary business processes, products, and services—where they are excellent and where they lag behind the competition. The CFO who understands the interrelationships of the organization's major business processes becomes more capable of evaluating whether or not the processes, and the resources allocated to them, are aligned with company priorities. Although CFOs are usually not technical experts outside their functional areas, observations and recommendations about resource allocations and process priorities can contribute much to the ways a CFO understands business process interrelationships.

This kind of ability to comprehensively see the organization's general business processes encourages the CFO to take more *initiative* to lead these methods from that widened perspective. Once a CFO understands current business processes, only a short walk is needed to making connections to financial results. Quantifying process improvement work is one of the greatest contributions the financial profession can make because nonfinancial employees usually do not have the expertise to see or articulate the financial connections. This action does not, however, happen automatically; the CFO must proactively learn about the processes and then find a way into cross-functional dialogues with process owners.

So far, so good. If the CFO stops the process improvement–related professional development with the *initiative* leadership competency, he/she will have succeeded in self-education but left important tasks undone for the people who participated in the process-owner dialogues. To actually make a difference, the finance chief should lead process owners and their respective functional executives in *achievement-oriented* analysis and process improvement planning and implementation efforts. Obviously, the steps from awareness to achievement require significant *relationship management* competencies. The very process of raising personal and peer awareness in subsequent dialogues *builds bonds* between the AFF and its customers. As the CFO participates in cross-functional process improvement projects, the *teamwork and collaboration* and *communication* competencies come into play.

CFO ↔ AFF People who participate in process improvement initiatives must have intimate knowledge of the business and its inner workings. In this regard, the CFO identifies AFF staff members who meet one or more of the following criteria: longevity with the company, long-term experience in the industry, previous work in related nonfinancial jobs, and formal training in process improvement methods. If none of these are present in any existing AFF staff members, a CFO should select people for process improvement work who are excited about doing it. Most project leaders are more than happy to have an enthusiastic team member no matter what their professional background. As for the CFO personally, participation in high-priority process work provides hands-on experience and the chance to contribute at a significant level. The CFO should also routinely invite briefings from AFF staff members who are on process improvement teams. If a finance chief chooses to assign staff members to these efforts, careful workload monitoring is necessary.

Identify Service Relationships   As the AFF becomes adept at process improvement work, the function runs the risk of compromising core AFF responsibilities. Staff members may find cross-functional process work often yields more tangible results and professional job satisfaction than routine, invisible accounting work. This stage is a good opportunity to accomplish two tasks: First, AFF staff members and the finance chief should look at those routine duties and ruthlessly critique them for their value and necessity. Desire (to do something else), as well as necessity, is the mother of invention. Second, if performed deliberately and conscientiously, process improvement work outside the function can lead directly to process improvement within the function.

Obviously, the AFF staff is hardly ever large enough or interested enough to participate in every process improvement effort. In organizations where there is an antifinance bias, AFF staff members may not even be welcome. In any case, the CFO discerns the competencies of staff and where they can contribute most to improvement projects. This approach may mean saying no to some requests for staff involvement in general business projects. Service relationships should not be based on a first-come-first-served basis, nor on an all-AFF agenda, but rather on where CFO and staff efforts can contribute most without compromising functional responsibilities. The finance chief keeps an eye on the level and kind of extrafunctional responsibilities.

AFF ↔ ORG   Remember that these discussions assume the most mature AFF/organization interactions. In such a firm, AFF staff members are expected to serve as equal partners in continuous improvement efforts, large and small. Relationships are built not so much on which function one belongs to but rather on what specific contributions one can make. Functional boundaries are not barriers in organizations that put the right people for the job above internal politics. The relationships grow from properly matching people and work, and being willing to alter organizational design as the need for process improvement requires. In fact, design adaptability is proving to be one of the most important aspects of company survival. In mature organizations, process improvement is a way of life, and transparent, accessible information is a necessity. The AFF relates to nonfinancial personnel as fellow students in the ever-widening horizon of improvement opportunities.

Getting down to the actual business of teamwork and collaboration between the AFF and operations units takes on a refreshing concreteness. No theory, no abstract financial concepts, just good ol' honest-to-goodness work. Continuous improvement and problem-solving make up the bulk of the world where these teams work. Accountants who work closely with operations must join them in a worldview of physical processes and actual people. Emotional intelligence competencies facilitate this work, but not much talk takes place about such inner factors. The concreteness of the work crystallizes team energy as it naturally focuses on tangible processes and related costs. In other words, interactions live and speak EI competencies as the norm without using the vocabulary of a model. See the sidebar about Marvin Windows and Doors where Mitch Cole, manager of the Wood Processing Product Group, spoke with Catherine Stenzel about his experience with teams matching this description.

General Business AFF Technical Requirements & GAAP/GAAS Vulnerabilities

The transparency and accountability currently demanded, especially of public companies, makes adherence to GAAP and GAAS standards essential.

Financial criteria: Knowledge and experience in conventional cost accounting, in strategic cost management methods, and a talent for extracting business-meaningful information from quantitative analyses.

Nonfinancial criteria: As stated above, longevity with the company, long-term experience in the industry, previous work in related nonfinancial jobs, and formal training in process improvement methods.

GAAP/GAAS: Rather than creating vulnerabilities, process improvement work contributes to discernment and proper judgment in cost and financial matters. An accountant who has never worked outside the AFF environment may find it much easier not to question cost reports coming from operations. In contrast, an accountant experienced in operations is more likely to catch discrepancies and to see opportunities when dealing with conventional financial and cost accounting data.

General Business Ethical Resonance

Process improvement work inherently strengthens a person's understanding of connectivity and relationships. Companies working within the mid-range of process maturity quickly discover that financial measures are lagging results that are dependent on leading operations activities, and measures. This insight typically leads to a variety of initiatives that explore the interrelationships of business processes and their cumulative contribution to financial success.

A CFO can serve a company while in this mid-range by simply keeping track and making visible all such projects and explorations. Resources are easily wasted during exploratory periods, as people become excited about the connections they are seeing and neglect to check out who else is working on similar investigations. Ethically, a CFO helps conserve human and material resources by coordinating these efforts to encourage synergy and cross-pollination.

An excellent way for the CFO to support process improvement is to engage serious improvement efforts in the AFF home territory. Charting, shaping, and streamlining accounting processes has several benefits. First, it is good practice for work in the larger organization. Second, improvements free up staff time for work on more valuable contributions. Third, and quite importantly, process work in the AFF demonstrates exemplary behavior and visibly proves to the rest of the company that the CFO is serious. One caution is in order when working on process improvement within the finance and accounting function. Many controllers and finance chiefs stop there and never move out into the larger organization. Although nothing is wrong with cleaning house internally, the savings to the organization are usually insignificant because of the relatively small size of the AFF group.

A sign that a company is moving from the midway point to the most mature level in process management comes when improvement efforts stop being boundaried projects and improvement practices become the common way of working. During this movement, most organizations continue to rely on conventional financial systems, sometimes including cost accounting systems. The CFO is ethically bound to improve ROI on accounting systems as rapidly as possible. Many financial professionals chafe at the work involved in the inevitable changes to routine systems. Many mature organizations choose parallel systems at first (e.g., a stand-alone activity-based system) and keep the conventional financial system on automatic.

The major dilemma of enterprise resource planning (ERP) systems is that integrated technical systems are force-fit into mature organizations. By not saying—or perhaps knowing—differently, ERP vendors allow customers to believe that the technical system is the solution to integration. So many ERP implementations have proved otherwise that a CFO would truly be acting unethically if an organizational maturity assessment was not conducted to determine readiness for such a sophisticated system. ROI calculations on ERP and other large IT investments have become quite popular of late. Because such investments deal with information value, predicting or assigning monetary value is next to impossible. The ethical CFO makes this point to executives and cautions them that software is never the solution.

A LOOK AT MARVIN WINDOWS AND DOORS

Background: Marvin Windows and Doors is a Minnesota company known for its health and longevity. Its roots date back to 1904 when George C. Marvin came to Warroad, Minnesota, to run a Canadian grain elevator. The Marvin Lumber & Cedar Company was established in 1912. In the 1930s, the company began building and selling frames locally and throughout the Red River Valley. The Marvin family managed the company for the entire twentieth century, and today, Susan Marvin is the company's chief executive officer. The company's combined workforce exceeds forty-five hundred people in six manufacturing locations in Minnesota, North Dakota, Tennessee, and Oregon.

Federal and state agencies recognize Marvin Windows and Doors as an environmental awareness leader, especially in recycling and activism in forest management. The company recycles over six thousand tons of waste each year, including aluminum, plastics, tires, cardboard, glass, metal and paper. Marvin Windows and Doors ships approximately four ninety-five-ton railroad cars of crushed scrap glass every month. From electric motors to printer cartridges, the company recycles just about everything. It purchases its wood products from lumber suppliers who subscribe to the Sustainable Forest Initiative (SFI), which supports sound forest management practices.

Mitch Cole manages the Wood Processing Product Group (composed of nine departments) and is responsible for managing the product group as if it were a stand-alone business, providing leadership and direction to help ensure that the company's two goals are met: profitable growth and increased customer value. His specific responsibilities include:

- Manage the production schedule to ensure delivery dates are meeting customer expectations. Carefully plan production so the schedule is balanced and shortages are minimized.
- Provide direction to ensure a quality product is manufactured in a cost-effective manner. Maintain charts and graphs to ensure quality is constantly improving.
- Solve problems as they come up on the production floor. Review current methods, procedures, and systems; implement changes that reduce manufacturing costs. Ensure safe work practices.
- Develop and monitor a budget that contributes to profitable growth. Ensure bills of materials and routings are accurate for the standard cost system.
- Manage projects and planning (capacity, engineering changes, new product, productivity, etc.) as required. Communicate and make suggestions as needed to management.
- Perform reviews, offer suggestions, and recommend training to develop employees. Administer reward and disciplinary action as appropriate. Ensure a good work ethic in the department.
- Communicate regularly and effectively with the departments.

Question: *It seems that the CFO in a business that depends so much on cost and waste containment would keep a close working relationship with operations.*

a. *What are operations' most important cost management priorities, and how have the CFO and accounting and finance function (AFF) helped you (or not) understand your cost management performance and options?*

b. *Given that waste is a key element of both quality and cost management, how have the CFO/AFF and operations worked together to improve waste management?*

MC: Operations' most important priorities for cost management are materials and labor because raw lumber is a big part of window cost; therefore, the closer we can control that resource (material), the more control we have on cost.

AFF and operations work together to establish good accounting practices. Our chief concerns are accurate bills of material (BOM) and accurate routings. During the last two years, accounting has implemented a recording process in final assembly where parts used or not used are kept track of and the results looked at once a month. Accounting rolls up the cost of the quantity of parts used versus how many should have been used to equal acceptable or unacceptable variances. If the variance is outside the acceptable level, operations is questioned about what is going on and what we are doing to continuously improve the unacceptable variance.

AFF is responsible for applying standard costs to actual work. Standards are set up annually by (manufacturing) engineering, production, and accounting. The process of determining what standards should be is quite involved. The role of accounting is to verify that the numbers are accurate; they work as go-betweens for engineering and production. Everybody wants "true costs," rather than what an engineer or accountant *wants* the cost to be or production *thinks* it should be. We work to identify all the steps that impact the cost.

Accounting often challenges costs produced by engineering and production, especially where there are differences of opinion when reprocessing a standard. There is usually some conflict, and not everyone is happy with the decision; however, each party has ample opportunity to go out and prove their viewpoint. The usual situation when there are disagreements is that the costs are in a gray zone; each party is partly right under certain conditions. For example, there was an issue between production and accounting about the cost value placed on fingerjoint material. Fingerjoint material is a production by-product, and the question was what to do with it. After hearing all viewpoints, accounting applies what is believed to be an acceptable cost, even though it may be higher than that proposed by production. The accountants have the final say, but they are open to changing the cost if proven beyond any reasonable doubt.

One of the problems with standards is that they are set on assumptions about the process. The second and bigger problem is that production is always looking at results (variances) after the fact. The third problem is that costs and variances are affected by more than what happens in production. Production gets pressure to keep doing the right things when the variance is positive, and to turn things around if the variance is negative, when actually some portion of change is not caused by what manufacturing is doing at all. Often, the business cycles create the plus or minus variance, or maybe material costs, such as the price of lumber, starting to rise, or the price of glue going up. Production works hard to get the costs right, but other factors, especially economies of scale, affect the variances.

Window parts have a pretty consistent product mix. If the cost of material usage for a window part profile is going up, we have an opportunity to look at it. For example, if the cost of the ultimate wood doublehung stiles is going up, we go after the causes. The variance reporting by product-profile part that the CFO and accounting implemented allows us to track trends and graphically put out the information about cost and usage. The fact that the CFO pushed for this reporting gave it validity. The really difficult part isn't reporting the variances by product-profile part. It is figuring out where the variance was caused. To make a point, I'll make up some numbers.

For example, say that one hundred pieces of cut stock go into the molder, and maybe eighty come out as usable wood for the ultimate style. This is a 20 percent reject rate. Then final assembly may reject 5 to 10 percent. So, to record pieces produced and rejected, wood processing must have a person at a spot at the end of the machine where they record produced/rejected. Then again, in final assembly, they do the same thing to record rejections. All along the way, waste and rejects are produced. That's normal when you're working with wood. The dilemma about material usage is getting well-defined specifications for the products and getting everyone to follow them. Disagreements crop up between the producing group that says the receiving group should be able to use their output and the using group saying the material doesn't meet specs.

Another issue relates to purchasing activities and material prices. Most of the time, purchasing survives variance scrutiny better than operations because the costs of purchased parts are more definite and easier to see. The variables in production are more numerous and more volatile. Typically, buying "bad parts" is not an issue for wood, but when it comes to replacement parts, a purchaser may get a deal on price, but not know it's quality. They think they have a good deal *and* quality replacement parts, but when we in production go to use the material, the durability of the steel and the hardness of belts is not there. We find ourselves going through parts faster than usual, so we go to the purchaser and *then* we find out the supplier has been changed.

Question: *Manufacturing organizations depend on team building, teamwork, and collaboration abilities. Giving some specific examples, how has Marvin Windows and Doors created a teamwork culture? Does the sense of teamwork extend between different functions such as between your various operations units and between operations and the AFF?*

MC: Teamwork is one of Marvin Windows's strong points. We have been working on formal team building since the late 1980s when we started out working with the Juran Institute. In the 80s, everyone thought that Juran and Deming gave Japan the edge. So, good organizations, like us, tried to figure out how to use their concepts. We worked hard for four to five years with Juran people, for example, learning to use their twelve-step problem solving to identify root causes. We used it here in Warroad and at our Ripley and Baker sites. Each location had site councils. The quality councils were organized to go after improvement in both quality and profitability. Marvin Windows's accountants were involved in this process to tell us about profitability. During this same period, for better analysis Marvin Windows split out the final assembly areas by functional product line and created ten product groups that were treated as work centers with budgetary responsibilities. While still looking at the whole picture of production performance, we looked at product groups and began to examine measures like quality performance and delivery service in addition to cost and profit.

The teamwork concepts were being worked on all through this period. The shift to product groups created a great deal of change, including in the management structure, which began to flatten out. During this time, there was a lot of anxiety and apprehension. Marvin Windows brought in a consultant who had done work for Motorola in educating supervisors and management about how to work through change and not be afraid. The training lasted for a week, and it really helped. For starters, it showed middle managers that executive vision was good and reasonable. Some of the other things that improved were being able to be more understanding of peers, fellow workers, and decision makers. We started to listen to those around us more deeply so we actually heard what they were saying. Once you learn to listen to people, going through change is easier because you can see their needs and help better, either by talking them through it or making changes so the person can survive. At one time, I was one of those task-oriented people: See it, do it. But if you don't manage above the task level, you can't get people to buy in and help. No matter how well a change is planned, something goes wrong, and then you really need people behind you.

One year ago, wood processing evaluated our part numbering system. We had eleven thousand part numbers for cut stock, and we wanted to get it down to four thousand. A few people got together and brainstormed to simplify the part number system. There were people from engineering who helped us see how the design of routings and BOMs was tied to part numbers. Accounting helped on how parts were costed. The central opportunity we wanted was to change from working with a part number for each specific cut stock length, to a general length of cut stock—say 36 inches—that could be used for multiple parts, say for 36, 35.5, 35, and 34.5 lengths.

Naturally, that approach created some wasted material, but other measures improved, such as on-time delivery and economies of scale. The new way also has the advantages of more organized warehouse space and fewer parts and part numbers to warehouse. Also, parts are now easier to find, and it is easier to see parts on hand. But the cost of the material waste has to be applied against all these savings to determine how big the combined impact is on profitability. The cost of material waste is calculated in board feet and includes labor to get the raw lumber in the cut stock state. We are in the process of negotiating with accounting on this.

The calculations have to recognize that under the old system, we had to have cut stock for each length—say, 1000 of 36 inch, and 250 of 35.5 inch, to total 1250 parts. By combining those two lengths, we don't have to have as much stock on hand or as many part numbers. It's a tradeoff. We have had to go through every part and calculate the cost under the old part system and the new way. Accounting set a limit: If the cost of combining the parts was more than $250 per SKU annually, then we couldn't combine the part numbers. It has been a long year of discussions between production, engineering, and accounting as to where the cutoff would be set on combining parts; if it costs more than $250, we can't combine.

Question: *Located in a small rural community with limited employee resources, Marvin Windows and Doors clearly needs to cultivate the abilities of all employees. What kind of programs does operations use to help employees to better themselves? Have you, yourself, benefited from any program? Has operations or the company seen any measurable benefit from these practices?*

MC: Marvin Windows has set up a program with the University of Minnesota, Crookston, and Northwest Technical College in Bemidji for employees to get undergraduate degrees in supervision and leadership (a two-year associate degree) and two four-year bachelor degree programs in manufacturing and technical engineering. Marvin Windows pays for all of it if you maintain a C average or better. They also pay for an on-site program manager, and instructors come to Warroad, so we don't have to travel. It's unbelievable. [Mitch completed his bachelor's degree in manufacturing in 2002.] Any of us who have completed one of these programs has an advantage within Marvin when, by policy, a job is posted internally that requires a degree. We now have the opportunity to go after it. For me personally, I have gained self-confidence in what I can do, and I can see how things operate more easily. The education has opened doors for me to get more information to do my job, and my work is easier and better because of it.

In my area, I center training on heavy machining equipment. Every other year, I bring in Weinig Molders to train operators on the basics of their equipment: setup, maintenance, and changeover. Weinig also brings in any new ideas and concepts they have incorporated into their machines. I also bring in specialists on optimizer cut saws. Every other year I schedule training for edge gluers and finger joiners.

The average person at Marvin Windows wants more time away from work. To address this, and for other good business reasons, in 2000 we changed our two-shift schedule with Crew 1 on days for two weeks, and Crew 2 on nights for two weeks. The old schedule meant people worked eight-hour days, Monday-Friday, for two weeks, and then they worked evenings for two weeks. We went to a four-crew rotating schedule working four ten-hour days on a rotating schedule. Now people only have to work one week a month on nights and they get five days in a row off once a month.

Question: *Manufacturing means that there is always a better way to build a better mousetrap. Along the way, good organizations need people who act as change catalysts and conflict managers. Please give examples of changes that have an impact on the entire organization, and examples of Marvin Windows and Doors's best conflict managers.*

MC: As in any organization, our conflicts are almost always over resources—competing for people, planning capital budgets and fighting for money there, and space. Susan Marvin, president; Joe Freud, vice-president of manufacturing; Ron Lund, plant manager; and CFO Elliot Larson are always trying to balance resources because all ten product groups compete for resources. The executives make decisions from backlog information, on-time delivery measures, and so on. They work hard to see if a department that is not performing well needs more resources. They try to allocate people where they are needed. The executives also take a look at where each area is at in technology.

From a higher level it must be hard to decide between all the requests. The executives are very good at giving resources to the areas that support the company mission and they try very hard to make their decisions on that basis. They don't give in to someone who cries "wolf." The plant manager and VP manufacturing get a lot of this. The executives also work with the accountants to get the picture right, and managers get consulted. All the operational areas present their budgets; then Susan, the CFO, the VP manufacturing, and the plant manager take the capital budgets and put the picture together. They work to identify the most serious problems and how the capital budget can help overall. After the budget is approved, each product group in the budget has to justify capital projects and get approval for expenditure.

Right now, the main focus is payback. If you have a one-year payback, you are in. If your project takes more than one year, you have to come up with tangible and intangible savings. This process could be improved; payback isn't the only way to judge capital investments. The company does postinvestment analysis to see how well the project performed, but this is an area that could also be improved with a more focused performance analysis.

C. STENZEL, *Conversation with Mitch Cole, May 11, 2003, Warroad, Minnesota.*

GENERAL BUSINESS: PERFORMANCE MEASUREMENT AND MANAGEMENT

Organizational performance measurement and management methods are arguably among the most mature approaches practiced widely in business today. Although the balanced scorecard is probably the best known, several other approaches are in use. The origins of performance measurement and management reside in efforts to balance nonfinancial with financial measures, but the practices evolved rapidly and soon encompassed strategic, value-based, and process-based approaches. The idea, as most people now know, is to align organizational energy and effort with measurable priorities and intentions. Easy to say, hard to do—especially in a market dominated by shareholder interests.

More than any other predecessor general business methodology, performance measurement and management seeks to include the entire organization and everyone in it, coordinating people, resources, and priorities to best effect. This comprehensive ambition necessitates an array of EI competencies on the part of the CFO. Perhaps for this reason performance measurement and management efforts have had no more or less success than any other innovative general business management approach. All are subject to failures of leadership, insufficient readiness, and continuing financial measurement myopia. In the best cases, companies have learned a great deal about articulating their intentions and have had success in better communication of those intentions during execution efforts. In the worst cases, a very expensive performance measurement and management project ends up as a fancy Web page on the Internet or the company's Intranet.

Attend to EI Performance Management–Related Competencies

Performance measurement and management work is, by definition, an attempt to increase *organizational awareness* through information distribution. Any executive leading a performance measurement and management project must have deep understanding of the business and a healthy level of *self-confidence*. In addition, a CFO, in particular, needs to be highly *adaptable* under performance measurement and management conditions. The financial system will be the one most frequently challenged by the initiative because (1) the project intention is to balance financial measures with operational indicators, and (2) if done well, the exploration unearths the cause-and-effect relationships between what the performance measurement scorecard calls leading indicators (operational) and lagging results (financial). The CFO must also be prepared to assist other executives in transitioning from management perspectives predominantly managed by financial measures to a more balanced approach. The CFO can do great harm by continuing to insist that financial-measure dominance should persist.

One of the greatest potential contributions of a performance measurement and management project to a CFO's leadership competencies is improved leadership *communication*. Performance measures that are aligned and connected from executive intentions throughout the organization, right down to the individual person, implicitly create an understanding of connectivity and functional interdependence, and contribute to the intrinsic satisfaction of being a part of something larger than local responsibilities. These dynamics naturally *build bonds* to the AFF throughout the organization. The need for *teamwork and collaboration* competencies when working across organizational functions becomes obvious in this context. When performance measures change, their modifications may impact performance incentives. CFOs are typically heavily involved in incentive design. Changing incentives is tricky business. The CFO can provide a great service to the organization by working to avoid *conflicts* and to mediate them when they occur.

CFO ↔ AFF   Performance measurement and management work is one of the greatest opportunities for the financial profession in a long while. By nature, performance measurement and management is quantitative. Few people in the organization have greater quantitative skills than high-level accountants. What they do not know they can quickly learn. Unlike process improvement work that usually originates in operational areas, performance measurement and management efforts commonly find a leadership management home in the AFF. Frequently, the CFO leads the initiative because the CFO position is one of two (the CEO being the other) that consistently looks for opportunities to see the functional needs of the entire organization. One of the greatest hurdles that financial professionals must overcome in performance measurement and management work is that it is not a general ledger process. Everything that moves need not be measured, and likewise, the objective in this kind of work is to find financial *drivers* (i.e., *leading* indicators) and not to tic and tie and balance the analysis targets.

Identify AFF Service Relationships   When the AFF is the project center for a performance measurement and management initiative, the service relationships, by definition, become holistic. This result is one of the great potential outcomes of performance measurement and management work: creation of a coherent picture of processes, how they relate to one another, and how together they contribute to success. In performance measurement and management work everyone is in the same boat, but not necessarily always pulling oars in the same direction. An organization must be very mature to handle and coordinate the many active leadership responsibilities and constant leadership attention this powerful method requires.

Every enterprise has core self-organizing principles that people use to characterize work and new work directions. For most businesses, this organizing principle is strategy. A public university has trouble thinking of itself in strategic terms. For health and education institutions, the central focus is usually not strategic, but rather expressed in terms of mission or vision. Manufacturing companies sometimes choose a process perspective to organize their work.

To be of the most help in performance measurement and management initiatives, the CFO and the AFF staff must identify and understand the self-organizing principles operative in the organization. Many consultants have made the mistake of entering a mission-driven institution and trying to force onto it a strategic paradigm. Such force fits have led to some of the most spectacular failures in the consulting world. The mistake most likely to be made by a CFO in this regard is to frame too many measures in financial or complex quantitative terms. The quantitative worldview of the financial professional can be almost incomprehensible to nonfinancial peers. The whole purpose of this kind of work is to create a balanced view of the organization so that financial and nonfinancial decision makers can better manage the work activities that eventually result in financial profit.

AFF ↔ ORG　A mature organization engaged in performance measurement and management work makes rapid progress in understanding the business, the conditions and forces that affect it, and the critical interdependencies that support the life of the company. Again, the biggest barrier to performance measurement and management progress is the cultural predominance of financial constructs. The CFO must be extremely *self-confident* and committed to being a *change catalyst* to endure the strong cultural pressures that financial abstractions and stockholder expectations exert. Because performance measurement and management is a discovery process where hypotheses are posed and tested, fruits of the labor do not appear in one or two quarters.

Performance Management AFF Technical Requirements & GAAP/GAAS Vulnerabilities

Popularized primarily by the balanced scorecard, performance measurement and management is currently one of the most pervasive methods in business. Performance systems may actually compete with GAAP and financial accounting for top billing as most able to reveal a company's actual conditions.

> *Financial criteria:* Because performance measurement and management work takes an organization from reliance on financial indicators to a more balanced performance perspective, the CFO and AFF need to remain deeply rooted in the conventional ground they are about to disturb. During the performance measurement and management transition, an AFF often discovers ways to more fully automate the financial accounting system. This allows them to spend more value-added time contributing to work such as performance measurement and management.

> *Nonfinancial criteria:* People best suited for performance measurement and management work are natural associaters. They see, hypothesize, and know how to test the strength of relationships. Statistical analysis skills add scientific validity, turning correlations into confirmed causal elements. Another key characteristic for AFF staff members working in performance measurement and management design and implementation is an ability to see patterns, which refers to the self-organizing principle discussed earlier. For example, if a company sees itself in terms of core processes, the AFF staff member needs to be able to see process patterns and understand process methodologies before appropriate contributions to performance management work can emerge.

> *GAAP/GAAS:* Like process improvement work, performance measurement and management contributes to discernment and good judgment in cost and financial matters. A CFO who understands the cause-effect relationships that are actually present between operational work and financial results has a

harder time consciously fabricating revenues, maneuvering costs, and performing other accounting sleight-of-hand. Similarly, performance measurement and management work immerses a CFO in the actual work of the organization, which can only improve one's financial analysis skills. One potential benefit is that when auditors find something amiss in operations, the CFO usually has enough insight to quickly solve the mystery.

Performance Management Ethical Resonance

Transitioning from a mid-range maturity-level perspective that continues to rely predominantly on financial measures to a comprehensive performance measurement and management system loaded with performance information from all key areas of the organization can be daunting. Chief financial officers frequently are among the first to see the advantages of performance measurement and management work. Weaning the organization from dependence on financial management sometimes takes heroic effort. A CFO can begin with some small steps inside the AFF, starting with service relationship measures and how those activities impact financial results. The most mature organizations can leap right into an examination of all manner of interrelationships, but the CFO should pace and lead. A specific task that typically comes up during performance measurement and management initiatives is reformatting performance reports. Here an old standby of the financial realm comes in handy: running parallel systems. A comfortable sequence includes (1) reporting measures the old way and the new way without affecting accountabilities for a predetermined time, (2) coordinating education and training on methods that show ways to affect targeted measures, (3) funding a few pilot initiatives, (4) carefully modifying any incentive systems, (5) and treating the whole transition as the organizational learning process that it surely is.

COST MANAGEMENT: COST ACCOUNTING SYSTEM

Process improvement and performance measurement and management contributions currently remain at the top of the list for CFO and AFF staff participation in the larger organizational community. The next most important AFF responsibility is cost management abilities. Perspective is very important here. Accounting and finance professionals immersed in their functional duties tend to forget that cost and financial accounting are dial-tone activities for the rest of the company. Yes, financial statements remain important, but their regular appearance is taken for granted.

Picture the responsibilities of the CFO and AFF as the surface of a calm lake. Below the surface, invisible to nonfinancial employees, AFF staff members churn out the workings and products of the cost and financial accounting systems. In general, the organization pays attention only in certain circumstances. People focus on financial statements when they are the primary means of performance evaluation. The same is true for cost accounting reports. As the discipline of cost management takes root and flourishes within an AFF, useful practices become visible to operations units. For example, activity-based initiatives often provide the first common ground for accountants and production employees to work together. Only at this point does the Function's work start to apply to the day-to-day work priorities of the nonfinancial members of the organizational community. This point is also the fertile ground where process improvement and performance measurement and management activities take root. Refer to Exhibit 4.6 for a detailed cost management view of the AFF Responsibility Diagnostic.

Attend to Cost Management EI Competencies

Organizational awareness is of great importance in cost management work. If an accountant is incapable of visualizing cost structures throughout the company, and uses cost accounting work simply as an input to the financial system, that person's work contributes minimally. Cost management methods such as target costing, resource consumption accounting, and life-cycle costing are very good and relatively easy transition points for the AFF to begin to participate in the workings of the company.

Just as an accountant must take personal *initiative* to break into the process improvement world, so too, cost management work requires proactive efforts to demonstrate its benefits to nonfinancial functions. A key difference between process improvement and cost management work is that process improvement brings in knowledge from outside the Function, whereas cost management knowledge flows in the opposite direction with the AFF driving cost insights outward. This difference makes *achievement orientation* more critical in cost management work because an accountant must prove cost concept advantages to nonfinancial workers. To accomplish this, real benefits must be demonstrated in the form of process improvement time and money savings, and in cost-based methods, such as target costing, that are capable of improving product/service design and production.

Building bonds and *teamwork and collaboration* leadership competencies typically arise naturally from cross-functional cost management work. Another EI competency rises to prominence during this work: *communication*. Information technology specialists are frequently criticized for using too much discipline-specific language when dealing with non-IT people. Accountants can also be guilty of this. Financial professionals must be keenly aware of the vocabulary they use. Few things

www.

EXHIBIT 4.6 AFF COST MANAGEMENT RESPONSIBILITY DIAGNOSTIC

Professional Status	In Trouble	Good Accountant	Great CFO
AFF Cost Management Responsibilities:			
Cost Accounting System	None or standard costing	Automated for G/L; stand-alone ABC	Integrated cost and financial system
AFF Technical Capacity	G/L product/service cost	ABCM is typical alongside G/L system	Advanced methods, e.g., target costing
AFF Service Relationships	Report cost and variances	Cooperative team members	Fellow explorers discovering cost structures
Organizational Expectations of AFF	GAAP costing accuracy	Make the cost structure visible	Improve processes to eliminate waste
Organizational Information Focus	Gross margin	Strategic cost management	Resource utilization and process excellence

deteriorate relationship bonds more than the sense that a person really wants to demonstrate expertise but does not care whether or not listeners understand. Accounting is an abstract language that must be learned, but in cost management efforts, the accountant's responsibility is to translate and interpret.

CFO ↔ AFF   People drawn to the accounting profession frequently gravitate toward either financial or cost accounting. When a CFO determines that a staff member has a much stronger affinity for the finance side and seems to struggle with cost accounting, task assignments become easy. In contrast, professionals like Jeff, the operations-oriented controller from Chapter 2, make an excellent candidate for cost management projects and responsibilities. The CFO should identify staff members who have the ability to discern between material and immaterial costs. Some financial accountants become annoyed when they cannot balance accounts to the penny (and actually celebrate when they find that penny). This professional profile is not the preferred one for cost management work. In contrast to financial accounting, cost management has much more potential to deliver actual value; therefore, a CFO should look for approximately a 60/40 ratio of staff time, with the 60 percent devoted to cost, process, and performance. This ratio applies to a mid-range firm that would probably find it difficult to lower the financial focus below 40 percent.

Identify Service Relationships   In the most mature companies, the AFF service relationships in a cost management context are easy to identify. AFF members can be found where the most significant costs and highest waste abide. For example, if industry demand is in decline, and the company finds itself with excess capacity, the Function works with a cross-functional team to identify new uses for the capacity (AFF calculates revenues and costs of selling capacity), options for disposing of the capacity (AFF helps construct opportunity cost scenarios), and partners with human resource professionals to plan for minimum impact on the people who will be affected. The last thing a mature organization does is engage in handwringing while waiting for the next month-end income statement.

AFF ↔ ORG   The 60/40 cost/finance accounting ratio is inflammatory in some circles, but only where financial constructs have dominated the AFF focus for so long that staff members have lost sight of the fact that operations creates the value captured in the financial numbers. The least mature companies will bluster and bellow, saying that such a shift away from the financial is impossible. They make their mistake with use of the word "away"; the move is not away from financial measurements, but rather putting them in balance and proper perspective during the mid-range maturity period. This change in viewpoint opens the organization up to several insights. The first insight is a simple one: Resources create financial results, with "resources" defined in terms of people and the work they do. This insight manifests in the form of increased process improvement, performance measurement and management, and other efforts directed toward operations. Typically, experimentation within resources and operations parallels the legacy financial performance system, while people adjust to the idea that financial measures cannot be managed because they reflect history.

Currently, the most mature form of cost management falls under the general term "strategic cost management." Strategic cost management (SCM) makes use of the same cost methods as a mid-range cost management system, but in a much more coordinated fashion. Mid-range cost exploration has delivered its lessons through trial and error. Based on those specific discoveries, the company strategically selects methods to accomplish targeted goals. For example, ABCM is put to work to drive out waste. CFOs use target costing to create a competitive edge. People begin to understand organizational resources at a deeper level and quickly see how work in product component management, capacity utilization, and other SCM methods connect to financial results.

AFF Cost Management Technical Requirements and GAAP/GAAS Vulnerabilities

Unlike financial accounting, cost accounting does not have a common set of standards and principles. The Institute of Management Accountants issues statements on a number of cost accounting aspects, but there is nothing like a GAAP assemblage to guide cost practices. Because worthwhile cost accounting aims to accurately reflect business conditions, a lack of hard-and-fast standards is not necessarily a bad thing.

Financial: Only AFF members who are facile with both cost and financial accounting in their conventional forms need apply for cost management duties. A staff member who has spent a career performing treasury duties will have a steep learning curve in the cost management arena. Most cost management methods have their roots in accounting, in that early explorers were interested in making accounting more relevant. Most mature cost management initiatives continue to be led by financial professionals. So, the AFF is in a very good position to continue this logic.

Nonfinancial: Staff members with previous work and credibility in operations functions should lead the way in cost management initiatives. AFF staff inexperienced in operations, but enthusiastic to learn, may play secondary roles on the team.

GAAP/GAAS: While working in the mid-range of cost management maturity, running stand-alone cost systems is the recommended path.[6] Because the organization is learning about cost structure and can not yet fully see how it integrates to financial results, the best approach is to continue the legacy financial system and conduct cost experiments separately. Some companies that have implemented ERP systems have tried to skip this step and find themselves all dressed up with no place to go—a powerful technology without the developmental learning required to use an integrated information system for decision making. One of three outcomes is predictable. (1) Scrap the system. (2) The integrated ERP modules seem to reinforce the financial perspective as the sensible way to see and manage the organization. (3) If the company has survived, executives must deliberately turn back to learning the lessons of mid-range cost management work. Unfortunately, not everyone survives, and few executive teams have this kind of time or patience. In the midst of such turmoil, allowing accounting and auditing principles to slip from priority status is easy. Such a scenario is far less likely when a company has spent appropriate learning and development time in the mid-range cost management work, and then attempts to move to the most mature.

Cost Management Ethical Resonance

During cost management development, the CFO's primary responsibility is conservation of resources. As stated earlier, mid-range cost management practices typically lead to a flurry of activity and projects that can be redundant and even generate conflict. The traditional duty of the CFO to safeguard company assets remains. To perform this duty, the CFO develops more and more expertise in both financial and human capital. Such vigilance manifests in many ways, including:

- Coordination of cost management projects. If the company is deeply into cost management learning, this coordination can feel like herding cats. The CFO makes a point to know about every cost effort, gather information about this work and its objectives, and most importantly, communicate this coordinated information to all parties. When one group becomes territorial about its efforts, the CFO serves as liaison and mediator to bring together people who are working on the same things.

- Every activity costs money, so a company has infinite opportunity for cost management work. With so many possibilities, the CFO makes a formal effort to identify and calculate the range of opportunities, discuss and strategically choose among them with the executive group, and communicate the decisions to the working groups complete with clear rationale for the choices.

Give It a Try

When deliberately paired with EI competencies, the maturity diagnostic supplies a powerful tool for CFOs to quickly move the AFF toward the most mature performance levels. "Lack of leadership commitment" is often cited as the chief reason for project and initiative failures, but this judgment is incomplete. Although negligent executives exist, the more correct general diagnosis would be lack of maturity and leadership competencies in executives and managers. This diagnosis is superior in that it can be directly remedied and the condition successfully treated.

As with any new capacity, practice is the key. Everyone knows that native talent is worth something, but that most people advance through hard work and skill repetition. Developing maturity and leadership competencies is no different. In that spirit, you are invited to try your hand at using the AFF Responsibility Diagnostic to assess the maturity of your own AFF and your own CFO leadership competencies. The practice example below continues in the cost management area. The focus is on inventory audits and budgets. As you work through the example, picture your AFF organizational structure as it appears now (probably hierarchical), and watch how the structure flattens and how the Function's boundaries open with more mature practices. The AFF borders are no longer marked with approval documents to sign and accountant guards to assure compliance. AFF territory becomes a place of rich resources and respected professionals.

Cost Management: Inventory Audits and Budgets   In the area of accounting responsibilities, inventory audits and budget cycles are what everyone, including accountants, loves to hate. The way the company structures its inventory audits and budget processes says a great deal about the prevailing maturity level. This section uses these two conventional accounting tasks for two reasons: (1) their broad familiarity, and (2) the immense opportunities for improvements they contain. You can apply this exercise directly to your current processes. All organizations have some sort of budget process, even if it amounts to monthly bank statement reconciliation with the goal of a positive balance. Not all companies have physical inventories. So, for service companies and others without inventories, substitute the primary revenue-generating resource within the organization. For a CPA firm, the primary resource generator is the complement of auditors and tax specialists. For an advertising agency, the primary resource generator is human creativity, intellectual capital, and marketing skills.

Please note that the process you are about to engage can be used for any AFF responsibility or task. The skeleton format without the matrix descriptions can be used by any discipline. With minor exceptions, this approach to assessing current conditions and levels of maturity remains the same regardless of the object of analysis. *Begin by addressing the following points of exploration, using actual current practices as the focus.*

- Refer to Exhibit 4.7 and read the descriptions across the maturity spectrum for inventory audits and budgets.

- Make no evaluations yet. Compare the maturity descriptions with the time perspective.

- Now assess where your company's inventory audits and budget practices sit on the maturity spectrum. If one process is at a higher level than the other, proceed with the process at the lower level. If your assessment places your company at the most mature end of the spectrum, spend some time analyzing the steps it took to get here. If you are fortunate enough to be in a very mature environment now, this kind of analysis may come in handy when conditions change—whether you change jobs, the company is sold, or a new CEO comes on board. Under changing conditions, development never ends.

Result: Selection of the maturity level—low, mid-range, high—for inventory audits and/or budget processes.

Now that you have given some thought to the crrent situation, consider the advantages and disadvantages of maintaining the status quo in the inventory audits and budget processes. To help work through this, think about the following:

- How much time do AFF staff members spend on these two processes every month or year?

- How much of this time do other functional executives think is valuable? Take a guess at the percentage.

- Make a list of what you consider the valuable outcomes from these two processes. Compare this to the list you believe the least accounting-friendly executive would make. Examine probable assumptions underlying each list.

- Write down explicitly and clearly what you believe the CEO thinks of these two processes.

Result: An assessment of inventory audits and budget processes that has a good chance of being 80 percent correct.

Decision point: Choose one of the following three decision points:

1. Inventory audits and budget processes match current company needs.
2. Both inventory audits and budget processes need improvement.
3. Only one of these processes needs attention.

If you selected number 1, end this exercise. If current practices satisfy organizational needs, no immediate work need be done. Come back to this exercise when

www.

EXHIBIT 4.7 AFF INVENTORY AUDIT AND BUDGET RESPONSIBILITY DIAGNOSTIC

Professional Status	In Trouble	Good Accountant	Great CFO
AFF Cost Management Responsibilities:			
Inventory Audit			
	Done by hand	Automated; statistical sampling	Immaterial inventory; no physical audits
AFF Technical Capacity	Records subject to error	Team performs semi-automated audit	Automated reporting
AFF Service Relationships	Adversarial	Cordial; routine process	Process versus inventory work
Organizational Expectations of AFF	Inventory valuation	Accurate counts and valuation	Help minimize inventory
Organizational Information Focus	Inventory turns and days	Inventory meets demands	Process performance
Budgets			
	One-time annual targets	Flexible structure	Real-time or no budget
AFF Technical Capacity	Forecast-based allocation	Adjust to demand modifications	Capacity and demand management
AFF Customer Relationships	Adversarial	Friendly watchdog; good analyst	Resource use partnership
Organizational Expectations of AFF	Cash flow and solvency	Budget control, variance analysis	Help guide resource allocation
Organizational Information Focus	Spending allocation	Identify causes of variance	Cause/effect and financial impacts

you sense this is no longer true. If you selected either number 2 or number 3, proceed to the next step.

Preliminary intentions: Identify the common process shortcomings for both inventory audits and budgets. This identification usually takes considerable thought. List three to five shortcomings. Select two of the shortcomings based on the aspects that nonfinancial employees dislike most about inventory audits and budgets. Construct a process improvement plan to rectify the shortcomings.

Attend to Inventory Audit and Budget-Related EI Competencies

- Use Exhibit 3.1 in Chapter 3 to identify the EI competencies most necessary to successfully implement the improvement plan.
- Identify specific people most likely to participate in the improvement effort.
- For your private use, draw a simple matrix with actual names on the x-axis and the selected competencies on the y-axis. Include yourself and likely candidates from your staff.
- Considering one person at a time, create a scattergram that depicts people and competency levels.
- This work is for your eyes only.

From here on, the sequence of steps in this approach begins to dovetail with conventional project planning and management. The critical difference is the work up to this point that informs and guides.

CFO ↔ AFF   Within the context of a regular staff meeting, include discussion of intended process improvements. This step assumes that regular staff meetings are already in place. If they are not, back up and do more critical foundational work before attempting process improvement.

- Encourage free-form discussion and brainstorm for ideas related to the improvement propositions.
- Choose an appropriate number of staff members (in small organizations, perhaps only one person) to continue the exploration in more detail. Make choices immediately and openly; at this point, discernment and intuition serve you well, and more time and thought do not guarantee better decisions. These immediate and open choices are also important for staff learning. They have just gone through a discussion process with you and are intelligent enough to see why you made the choices that you did.

- Give your staff members the option to decline and check on the reasons later privately. If you discover the staff member is actually interested but has too heavy a workload, work on a temporary job redesign. Likewise, provide staff not chosen with the opportunity to ask to be included in the effort; they should do so within twenty-four hours of the discussion.

Identify Service Relationships

- Name all people and groups most likely to be impacted by, and therefore interested in, the process improvements you intend.

- If you have not already done so, complete an informal EI competency assessment for each person and group.

- Meet with the AFF staff you have chosen for the improvement work and discuss their impressions of who the beneficiaries are of this improvement work. Compare with the impacts you identified.

- List and discuss potential methods, specific objectives, and appropriate performance measures for the improvement work. Your job is to make sure the choices align with organizational needs and maturity.

- Prepare a draft project plan to share with potential nonfinancial team members.

These steps are not the AFF staff members working in isolation; this structure builds AFF teamwork.

Although this approach may take longer the first few times it is used, the method soon becomes second nature, and all the activities up to this point can be accomplished within a week. The work done so far provides a firm base for discussion with other functions. Nothing has been decided and no action has been taken, but the AFF has put in a sincere effort to begin a productive dialogue. This foundation is much better to start from than simply calling and fumbling through an ad hoc meeting.

AFF ↔ ORG   The most important focus in this segment of the process is to discover the nature and kind of information that is currently being used—in this case, related to inventory audits and budgets—for decision making. Determining the units of information that members of the organization currently use to make decisions is a very good indicator of their maturity level. For example, signs of immaturity include being more worried about inventory *valuation* and related ratios than in the *value* in inventory. Similar budget-related symptoms of low maturity include low balling sales forecasts for incentive purposes, and spending frenzies near the end of the fiscal year to avoid lower allocations in the next budget round. You know the games. Everybody is tired of them, yet few know how to fix them. So, here are four steps related to taking the proposed improvement projects to the larger organization community.

1. Determine the types and units of information currently prized by nonfinancial decision makers. This is not guesswork. The CFO directly asks decision makers to describe their most frequent decision types, recurring operations challenges, and how much of their information base relates to human beings.

2. Assess the current users of AFF information for their readiness to move on to more mature ways of seeing. Take, for example, potential improvements to the budget process. A few straightforward inquiries determine a person's appetite for change in this process.

   • *What do you think of our current budget process?* If the person replies, verbally and nonverbally, "It's just fine," this person is not ready for any significant changes. Look for a response to this budget question that is directly opposite of the one just described. A person who is less than satisfied and may have ideas for better ways to budget almost never can restrain the nonverbal cues that tell the story.

   • *If you were emperor or empress of the budget process, what would you do?* Invaluable information and suggestions can appear in the spontaneous responses that follow. This inquiry indicates readiness (i.e., the least mature will see nothing wrong with a conventional budget process), and also opens the door for improvement suggestions.

3. Refine and publish project planning based on the results from these questions.

4. Get on with implementation. Follow that with the usual project management feedback loops and adjustments.

AFF Inventory Audit and Budget-Related Technical Requirements & GAAP/GAAS Vulnerabilities

Financial: This is an easy one for a CFO. The answer undoubtedly looks something like the following: Using inventory audits as the example, staff participants should have strong theoretical, if not practical, background in managerial accounting and alternative inventory practices. They should also be familiar with GAAP and GAAS concerns.

Nonfinancial: In lean manufacturing and total quality environments, the goal is to keep inventory levels as low as possible while still satisfying customer demands. Inventory audits thus decline in significance, and in some cases may not be "material" in the sense of the accounting principle of materiality. The more the staff knows about leading operations practices that affect inventory, the more they can concentrate on the value of inventory, as opposed to valuation of inventory.

GAAP/GAAS: CFOs are only too familiar with the importance of GAAP related to inventory. Moving external auditors smoothly in and out of the inventory portion of the audits is also a familiar CFO skill.

Inventory Audit and Budget Ethical Resonance

Of course, this process sounds like a great deal of work. At first it is. But the length it takes to describe the process is deceptive, simply because it takes much more space to explain human-based dynamics than it does to describe a numerical calculation. The good news comes in several parts: (1) every human being comes naturally equipped with the capacities to quickly learn these competencies; (2) development of maturity and leadership competencies is a great deal more enjoyable, in the long run, than a lifetime of quantitative work in isolation; (3) the approach works. Only three repetitions of the approach just described are necessary to gain a reasonable level of confidence and success with nonfinancial customers. The size of the project and the methods applied do not matter. The process itself is what is being learned. A CFO should select initiatives with relatively narrow scope to try out this new way of doing business.

As a personal accountability check, address the following five items:

1. How wisely are inventory resources used here? What parts do I play, or not, in entrenchment of past inventory practices? (Same question for budget processes.)

2. Do I feel any shade of arrogance or condescension during inventory audits or budget discussions?

3. Can I honestly say that I am doing everything I can to promote simple inventory and budget processes?

4. Am I at all afraid that simplification of inventory and budget processes means less recognition for my staff and me?

5. What emotions do I most frequently feel during an inventory audit or during budget work?

You get the idea. These questions are some of the most important kinds that a CFO can ask. Answers to such questions applied to the range of AFF responsibilities have the potential to change companies far more than all the financial calculations in the world of accounting. This alternative approach is not difficult, but it does require a significant shift in mind-set. Once a financial professional is aware of the options, the choice becomes an ethical one. Will I continue to encourage the use of financial symbols and abstractions as the primary information to run our company? Or will I begin to put financial information in proper perspective and pay more attention to the dynamics that created financial results: People and the work they do?

Again, as you engage this process, please note that the diagnosis and assessment process can be used for any AFF responsibility or task. Furthermore, the skeleton format without the matrix descriptions can be used by any functional discipline. With minor exceptions, this diagnosis of current conditions and levels of maturity remains the same regardless of the object of analysis.

FINANCIAL ACCOUNTING: MONTH-END CLOSE AND INCOME STATEMENT

At last, we arrive at the point from which most good accountants start. The way a company conducts its month-and close and how it views the release of its income statements are the litmus tests of organizational maturity. This lengthy discussion based on the AFF Responsibility Diagnostic has intentionally moved from the business at large to financial accounting by way of cost management. Financial accounting belongs at the end of a long line of prior AFF activities that create value for the organization. Financial reports express the results of decisions already made and actions already taken. Financial measures have an important place in the pantheon of performance indicators, but at the end of the process, not at the beginning. Exhibit 4.8 details some of the AFF's more important financial responsibilities.

With that in mind, any CFO should now be able to use the AFF Readiness Diagnostic and quickly apply it to AFF responsibilities. Complementary to the diagnostic, the CFO practices from a broadened perspective that includes the exact maturity and leadership competencies required for predictable performance success. Based on EI competency research, this statement is not a flashy opinion, but a fact. Accepting that fact builds an entirely different and stronger platform from which the CFO structures AFF responsibilities, expertise, and staff members into an organizationally aware, confident, and trusted group of people. The final section of this chapter provides more specifics about that claim.

TRIPLE HELIX AND PSYCHOSOCIAL DEVELOPMENT AT WORK IN THE AFF

By now, no one should be surprised to discover that the accounting and finance function mirrors the parts of the triple helix: individual human beings, organizational form, and environmental conditions. Every function mirrors the triple helix. Differences are only a matter of the size of the group. All groups of people must contend with environmental conditions as they structure their group activities. Individuals who wish to be part of the group must honor the group norms. Although all developmental systems rely on relationship perspectives to some degree, the psychosocial developmental subsystem most capably examines how and why groups are formed and how members structure their relationships to carry out their chosen activities.

This section and the next three sections explore the workings of the psychosocial subsystem within the helix triad in the ways that the CFO leads the AFF. Exhibit 4.9 on page 190 characterizes the CFO's leadership relationship with the AFF in several important relationship contexts:

- The triple helix
- AFF structure and profile
- CFO competencies as related to functional responsibilities
- Psychosocial results of mature leadership

If the exhibit were drawn as its elements actually interact, every element would appear linked with all other elements. Because every constituent part represented in Exhibit 4.9 has the potential to influence all other parts, for demonstration purposes the discussion looks at each of the four components one at a time. The object of analysis is the AFF composed of triple helix parallels.

- Organizational environmental conditions
- Function form and group identity
- Individual staff member

When examining a specific organizational form, such as the AFF, *group identity* is an important part of the Function's design. Group identity is not a fourth aspect of the triple helix, but rather a point of connection between the AFF function design and the people who work in it. In other words, when people serve in a functional group such as the AFF, they retain a personal identity and accept a group identity. People serving in the CFO role most significantly influence the group's overall identity. This influence combined with the formal authority of the role helps characterize the CFO leadership competencies required to successfully carry out those responsibilities, which are addressed in Exhibit 4.9 under the headings *CFO competencies* and *CFO responsibilities.* For the most part, the competencies relate to emotional intelligence. So far, the exhibit directs leadership attention to the AFF using concepts familiar from prior chapters.

The payoff for all the previous work shows up in the final section at the bottom of Exhibit 4.9, *psychosocial results,* when reading each column from top to bot-

www.

EXHIBIT 4.8   AFF FINANCIAL RESPONSIBILITY DIAGNOSTIC

Professional Status	In Trouble	Good Accountant	Great CFO
AFF Financial Accounting Responsibilities:			
Month-End Close/Income Statement			
AFF Technical Capacity	Many forecasts/pro-formas	Reduction of forecasts/pro-formas	Leading indicators/no surprises
	Conventional month-end close	Closing routine, automated, rapid	Virtual close; compliance automated
AFF Customer Relationships	Operations serves accounting	Operations data imports minimize interaction	Closing is nonevent; supports operations
Organizational Expectations of AFF	Financial solvency	Accurate/timely; profit analysis	Identify/interpret cause and effects
Organizational Information Focus	Profit	Product, service, quality=profit	Long-term wealth and health
Government/Regulatory Compliance/Tax	Mechanical compliance; errors	Compliance, currency, minimum work	Performs above compliance requirements
AFF Technical Capacity	Compliance	Process routines/automated systems	Transparent, fully automated compliance
AFF Customer Relationships	AFF—internal only	AFF—internal only	Integrity and accountability obvious
Organizational Expectations of AFF	Comply timely and accurately	Comply timely and accurately	Comply timely and accurately
Organizational Information Focus	No IRS/government visits	No IRS/government visits	Cordial relations with compliance agencies
Internal Control/Audits	Few controls; no internal audits	Onerous on nonfinancial employees; activity waste	Control embedded in routine processes
AFF Technical Capacity	Payroll and cash controls	Conventional control systems and policies	Design accountability into processes
AFF Customer Relationships	AFF—internal only	Adversarial as in T&E and policy complexities	Control updates as needed
Organizational Expectations of AFF	Safeguard cash/physical assets	Control cash/physical/information assets	Wise use of resources
Organizational Information Focus	Theft, fraud, embezzlement	Control breaches and their costs	Malfeasance exceptions rare

Professional Status	In Trouble	Good Accountant	Great CFO
AFF Financial Accounting Responsibilities:			
Asset Valuation	Ad hoc purchasing; no capital budget	Capital plans, tagging system, audits	Strategic asset acquisition tracking and disposal
AFF Technical Capacity	Book value; tax depreciation	Book value; depreciation method analysis	Capital investments aligned with priorities
AFF Customer Relationships	AFF—internal only	AFF—internal only	Cross-functional investment decisions
Organizational Expectations of AFF	Safeguard physical assets	Positive return on investments	Help guide the wise use of resources
Organizational Information Focus	Income statement impact	Utilization rates, downtime, etc., ROI	All before, plus focus on human assets
Cash (A/R, A/P, P/R, ST Investment)	Minimal to no management system	Standard cash management practices	Strategic cash/investment management
AFF Technical Capacity	Delay payables, meet P/R; minimum A/R	Cash flow forecast; support/credit management	Contract-based, automated funds flow
AFF Customer Relationships	Adversarial	External and internal: cordial/cooperative	Partnership
Organizational Expectations of AFF	Monitor solvency	Cash flow forecast; support/credit management	Cash treated as resource
Organizational Information Focus	Cash position	Short-term cash management	Wise use of resources, including people
Debt Instruments	Many covenants	Lines of credit, debt:equity monitored	Seasonal LOCs, tailors debt to purposes
AFF Technical Capacity	Make payments	Cash flow forecasts to minimize debt balance	Debt/equity are part of strategic design
AFF Customer Relationships	None internally; bank compliance	None internally; bank negotiations	Decide use of debt/equity with executives
Organizational Expectations of AFF	Timely payments; no penalties	Favorable lending entity relationships	Optimized debt/equity structure
Organizational Information Focus	Debt balance; interest paid	Wise use of LOC; ROI>cost of capital	ROI on debt-funded operations

tom. Notice how the results are described both in terms of emotional intelligence competencies and healthy psychosocial development. Significantly, work within the AFF related to individuals, the group as a whole, and the structural design of the function—when done well—creates environmental conditions of their own for Function members: *influence, inspiration,* and *achievement.* In concrete terms, the CFO and the AFF staff members become influential within the organization and inspirational to others, both based on their achievements. With these leadership interrelationships in mind, this discussion addresses the dynamics of each part of the helix.

The Work Space: Environmental Conditions

ENVIRONMENT—structure—group—individual

People work better when they are comfortable. Ergonomics, climate-controlled buildings, private offices, or bullpens and mazes of cubicles either add to or detract from workplace comfort and worker efficiency. This section speaks to a quite different set of environmental conditions, namely the cultural space within which the CFO and AFF work. Beyond mere physical requirements, the working qualities of this "space" are determined by the prevailing organizational cultural norms and values, the general health of the organization, the working culture values of the CFO, and the impact all of these forces have on the structure, services, and personnel composition of the AFF. As a leader, the CFO must have accurate, incisive environmental scanning capabilities to shape the AFF to meet individual staff and company needs while building the appropriate skills and services that the AFF staff members need to fulfill the CFO's vision.

Relevancy Criteria   What makes the CFO and AFF relevant? While no single answer fits all organizational environmental contexts, methods are available to determine relevancy within a specific organization. "Know thy customer" has long been a commandment of sales, marketing, and quality disciplines and is manifested in specific ways. Once more, "understanding the business" entails knowledge and experience not only about physical operations, but also comprehension of ambient culture, values, biases, and of course, existing management maturity levels throughout the organization. The AFF Responsibility Diagnostic contains two perspectives useful in beginning to formulate an organizational profile: the organization's expectations of AFF and the organization's most valued information focus.

To illustrate, consider a mature and experienced CFO who somehow ended up in an engineering firm that keeps accountants around to write checks and pay taxes—in other words, a culture with an antifinance bias. Confronting and resolving such bias is another matter altogether, but the CFO's immediate leadership

concern focuses on what is most relevant to this finance-unfriendly group of people. This kind of organization is definitely not ready for what a mature CFO can
offer, like a full-blown performance management initiative or even help with
process improvement. What is relevant to a group with this profile is getting paid
and avoiding visits from the IRS.

Moving from this extremely negative example of the organization's cultural environment for mature AFF responsibilities, a positive extreme can be equally challenging for the CFO. Imagine an experienced CFO accepting a position in a
company that is an industry leader. One of the first requests from the CEO directs
the CFO to organize and lead a performance measurement and management initiative, one that is explicitly aligned with actionable strategic objectives. The CFO in
question is an excellent mid-range practitioner with no experience in performance
management initiatives. In this case, performance work is relevant to the CEO and
presumably to the company. The CEO expects the CFO to rise to the opportunity.

Relevancy Guideposts   Both these examples characterize conditions where a
mismatch exists between organizational expectations and CFO/AFF capabilities.
Here are some guidelines for discovering relevancy criteria.

> *Guideline 1*: The CFO is always the one responsible for matching function serv-
> ices to the organization's needs. Discover or describe the organization's view
> of the accountants and their responsibilities. When interviewing for a new
> position, this concept should be an explicit discussion between the CFO
> candidate and the CEO. For the incumbent, the finance chief should clearly
> articulate this aspect of the organization's profile.

> *Guideline 2*: Know what the CEO wants. Clarification of CEO expectations is
> one of the primary factors in shaping an AFF group. Second, determine the
> requirements of other major functional areas. Again, the AFF Responsibility
> Diagnostic can be a helpful tool for creating and interpreting a template
> based on organizational expectations. A warning: Performance of these
> guidelines can lead to a rude awakening or a pleasant surprise for the CFO.
> The rude awakening comes in the form of the discovery that the CEO is, at
> best, neutrally disposed to the finance function. The pleasant surprise appears
> when the CFO discovers that the CEO has been waiting for the finance
> chief to take more initiative in defining and developing the Function.

Explorations such as these create a reasonably clear picture of existing conditions for the AFF in the organizational environment. Most business professionals,
CFOs and otherwise, rarely take the time to perform scans of their functional environmental conditions. Consequently, those who do so have a great deal more information and insights than their peers. Failure to conduct environmental scans
predictably results in mismatches between AFF supply and company demand. An

energetic CFO can easily construct the equivalent of a luxury yacht when the company expects a rowboat.

So far, relevancy criteria relate to cultural and individual attitudes and beliefs within the four walls of the organization (or five if you work in the Pentagon). External environmental conditions include sector and industry conditions, general economic health of the marketplace, the company and its competition, and identification of the company's central self-organizing perspective discussed earlier in this chapter: strategy, mission, process or other means of understanding the purpose of the company's work and outputs. With a combination of internal and external information generated by these scans, the CFO is in a good position to continue on to the next step in shaping the Function. A summary of relevant environmental conditions based on internal and external environmental conditions include:

- Attitudes toward the CFO function
- Company expectations of the AFF
- CEO and functional executive expectations of the CFO
- Executive maturity and readiness
- Sector and industry conditions
- Economic conditions
- Central self-organizing perspective awareness

Two additional considerations: Recognize that just as marriage partners find they can rarely change their spouse after the wedding, a CFO should not delude himself into thinking that she/he can change a CEO or an entire company. Development is possible, but quick changes from one specific set of beliefs to another (e.g., from antifinance to profinance) are rare. Additionally, and perhaps central to this whole discussion, the customer is *not* always right. Specifically, organizations hire the CFO as the accounting expert. Demands on the AFF by a CEO or another executive do not equate to the demands being correct. With greater knowledge of the range of accounting and finance possibilities, the CFO has the obligation to share information on alternatives at every opportunity.

Working Lean and in the Stream

environment—STRUCTURE—group—individual

Organizational design is quite the buzzword of late. Apparently, some people have figured out that if force-fitting an ERP system, a performance scorecard, and so on *into* the organization is not possible, then perhaps it's time to change the parameters of the organizational structure itself. The part about creating the company design to facilitate company objectives is absolutely correct. Good principle.

Unfortunately, because it deals with a popular and expensive consulting venue, organizational design contracts line the pockets of gurus and experts as fast as any other management trend. A commonsense, relatively inexpensive alternative is as follows: Organizational design and the structure of a company—or a function—can only be successful when actual environmental conditions are well understood by its leaders, and when those leaders commit to developing and appreciating the human beings who populate the organizational/functional design. A briefer version of the same concept is that design is only as good as the people who bring it to life.

Work Design   Another way to think of organizational or functional design—hereafter called "Function design" with an AFF focus—is *work* design, for that is what structure facilitates: structuring work conditions to enable people to perform their best work. Of course, these "structuring conditions" are embedded within the environmental conditions described in the last section, and AFF staff members are continuously immersed in the energy and movement of the larger company community and culture as it responds to the mandates of the greater competitive environment. Many managers do not design their functions to reflect the larger ambient conditions because more immediate priorities within the organizational environment demand all their attention. The CFO's environmental scans of the organization come into play here. The scans help minimize Function design time and increase the appropriateness of design strategies. This approach all boils down to two leadership imperatives for the CFO:

1. Design and structure the AFF function to align with the organization's current needs and development readiness.
2. Guarantee conditions that enable AFF staff members to do their best work.

The quality and fit of the design and structure contribute significantly to work efficiencies. Some concrete examples of design/structure impact on AFF members include the following:

- Approval routing structures—the greater the complexity, the less the efficiency.
- Access to IT infrastructures—the greater the access, the greater the efficiency.
- Opportunity for cross-functional experience—the greater the exposure, the better the AFF staff understands the business.
- High degrees of hierarchical form within the function are at odds with collaborative and team-building efforts.

Controls, restrictions to information, hierarchies of approval, and the like are all attempts to manage exceptions. Both organization and function should be designed to prevent the exceptions—for example, limited access to liquid assets, just-in-time (JIT) inventories to minimize opportunities for theft, and so on. The structural design becomes the guardian.

Working Lean   Any number of people take credit for inventing or enhancing lean operations processes, but lean thinking has its roots in the legendary Toyota Production System. Business professionals owe Toyota and all the other lean thinkers a debt of gratitude. To date, there is no better way to create functional agility and adaptability then to follow the principles of lean processes. Manufacturing operations are probably home to more lean advocates that any other disciplines. However, these lean properties are quite transferable to service organizations. A few examples demonstrate how lean and agile thinking applies to improved AFF structural designs.

Lean tactics precede agile tactics. In the most general terms, lean management practices work to eliminate all forms of waste that occur during product/service production and delivery. Agile management tactics work to eliminate the rigidity of the traditional dependency on economies of scale by increasing production/service delivery flexibility without sacrificing quality or incurring added costs. Lean and agile management practitioners emphasize resource, operations, quality, and continuous improvement perspectives in the design of their tactics.

A finance and accounting function that forms an intention to have a lean and agile identity sets in motion a pattern of continuous improvement that in turn becomes part of all the organization's operating and service procedures. AFF staff members make it their way of life to continually look for leaner, more streamlined methods to maintain a specified level of quality while building greater functional flexibility. People take pride in finding and eliminating waste—automating manual tasks, eliminating reports that go unused, identifying tasks where a team of two is more efficient than one—when their efforts are acknowledged. One of the problems with lean and agile identities is that they tend to be overly focused on in-house processes and sometimes miss seeing external changes in environmental conditions. The introversion tendency of accounting professionals makes this risk concrete. Another danger is that a lean and agile identity can become stingy and mean (as with cost cutting), unless the CFO sets a consistent and balanced tone. Again, the traditional focus on cost invites caution and vigilance for AFF professionals.

Lean thinking favors some particular methods (discussed shortly) but is more an attitude of conscientiousness than a particular technique. An AFF function uses lean and agile management principles to shape its image as a serious and efficient supplier of decision-quality goods and services. The Function should be in love with its own processes, wanting to know everything about them, to provide the best input resources to those processes, and to check in regularly to see what adaptations are needed to meet the demands of changes in structure (an acquisition) and priorities (competitor's disruptive technology). However, this internal process dedication should be largely invisible to customers because purchasers value only the results of lean management: value for money, process speed, and information-quality insights. The last of these, information-quality insights, is the check-and-balance point on lean, waste-elimination company values. For example, lean enthusiasts can become so lean that they stop spending time analyzing the reports they produce. The report may be of the highest quality, but if equally high-quality interpretations and recommendations are not a part of the report, the positive value of the report suffers.

A lean function cultivates a waste-not-want-not mentality. As long as people feel confident that they do not endanger their own jobs or those of coworkers, they participate in work that discovers and eliminates waste. A pattern of reward for innovative, high-dollar waste elimination reinforces such participation. In contrast, when the CFO begins a pattern of eliminating people and departments without satisfactory reassignments and/or reliance on attrition, the lean effort is almost always short-lived. A mid-range maturity Function (or company) that makes this mistake commonly regresses to cost-cutting procedures.

An agile Function cultivates quick, coordinated reflex responses to its customer preferences to improve its technical methods. "Stay three steps ahead of everybody" would make a good motto for an agile AFF function. A mature Function adds, "Be ready for them, and make certain they are ready for us." This is especially true when moving paper-based reporting to the Web. Some customers are very attached to their paper. Agility is an attractive quality and typically generates innovation and creativity. However, agile practices may be too focused on adapting quickly to the trends of customer preferences outside the organization. Some adaptations can generate too much change, at too great an expense in the interest of customer preferences that shift before the agile implementation is fully justified in terms of ROI. Where people are concerned, a rapid series of agile adjustments can induce burnout, and management must take care to advocate for balanced work perspectives, or there will be fewer agile employees to care for customers.

Lean/agile management tactics take many forms. One of the more mature subsets is the JIT production model. JIT can be a set of lean accounting practices used primarily in repetitive tasks (e.g., A/R invoicing, A/P matching), and reporting processes (e.g. credit and collection, month-end close). Lean principles work to minimize waste by creating efficient flow processes through linked work centers (purchasing, receiving, A/P) that eliminate any activity that adds cost without adding value, such as redundant approvals within AFF. JIT managers learn to streamline process operations and focus their waste elimination efforts on the interactions of three principal process resource components: materials, space, and people.

Resource flexibility is a key feature of JIT tactics. JIT managers increase the number of multiskilled workers in all processes and select nonspecialized equipment (e.g., general ledger software applications) for any largely automated process. One of the most important features of JIT process management is the integrated "pull" dynamic of process workflow, in contrast to more conventional "push" systems, which in accounting and finance processes means the radical reversal of users "pulling" reports, rather than AFF staff "pushing" reports to them. If monitored, the very process exposes waste—reports never pulled by anyone. JIT management coordinates workflow pull according to eight principles with significant cost and performance management implications, some of which, with a little imagination, can be applied to AFF processes.

1. *Small lot production* saves space and capital. Work groups can be moved closer together and wait time can be reduced, thus generating more rapid total cycle time. Credit applications are prime candidates for this principle.

2. *Process setup efficiency* to minimize human downtime.

3. *Lead-time* management focuses on the interrelationship of services dependent on cross-functional cooperation such as activity-based reporting and performance measurement refresh cycles. Nonfinancial workers responsible for activity rate calculation, measurement analysis, and the like can be put on a staggered schedule. When ABC and performance design integrity are important, the AFF can receive the staggered updates, make the adjustments in another version of the model, and periodically, just like month-end close, release the aggregated, updated version all at once.

4. *Kanban* control system. This one, like setup, takes some real innovation to apply.

5. *Uniform production levels* smooth processes during final assembly and permit more accurate output forecasting. This principle dovetails nicely with the approaches in number 3.

6. Internal process management depends upon the sixth JIT management focus, the *supply network,* which is especially applicable to multidivision companies that need to periodically collect "supplies" of data at the corporate or intermediate levels. A CFO attends to information supplier relationships in the interest of greater quality and responsiveness. The AFF equivalent of locating processes near the customer is standardized data/report electronic delivery schedules. Here the upstream AFF staff members, as customers of downstream providers, *pull* the data/reports needed rather than waiting for them to be delivered. Naturally, this requires a high level of interconnectivity via the IT architecture.

7. Finally, *quality at the source* and (8) *total process maintenance* ensure quality while processes become more efficient and cost effective. Total process maintenance

in an accounting/finance context means practices that address process breakdowns and breakdown prevention within the process. Careful records may track breakdown costs, frequency, and intervals so that AFF staff can design improved processes.

Importantly, a Function that practices lean and agile management integrates vast amounts of cost and performance information into a single decision support system whenever possible. However, these same organizations thrive only when the same information is integrated into the processes themselves. Cost-to-benefit ratios still matter.

Working in the Stream   "So, what happened to EI competencies and psychosocial development?" A very good question. Naturally, an environmental scan will reveal conditions related to maturity and leadership competencies; however, in the scan phase there is no fixing. The CFO must align with current conditions and serve the requirements of those conditions *before* embarking on development work in the rest of the company. Of course, the finance chief must be working on personal development to even be thinking in this mode. So, the rule is *scan, don't fix*.

Similarly, during the process of work and Function design or redesign, the focus is on providing services needed now, but at every opportunity, designing Function work to be adaptable to future development efforts. For companies and Functions that truly work at the "most mature" end of the spectrum, the approaches in this and subsequent chapters provide a robust framework for testing the maturity of current practices. Naturally, as the Function design takes form, the finance chief identifies and considers the EI competencies and the psychosocial scenarios likely to arise when the design matures. The EI competency, *transparency*, comes in very handy at this point. No good comes from rumors about everyone's job being redesigned, and worse, positions that might be eliminated. Therefore, the CFO must be very transparent about the reorganization process. An effective approach entails town hall meetings where the CFO gives updates and asks for comments and recommendations. This approach has several advantages:

- The CFO gets the benefit of more information directly from staff
- The staff actually participates in the design of its own work
- The CFO may authorize trial runs of the reorganization on a modified basis
- The rumor mill has nowhere to go

The EI competencies are beginning to seamlessly integrate specific CFO leadership responsibilities for the AFF. At this point, all the work begins to come together. The Function is cognizant of environmental conditions, organizational expectations, and information focuses. Based on that knowledge, the CFO with staff participation has designed a structure of services, schedules, and intrafunction relationships and reciprocal responsibilities. In short, the Function is ready to get to work in a new and better way. This sort of process must be described sequentially for clarity's sake; however, the common experience is not a blank-slate Function design, nor a stretch of time when the CFO and staff can work on nothing but re-design. The sequence, the timing, and the magnitude of the design effort are not nearly as important as the mind-set behind them. Following the spirit of the ideas and principles described here paves a solid road of progress, avoids guesswork about customer needs, and saves a great deal of backtracking and apologies. Attending to development of personal and functional maturity and competence, in fact, keeps the CFO and AFF in the stream.

The approaches outlined in the *CFO Survival Guide* do not tell the CFO how many accounts payable clerks to hire. They do not prescribe the exact responsibilities the CFO should oversee. They do not explain how to conduct an internal audit, or which internal controls will guarantee safety. The *Guide* does not identify the right budget system, the right performance management system, or a list of measures guaranteed to keep executives honest. What this alternative approach does do is answer the three enabling inquiries: *Why* is the CFO here? *What meaning* does the CFO's presence have in the organization? What are the *differences* between a good accountant and a great CFO? By rigorous and persistent work, answering such questions offers the possibility that the CFO and staff can become absolutely clear about their purpose in the organization.

The Functional Group: Attracting and Retaining the Right People

environment—structure—**GROUP**—individual

At the moment, sluggish economic conditions drive AFF emphasis more to retention than recruiting, but as with economic cycles, this pendulum swings both ways. So, the CFO attends to both a continuous scan for new talent and the development of current group members. Staying aware of people who need to be liberated from the AFF is a third point of attention. Coming in—staying/developing—moving up/cleansing: These are the highest-level considerations when shaping, developing, and cleansing an accounting and finance function. Since "moving up/cleansing" activities are far more emotionally charged, a measure of CFO success could be a triple ratio of all three. By the way, "moving up" is a feather in the CFO cap when defined as a person who has matured and developed beyond the Function's current needs, and who with good wishes all around moves up to the next rung of the profession. When a great employee leaves with warm regard toward the company, a chance of return at a more mutually propitious time is put in motion.

The finance chief is the guardian of the composite AFF team profile. In smaller firms, every single person may be directly under the CFO wing. In larger organizations, the top financial executive has an obligation to train and monitor direct subordinates so that the most important aspects of the corporate profile are retained, while customizing the team for local necessities. Two good ways for a CFO who sits atop a multilayered organization to keep tabs on the global AFF profile are standardized technical and competency profiles for everyone, and making a point to regularly spend time with people, one-on-one, who serve in the far corners of the corporate universe.

What does the composite technical and competency profile look like? From a technical and subfunction perspective, the profile depends on the size, location in structure (i.e., division, shared service unit, specialist group; e.g., tax, M&A), and the expectations of the CEO or unit head. Should we have a formal internal control system in our three-person enterprise? Probably not. Are supervisors necessary in a ten-person department? Maybe, maybe not. Can one CFO guide, develop, and supervise fifty staff members? Some try, but such an effort probably is not based realistically on human physical/mental capacity limits. Yet, a few core specifications do mark the way to create the best possible composite of AFF skill and competence. The overarching CFO responsibility is *build and sustain the Function*.

- Align services with the current needs of the organization.
- Pace and lead development of maturity within the AFF and the organization.
- Shape collaboration as a way of behaving in relationship.
- Serve holistically.
- Design Function-generated information to show the appropriate blend of short-term necessities and long-term health.
- Encourage and reward widening of functional identity to include ever-larger relationship circles.
- Regularly check service to and knowledge of primary constituencies: the profession, each other, the home community of the firm, the company, and the industry. Some very mature practitioners may even wish to attend to these in rank order.
- Model, develop, and reward maturity and leadership competencies.

The AFF group helps people make appropriate decisions between local/holistic, routine/exceptional, and cost/benefit parameters. People make the most of their decisions from a local perspective even when working holistically. Local perspectives cause intentional and unintentional impacts. A focus on local stimuli is natural: a vendor call, a reconciliation error, an irate staff member; however, the true and ethical professional maintains a multivariate perspective: humane, technical, the good of the one, the good of the many.

Start with Trust   Review of the psychosocial results at the bottom of Exhibit 4.9 reveals the inner spirit of a healthy AFF group, respected and appreciated by their finance chief. Observing from right to left, and remembering that none of these dynamics is linear and all simultaneously impact each other, a strong individual staff member identity contributes to a powerful group identity that yields an internal-AFF experience of autonomy and confidence that permits great adaptability and innovation, and a confident mind-set unafraid of transparency. A group endowed with this inner capacity and competence generates notable achievements that influence and inspire each other and the rest of the organizational community. This sequence is relatively easy to comprehend, yet rarely built and sustained. The starting point is always the same: Trust and trustworthiness.

Ethics is, of course, very much on everyone's mind, and all ethics begin with honesty—honesty with self and with others. Telling a lie in an important relationship is the quickest way to end intimacy and trust. When average honest people on the street are asked for their reactions to Enron-like scandals, their gut reaction is almost always one of two responses: outrage and disgust mixed in varying proportions, and/or deep sadness and a feeling of betrayal. When asked what executives could do to remedy the situation, the spontaneous answer is some version of "Tell the truth!"

The swift demise of Arthur Andersen is grim evidence of how seriously people expect and need trust in the accounting profession. As emphasized in the discussion of psychosocial development, trust versus mistrust is at the root of relationship development. Untrustworthy behavior quickly diverts creative energy to organizational survival activities because lies make relationship conditions uncertain. Untrustworthy behavior robs group energy that could go toward sustaining and enhancing group function—the energy necessary to work productively.

Everyone, but especially a person in charge of an accountability function, must be the model of trustworthiness. In the Function, trust should be implicit, not flaunted or preached. When a CFO works with staff, the focus should not be on setting an overt example for the rest of the organization (not, "Let's be good, and show everybody else how good we are"). Rather trustworthiness, as a value and as a competence, underlies all services. Demand integrity within the Function, and the probability increases of staff naturally carrying out responsibilities in trustworthy fashion with no overt emphasis. The CFO has two perspectives when it comes to trustworthiness: (1) My values and behavior within and for the Function so staff can work according to clear expectations and suffer no doubts or disturbances because of my behavior and (2) My responsibility to introduce working values into the AFF so that staff members implicitly model trustworthy behavior for the rest of the organization. The latter may manifest in the form of honored service agreements and making sure information users receive complete information, even if some of it is bad news. For further discussion on the dy-

CRACKING SHELLS: BUILDING BONDS WITHIN THE OFFICE OF THE CFO

Building bonds is a necessary and natural process for human social structures. Bond building is a process. Unlike mechanical processes, all participants also influence the final result, so there is no way to predict the outcome, and in the workplace, forging connections is a continuous process. The relationship between the CFO and the AFF staff represents a particular type of bond building. A patient getting-to-know-you period gives the CFO and staff members a chance to gather some firsthand information before making snap judgments, which is especially important if the CFO has inherited a staff. The CFO has the responsibility to make the first move.

When a new CFO arrives on the scene, building bonds with the AFF staff is second only to developing a relationship with the CEO. Although the CFO does not know the staff members, they will have heard a great deal about the *virtual* CFO, most in the form of rumors and half-information. You can begin by checking and verifying or correcting this information. Concurrently, you must consciously and deliberately create *actual* first impressions. If the rumor mill has been exceptionally active, this warming-up time period can be lengthy.

Who is getting to know whom? The process is taking place on both sides. In a best-case scenario, a healthy curiosity drives all participants during the getting-to-know-you period and trust develops quickly. Almost everyone begins a new relationship with a little bit of protective armor that breaks down over time as the relationship matures. A good analogy for this process is the way a chick and hen work together to crack open the egg. The process is a natural one, and there must be effort on both sides. In the case of the CFO, it is sometimes difficult to tell who is inside the shell trying to get out, and who is outside trying to get in. Some people seem almost impossible to reach, often as the result of unhappy conditions with former supervisors. In such a case, the CFO patiently practices the best relationship skills.

The most skillful CFO breaks down relationship shells gently and gradually by practicing listening skills and appropriate responsiveness that engenders trust throughout staff relationships. Such an approach has amazing results, but it takes time. Some business cultures use an unfortunate mandate for leadership expectations: "Just do the job." But the leadership job becomes harder and harder as staff relationships deteriorate. Up-front relationship work has a huge payoff in the long term.

EXHIBIT 4.9   TRIPLE HELIX AND PSYCHOSOCIAL DEVELOPMENT AT WORK IN THE AFF

Triple Helix			
Environmental Conditions	Structure	Group	Individual
AFF			
Organizational Conditions	Function form	Group identity	Staff member
CFO Competencies			
Organizational awareness	Design form to suit purpose	Attract and retain the right people	Inspire and influence
Environmental scanning			
CFO Responsibilities			
Determine AFF skills and competencies	Guarantee conditions to perform work	Build and sustain AFF Shape collaboration	Develop and mentor
Psychosocial Results			
Influence	Self-confidence	Trust	Industry
Inspiration	Autonomy	Group identity	Conscientiousness
Achievement	Adaptability	Transparency	Initiative

namics between the CFO and individual staff members, see the "Alliances" feature in this chapter.

Group Identity   Much has been written and publicized about finance for the new millennium, building customer-oriented finance departments and accounting transformations of many shades. All are worthwhile as far as they go, but most miss specifically addressing the importance of the cohesiveness of group identity. Membership comes just after safety and survival on Maslow's hierarchy of needs; that's how deep our social natures go.

The following analogy can be applied to any living organism, but here the focus is on the AFF as a group within the organization. First, think of an organism, a human being, for example. Within the whole human organism, many organ systems contribute specific functions for the care and maintenance of the human entity. Each organ system, in turn, is composed of specialized cells. The body needs each type of cell to survive. Some organ systems in the body, like the circulatory system, inherently function in more holistic tasks than others. These more global systems function continuously, in contrast to the digestive system, which works intermittently. As an organ system, the circulatory system analogy exhibits four principles that are directly applicable to the ways the CFO can work to sustain and enhance the AFF group identity. In the AFF context, call them group values. These values include some of the most important characteristics of healthy accounting and finance groups, the information circulatory system of the organization. Attention to these four values yields far more concrete and desirable behavior than a cloudy mission statement hanging on the office wall.

1. Collaboration
2. Intimacy
3. Continuous work
4. Self-referencing (centering) locus—identity

"Collaboration" along with the more common term, "teamwork" (EI competencies), is the natural outcome of applying all other relationship management competencies. Leading a team is one thing; an entirely different matter is being *part of* a team. Great CFOs know when to simply blend and the right contexts to join in performing activities beyond those that go with leadership authority. In the process, they model collaborative work behaviors for others.

Outside of the human resource discipline (e.g., Dave Ulrich, *Results-Based Leadership*), only bold sales and marketing types have dared use the provocative word, "intimacy." But think about it. Where there is no intimacy, there can be no trust, and without trust, there is no relationship. Sharing observations invites intimacy far more than asking questions. This kind of leadership requires personal and professional self-confidence. Intimacy in a work group has many manifestations. Here are two.

- In a caring context, people are free to tap a collective wisdom, and they draw on it to inform their work: when to be silent, when to speak up, who is ready for something more from the AFF, who is not.

- "Mutual esteem" is synonymous with friendship. What a powerful antidote for the unhealthy aspects of psychosocial development: mistrust, shame, doubt, inferiority feelings, role confusion. Mutual esteem is a way of appreciating that extra effort to help close a difficult month, the pleasure of sharing success in a new process improvement initiative, the communal pride of eliminating functional waste. What a great way to *build bonds* and to cultivate *empathy* for coworkers. Notice the interplay of one competence energizing another.

"Continuous work" does not mean that the accounting shop runs 24/7. It does mean that AFF systems must be ready and receptive to information whenever it arrives. Like the digestive system's intermittent activity, some organizational functions can afford periodic downtime: two-shift production units, compensation and benefits specialists, and to varying degrees, customer service staff. Although the work of the AFF is characterized by repetitive processes and recurring cycles it functions much like the human circulatory system, which shuts down at its own peril and that of the entity serves.

All living entities stay within *self-referencing* parameters. Self-referencing parameters provide adaptation and pattern limits that keep horses from giving birth to cows, and prevent humans from flying without artificial aids. Self-referencing in the case of an AFF is a *centering locus* of identity and operation that keeps accountants from tromping on the territory of marketing specialists, and functional specialists from trying to take the place of accountants. All four principles themselves based on trustworthiness are the elements of an ever-sensitive, ever-adjusting system that remains true to itself. Situational ethics for personal gain and fragmented assemblages of people who are supposed to be working together exhibit the opposite attributes: in-fighting, distance, continuous personal agendas, and no group identity to center on and reference to.

The circulatory organ system analogy offers another helpful frame of reference related to the various kinds of work the AFF performs. Some functions are routine but vital (heartbeats/payroll). *Nonroutine* tasks usually entail temporary redistribution of resources, as occurs when the body is pushed beyond the resting level. The heart responds by increasing cardiac output, and blood vessels redistribute flow to the site that needs the most oxygen: muscles. Importantly, nonroutine tasks always mean extra work, and unless available resources can be expanded (training to deliver more oxygen to the lungs for running, more staff time on major initiatives), the stress of working above and beyond the routine results in collapsed joggers and burned-out staff members. Nonroutine work mandates usually come from executive and manager levels, which in itself creates a layer of stress and performance intensity. An emotionally intelligent CFO has empathy for staff (and self) and runs interference with other executives and managers who may honestly believe that their request is the only ad hoc priority.

In essence, the CFO monitors the aerobic and anaerobic states of individual members and the Function as a whole. Routine, dial-tone services should be low-key, autonomic, and automated. Exception work of short duration (i.e., less than two weeks) may be left to staff discretion who have proven to be self-aware enough to self-assess priorities and workloads. For long-term, exceptional work, the CFO or direct supervisor should always be involved, for at least two reasons: (1) To keep current on workload changes, and (2) To assist in assigning appropriate resources and calling on nonfinancial resources from peer managers, as appropriate. An individual staff member does not have these perspectives and powers.

Best Practices for CFOs   Benchmarking and best-practice approaches have found their way into the CFO's world. Some great ideas out there on concrete practices have proven that they build group strength and motivate individual staff members. Here is a sample from *CFO Magazine*'s 2002 annual study that benchmarks "best workplaces."[7]

- Work elimination teams inspired by tremendous redundancies and unnecessary complexity after merger with Nabisco. (Kraft Foods North America)

- Job mobility and flexible work arrangements. (CNA)

- Individual development profile summarizing "technical skills and leadership competencies." (Kraft)

- Desktop dashboards for staff to track their performance and related incentives. (Vanguard)

- A CFO who stays in touch with staff by actually doing his work in vacant cubicles near finance workers. (Robert Deutsch of CNA)

Great ideas, but just as dozens of inspired operations professionals visit Toyota to look at their legendary production system and come away feeling the presence of a factor they are not grasping, a CFO might visit any best-practice accounting and finance function, look deeply into processes, procedures, and priorities, and still come away *without* that Toyota marketing "I-got-it" feeling. The reason is that business professionals in general, and accountants in particular, see the linear, the physically obvious, and the end results. Only the rare and mature executive sees the inner competencies, the aspects of maturity, and the intangible underlying causes of success.

Performance measurement and management experts encounter a similar dilemma. Clients and seminar participants almost always want the "experts" to "give them the list of the right measures," or to direct them to "somebody who does it right." Just like the best customhouses and the best burger joints, the best AFFs must be built one at a time. Consider the following ten steps:

1. Conduct *gap analyses* for the Function and the company, not only for maturity levels, but also for the specific tasks the AFF performs (or not) for the company.

2. Construct a *concrete matrix of services* performed and customers of those services. Use this for discussions with nonfinancial functions: adequacy of current service, too much or too little attention, pencil in suggestions where AFF could contribute more, and so on.

3. Likewise, construct a grid on all staff members including yourself, by name, (horizontal access) and the *skills and competencies* required for tasks identified in numbers one and two. Consider using some standardized skill/competence inventory such as Kraft's individual development profile to summarize technical skills and leadership competencies. If these are in a database, creating a Functionwide view is expedited. Periodically evaluate the blend and balance of skills.

4. Remember that *outsourcing* specialty services (e.g., tax) and routine processes (payroll) is sometimes more efficient, effective, and cost-wise, but not always.

5. Whenever an AFF staff member regularly spends half or more of his/her working time with one or more specific functions, physically locate that *person near the serviced function.*

6. Institute *job rotation and cross-training* as formal performance objectives.

7. When planning assignments with staff members who serve largely outside the AFF, go with the staff member to meet and discuss services with appropriate customers. A staff member should never be allowed to serve a customer without a personal meeting, and should not continue to serve without *regular personal contact.* As CFO, help the staff member to visualize all parties' positions in the interdependent organization flow.

8. *Coordinate staff relationships* between members who serve closely related constituents, for example, proximate manufacturing departments/divisions, sales and R&D.

9. Hold regular general staff meetings for many purposes, but always to review Function priorities and workloads in a public forum. This cross-pollinates ideas and *understanding of relationships and interdependencies.* Staff members have access to the facts about who is doing what and the load each person

is carrying; people prone to burnouts are encouraged to rely more on the group.

10. Sustain and enhance everyone's *emotional intelligence competencies*, especially your own.

Service with Style

A long time ago in a far corner of the country, an airline decided to drop its most elite perks: seat assignments, food that tried to be fancy, and preboarding to name a few. The company is Southwest Airlines (SWAL), the only airline not to need or accept a government rescue after September 11, 2001. What gives? Don't customers like to be treated as if they were special? Isn't the customer always right? SWAL has a different answer. It's called "service with style." A CFO and AFF could easily adopt such a profile.

So, how special is it when another airline allows customer preboarding overseen by snarly gate agents? How special is that seat assignment, a practice so ubiquitous that it is now seen as entitlement? The Southwest style makes people feel (1) part of a community (entertainment by counter agents, little games involving passengers), (2) in it together (I see you don't have a seat assignment either. Care to rush on board together? What fun!), and (3) engaged, because you never know what will happen next when you're in SWAL territory.

Let's face it, Southwest Airlines has a unique identity amid the long faces and predictable service of the airline industry. Southwest is profitable, not in financial trouble, and has a high employee retention rate. Group identity: It's worth a lot to profit, to longevity, to competitiveness, and to real live human beings. Although the airline business is, admittedly, a bit more exciting to most people than accounting and finance, anything can be made engaging with enough creativity. A sense of humor should probably be added to the list of leadership competencies. People love to laugh—anywhere they can get it.

Developing Individuals: Essential Work Resources

environment—structure—group—**INDIVIDUAL**

Developing individual staff members is the easy part. A CFO can only make one mistake at a time. Developing people is easy for a mature, emotionally intelligent CFO, with a larger-than-usual supply of empathy. In fact, development is not only easy for such CFOs; it is the most valued part of their work, the reason they look forward to going to the office every day. Leaders interested in developing others use specific techniques like mentoring, delegation, job rotation, and cross-training. Good as these are, they are only the beginning.

Less well-known approaches include the following:

- *Staff motivational profiles* for better alignment of people and tasks. A person who measures high on a *generativity scale* may very well be highly effective in working with process improvement teams in manufacturing operations, where changes are physically visible and everyone's hands get dirty. Another person highly motivated by *networking* is probably an excellent member of a performance measurement and management team.

- *Individualized training.*

- *Technical and leadership competence profiles* for better assignment of roles. A staff member high on analysis skills but low on self-confidence may gain that confidence with a temporary assignment to a small technical analysis team— plus some mentoring on the side. Another member who deals well with difficulties but gets overly excited, boastful, and arrogant could use a boot-camp experience with a master chief personality.

- *Craft role identities within the Function.* Honor the bookkeeper's bookkeeper who truly finds joy in balancing the books. Go to him for that expertise. Recognize someone who is particularly good at articulating accounting concepts to nonaccounting workers. Put her in the liaison/interpreter spotlight every time there is a cross-functional language dilemma. You know what to do with the natural born troubleshooter who loves it when someone says, "I've got a problem." Honoring and utilizing specific, inherent talents requires leadership flexibility and a willingness to delay or reassign some tasks.

- *Grow internal consultancies.* This area is another one for those trouble-shooters and interpreters, as well as the technical geniuses. Going out into the company as virtual SWAT teams, groups can be developed to do just about anything: specialize in training new divisions or acquisitions, analyze operations cost structures, and mentor entry-level staff. Who knows, the AFF might even become a revenue center?

- *Formalize mentoring and grooming as standard practice* for all managers and supervisors reporting to you. Make it part of their performance review: specific names with specific development plans and progress reports. This tactic is a good way to clone your competencies.

- *Practice the watch one/do one/teach one cycle.*

A CFO is limited only by an underdeveloped ego, restraints on personal innovativeness, and lack of passion for people and the work they do. All these are under personal control. More good news is that most of this activity doesn't cost more than petty cash. The next piece of good news is that you get to practice all this wherever you are. Maturity and leadership competencies can be developed, the materials are free, and you don't have to take time off work to do it. Every encounter is a practice opportunity, but some are more important. Those encounters are the ones that make you wince, feel guilty afterwards, or make you feel like firing somebody. Thank every difficult encounter that walks into your life as a teacher and a chance to develop faster.

It's Not All Roses   Negative things happen, which is one of the most important reasons for leaders. Here are some of the guideposts that mature executives acknowledge and use to help themselves and others through the difficult times.

- Correcting others is part of a leader's job. Correction is about a technical mistake or inappropriate behavior, never about the person's worth.

- Teams fall apart due to malicious gossip, the arrogance of a member, someone's stubborn refusal to see a truly better way. These difficult circumstances are also the working ground of leaders, who adjust incorrect perspectives, guide difficult people, overlook ingratitude, and only give up on someone when that person carries a virulent behavioral pathology that is contagious to the community. Not everyone wants do the work needed to grow up and become part of a team. Let them go.

- Disturbing emotions intensify and spread when left unattended. Address them as you recognize them.

- Seek dialogue entry points that are direct and closest to the suspected sources of suffering, anger, and pain.

Every Soldier a General   The very best CFOs see every staff member as the CFO, just as the Marine Corps sees every solider as a general. The perspective of this armed services branch is, first, unit survival, followed in order of priority by the Marine Corps and then the country. If the individual marine doesn't survive, and if that soldier can't step into a command position when all the commanders are dead, well, then the unit won't survive, the Marine Corps will be history, and the country will lay open and vulnerable. The logic is simple and elegant. The Marine Corps is expert on interdependence, common resources, and unified community. They aren't the only ones but they are really, really good at it. Have you ever known anyone who wasn't changed by being a marine? Have you ever met a former marine who isn't fiercely proud of that identity? Certainly, some people come away from the experience with no love lost for the Marine Corps, but they remain forever changed at the identity level.

Along with trust, seeing every individual as uniquely valuable builds strong group identities, which means being able to recognize what a staff member is capable of and continuously supporting development of that person. Concretely this outlook means:

1. Accepting the fact that every individual's behavior reflects on the group identity.

2. Acting with the understanding that in every service encounter between a staff member and another worker, you, the CFO, are being judged. This person is your work, your problem, and your gift to the greater company community. That's specifically why every staff member must be able to be a CFO—not forever, not for even very long, but just long enough to exhibit the integrity, trustworthiness, and service orientation that you, the CFO, have instilled in every individual. Even the solider won't be asked to be a general permanently. But the solider, the staff member, is motivated to do self and corps/group proud when called upon.

3. A CFO who accepts and acts on these first two facts cannot help urgently develop leaders.

4. The CFO who accepts the fact that he/she won't be around forever (i.e., hopefully, the company life can outlast the CFO's life) puts heavy weight on succession planning,—and acknowledges that not just technical skills, but also the maturity and leadership competencies discussed in Chapter 3 and beyond. Some ways to develop leadership competencies include (1) skillful employee counseling, (2) exposure to executive/manager-level work, (3) sitting in on strategy planning sessions, (4) and senior staff members mentoring junior staff members.

A CFO who follows this pattern bestows a triple gift: a fine worker for the home group, a potential stand-in (or replacement) for self and other key group members, and from these first two, a treasure to the company that employs them all.

RUNNING THE AFF

Extending the reach of the professional self-assessment tools in Chapters 2 and 3, the following technical and leadership skills/experience/competencies focus specifically on running the AFF. Each CFO must adapt and align the AFF with the needs of the organization.

ASSESSMENT CHECKLIST AFF

Circle **S** if this is a strength or **W** if this is a weakness.

Technical
S   **W**   I make sure that staff members have regular opportunities to update their own technical skills.

S   **W**   I make every effort to keep purely financial and regulatory (e.g., tax) work in its own cage.

S   **W**   I instruct staff members on the technical and ethical aspects of GAAP.

S   **W**   I look for opportunities to assign staff members to support specific, nonfinancial functions, and where appropriate, physically relocate AFF staff members to those functions.

S   **W**   I do my best to provide staff members with appropriate physical work space to support productivity.

S   **W**   I make sure that staff members understand the nonfinancial reasons for all their work assignments.

S   **W**   I work directly with the AFF staff to review the appropriateness of reporting formats, i.e., easy to understand and accessible to nonfinancial managers

S   **W**   I eliminate unnecessary reports and design new reports with AFF staff.

Leadership
S   **W**   I personally inform and teach technical skill updates to AFF staff.

S   **W**   I regularly inform staff of important organizational priorities and how they can support them.

S   **W**   I recruit and hire personnel according to the needs of the entire organization.

S   **W**   I consciously attend to the retention of all valuable employees.

S   **W**   I meet with AFF as a group on a regular basis.

S   **W**   I meet with individual AFF staff members at least once a quarter to formally review their assigned functional objectives, their performance on these objectives, and their workload and resource reasonableness.

S   **W**   I have a formal plan that I actively work on for my own succession and other key AFF positions.

S   **W**   I train, coach, and mentor my staff on the appropriate interpersonal competencies.

S   **W**   I periodically follow up with the customer-managers to assess satisfaction.

S   **W**   I stay alert for opportunities for self and staff to participate in nonfinancial projects and initiatives; I do not wait to be asked but proactively seek the opportunity.

S   **W**   I regularly teach staff members about ethics, show them ethical challenges, and guide ethical conduct for each important AFF cross-functional relationship.

NOTES

1. Lao Tzu, *Tao Te Ching*, trans. Victor H. Mair (New York: Bantam Books, 1990) 61/17, p. 35.
2. John Heider, *The Tao of Leadership* (New York: Bantam Books, 1988), 3.
3. Lori Calabro, "Grooming a Replacement: Who's Next," *CFO Magazine*, April 2003, 74–75.
4. Thomas Walther, Henry Johansson, John Dunleavy, and Elizabeth Hjelm, *Reinventing the CFO: Moving from Financial Management to Strategic Management* (New York: McGraw-Hill, 1997).
5. For an excellent history of the rise of institutional investors, as well as a review of the evolution of corporations, see "The Corporate Paradox," in John Micklethwait and Adrian Wooldridge, *The Company: A Brief History of a Revolutionary Idea* (New York: Modern Library, 2003), chap. 7.
6. See Joe Stenzel and Catherine Stenzel, *From Cost to Performance: A Blueprint for Organizational Development* (Hoboken, N.J.: John Wiley & Sons, 2003), chap. 1.
7. Roy Harris, "Benchmarking Workplaces: What Works," *CFO Magazine,* November 2002, 60–68. Note: 2003 is the third year of this CFO "search," with results published in November. Other sponsors: The Hackett Group, Association for Financial Professionals.

CHAPTER 5

Working Governance: Leadership Maturity in Action

The current is becoming wilder, more capricious. It's all absurd, and I'll never understand why I set out on this enterprise. It's always the same at the start of a journey. Then comes a soothing indifference that makes everything all right. I can't wait for it to arrive. . . .

Now I understand how those incredible cavalry charges were accomplished. I wonder if what we call courage is simply unconditional surrender to the uncontrollable, neutral, overwhelming energy of an order issued in that tone of voice. More thought should be given to this.

Maqroll the Gaviero[1]

Breaking the cycle of bad behavior will take more than convicting executives, shutting down auditors, and instituting new rules and regulations. It will take a seismic shift away from the short-term mentality that grips corporations. . . . Companies grappling with how to regain public trust should start focusing on the long-term health of their businesses. Only then can the ethical temptations wrought by quick fixes and rapid rewards be replaced by the ethical resolve to build companies for the long term.

Jeffry L. Seglin[2]

T he history of human social and economic life is the history of resource possession and distribution. Some of these resources ensure survival itself. The competition for resources always begins with situations of relative scarcity. Vying for resources eventually escalates to the imperialist exploits of the best-armed groups backed by the greatest wealth resources. From there it was a short step to the present heavyweight profit imperative, the shareholder-dominated economic marketplace.

Today, in its quest for ever-greater resource ownership, an entity called the corporation operates largely without concern for the boundaries of sovereign states or their laws and ways of maintaining order. Many companies still consume essential planetary resources in medieval terms, as if they were divinely bestowed, unlimited, and everlasting. The corporate hunger for these resources severely disturbs the natural order of our planet. This disturbance is the worst expression of a "sovereign" hierarchy in action: a two-year-old prince left alone within reach of all the household's electric, gas, and other utility switches, possessing the self-discipline and governance capabilities of, well, a two-year-old.

Other than the capabilities of the U.S. military, no other organized, coordinated group has greater power to influence world policy than multinational corporations. With such power comes great responsibility, but wait a minute! The corporation, like financial reporting, is a symbolic (though legalized) abstraction, and abstractions cannot wield great power for good or ill except in the minds of the people who accept their legitimacy without question. So, the next order of developmental inquiry asks the question: How did this terrible two-year-old come to power, and what should society do to correct the situation?

CORPORATE HISTORY *CLIFF NOTES*

Making a study of the history of the corporation is like unearthing the story of an immediate family member that you were (mostly) unaware of, and who, frankly, does not fill you with pride. In the case of investigating corporate genealogies, the first shock comes with the discovery that the "family members" are not actually human, but they have acquired at least equal rights and privileges. The second stunning discovery is that these legalized nonhuman entities are virtually immortal. As long as someone feeds them enough, they never die—a new twist on *The Little Shop of Horrors* story. The ultimate blow comes with the realization that the rest of the "family" is a collection of living, breathing people who have voluntarily exchanged their personal identities and status in a democratic society for a job in a corporate identity, as in "I am with Big Blue" or "I am a 3Mer."

Our ancestral corporate past reveals that in the pivotal centuries of early governance, people first partnered to shoulder the risks of business ventures. Partnerships lasted through clear-cut intervals of risk such as sea voyages or caravan passages whose ending signaled that the contract was complete. Every member of the partnership was in effect, a shareholder, but a far more up-close and personal investor than the majority of modern shareholders. For a very long time, technology demanded that such businesses remain small and predominantly family-owned. This form of business persists in less industrialized nations, but it may be headed for extinction because of the encroachment of the giant multinationals.

The invention of the representative abstraction called *currency*—as opposed to the limited supply of physical items of value: gold, shells, animals, and sometimes people—began the separation of business owners from actual workplaces and from work itself. Currency, of course, was the progenitor of the paper share that remains the forebear of today's digital wealth. The abstract nature of currency and other paper instruments of value also set the foundation for professional managers whose presence began the still-unsolved problem of aligning the interests of absentee owners with on-site managers and workers, so that executives would govern in the interest of shareholders. Again and again, company owners have tried to make managers think and act like owners; stock options are one recent attempt at solving this ancient accountability enforcement problem.

The lineage of the corporate charter started in countries like England, a leader in granting royal charters that guaranteed a monopoly for a specific time period, usually less than twenty years. Then came the Magna Carta ("really big charter") where monarchy lost the privilege of sole ownership of everything, everywhere, always, to the aristocratic rabble of the day. Not long after, the first 150 years of American history created a whole new way of doing business free of the notion of elite ownership privilege, and by the end of the nineteenth century, incorporation had become easy, at least for those matching the title of Michael Moore's recent bestseller.[3] At that time, however, most states still limited the duration of corporate charters. Wherever a charter monopoly was granted or a company grew too large, some people vociferously protested. Likewise, fraud, scandal, and lies are as old as commerce. Enron, Tyco, HealthSouth, and the rest have done nothing original.

In more recent decades, companies and corporations—especially American ones—morphed into political animals with all the favoritism that bureaucratic environments bring, and all the legislated logic accorded the IRS tax code. In short, the corporation grew up like a precocious, spoiled child left to its own devices. Intentional, conscious development never entered the public governance debate. So, today, we have an organizational entity with tremendous inherent worth, but reared with many antisocial traits that are simply unsustainable in the long-term:

- Ease of incorporation with almost no reciprocal obligations
- The corporate veil limiting the culpability of owners and managers—still largely intact
- The same (or greater) legal rights as a human being

- Unequal status between shareholders as the extractors of wealth and employees as the producers of wealth (with the possible exception of on-site shareholders)
- Freedom from national control and lack of enforcement of state control[4]
- Immortality

Corporations have not completely failed to contribute to the social and economic public interest. None of the following were standard practice before the twentieth century: prohibition of child labor, pension and retirement benefits, or employee health care. Some early corporate leaders remain revered to this day. For example, the citizens/workers of Hershey, Pennsylvania (a company town built by the Hershey legacy), rose en masse to protest the acquisition plans of a suitor.

As recently as a century ago, companies were generally expected to operate in the interest of the public good. In fact, many original royal and legal charters explicitly required that the mission of the enterprise directly impact the public good for the better. This expectation remains active in cultures such as Japan, but is deteriorating even there. Beginning with expansive business ventures like building railroads, that obligation to public good began fading rapidly. In its place, the investor culture arose, which led to an emphasis on growth, which in turn led to multidivisional companies that eventually became multinational corporations (with a bit of obligate antitrust law thrown in along the way). In parallel, the audit profession soon sprouted and flourished as a comfort to all those absentee owners and creditors.

The social responsibilities of the corporation began to muddy soon after. Whereas pre-twentieth-century attitudes primarily viewed business as having an obligation to be responsible to the public good, post-1900 perspectives began to explicitly emphasize the interests of shareholders. After a long gestation, and contrary to expectation, a lengthy but largely unattended corporate labor birthed a spanking new, culturally validated corporate prime measure: Maximize Shareholder Wealth. This baby prime measure looked healthy (and historically upright), but an evil twin was part of the parturition: the Profit Imperative. As the twins enter their second century of life, the fairhaired firstborn has been corrupted by its sickly twin and now harbors a pathology that has spread throughout the entire corporate body. The evil twin has a long but appropriate alias: Profit at Any Cost. Shareholder wealth maximization and the profit imperative are identical twins, and telling them apart is almost impossible.

By the mid-1950s, financial numbers and the mythical status of the shareholder ruled. William H. Whyte chronicled these changes in *The Organization Man* (1956)[5] within the diversified conglomerates that were well on their way to institutionalizing the "sovereign" hierarchy and its obsession with growth, economies of scale, and conformity. At the top of the hierarchy sat a historically unlikely sovereign—

not kingly, papal, or even aristocratic, but the bourgeoisie shareholder. The preeminence of sovereign shareholder wealth grew as the prime measure of organizational performance until it looked too concrete and institutionalized to question, just like sovereign rule in the Middle Ages.

Fast-forwarding to the last quarter of the twentieth century finds what John Micklethwait and Adrian Wooldridge call a story of "unbundling the company."[6] This most recent chapter of corporate history is the story of the sovereign hierarchy standing at a great developmental divide between unbundling forces and investment interests. Everything from brands, core competencies, and the Japanese to the ascent of the computer and the unorthodox dot-com new economy played a part in this corporate unbundling that distracted from investment priorities. In the other direction, investment instruments based primarily on mathematical constructs that magically created hedging, swapping, options, and derivatives are creations of the evil twin. In no time at all, digital wealth took the place of bricks and mortar and actual sales revenue. (Remember that odd asset called cash?) Financial voodoo was loosed upon an eager investor public. But recently, two conditions have opened the eyes of the public, which is now scrutinizing the corporate social contract.

> To keep on doing business, the modern company still needs a franchise from society, and the terms of that franchise still matter enormously. From the company's point of view, two clouds have gathered on the horizon: the cloud of corporate scandals, and the cloud of social responsibility.[7]

These words are among the concluding remarks made in *The Company*. Today, sitting atop the long and exciting history of "the company," some fundamental elements of the human condition endure: ethical behavior, good governance, and "virtuous lives,"[8] all depending on developmental maturity and competent leadership. So, this discussion brings the inquiry to the following question: *How much can any one person govern and be responsible for?* How can those people, like the CFO, who guide organizations identify their own level of governance maturity, and uphold or develop those standards in the face of the influence of enormous pressures of personal wealth? For how much can, and should, a corporate entity be responsible? For the sake of honest discussion, let us start with a sincere answer: "I don't know yet."

OLYMPIAN EXECUTIVES

Everyone expects executives to fall into the "mature leader" category, but few people see the executive as being beyond human foibles, unaffected by the conditions and influences that the rest of us chalk up to being "only human." Like the protagonist in a Greek tragedy, when executives fail, they appear to fall harder and farther than mere mortals.

Take the chief financial officer, for example—the classic role for such a tragedy. The CFO is looked to for complete, truthful decision-quality information, expected to advise wisely and correctly, and in some cases counted on to deliver numbers that make everyone smile all the time. The CFO shoulders executive burdens second only to the CEO, but with added expectations. Everybody wants somebody else to choose the right way, and to take responsibility for outcomes. Many want someone else to do the hard work and have the discipline to see things through. Most people want someone else to govern their lives. *Or do they?*

Do people doubt themselves so much that they actually want to defer their personal autonomy to a leader? The answer seems to be yes, in hierarchical organizations, but not always for reasons of self-doubt. Borrowed from the military, the hierarchical chain of command is an excellent means to coordinate large numbers of people through a complex, changing environment toward a common goal. Hierarchical governance as a chain-of-command structure is the chief means of organizing the corporate workforce, but its strengths come with significant developmental dangers. One of the most significant dangers of hierarchical organizations is the concentration of power in the positions of leadership. While even highly autonomous, self-confident people depend on leaders to shape their work identity, and to help them see where and how their work has meaning and purpose, some of history's most intriguing stories describe how the immature abuses of concentrated power toppled otherwise unimaginably powerful social structures (the Roman Empire, the Roman Catholic papacy, Napoleon, Elvis). The caution here is that even an ineffectual, unethical, or irresolute person in a leadership position influences, and sometimes controls, people's work lives, making mature leadership so essential—especially where good governance is concerned.

A first-order question needs an answer at this time: *Why exactly do we place this continual emphasis on development?* Development, the science of becoming, is grounded in massive amounts of hard data and extensive research. This topic should intuitively appeal to a business-minded person: reliable numbers *and* a proof of concept. Just as significant, business needs a science to hold leaders accountable for the measures and behaviors that actually count, the ones that determine organizational health and longevity. Accounting and financial methods are conceptual models; they are not a science. No matter how much good comes from research done on strategy, marketing, and information technology, their contribution is suboptimized without the cohesive knowledge and practice of human development.

Recent research indicates that executives and managers have more difficulty than one might anticipate taking action and following through during turbulent times where only about 10 percent perform with obvious, clear intentions. Although the other 90 percent could articulate what needed to be done, they took no action on that knowledge.[9] The adage, "Talk is cheap," applies here. Anyone who is halfway articulate can share great ideas. Taking action and following through to completion requires mature leadership. How many of us start a degree program, a diet or exercise regimen, or a family, and although we know what should be done, we often find it difficult to navigate the course of action? Executives are often the same way. Perhaps taking a public stand, making a commitment, *and* achieving it are rarer in the human condition than we commonly realize.

Ever wonder why executives seem vulnerable to word-of-the-week slogans, to solution-of-the-quarter methods, and lately to big information technology (IT) investments that promise to ease business life? Sometimes they are looking for the magic in the short-term fix because their companies really need something fast. Other times, approach adoption is based on the perception that the method worked well somewhere else. Typically, executives are wired to recognize good ideas when they see them; these people have good intentions and sincerely want to help their organizations and themselves. But often, something goes wrong; the technology fails to work as advertised, and people resist yet another initiative that they must add to their full workloads. Sometimes the technology works beautifully and everyone is on board, yet business results stagnate, show little change, or even decline. This last situation is the most frustrating, and the cause almost always goes unrecognized: The technology, method, or tactic does not match the strategic needs of the company. How many of the rest of us begin a career that turns out to be unfulfilling, marry a person who is not a good match, or hold beliefs that do not serve us well? Executive choices are the same way. Perhaps making the best choices is a matter of trial-and-error experience and is more intimidating than we commonly admit.

Executives are expected to run an entire organization across areas of expertise for which they have no training. They are expected to know what to do whenever there is a problem anywhere, in any domain. Executives are supposed to make incisive evaluations; sound, fair judgments; and optimal decisions. Their assessments, though, not infrequently leave out some vital piece of information. At times they don't have a clue what is going on in functions outside their expertise. From time to time their human biases cloud their judgments and decisions, and they must move forward with imperfect information. How often have you heard an executive say, "I don't know" or "I can't decide"? Is executive behavior so much at variance with the balance of the people on the planet? Who has not at one time or another plunged forward because there was no apparent way back, made important decisions beyond personal expertise, and erroneously evaluated and judged other people and situations? Sometimes even knowing what information is needed for a decision and what questions need asking for a fair evaluation is more arduous and involved than people commonly concede. Still, just about everybody expects executives to get things done, to choose the right tactics, to know. With all the challenges faced by corporate leadership, none is greater than the expectations others have of leadership.

Leadership excellence can be measured in terms of an integrated profile of actions, comprehensive worldview, and emotional competencies. A person who has steadily and conscientiously developed an integrated leadership profile sees more, has more information, and therefore is more likely to confidently and ethically use authority to govern well. Remembering that 90 percent of executives seem to know what to do but take no action, the question remains: What are the barriers to corporate leadership and governance maturity? Emotional intelligence research suggests that only self-aware executives can hope to break through the barriers to maturity.

For example, consider the CFO who abdicates any active role in corporate governance out of fear and intimidation not to mention the structural barriers dictated by the hierarchical governance form. The barrier to leadership maturity is not lack of skill and experience, but rather overcoming the emotional obstacles as well as the challenges of a workplace divided between shareholder and employee interests. In contrast, the self-aware CFO conscientiously discerns what needs to be done, takes initiative, and commits self and others to achieving organizational intentions. This CFO does not retreat from the gates of hierarchical power structures, because self- and relationship awareness allow the more mature CFO to see through the artificial hierarchical constructs and subsequent emotional barriers that obstruct the path of the less mature CFO.

Exhibit 5.1 identifies the position of the CFO with the executive team in the rank-order hierarchy of corporate structure. While the left side demonstrates the flow of power, the right side characterizes influences on governance and the uses of power at each level. In rank order, the executive team members who work in the same buildings with hundreds of people who are actually working to follow their orders must first and foremost attend to increasing shareholder wealth as directed by the board while meeting customer needs and employee demands. Those troublesome employees—always undermining shareholder wealth with their salaries and benefits!

For the CFO this all boils down to a simple question: How can a mature financial officer lead maturely in an immature organizational governance structure? Some notable historic leaders provide the answer. Based on their ability to articulate new, more mature ways to see relationships between people, Lincoln, Gandhi, and King led entire nations through long, difficult phases of immaturity. Maybe there's a more mature way to organize the ways people structure work, work governance, and work outcomes.

EXHIBIT 5.1 EXECUTIVE LEADERSHIP INFLUENCE IN THE CORPORATE HIERARCHY

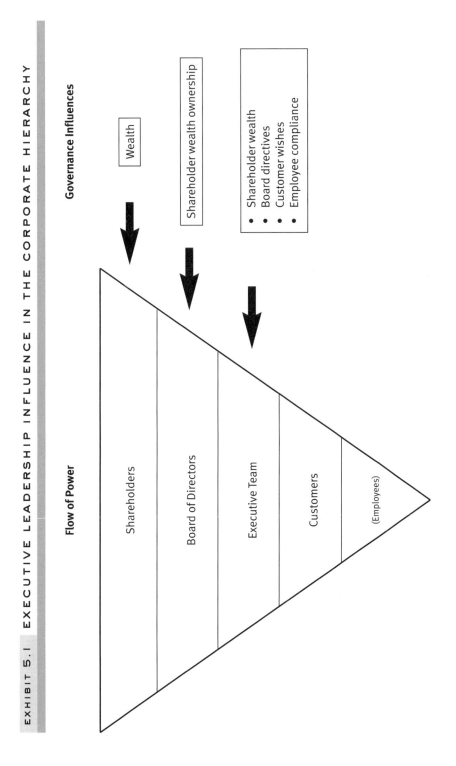

Flow of Power

Governance Influences

Shareholders

Board of Directors

Executive Team

Customers

(Employees)

Wealth

Shareholder wealth ownership

- Shareholder wealth
- Board directives
- Customer wishes
- Employee compliance

GOVERNANCE

Governance is another area of human maturity with its own progression of milestones intimately linked with the moral subsystem. Governance is much in the news of late. As pointed out in the "Ethical Resonance" feature in Chapter 2, the current scene is one where the law-and-order moral types are trying to spank those instrumental hedonists back in line. But already thoughtful commentators are saying that the ethical "shenanigans" are still afoot, or more cynically, "Enron never happened."[10] In essence, war and the continued poor economic conditions of 2003 have diverted public attention. At the same time, the commentaries focus on the futility of immature governance policies and methods. The Chinese identified these patterns hundreds of years ago, shown in italics.[11]

- Sarbanes/Oxley and the like are not enough to ensure that instrumental hedonists don't do unethical things. *[They] draw their bow[s] after the thief has gone.*

- The attitudes of unethical people in corporations haven't changed; they just have more financial disclosure paperwork to do. *[This is like] washing a lump of dirt in the mud.*

- Corporate governance remains immature; investors remain at risk. *In the same pit, there's no different dirt. If you see cheeks on the back of their heads, don't go along with them.*

The governance predicament has at least two troubling aspects from a maturity perspective. First, the current legislative and professional efforts are vintage Nancy Reagan[12]—a relatively more mature contingent of professionals and the Congress attempting to enforce codes of behavior on people too immature to accept the codes voluntarily. Imagine training a feral dog by kicking it every time it fails to follow a command. In short, people who would enforce ethics have no idea how to change the ethical behavior of immature human adult professionals. Punishment and monitoring thus emerge as the norm, and the crooks just get smarter.

The second characteristic is that ethical executives have no formal structure for governing maturely. The dynamics of Exhibit 5.1 certainly don't suggest such a structure. They have no pattern, no guide, and no logical progression to follow. Instead, they are the beneficiaries of a great deal of reactive emotionalism and popular opinion from the media, the legislature, and professional pundits. *The sound of thunder is tremendous, but there isn't even a drop of rain.*[13] Executives who have not been and who do not want to be associated with unethical practices often interpret all this as follows:

- Do better corporate reporting, containing more honest, open information (e.g., nonfinancial measures, industry benchmarks)

- Be very conservative in interpreting GAAP
- Just say no to earnings management
- Better not to use stock options as incentives

This kind of advice grabs at the empty space of financial abstraction and goes much too lightly on the subject that is of most interest to everyone: Trust. Now there is a paradox. The four bulleted points just mentioned express what good, honest professionals do without thinking. So, those professionals who are trustworthy attempt to do more work to display their integrity, while the untrustworthy arrogantly continue to find ways not to get caught. No amount of regulatory changes, GAAP clean-up, or monitoring ever changes anyone's leadership maturity for the better.

Because governance, like finance and accounting, is an abstract concept, it can only be *seen in action*. Correspondingly, only individuals and groups of people can be held accountable for good governance, not corporations or institutions. Governance has its own maturity curve. In general, it aligns with moral development milestones. Second, the maturity profile of governance milestones also parallels the development of social groups over the history of humanity. Of great interest in the business context is executives' *perceived scope of governance*, a third parallel describing the governance maturity path. Exhibit 5.2 shows these three parallel aspects of governance maturity: the familiar moral path, the milestones of social group configuration, and the development of wider perception of executive responsibility in the organization. Paralleling organizational *moral maturity*, governance maturity can be more completely evaluated by observing *internal social configurations* within companies and the behaviors they advocate. These first two criteria of governance maturity—moral codes and internal social configurations—can be difficult to observe; however, the third criterion is both observable and reliable: *executive behavior based on perception of personal scope of governance*. While exploring the three governance criteria, discover where your (and your organization's) governance maturity currently sits.

Importantly, just as with development stages, *internal social configurations* are not inherently right/wrong, better/worse. They are what they are, and under varying conditions, each can be exactly appropriate. Aircraft wrecks sometimes create survival situations where tribal behavior may be the best governance structure. The beauty of developmental frameworks is that each new milestone incorporates and integrates all previous milestones. A person or an organization goes beyond earlier behaviors, but values and appreciates all prior development achievements. The utility of developmental awareness is the ability to see and act on a variety of perspectives, activating behaviors accordingly. Similarly, the capacity to adapt social configurations to conditions as they present themselves is the hallmark of highly mature people.

EXHIBIT 5.2 GOVERNANCE MATURITY PARALLELS

Moral Code	Internal Social Configuration	Executive Responsibility Perception	Profile of CFO Governance Participation
Punishment and obedience	Tribe	Local function	Not applicable
Instrumental hedonism	Loose confederation	Loose consortium of independent functions	Governance resource
Law and order	Hierarchy	Company	Compliance regulator and administrator
Universalism	Heterarchy	Diverse plurality	Arbiter

Perhaps most important of all, when one works toward and reaches each developmental milestone, not only are more personal competencies at hand, but interpersonal encounters benefit as well. Take a CFO who is at the *universalism* stage of moral development. Say that the CFO has apprehended a staff member embezzling. Nothing can change the unethical state of the behavior. However, the CFO *can see* beyond the scope of right and wrong, yet still deal with the undesirable behavior. In other words, such a person understands why the staff member engaged in criminal behavior, while still maintaining clarity about the unprincipled behavior. This CFO responds firmly, yet compassionately, whereas a law-and-order CFO would probably leave out the compassion because of the belief that people operate as part of a social unit, and certain rules apply to everyone. Make no mistake, the law-and-order CFO has made a significant beyond from the hedonist's "I will do whatever I can get away with."

Internal Social Configurations

The embedded structures of natural systems is another dynamic attribute of development and social configurations. "Embed," with connotations of "implant" and "insert," is apt for discussions about developmental subsystems and social groupings. As demonstrated in earlier chapters, human development is a set of subsystems embedded in the nervous system that unfold and work interdependently. Similarly, social configurations are naturally embedded within one another from the individual to the nuclear family–extended family–neighborhood–community–township–marketplace–nation–continent–planet–solar system. We cannot avoid the embedded nature of the multiple social groupings within which we live. Just try to extract yourself from this conglomerate!

This chapter discusses social configurations specific to the internal relationships of governance within an organization. When it comes to governing a workplace, the same embedded qualities apply. Some people behaving at less mature levels try to separate one social group from another or enforce rigid hierarchies within organizations. In that regard, three insights emerge from Exhibit 5.2. The first three columns in the exhibit portray a high-level composite of the interdependent maturity influences that shape organizational governance and governance relationships. The "internal social configuration" column contains the second insight: Organizational form reflects and dictates particular governance patterns and maturity milestones for people's internal relationships. The next column conveys the third insight: An executive's own perception of the scope of his/her governance responsibilities is the acid test of applied governance maturity.

Moral development is embedded in executive governance behaviors and the ways they shape internal social configurations in the organization. The executive's behavior and speech clearly reveal the operative beliefs about the size of the circle of relationships to be governed. In combination, the three—moral code, internal social configuration, and executive responsibility perceptions—characterize governance maturity, as well as the most influential accountability expectations. For instance, if tribal groups are the social configuration norm, local loyalties govern behavior. Think Robin Hood and the Sheriff of Nottingham.

Naturally, the appearance of these social forms, moral behaviors, and responsibility postures do not actualize in a single format. They emerge more dynamically based on the number of relationship structures the organization creates for employees to perform their work. An overarching hierarchical form usually dominates, but some portions of the company may behave in tribal contexts, and a few individuals do their best to work holistically. These nonlinear conditions are significant because the common experience consists of many interlocking layers of group and individual maturity, across many developmental subsystems, interacting without awareness of their developmental differences. Is it any wonder that organizations, trapped in mechanistic viewpoints, can't seem to get the "human element" right? Picture, for example, one executive who thinks of a peer as wise, calm, and understanding, whereas a third peer perceives the "wise one" as arrogant and aloof. Two other executives share mutual animosity based on conflicting (but never expressed) beliefs in behavior rules. The end result is what is observed in most organizations: people spend as much or more energy "getting along with others" as on technical work. As an applied practical example of developmental governance, an executive group using developmental constructs in their decision making dialogue (1) takes blame out of the picture, (2) gives people a common framework to work within, (3) encourages the next right steps for a group and for individuals in the group, and (4) moves the executive team rapidly into cohesive collaboration.

Learning to use developmental concepts and language at work takes determination and an absence of ego agendas. This process is one of progressive learning, experience, and mastery. A *tribe* dynamic may be the right form to govern and energize an entrepreneurial start-up where loyalty, mutual support, and shared responsibility enable the fledgling company to survive. In larger companies, one can easily spot a tribe operating within a governing hierarchy. Tribes consistently take breaks together, eat together, and socialize outside of work. They are very hard to "join," as one controller discovered. The first day on the job, a sociable new controller in a fifty-year-old manufacturing firm made the mistake of sitting down with her department members in the cafeteria. All conversation stopped as the controller took her seat. Being aware and empathetic, she noticed right away and asked directly what the trouble was. "That chair belongs to Barbara," said Kathy, who the controller discovered later was the tribal leader. "She sits there every day," Kathy continued, explaining the rules of governance in a respectful, matter-of-fact tone. "In fact, we all sit in these exact same six chairs every day." The controller acknowledged the ritual and with friendliness moved to another table.

A *loose confederation* can be identified by its self-governing functional silos, limited interaction outside the function, and conflict whenever groups need to work cross-functionally for any length of time. Loose confederations commonly exist symbiotically within a *hierarchy*. Hierarchies operate in all group types from nation to family, whenever a power of governance imbalance exists, that is, where power is explicitly stratified, and a limited number of "sovereigns" hold and distribute almost all the actual power to govern. Hierarchies are without question the current dominant organizational form. Because all people want to have power over their own lives, and many want to participate in the power structure, this form is also marked by interdepartmental conflicts. In addition, the hierarchy contains layers of formal authority-management that is often less potent than informal power structures. Executives and managers in hierarchical organizations are rarely aware that the informal power structures actually drive the production of their typically profuse policies and procedures that prescribe behavior norms. This kind of organization really wants to be sure things are done right, although the very complexity of policies and procedures makes "doing right" more difficult.

The social configuration equivalent to moral universalism is rare as a workplace paradigm except in small businesses, local areas in a big business, and small cooperatives. A *heterarchy* distributes authority as needed according to knowledge and functional application—those who know best and can do best lead, and leadership configurations change as the work changes. Even though moral universalism with its holistic perspective and heterarchical social configurations are currently rare in the workplace environment, they nonetheless appear to be the next stage of governance maturity. They certainly suggest ways to begin untangling the immature governance knots in Exhibit 5.1. As unlikely as this move may currently seem, the seeds of transformation are already sprouting.

The following discussion of assessing and applying principles of governance maturity in the workplace focuses on the challenges a CFO faces while integrating the most mature governance practices. The developmental focus for this chapter is the executive passage from the law-and-order-based hierarchy mind-set to moral universalism within a heterarchy where executives perceive their scope of responsibility as more extensive, diverse, and pluralistic. Chapter 6 examines ways to free workplace governance from the cultural dynamics that have placed the governance of almost all social systems in a state of developmental arrest.

Consider the far right column of Exhibit 5.2. Because this *Guide* is built for the CFO on the path of comprehensive professional developmental, examples and discussion focus on the governance experiences of the finance executive, although many of the behavior guidelines apply to all executives. Notice up front that the governance role of the CFO does not really emerge and become concrete until the fourth stage and the heterarchy. But the CFO is not alone. The fourth stage is also the first time that individuals come to be seen as part of the governance responsibility plurality; stakeholders become more numerous, and work governance considers more than shareholder wealth. Prior to that, employee stakeholders and the CFO are mere producers and resources.

Executive Responsibility Perceptions

Every human being has a sense of responsibility, even if that sense extends only to oneself. The question is: How much can any one person govern and be responsible for? How much *self*-governance? Family governance? Corporate governance? The answer depends on the maturity and capacity of the person or organization. When any two or more people form a purposeful group, they rely on trust, shared responsibilities, and some form of leadership to sort out practically their best mutual interests. "How much *can* I be responsible for?"

So much meaning is contained in that one, simple word, "can." One word sums up the potential breadth of governance responsibility for a CFO. "Can" encompasses skill and experience (as in "know-how") and competence capacity (as in "capable of"). But remember the statistics that opened this chapter? Although 90 percent of executives and managers could articulate what needs to be done, when the going gets tough they take no action. The third component o "can" (as in *equal to* the task) takes the grand idea into the arena of intentional follow-through and execution. In the vernacular, "can" means saying yes to questions like "Are you up to the job" and "Can you handle it?" Let us take a close look at the developmental range in executives' perception as to their personal scope of governance responsibility. This scope of responsibilities—how executives, individually, and as a group, perceive the extent of their governance responsibilities—is the second major indicator of the level of organizational, governance maturity.

Looking at the third column of Exhibit 5.2, perception is based on belief, and beliefs are shaped by how much a person is capable of seeing. Anyone in an executive position, by default, holds some measure of governance responsibilities. Take a CFO. No matter how well or poorly a CFO performs, a broad spectrum of responsibilities is possible. Previous chapters address the range in detail. To review, a CFO *can* function as bookkeeper, analyst, scorekeeper, business and strategic partner, people developer, and emotionally intelligent and mature leader. As an organizational leader, the CFO works within the context of five governance alliances.

THE FIVE INTERDEPENDENT GOVERNANCE ALLIANCES

A governance alliance is a relationship between individuals and groups charged with organizational governance responsibilities. The current predominant governance structure includes three formal groups. For the corporation, the standard three are (1) the executive counsel of the CEO, (2) the board of directors, and (3) the shareholders.

The equivalent of these three standard elements in the not-for-profit sector follows a similar pattern, except that constituents take the place of shareholders and the board usually goes by a different name. For example, at a public university, the board members are most often called "regents," and the constituents include taxpayers and students. The appellations may differ, but the triads function similarly: executives lead and manage, and the board oversees and guides, in the interest of serving shareholders or taxpayers and students. The groups exist interdependently in the form of a mandala of governance interests, distinct groups with interconnected work and concerns. Exhibit 5.3 portrays a simple mandala form that expresses such complex corporate interactions. The position of the CFO in such a configuration typically lies within the executive circle barely touching the board and shareholder domains. Not uncommonly, the CFO conducts shareholder relations exclusively through investor analysts and formal shareholder public relations mechanisms. Shareholder activism is on the increase, so steady convergence can be expected in the shareholder, board, and executive domains.

Clearly, these governance groups can be reconfigured in a number of significantly different patterns of influence and alliances. For the CFO who seeks to find more and better ways to govern, five primary governance alliances focus the work for greater governance maturity:

EXHIBIT 5.3 GOVERNANCE MANDALA

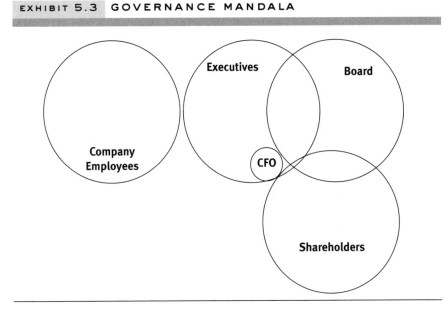

1. CEO–CFO Alliance
2. CFO–Executive Counsel Alliance
3. CFO–Board of Directors Alliance
4. CFO–Shareholders Alliance
5. CFO–Employee Stakeholders Alliance

This fifth CFO governance alliance deserves a brief discussion before moving forward. The discussion turns to the crucial CEO-CFO alliance shortly, but first, a complete representation of workplace governance relationships necessitates the identification of one more alliance: the *missing* one that is discussed briefly at the end of this chapter and in detail in Chapter 6.

Even though putting an employee perspective in performance scorecards has recently become popular, in a hierarchy devoted to shareholder interests, employees are not considered allies. Within the constraints of a hierarchical corporate governance structure, employees may be treated well, but in a corporate hierarchy, employees are an expense (wages and benefits) and a burden (another name for overhead traditionally allocated on the basis of labor dollars or hours). On the income statement, the expense of people pulls down profit; on the balance sheet, people show up as liabilities (e.g., wages) and never as assets.

To reach a stage of governance maturity that includes the wisdom of the hierarchy—and more—this valuation of employees must change. Exhibit 5.3 suggests the only place in a governance hierarchy where people and their work touch governance is by way of representation through the executive counsel. One executive ally—the CFO—can change this condition of exclusion better than any other. When the CFO proactively enters and represents the interests of people and their work, the possibility of their inclusion in governance begins. Other than the CEO, the CFO is the only executive who has a chance of merging rank-and-file people into the governance structure. The CEO can do so by mandate, but unless the chief executive is either a financial expert or has a CFO who understands this exclusion, a mandate goes only so far.

The mature CFO's governance participation agenda starts with a commonplace but subtle point of information: The workplace creates wealth. The finance executive can change the perspective on resources by revealing people as the actual source of value and wealth creation in terms other executives immediately understand: abstract financial representations. Thus the finance chief creates a bridge from a mental construct to the actual life and purpose of the workplace. In doing so, the finance executive becomes a catalyst for changing the governance structure. In development, nothing ever goes to waste, not even financial abstractions.

The remainder of this chapter speaks to how the mature CFO plays a role in the reconfiguration of the executive, board, and shareholder domains. Chapter 6 explores how the CFO can work to include employees in organizational governance—directly and indirectly.

ASSESSING ORGANIZATIONAL GOVERNANCE MATURITY

The science of human development is one of very few disciplines that could attempt governance assessment. Specifically, hierarchies are a very efficient and effective way of organizing a complex, multifaceted workforce. In fact, they may constitute the most efficient and effective way to do so. However, as already suggested, hierarchies are a very dangerous way to structure governance authority, perhaps second only to a committee of academicians. To distinguish between the ways large organizations coordinate their work and the ways they govern their people, diagnostic assessment helps tease apart these important distinctions. As such, the diagnostic discussed in the rest of this chapter has three purposes:

1. To assist people in their workplaces to see the patterns of mature governance.
2. To identify the presence or absence of leadership competencies allied with mature governance.
3. To explain the emerging governance role—*arbiter*—of chief financial officers.

Illustrated in Exhibits 5.4, 5.5, and 5.6, the organizational governance diagnostic assesses the three governance maturity indicators in Exhibit 5.2: moral, internal social configurations, and executive perception of scope of governance responsibility. At each point in the discussion that follows, the governance diagnostic emphasizes the developing role of the finance executive in terms of the CFO's primary government alliances. The three diagnostic templates in Exhibits 5.4–5.6 should be customized for the specific conditions within each company. Detailed instructions for using the diagnostics are located in "Guidelines for Diagnostic Use and Customization of Exhibits 5.4, 5.5, and 5.6" on the Web site.

The governance maturity assessment method presented in the remaining sections of this chapter charts important aspects of the CFO's five interdependent governance alliances, one at a time, using the instrument in Exhibits 5.4, 5.5, and 5.6 with a focus on hierarchy and heterarchy. Two of the governance indicators appear in sequential parts of the diagnostic: internal social configuration and executive responsibility perspective. The discussion integrates the concepts of the third indicator: the parallel moral development stages—law and order and universalism—discussed in previous chapters. The diagnostic demonstration proceeds as follows:

Alliance Focus	Diagnosis Segment
The CEO–CFO alliance	Competencies specific to CEO-CFO team
The executive counsel alliance	Executive responsibility perception
Board alliance	CFO governance participation

Other maturity diagnostic focuses include:

- Discussion of CFO governance maturity in all five alliances with emphasis on the *arbiter* role in heterarchical governance.
- Mature/immature governance examples, using actual excerpts from the SEC allegations/charges related to the 2003 alleged scandal at HealthSouth.
- Primary attention to the developmental work and milestones in the transformation from hierarchy to heterarchy governance practices.
- Identification of actual workplace achievements that express successful navigation of governance maturity milestones, executive leadership, and workplace form.
- The EI competencies most relevant to each governance indicator.
- Governance maturity assessments that rely on foundational principles of the three interdependent components of the triple helix: people, organizational form, and contingent environmental conditions.

In the context of the *CFO Survival Guide*, the nascent emergence of the arbiter role for finance executives places the profession and its members in a position to

www.

EXHIBIT 5.4 CEO-CFO RELATIONSHIP DIAGNOSTIC

Context: Internal social configurations

Assessment: Role relationships and power

Choose a place on the scale from 0 to 5 that best represents how power and authority are distributed in your relationship.

(0) *Hierarchical:* power flows through formal, rank-order authority

(5) *Heterarchical:* power and authority flow according to knowledge, utility, and circumstances

Hierarchy	0	1	2	3	4	5 Heterarchy

EI Relevant Competencies:

Social awareness: Empathy, organizational awareness, service

For each of these three EI competencies as they are evident in your workplace, choose a place on the scale to indicate how governance relationship partners embrace the competency as a governance team and apply it to the organization's governance structure.

Empathy

Hierarchy	0	1	2	3	4	5 Heterarchy

Empathy not applied

Empathy used to sense/ discover best available sources of knowledge and specialist expertise

Organizational Awareness

Hierarchy	0	1	2	3	4	5 Heterarchy

Rank order by structural hierarchy; department function, unit, division

Employee knowledge and utility shape relationship form and determine group/ team configurations

Service

Hierarchy	0	1	2	3	4	5 Heterarchy

Only serve the next highest rank authority; executive service always takes priority

Serve priorities according to the common good; service decisions are autonomous and discerned by people closest to the point of service requirements

lead ethics and accountability at an entirely new level of organizational maturity, while continuing to rely on the foundations of the profession. A CFO who learns to see the work that people perform in the organization from a universalist perspective participates more fully in the organization's pluralistic governance interests. Once the finance executive develops this perspective, the path opens to the concrete possibility of employees joining the governance circle as it reorganizes and matures into a governance heterarchy in which they participate in shaping organizational form, presence, and function. This prospect is exciting: witnessing the deliberately exquisite, if not graceful, and very human transformation of workplaces from the power structures of the hierarchy to the diverse plurality of heterarchy interests. After that, who knows?

The type of work outlined throughout the governance diagnostic focuses the CFO on developing *organizational* and *self*-awareness, two foundational EI competencies with direct relationships to governance maturity. Using these objective assessments allows one to see the relationships between more and more perspectives simultaneously, and how they interdependently relate to one another—shareholder, customer, employee, to name a few. In the making of a great CFO, this section is also one of the most developmentally important for personal learning and evolution from hierarchical to heterarchical governance responsibilities of the financial executive role.

FIRST GOVERNANCE ALLIANCE: THE CEO-CFO

> *Ask one, answer ten. Raise one, understand three. Seeing the rabbit he looses the falcon—he uses the wind to fan the flame—he doesn't spare his eyebrows.*[14]
> The Blue Cliff Record

The first governance alliance is informal and quite personal: the partnership of the CEO and the CFO. While not in the position of sovereign power, the CEO is the leader of the business, and because the language of the corporate hierarchy is financial, the CFO often serves as advisor, confidant, enforcer, liaison, and stand-in for the CEO. Most of this relationship happens internally on a continuous, informal basis. In an organizational governance hierarchy, the CFO functions as an internal governance regulator/administrator. Although the CFO is usually present at all governance-related meetings, governance authority is in other hands. The developing CFO in a governance hierarchy works toward the next stage of organizational and executive development to establish a concrete governance role.

A chief financial officer working seamlessly with a chief executive officer is a thing of beauty to behold. The business news profiles a number of star CEO-CFO pairs. These teams often have a characteristic pattern; when the CEO moves up or out, the CFO follows in short order. A synergistic CFO is a rare treasure for CEOs fortunate enough to have such a partner. A true leader graces the work life of a CFO. Together, these two constitute the cornerstone for a sound organizational governance foundation. The best way to explore the diagnostic is to take it yourself, beginning with the section that assesses perhaps your most important governance alliance, the one you have with your CEO.

After reading through the general instructions in "Guidelines for Diagnostic Use and Customization of Exhibits 5.4, 5.5, and 5.6" on the Web site, turn to the CEO-CFO Relationship Diagnostic in Exhibit 5.4. The first indicator examines the structure of governance power between the CEO and CFO. Does your alliance with your CEO employ a rank-ordered structure in most or all of your mutual activities and communications, or does the alliance work as a partnership that allows each of you to serve in a primary leadership capacity as the need arises? After all, development starts at home. Similarly, examine the ways that you and your CEO deploy some of the most important governance-related EI leadership competencies. When it comes to empathy, is the competency even practiced or is it valued and openly discussed in your alliance activities to identify unexpected information and value creation resources from all employee levels? Do you work together and each share information about organizational awareness with one another? If so, do you structure your insights in terms of hierarchical organizational units alone or can you also identify insights in terms of new or unconventional configurations? Finally, when you speak together of serving the organization in a leadership and governance capacity, do service responsibilities come in the form of rank-ordered assignments or do responsibilities change according to the time, place, and specialty focus?

One of the best ways to demonstrate the range of a good diagnostic tool is to test its specificity and sensitivity across a wide spectrum—in this case, a maturity spectrum. As a case of immaturity, this chapter applies all sections of the diagnostic to the governance of HealthSouth Corporation.

HealthSouth: How Not to Govern Maturely

> *"What is accomplished by hitting a dead man?"*[15]
> *"What is the real truth?"*[16]
>
> The Blue Cliff Record

HealthSouth Corporation (HRC) would seem to be a classic example of governance immaturity, judging from a document filed with the United States District

Court of the Northern District of Alabama, as Civil Action No. CV-03-J-0615-S, wherein the plaintiff, the Securities and Exchange Commission (SEC), filed a Complaint for Injunction and Other Relief against two defendants: HealthSouth Corporation and its CEO, Richard M. Scrushy. Within Civil Action No. CV-03-J-0615-S lies the bones of a purported failure in governance and the CEO behind the alleged offenses. To remind executives exactly how not to govern, excerpts from the Civil Action are inserted at appropriate points throughout the rest of this chapter. For starters, here are the seven Claims for Relief:

COUNT I—FRAUD

Violations of Section 17(a) of the Securities Act [15 U.S.C. § 77q(a)]

COUNT II—FRAUD

Violations of Section 10(b) of the Exchange Act [15. U.S.C. § 78j(b)] and Rule 10b-5 thereunder [17 C.F.R. § 240.10b-5]

COUNT III—REPORTING PROVISIONS

HRC Liability for Violating Section 13(a) of the Exchange Act [15 U.S.C. § 78m(a)] and Rules 12b-20 13a-1 and 13a-13 thereunder [17 C.F.R. §§ 240.12-20, 240.13a-1 and 240.13a-13]

COUNT IV—AIDING AND ABETTING REPORTING PROVISIONS

Liability of Scrushy for Aiding and Abetting HRC's Violations of Section 13(a) of the Exchange Act [15 U.S.C. § 78m(a)] and Rules 12b-20, 13a-1 and 13a-13 thereunder [17 C.F.R. §§ 240.12-20, 240.13a-1 and 13a-13]

COUNT V—BOOKS AND RECORDS AND INTERNAL CONTROLS VIOLATIONS

HRC's Violations of Sections 13(b)(2)(A) and 13(b)(2)(B) of the Exchange Act [15 U.S.C. §§ 78m(b)(2)(A) and 78m(b)(2)(B)]

COUNT VI—AIDING AND BETTING BOOKS AND RECORDS AND INTERNAL CONTROLS VIOLATIONS

Liability of Scrushy for Aiding and Abetting HRC's Violations of Sections 13(b)(2)(A) and 13(b)(2)(B) of the Exchange Act [15 U.S.C. §§ 78m(b)(2)(A) and 78m(b)(2)(B)]

COUNT VII—BOOKS AND RECORDS AND INTERNAL CONTROLS VIOLATIONS

Liability of Scrushy for Violating Section 13(b)(5) of the Exchange Act [15 U.S.C. §§78m(b)(5)] and Rule 13b2-1 [17 C.F.R. § 240.13b2-1] thereunder[17]

"Fraud." "Violation of SEC reporting provisions." "Books and records and internal control violations." These serious allegations offer a vivid example of how not to govern. Let us look at some of the particulars of the defendants of these serious accusations. *Fortune* magazine columnist Geoffrey Colvin[18] took up a large portion of his column one month addressing these accusations with a cartoon caricature of an obese businessman dressed in top hat, tie, striped trousers, complete with gold watch chain and handkerchief in vest pocket. A pacifier plugs the mouth of his tiny head atop a corpulent body; a teddy bear is clutched in his right hand, his bulk hunkered down on a baby carriage. The caption reads, "HealthSouth had a baby company's culture in a giant company's body." The picture and caption reflect the developmental governance dilemma perfectly. One might suspect Mr. Colvin of being a student of human development as he deftly analyzes three common pathologies, not only with HealthSouth, but also in all the "scandal companies."

The number-one pathology is the baby-company-in-a-giant-body characteristic already mentioned; however, Colvin astutely notes that all the unprincipled actions occurred in companies that were *real babies* in terms of the number of years they had been in business. The number-two pathology is greed. Colvin also puts a developmental spin on "greed," in that the unethical behavior stemmed from a deluded "personal greed" of founders and other executives who "believed deeply that they deserved everything they got, regardless of how they got it, because they had created their success."[19] Number three is short-term thinking, but again the twist: the unprincipled executives demanded slavish adherence to Wall Street expectations, and making the numbers grew into an obsession. To summarize, immaturity may well be spotted when all three deficiencies are present in a youngster of a company, run by a greedy founder (aided and abetted by equally greedy sidekick executives), that treats Wall Street expectations like royal wishes.

And the CEO-CFO connection? Defendants' profile: HealthSouth Corporation (HRC) headquartered in Birmingham, Alabama; incorporated in Delaware in 1984; went public in 1986. HRC has a presence in eighteen hundred U.S. and non-U.S. locations. In the United States, HRC is the largest provider of outpatient surgery, diagnostic, and rehabilitative healthcare services. HRC stock is listed on the NYSE; for fiscal year 2001, HRC reported revenues of $4 billion and net income of $76 million.

The founder of HRC is forty-nine-year-old Richard M. Scrushy. He took the HRC chairman position in 1994; he has held the position of CEO of HealthSouth for most of its history. According to testimony, a short time after HRC went public, Scrushy began directing HRC accountants to "materially inflate HRC's earning to match Wall Street analysts' expectations." In conjunction with the 2003 SEC lawsuit against HRC and Scrushy, *CNNMoney* reported (March 19, 2003) that forty-two-year-old Weston Smith, former CFO of HealthSouth, agreed to plead guilty to fraud charges and to cooperate in the investigation of HealthSouth begun by the SEC in September 2002. The SEC corroborates the maturity of this governance alliance:

> Since 1999, HealthSouth Corp. ("HRC"), one of the nation's largest healthcare providers, has overstated its earnings by at least $1.4 billion. This massive overstatement occurred because HRC's founder, Chief Executive Officer and Chairman of the Board, Richard M. Scrushy ("Scrushy"), insisted that HRC meet or exceed earnings expectations established by Wall Street analysts. When HRC's earnings fell short of such estimates, Scrushy directed HRC's accounting personnel to "fix it" by artificially inflating the company's earnings to match Wall Street expectations. To balance HRC's books, the false increases in earnings were matched by false increases in HRC's assets. By the third quarter of 2002, HRC's assets were overstated by at least $800 million, or approximately 10 percent of total assets. HRC's most recent reports filed with the Commission continue to reflect the fraudulent numbers. Despite the fact that HRC's financial statements were materially misstated, on August 14, 2002, Scrushy certified under oath that HRC's 2001 Form 10-K contained "no untrue statement of a material fact." In truth, the financial statements filed with this report overstated HRC's earnings, identified on HRC's income statement as "Income Before Income Taxes And Minority Interests," by at least 4,700%. Defendant HRC has engaged in, and unless restrained and enjoined by this Court, will continue to engage in, acts and practices which constitute and will constitute violations of [sections of the SEC Exchange Act].[20]

A long line of defendants precedes the accused CEO and CFO at HealthSouth. If Scrushy and Smith are found guilty, they will join a cadre of people in other companies who have been tried and found guilty. For the Tycos, WorldComs, Enrons, and now potentially HealthSouth, law-and-order regulators like the SEC deal with people in executive positions who reside nowhere near the hierarchy/law-and-order level of development. Convicted executives and others facing charges have another thing in common: The word of the CEO (and often founder) is viewed as a divine decree that carries severe punishment if not carried out. Executives who live in the early stages of moral and psychosocial maturity cannot possibly see and understand workplace conditions as they are. Perhaps that is what makes them easy to spot, if only someone is looking—that is, these people actually *see* many fewer perspectives (i.e., everything is "about me") and govern accordingly. In short, fewer governance perspectives mean fewer options, so their patterns are more predictable. Check any workplace for the unethical pattern discussed so far:

- CEO's word is the law.
- The company is a relative youngster, often still run by its founder.

- Executive greed is based on a belief in personal entitlement because of perceived personal effort.
- Pathological obsession and obeisance to Wall Street and capital markets versus attention to company internal health and well-being. In fact, the latter are regularly sacrificed for the former.

There is a timely message for CFOs in this kind of pattern as they work out their governance relationships with their CEOs. Before entering the heady domain of governance, pause to review and renew personal commitment to the responsibilities that count the most in the work life of a CFO. First and foremost, running the accounting/finance function is always the first priority of the chief financial officer. No matter how great and mature the finance executive, without the AFF staff and the systems they manage, there is minimal substance to the executive position (very small companies with a one-person AFF being the exception). The CFO is no different from anyone else; people and the work they do hold up the leaders.

Governance Development Work: Hierarchy to Heterarchy

Hierarchies are not the dark lords of the business governance world. Contrary to some radical activist statements, a hierarchy is a relatively mature form of social organization. In stark contrast to the HealthSouth story, more mature executives who govern hierarchically are more likely to conform to standard principles of ethical behavior, and eventually become open to a universalist moral view. Some of the developmental work required for CEOs and CFOs as they move their workplaces from a governance hierarchy structure to a heterarchy that focuses on moral universalist milestones include:

1. In most organizations today, the CEO and CFO are the leaders. Whereas the hierarchy assumes one primary leader, the heterarchy opens to *coleadership,* even if the official titles remain hierarchical.

2. The increasing self- and organizational awareness contributes directly to the emerging ability to see other points of view; this expansion becomes a definite asset when the perspectives of the CEO and CFO are allied. "Allied" does not mean exactly alike, but rather complementary.

3. Expanding awareness and multiple perspectives hone the ability to see more contingent conditions depending on specific situations.

4. The CEO and CFO understand that their ethical maturity creates fertile ground for other kinds of maturity. Specifically, when the CEO and CFO openly challenge one another's postures in an attempt to learn more from one another, other executives are encouraged to act more conscientiously

and to learn more about their own significant leadership identities relative to peers.

5. Because of the openness of the CEO and CFO, others feel more self-confident in expressing their own views.

These five earmarks of a CEO-CFO partnership characterize executives who model the way into more mature forms of organizational governance and governance priorities. In fact, to assess CEO-CFO maturity, turn your attention to the first part of Exhibit 5.4 and assess role relationships and power within the current internal social configuration. Next, assess with your CEO the list of five CEO-CFO partnership characteristics presented here, each rated 1 to 5. Then average—and perhaps weight each average for relative importance. Parenthetical numbers are sample assessments.

1. CEO-CFO demonstrate coleadership (3)
2. CEO-CFO see from multiple perspectives; diverse yet allied. (4)
3. CEO-CFO appreciate that conditions vary in each specific situation. (2)
4. CEO-CFO create a learning environment by respecting, yet challenging viewpoints. (4)
5. CEO-CFO make others feel comfortable enough to express their own views. (2)

Internal social configuration simple-average calculation:
$$3+4+2+4+2 = 15/5 = 3.$$

The precision of this calculation comes about as close to indicating the CEO-CFO place on the maturity scale as GAAP statements come to exact depiction of financial position. In fact, one could argue that the maturity calculation indicator is a better predictor than the GAAP statement because financial position changes constantly—only convention holds that the month-end picture is *actual*—whereas human behavior matures over long periods, sometimes lifetimes. But then, human behavior is the real thing.

The diagnostics broadly place the analysis group or individual (here, the CEO-CFO) on a relative maturity scale; however, because the whole point of maturity measurement is to discover a starting point and enhance the rate of development, the CEO-CFO team can use the individual criteria to identify where the governance relationship can be made more mature. The "3" average is exactly like the profit/loss line on an income statement: an interesting indicator, but only a starting point. Companies that have a mature performance measurement and management system know that financial measures are a balanced part of a much larger set of measures (e.g., customer, community, suppliers, process, and so on), and executives guide performance by working with the precursor or leading measures (e.g., customer, supplier) to affect the lagging financial results measures. So, in this CEO-CFO example, the team needs to attend most to their "2-rated" criteria, that is, numbers 3 and 5 on the assessment. Actual developmental work should be focused on areas of weakness. The subsequent four governance alliance discussions do not present sample calculations; fictitious numbers aren't very interesting. However, in actual application, using quantitative maturity scales is important, because:

- When the diagnostics are applied to actual individuals or groups, an income statement–type maturity number on the hierarchy-heterarchy maturity scale directs developmental action, like using the profit/loss figure as a starting point.

- The maturity number means nothing without additional context. Construct specific criteria for a successful CEO-CFO relationship, such as the quantitative example just given.

- The thinking process during the crafting and quantification of criteria naturally yields rich information and anecdotes that greatly clarify future development work of the CEO-CFO governance alliance.

- Periodically (no less than every six months because behavior changes take time) reassess the governance alliance criteria being worked on privately (CEO and CFO) and with selected peers, subordinates, or whatever group composition is appropriate. Reassessment provides a rough indicator of progress.

- Importantly, a trusted group of governance alliance comrades who know the competencies help each other when they observe slips into old behavior. This support can only exist when targeted maturity criteria have been specifically identified.

So, just because the next four governance alliance sections do not present numbers, don't skip your own quantitative work when taking the assessments. The next point of attention becomes obvious: How to improve the less mature criteria, for example, the "2-rated criteria" in the CEO-CFO example. Some answers will be specific to the context of the individuals themselves; however, when navigating from hierarchy to heterarchy behaviors a common set of EI competencies serves in all cases. In this CEO-CFO alliance example, the competencies are empathy, organizational awareness, and service orientation as shown in Exhibit 5.4.

Best Corporate Citizens

The term "best corporate citizens" owes its origin to an annual report published in the bimonthly, *Business Ethics: Corporate Social Responsibility Report*.[21] *Business Ethics* publishes a report called *America's 100 Best Corporate Citizens*. The ranking is based on "companies that serve a variety of stakeholders well." The "stakeholder" groups are shareholders plus an additional seven "social stakeholders": community, minorities, women, employees, environment, non-U.S. stakeholders, and customers. Data and ranking make use of independent research and data bases (the socially screened Domini Index and KLD Research and Analytics). Some CEO-CFO alliances are a major factor in governing these best corporate citizens. Let us take a look at a real CEO-CFO team to see how they are doing on the maturity indicators.

Growth and Investment in Balance   If one CFO's name in the United States is commonly recognized for reasons other than the perp walk, that name may well be David Shedlarz, CFO of Pfizer.[22] In 1976, as a fresh MBA from New York University, Shedlarz came to work at Pfizer and has been there ever since (*longevity with the firm shows long-term interest in Pfizer's well-being*). He began as a financial analyst in the Brooklyn manufacturing facility, Pfizer's first home. Shedlarz, now in his mid-fifties, was promoted from vice president of finance to CFO in July 1995.

Almost from the start, his career paralleled CEO William C. Steere's. He rotated with the future CEO through several assignments before following him to headquarters in 1992[23] (*executive teamwork and collaboration; commitment to relationship*). After Steere's retirement in 2001, his successor, CEO Hank McKinnell, formed the same sort of collaborative arrangement with Shedlarz, as evidenced in a September 16, 2002, vignette in *Fortune:*

> At 8:30 in the morning of Aug. 13, one day before the executives of 947 American corporations had to swear, so help them God, that their financial statements were true, 15 people piled into a conference room on the 22nd floor of Pfizer's Manhattan headquarters. Awaiting them on the table were 300-page binders containing a year's worth of financial statements and detailed explanations—what is considered revenue, how Pfizer accounts for capital expenditures, how data come in from distant locations to headquarters, and so on (*trustworthiness, transparency, conscientiousness*). CFO David Shedlarz asked the two KPMG auditors a simple question: "If you were me, would you prepare the statements differently?" No, they replied.
>
> Shedlarz signed off. For Pfizer the two-hour ceremony was largely perfunctory, because the company already thinks of itself as one of the good guys (*self-confidence, organizational awareness*). It doesn't report pro forma earnings (*beyond conformity*), doesn't pay auditors for consulting work (*ethical behavior before Sarbanes/Oxley required it*), maintains a 15-person governance department (*attention to governance before it was a public issue*), and is regularly praised for the independence of its board (*inspiration, initiative*). "We had no hesitations whatsoever," says CEO Hank McKinnell, who also certified the numbers

(*self-confidence, transparency*). Other companies, though, fretted"[24] (*not as mature, transparent, self-confident, and so on, as Pfizer*).

Steere, McKinnell, and Shedlarz all believe firmly in balancing growth and investment, and their consistent actions make good on this belief. The first time Shedlarz articulated the notion of balancing growth and investment was in 1997: "We thought framing the issue in those terms was an effective way to put forward the strategy of the company.""[25] Another example: in 1998–99 (the era of the Viagra rollout and Celebrex launch), Pfizer's share price soared, and the company's stock held "the highest price-earnings ratio in the drug sector." Shedlarz could see (*multiple perspectives*) that analysts were uncertain whether or not Pfizer executives would stand by their "balanced growth and investment" story. "We saw that the analysts were waiting for guidance," Shedlarz said. "It was clear they hadn't concluded whether the balance theme would prevail, or that more smoothing of earnings would be seen."[26] So in mid-February, Steere, Shedlarz, and seven other executives on the corporate management committee gathered to consider what earnings would be for the upcoming quarters, and what Pfizer should say about them, if anything (*collaboration, teamwork, participative decision making*).

On the more personal side, Pfizer's pain reliever, Celebrex, is personal for David Shedlarz. He has taken the analgesic to

> help combat the near-constant pain he feels from a horrific accident he suffered in the summer of 1996. Although reluctant to talk about it, and visibly emotional (*emotionally aware, transparent*) as he does, Shedlarz recalls that it happened two days into a rare two-week vacation. He was riding his bicycle when he was sideswiped by a minivan. His pelvis was broken in five places. His doctor said he'd never seen anyone with such bad breaks live.
>
> As frightening as the accident was, Shedlarz wouldn't let it slow him down. Within a month, while still convalescing at home, he put in as many hours as he could (*achievement, self-control, adaptability, initiative*). Within two months, chairman and CEO William C. Steere Jr. called to say he wanted Shedlarz to add some operating experience (*mentoring; cross-functional experience*) to his résumé and run Pfizer's then–$1.5 billion medical-technology group. "This is either a very wonderful thing or a cruel joke," Shedlarz had quipped.[27]
>
> Running a business that makes medical devices for people who have suffered through traumatic accidents like his wasn't a joke. And Shedlarz wasn't joking when he came back a year later and advised Steere to sell the group (*self-confidence, adaptability, organization awareness*). If the company was serious about its pharmaceuticals focus, then medical technology didn't make sense (*analytical and strategic skills*).
>
> The sale was completed in 11 months, because, Shedlarz said, "it was the most humanistic way to deal with a tough decision" (*moral universalism*). Pfizer had sold many businesses in previous years, and intellectually, Shedlarz had al-

ways understood the impact of a divestiture—jobs lost, people with a long history at Pfizer forced to leave the fold. But this time it was different. This time he found the experience so "heart-wrenching" (*empathy*) he surprised even himself. "My own feelings of empathy were heightened by the accident," he acknowledges.[28]

After reading this kind of CEO-CFO executive profile, pick up any popular business magazine—*Fortune, Forbes, CFO*—and at random read any article that focuses on one executive. You will probably have to settle for a CEO unless you consult a publication like *CFO Magazine*, because only "scandal company" CFOs seem to make the general business press. As you read, do your own annotation based on the developmental knowledge you have gained so far. At the end of the article, there is a very good chance that you can name the executive's moral and psychosocial maturity, and the maturity of his/her identity. You may be surprised at how much you know and how much you are ready to practice developmental assessment.

How does this relate to governance maturity? In just about every way. Governance isn't a banner to be brought out and waved on appropriate ethical occasions. Plainly stated, if you want to really understand the governance system of any organization, there is nowhere else to look but to the competence or incompetence of the leaders themselves. Exhibit 5.2 is only a high-level picture of governance. To see where governance lives and breathes, examine the leadership competencies of the executive team, especially their presence or absence in the CEO-CFO partnership.

Relevant EI Competencies

The EI competency set used to assess internal social configurations in the CEO-CFO governance alliance is social awareness: empathy, organizational awareness, and service. The scales on Exhibit 5.4 measure role relationships and power. The scale continuum moves from a formal, rank-ordered authority to power distribution according to knowledge, utility, and circumstance (i.e., hierarchy to heterarchy). Developmental work goes on between 0 and 5, with 5 representing the developmental milestone goal. The work itself is development of the EI competencies. The progression has a sequence.

- Exhibit 5.4 must be used first, to assess the entire workplace. This is the index against which all other groups or individual maturity is gauged.
- Then Exhibit 5.4 can be utilized to diagnosis any other specific individual or group role and power relationships, and to discover a governance maturity level on the overall internal social configuration scale.

While each EI leadership competency is of interest in governance work, particular competencies rise in importance when addressing the CEO-CFO governance relationship and its impact on the workplace.

Empathy. As David Shedlarz speaks of his own empathy being heightened by his serious accident, and his consequent ability to feel the pain of longtime Pfizer employees terminated during divestitures and the resultant disruption in their lives, he means what he says. When he uses the words "heart wrenching," he is describing emotional distress. This classic description of compassion is gained from personal experience, often from deep emotional traumas or life-and-death incidents like Shedlarz's. Empathy is not an intellectual experience; it is an emotional experience wherein one person shares the deep emotion of another— any emotion, not just disturbing ones. Empathy is frequently joyous and cause for celebration.

Only a person who has reached some level of moral universalism and a conscientious self-identity can experience empathy, the capacity to see through others' eyes. The governance work of leaders includes creating opportunities that allow people in the workplace to cultivate empathy. These opportunities can come unexpectedly. Several years ago, a project team at Sikorsky Helicopter was building a new cost system. For some participants, it was the first time they had ever sat across the same table from their counterparts from other functions. In the process of describing the cost information that was important to them, team members explained a great deal about their functions, and a mutual sense of work empathy began to arise. Heartfelt remarks clearly exhibited a breakthrough far beyond a technical cost system. One representative observation: "I had no idea that the subassemblies I sent you were causing you so much trouble. We'll have to take a look at this right away." Empathy takes courage and the will to change things for the better.

Organizational awareness. Empathy leads naturally to organizational awareness. Organizational awareness depends upon official and unofficial sources of information. The more coworkers interact to identify mutual areas of improvement or to collaborate on innovations, the more they learn about one another's roles. From there it is a small step to seeing more about self and others, and how workplace processes can go more smoothly. Notice the interdependence of organizational awareness with increasing self-awareness. Executives and managers should go out of their way to create work structures that inherently raise organizational awareness.

Service. Awareness and genuine empathy generate a desire to serve others well. At the very least, one might do so in hopes of reciprocal treatment. Notice how all three competencies working together begin to bridge and shape social configurations that shift silo functions working in isolation toward collaboration.

Role Relationships and Power: The CEO and CFO

Within the CEO-CFO governance alliance, three additional leadership competencies rise in influence: transparency, optimism, and teamwork and collaboration. The importance of the third competence in this set, teamwork and collaboration, should be obvious. These same three competencies can serve for other executive and management governance assessments.

Transparency. The CEO-CFO relationship is the right place to begin working toward more organization-wide transparency. Practicing personal transparency in important professional relationships significantly sustains and deepens trust. Mistrust is especially damaging at the executive level because of the trickle-down effect. Between a CEO and CFO there is absolutely no room for mistrust. From a governance point of view, if the CEO and CFO cannot be candid and transparent with each other, how can they hope to lead the workplace in such an attribute? The CEO-CFO team who demonstrates mastery in the transparency dimension leads openly; they readily discuss what they believe and value, why they do what they do, and yes, how they feel. Such honest dialogue about values and behavior cannot help but lead to better discovery of governance issues and their remedies.

Optimism. The CEO-CFO team carries an enormous load in terms of overall responsibility to everyone else in the workplace. Still, to inspire and influence, the two executives must generally lead with optimistic energy. Things often go differently than expected and sometimes go terribly wrong. When a leader throws in the towel, everyone else follows. To ameliorate the inevitable effects of bad news and thorny problems, the CEO and CFO can pledge a private pact: no matter how bad things get, together we will search and find positive alternatives. In their governance role, the CEO-CFO can never go wrong in guiding the firm from an energized posture rather than from an attitude of gloom and doom.

Governing Patterns: With Good Work, There Is Nothing to Hide

Good governance, like profit and loss, is the result of prior efforts. Therefore, the best way for CEOs and CFOs to assure a healthy governance system is to attend to its inputs: mature executive behavior, ethical decision making day after day, and appropriate acknowledgment of anyone in the organization who behaves more or less according to mature standards. Governance is built one person, one decision at a time. No corporate-wide integrity program ever outweighs the actions of its leaders.

The best way to make progress in developing leadership competencies is to learn from example, and of course to create deliberate forums for practice. Intentional developmental work, as seen in the following examples, sets foundational patterns necessary for expansion to group interaction. These practices, in and of themselves, begin to spin out into ethical governance patterns.

- Find a mentor with the qualities you wish to develop and meet regularly to discuss the specific competencies you are working on.
- In a very good CEO-CFO relationship, the twosome might mentor each other.
- Taking the lead, the CEO and CFO should consciously demonstrate empathy, transparency, optimism, and an attitude of service in all encounters, but especially during executive counsel meetings and other formal public gatherings. (The word choice of "counsel" is deliberately preferred to "council." Anyone can sit around a conference table and look like a council, but it takes hands-on executive leadership to *counsel* the CEO, one another, and the rest of the people in the workplace.)
- Encourage openness and participation at all times with everyone.

Changing the patterns of relationship behavior takes practice, but soon the affinities and connections that grow from the practice make it inconceivable to return to less mature ways. In short order, the process comes quite naturally and feels more humane. Reading about the method here is no substitute for applying the developmental work to self and others. The faces of an actual group or individual make the exercise come alive.

The single most important governing pattern for the CEO and CFO to establish in their governance alliance is balance. In this case, balance is interior and exterior. Interior balance focuses on the two people; exterior balance focuses on governance in terms of the needs and interests of all organizational stakeholders. This interior/exterior balancing act is perfectly suited to these two roles. More and more, the person in the CEO role works to constantly scan the exterior environment of the organization in terms of Wall Street, shareholder, board, customer, community, and competitive interests. In a complementary fashion, by nature of the managerial accounting responsibilities that go with the role, the CFO knows the internal organizational environment as well as any senior executive. Working as a governance alliance team, the CEO and CFO complement one another with their external and internal focuses as they see to the needs of the organization's business units and other internal stakeholders.

When the CEO-CFO governance alliance works in the broad community of all organizational stakeholders, including stakeholders that never set foot inside the organization, balance is essential. Closer to home, employees remain underrepresented stakeholders in organizational governance, and the top-heavy situation depicted in Exhibit 5.1 places too much influence in the hands of people who do no work and only extract wealth. Developmental systems overwhelmingly suggest that such a system is unsustainable and, as such, will fail as people learn to recognize and correct the imbalance. This kind of process generally takes two forms: gradual evolution or sudden revolution and collapse. Which would you rather lead?

In the evolutionary scenario, the CFO uses the capacity of the office to learn about and represent employee interests vital to the success of the organization—profitable and otherwise. Depending on how the financial executive negotiates this new role with other employee groups, the CFO becomes a classic representational spokesperson in a truly democratic sense—speaking for the employees to balance their needs against those of other stakeholders. Importantly, as a governance alliance that first and foremost must address the overall, sustainable, long-term needs of many constituents, the CEO-CFO alliance works within the greater executive counsel to ensure that the work-related decisions (the ones that lead to any hope of value creation) represent sustainable internal and external goals. Shareholder wealth only cuts one way.

THE SECOND GOVERNANCE ALLIANCE: THE CFO AND EXECUTIVE COUNSEL

> *Social behaviour in wolves is based . . . on a dominance—subdominance—submission basis. A hierarchy develops and is maintained within the pack through ritual behaviours. The dominant wolf shows confident postures, makes confident sounds and marks his territory with confidence. He walks with stiff legs and high, moderately wagging tail. He sniffs nose to nose. . . . The subdominant tag along in a contented fashion with more subdued behaviours while the submissive perform ritual passive behaviours, groveling with the head and tail down, crawling on the belly and trying to lick the lips of the dominant wolf. The supersubmissive might urinate in abject submission at the same time.*[29]
>
> Bruce Fogle, D.V.M.

People are almost as transparent as wolves in physically displaying their places in a governance hierarchy. Such displays can even be observed at the executive level, but a heterarchy is a place of equals. The internal social configuration of an executive counsel drives ethical or unethical behavior in several ways. Even the most mature governance hierarchy by the very nature of its rank-order authority creates some uneasiness, thoughts of job insecurity, and a consistent low-hum of not-knowing in the chain of command. The work in Exhibit 5.5, *Executive Responsibility Perceptions,* maps the way to a more pluralistic form of organizational governance. The focuses included in the diagnostic bridge the development work between the foundational CEO-CFO governance alliance and the second governance alliance: the executive counsel as a larger, better informed governance team.

The executive counsel truly committed to the health and longevity of the workplace walks a clear path: attention to people and the work they do. The volume of the buzzing and mumbling about this "people" realization is increasing in many moderately mature hierarchies, but the methods to capture the human-resource potential remain elusive. Just as with governance itself, this human potential does not reside in a project or program, or in posters and banners, and certainly not in complimentary doughnuts every Friday morning. *Executive counsel governance guides work priorities, increases work effectiveness, and orchestrates encounters that increase employee self- and social awareness in the scope of their governance responsibility.* This definition of executive governance is a pretty good one. Let us examine it more closely.

Executive counsel governance activities and perspectives center on how the organization relates to other organizations and stakeholders, particularly employees. With executive counsel governance relationships as its focus, Exhibit 5.5 provides the format for exploring governance maturity in the executive counsel. Take a moment to read the descriptive statements in Exhibit 5.5 beneath "Executive Responsibility Perceptions." Three major focuses lead to greater governance maturity: (1) seeing the organization as a set of interdependent networks, (2) rethinking the competitive paradigm in terms of cooperative relationships, and (3) enhancing work conditions rather than controlling workers.

Specifically each of these three focuses significantly expands the scope (and maturity) of executive counsel governance responsibilities in the following three ways:

1. The current predominance of *financial abstractions* and the focus on creating *shareholder wealth* supports rigid hierarchical governance structures, especially like the one in Exhibit 5.1. Financial symbols make it easy for executives to perceive one undifferentiated company in a competitive paradigm. The developmental work to reshape perception so as to see the workplace as a network of many interdependent systems focuses on:

   - Executive orchestration of cross-functional project teams, problem-solving groups, and any other opportunity that encourages people to learn about and from one another.

   - Executive-led IT system projects intended to make information accessible, linked, and relevant.

   - For the CFO, steadily moving the AFF function out into operational areas.

2. The *competitive paradigm* builds barriers (i.e., the company against everyone else). As reported in *Fortune,* for example, Jamie Dimon, CEO of Bank One, demonstrated this perfectly in an opening statement to a "rank-and-file" crowd of Bank One employees: "'What do I think of our competitors?' Dimon shouts by way of intro. . . . Dimon yanks off his turquoise tie and

www.

EXHIBIT **5.5** THE EXECUTIVE COUNSEL

Context: Executive responsibility perceptions

Assessment: Perspective on role in company-wide governance

Choose a place on the scale from 0 to 5 that best represents how executive(s) perceive their scope of governance as characterized for hierarchical and heterarchical governance forms on the scale below.

Hierarchy 0   1   2   3   4   5 Heterarchy

Company as machine; financial abstractions	Company as network of interdependent systems
Competitive paradigm for all relationships	Cooperative paradigm whenever possible
Governance focused on employee control	Governance focused on work enhancement

EI Relevant Competencies:

Relationship management: Influence, conflict management, change catalyst

Characterize the ways that the executive counsel uses the following three EI leadership competencies in its governance activities that apply to employee relationship management.

| Influence |

Hierarchy 0   1   2   3   4   5 Heterarchy

Mandated compliance   Participative

| Conflict
Management |

Hierarchy 0   1   2   3   4   5 Heterarchy

Mandated compliance   Bipartisan consensus

| Change
Catalyst |

Hierarchy 0   1   2   3   4   5 Heterarchy

Authority-based   Participative and
                                                       investigative

---

chops the air like a karate master. 'I hate them. I want them to bleed!'" The *Fortune* writer reports immediately after this that Mr. Dimon made a "masterful tonal switch." Still, the very next thing he supposedly said in what one might assume was a softer tone was, "Winning [is] about one thing—how much you want it!"[30] And the crowd goes wild, or something to that effect. This example shows a large hierarchy reverting for just a few hours to a tribal mode. Elsewhere in more mature organizations, developmental work to reshape perception and see the workplace as part of an interdependent, *cooperative* world is actually starting to be quite evident:

- Strategic alliances and joint ventures to draw on the strengths of partners outside the company.

- Interorganizational cost management (see the work of Robin Cooper and Regine Slagmulder).[31]

- The emergence of a business philosophy dubbed *coopetion* (versus competition).

3. Regarding employees, the hierarchical governance statement, "You are either with the company or against the company," suggests that employee control is the governance priority. Work enhancement is the priority in the heterarchy.

So, the governance work of the heterarchy-bound executive team is to break down every barrier to productive relationships that it comes across. With this objective in mind, the governance responsibilities and developmental work of executives include:

- Care and attention to the resource needs of interlocking systems comprised of individuals and groups of people within the company.

- Informing decisions with actual economic conditions and market demand as opposed to setting the workplace up for failure with unrealistic revenue and profit targets.

- Assuring ecological sanity so that resources will be available to the workplace long into the future.

- Contributing as good community citizens to home communities.

Relevant EI Competencies

Governance cannot function outside of relationship. A governor must have people to govern. So, it makes sense that the three EI competencies most relevant to the executive governance alliance would come from the relationship management set. The relationship management competency assessment at the bottom half of Exhibit 5.5 reinforces the importance of stakeholder relationships in executive counsel governance activities.

Influence   Governance cannot exist without influence between the one who governs and the one governed. The form of influence a leader uses changes with leadership maturity. In models of hierarchical governance, "influence" is usually autocratic—ruling by oneself. All executives, but especially the CFO, must look for employee participation opportunities as more heterarchical governance practices unfold.

Influence is an EI leadership competency closely linked with the dynamics of another—inspiration. Inspirational CFOs sense and deliver a persuasive argument with just the right appeal to match the disposition of the listener dozens of times every day. As heterarchical governance takes root, so do decision-by-consensus practices and more direct participation in broader aspects of the workplace by more people. The CFO must recognize that more people need to have more information about the business, such as what measures and drivers influence their work. Specifically, how well does your company's executive counsel influence stakeholders, especially employees, to participate in important areas of organizational governance? The alternative is a workforce that follows autocratic protocols and remains untapped in terms of more effective ways to govern.

Conflict Management   Similarly, does your executive counsel manage conflict by mandating compliance to a rigid set of rules for employee work and behavior or reach resolutions based on bipartisan representations of executive and employee positions? As the primary resource guardian, the CFO leads the way to conflict resolution, not by avoiding confrontation, but by heading purposefully into it. In a governance hierarchy, conflicts are settled by fiat and decree by the first person up the ladder who is willing to do so. A great deal of time can be wasted as each authority level defers to the next, sometimes all the way up to the CEO. In a governance heterarchy, differences of opinion are looked at as opportunities for all parties to learn more—around the same table—all at once.

Change Catalyst   Given that organizational change is an essential component of relationship management in governance activities, does your company's executive counsel manage organizational change initiative with significant employee implications with an authoritative posture or one that encourages broad-based investigation and participation? Change management is a big topic in executive circles, and executives are supposed to be change agents. Companies that use hierarchical forms of governance are not built for agile forms of change. Like an aircraft carrier built for stability, on the strength of rank and authority, executive counsels and the people they lead change course very slowly. In contrast, the heterarchical governance structure focuses more on the people and less on the structure. As such, like an America's Cup yacht, employees at all levels of the heterarchically governed organization work to navigate change more quickly as a team coordinating many individual levels of expertise toward a common new challenge. What might an executive counsel member do to model and facilitate this kind of greater governance maturity for employee stakeholders? A very simple and effective entry point is to debunk the myth of the all-knowing executive.[32]

The Power of "I Don't Know"

Used well, the words "I don't know" deepen relationships, uncover innovations, and swiftly develop leadership competence. The statement also makes a fine entry point to the questions of governance and responsibility. "I don't know" used well means that the assertion is *not* employed to evade the truth or to withhold information, but rather to set knowledge boundaries. So, start from the premise that executives do not know. In particular, that they do not have a skillful and articulate answer to the governance question. In fact, executives, just like any group of human beings, rarely *know* what to do, where "know" means absolute certainty about how to run the business. Not many things in the workplace world fall into the "absolute and certain" category, and the work of executive leadership certainly does not.

"I don't know" can be a powerfully human statement—a tacit admission of the need for the participation of other experts and the inadequacy of solo decision making in complex scenarios. "I don't know" means taking responsibility for the limits of personal knowledge and expressing genuine reliance on others' participation for choosing best alternatives. Used well, "I don't know" also means "I am not lying." Imagine the warmth or shock and amazement some workers might feel hearing a top executive say, "I don't know, do you?" for the first time. Better still, imagine the gratification workers can feel when they know they have contributed to explanations, innovations, and workplace improvement. These kinds of interactions create ease between people, and build bonds and collaboration. Even if an executive has never used this three-word sentence before, it is never too late to start. For executives, the patterns of connection with coworkers generated by the statement are worth it in themselves, not to mention the added decision-support information. Depending on who an executive is speaking to and the exact nature of the inquiry, see the "Alliance" feature called—of course—The Power of "I Don't Know" for a pocketful of follow-up statements that intrinsically require more dialogue and next steps. The follow-up creates opportunities for building bonds, collaboration, and above all, trust.

Executive Counsel Governance That Never Grew Up

Executives who have trouble saying, "I don't know," or the equivalent, may also have trouble telling the truth. Here is more from the HealthSouth document.

- On a quarterly basis, HRC's senior officers would present Scrushy with an analysis of HRC's actual, but as yet unreported, earnings for the quarter as compared to Wall Street's expected earnings for the company.

THE POWER OF "I DON'T KNOW" IN BUILDING RELATIONSHIPS

Admittedly, an executive feels momentary discomfort when saying, "I don't know." The disturbance is easily remedied by having a few other statements and questions at hand. Using the I-don't-know mind-set genuinely assures a more rapid increase in the quality and maturity of governance dialogue. First, let's take a look at a leader who definitely knows how to use "I don't know."

Thomas A. Stewart, editor of *Harvard Business Review (HBR)*, has the right idea. In Mr. Stewart's May 2003 editor's letter, "Dear Shareholders," he writes what has to be one of the most honest leadership communiqués on record. The letter's direct and elegantly simple style alone makes it worth reading, and for executives ready to forego business-speak, the column serves as a model for telling the truth in shareholder letters and other forms of stakeholder communications. Mr. Stewart says things like, ". . . I haven't got a clue. . . . [A]m I confident we know the way forward? In a word, nope. . . . [and,] Here's the worst of it: It's in tough times like these that I most need people who will tell me whether the emperor has no clothes, but it's in tough times that these people are most likely to keep silent."[33] Then he makes some remarkably guileless statements about what he does know.

First he says that *HBR* staff members have promised themselves that they are not going to take their customers for granted. In doing so, he suggests that he and his staff members have taken their customers for granted. The second thing Mr. Stewart knows is that *HBR* experts don't understand the twenty-first-century corporate environment any better than anyone else. The last thing he knows— something that every executive needs to know—is "the days of easy promises are over."[34] Imagine your company's shareholder letter taking this tone. Imagine really hard, because "telling the truth" is always the peerless entry point when dealing with human beings. Telling the truth takes on renewed urgency during and after exposure of intentional deceit and betrayal.

These follow-on statements when using the "I don't know" approach are worth memorizing. They intrinsically require next-step action that presents yet other opportunities for building bonds, collaboration, and, above all, trust. Try them out, and see the results for yourself.

- "That's a good question. Let's find out."
- "I'll find out and get back to you."
- "I'm curious why you ask that question. You must have something in mind." (This is a great one for developing listening skills and for providing more context to allow you to respond more precisely.)
- "Let's ask [person's name]." (This one implicitly indicates reliance on others' participation in choosing best alternatives.)
- If the person is in the room, provide an "out" in case that person doesn't know either: for example, "I'm not sure Joe will have the answer either, but let's ask him." Followed by an easy, relaxed, "Joe, I'm wondering if you have any thoughts on this."
- If the person is not present, make sure you or someone else present gives

swift attention to the consultation, and provides feedback to all concerned. If you do it yourself, you create another excellent opportunity for building relationship bonds.

Notice the complete lack of questions in response to a question in this list. This communication principle is important. Questions create barriers to dialogue between leaders and other workers, even executives. Feel the difference between "What are you thinking?" and the above, "You must have something in mind." Questions jar, put people on the spot, and deteriorate intimacy. No matter how well intentioned, questions usually feel like interrogation. A parallel benefit to the executive who practices changing questions to statements should be obvious. Which is better: (1) an executive asking a question, or (2) an executive making a statement? The answer, of course, is the latter. Feel the difference. The question form runs the risk of putting the executive in the light of not knowing, as in incompetent. The statement—unless truly stupid—rarely does.

- [If there was a shortfall] Scrushy would tell HRC's management to "fix it" by recording false earnings.

- HRC's senior accounting personnel then convened a meeting to "fix" the earnings shortfall. By 1997, the attendees referred to these meetings as "family meetings" and referred themselves as "family members."

- Senior accounting personnel discussed what false accounting entries could be made and recorded to inflate reported earnings.

- HRC's accounting personnel designed the false journal entries to the income statement and balance sheet accounts in a manner calculated to avoid detection by the outside auditors. HRC also created false documents to support its fictitious accounting entries.

- While the scheme was ongoing, HRC's senior officers and accounting personnel periodically discussed with Scrushy the burgeoning false financial statements, trying to persuade him to abandon the scheme.

- HRC's accounting personnel advised Scrushy to abandon the earnings manipulation scheme. Scrushy refused, stating in substance, "not until I sell my stock."[35]

If the SEC's claims turn out to be true, what a horrendous story the Health-South saga makes. From a moral developmental viewpoint, the claims paint a picture of extremely immature executives. Observe the obedience to Scrushy's commands, as if no other choice were available. In the allegation statements, Scrushy treats subordinates from the least mature moral stage, while viewing himself through the moral lens of instrumental hedonism. As an internal social configuration, notice the tribal references to "family meetings" and "family members." Feel the psychosocial doubt and shame of the senior executives and accounting personnel that probably motivated them to advise Scrushy to abandon his scheme. For the purposes of this executive governance discussion, notice especially

- The implicit narrowness of the executive perception of the scope of their responsibility.
- The absence of anything resembling hierarchical checks and balances or heterarchical respect for expertise as circumstance dictates.

Notice, too, how the definition of executive governance gets turned inside out: The executive counsel

- Misguides work priorities.
- Decreases work effectiveness.
- Orchestrates encounters that distort employee self- and social awareness.

Best Corporate Citizens for Executive Counsel Governance

Ever notice the tons of articles and books about chief executive officers, but few about a great executive team? Think hierarchical governance. Hierarchies prefer to concentrate authority in a single place. Voila! The story of the CEO emerges. Japanese organizations surface over and over as the best models of heterarchical governance practices. Most notable are The Taiyo Group,[36] and of course, the legendary Toyota Production System (TPS). Toyota—specifically, Toyota Motor Manufacturing in Georgetown, Kentucky, aligns with the heterarchy governance principles in this book. What does Toyota's system have to do with governance? Well, just about everything. The answer has two parts, and both are based on values: heart values and work values.

Heart Values   Toyota plays by Japanese ethical rules, and honor is a very big deal in Japan. Contribution to society versus self is an ancient, respected value in Japan.[37] One could find worse places to explore ethical governance than the values of honor and contribution to society. In the last half of the twentieth century, both honor and contributions to society greatly influenced the rapid rise of the rising-sun country into the world marketplace. The original, prewar *zaibatsu* were huge conglomerates run from the heart of a relatively small, controlling, family-owned umbrella company that considered mutual shareholding across companies an important bond, not a conflict of interest, and intertwined boards of directors as a pooling of knowledge, not a problem with independence. This approach was possible because losing one's honor was unthinkable in this organization form. All these values evolved to the modern *keiretsu,* and the rest is history.

The American business obsession with things Japanese may have been in part a reaction to diversity in values: Honor and contribution to society versus rugged individualism and the profit imperative. "At the heart of the Japanese model was Toyota's system of lean production."[38] The Toyota system and the Japanese cultural values combine to form a highly mature organizational governance model that allows the executive counsel to balance and look after the needs of all company stakeholders, external and internal.

In a heterarchical governance team, the executive counsel fit to governance is not necessarily executive—that is, in terms of being cut off from people and the work they do, as is true in most corporate governance structures. On the Toyota production floor, distinguishing management from workers is quite difficult, basically because, in actual practice, authority on the line is very blurred. No layers of hierarchical administration exist to create political and social distance between management and workers. In hierarchical governance structures, this distance predictably generates two situations: (1) executives know much less about their workplaces, and (2) workers wonder what executives are doing "up there."

Leaders in a heterarchy work with and relate to other employees quite differently from their corporate hierarchy counterparts. Here the Japanese model lays down some underlying governance principles:

Governance Beliefs

Heterarchical	*Hierarchical*
Everyone is worthy of respect	The elite are worthy of more respect
Participation yields better decisions	Mandates and directives make things happen
Long-term community interest	Short-term profit
Market share is best measure	Profit is best measure
Funding from long-term creditors	Funding from short-term investors
Modest ROI on internal investments	High ROI on any investment
Government protects	Government regulates

The characteristics on the left fit heterarchical governance principles and echo Japanese business values. Note the interdependencies on the left as opposed to the relative isolation between people, groups, and ideas on the right. Note the relationship emphasis on the left; on the right, note shareholder wealth priorities. Of course, room exists in the middle for a blending of these two systems and their governance values, just as degrees of maturity exist on the governance scale in each of this chapter's assessments. As for governance, one can easily see that governance relationships, interdependencies, and long-term views naturally cultivate more fertile ground for ethical behavior than do money, mandates, and a short-term perspective. Again, governance is the result of prior ethical decisions and actions based on moral universalism and conscientiousness.

Work Values   How do the heterarchy governance maturity values translate into workplace values? Some points are obvious, like market share and funding sources. The first three heterarchy governance principles listed have the most direct influence on day-to-day operations. The last four have direct impacts on financial functions. As a CFO, imagine a few if/then scenarios:

- If market share were more important than profit.
- If funding came from banks and creditors with whom you have healthy, long-term relationships.
- If capital projects didn't always have to earn the capital rate.
- If government agencies existed to smooth the way for business ventures.

You can probably quite easily daydream about the "then" side of these scenarios:

- Then I could concentrate on market-driven measures instead of financial measures.
- Then I would have so much more time to do real work, not having to deal with analysts and short-term shareholder interests.
- Then I actually can help create some of those great ideas that the production people design.
- Then I would have so much more time to do work that might create new value instead of filling out an unending sequence of government reports that do nothing to change unethical behavior or to assure shareholder security.

In these ways among others, CFO life in a heterarchical governance structure would change. This time is a long way off developmentally because not only does the workplace need to move to the more mature model, but so do government agencies, banks, and capital markets.

The most widespread impacts come from the first two heterarchy beliefs: (1) Everyone is worthy of respect, and (2) Participation yields better decisions. In *Profit Beyond Measure,* Johnson and Bröms explicate the "G factor" that few Western business people can easily understand. The G factor is whatever Toyota does that we in the West don't do, because we already do (a) just-in-time, (b) kanban, (c) andon cords, (d) quality circles, and (e) statistical process control. Basically, to paraphrase Johnson and Bröms, the G factor comes down to this: Toyota operates on the belief that the most important purpose of business is to provide the means for "people to serve people," where everyone is someone else's customer and all employees see the interdependencies in the many interlocking work systems. Relationship is everything, and where that is true, hierarchical forms of dominance governance become archaic.

There is no better way for a leader to practice and assure good governance than to safeguard and nurture the assets of the workplace. These assets are not the financial symbols on a balance sheet. They are people, material, information, space, and relationships. If one accepts Toyota's version of the purpose of work, several principles follow. These principles directly translate and transform work practices and cost structures. The following is a highly condensed summary of the work of Johnson and Bröms at the Toyota manufacturing facility in Georgetown, Kentucky, as described in *Profit Beyond Measure*. Where an asterisk appears, the CFO can make particularly significant contributions, especially if he/she has prior experience in quality work, process improvement projects, and performance measurement/management.

- At every point, work activities must be connected to a customer, so that every worker is both customer and supplier.★

- In the interest of good service and stewardship, this connection conserves resources and uses only what is necessary to meet the downstream customers' needs.★

- The natural environment and its resources are precious.

- Work is carried out through relationships, not by moving material objects (or financial abstractions) around.

- Management work is based on human relationships, not financial symbols.

- Management's responsibility is to assure adequate conditions and resources for everyone in the workplace.

- Cost is a financial abstraction. Only resources can be managed and utilized. Proper utilization of human beings depends on relationship connections.★

- Long-lived and healthy companies (Royal Dutch Shell is the classic example) consider financial measures natural results of work done in ways that are natural (as in natural systems), and they spend most of their time assuring that the workplace is a good place to live.★

- Over the long run, people work well because they are intrinsically motivated, not because of external incentives. Quantitative measures and scorecards kill people's motivation to work. (Incidentally, D. Edwards Deming also held this view and considered such practices "deadly diseases.")★

- Waste is the chronic ailment of hierarchy configurations:
  - Whatever is called "overhead" is waste.
  - Work processes, not costs, need to be managed.
  - Focus on resource utilization within processes, not cost of resources.

- Economies of scale are wasteful; producing "just enough" leads to lower costs.
- Rely on the work itself for the information needed, not on externally produced reports, targets, and analyses.

Anyone who hasn't come across such principles before is bound to be overwhelmed at the magnitude of the shift in worldview. In that case, the following distillation of these work focuses clarifies a CFO's governance duty at every step of the way:

> [M]anagement's job is to help people in a business create and nurture patterns of relationships that connect human talents with human needs in a context that provides everyone a proper livelihood while pursuing activities that ensure a healthy community and a robust natural environment.[39]

Governing Patterns

> *It's like a great mass of fire; approach it, and it will burn off your face.*[40]
> The Blue Cliff Record

Force of governance is felt person to person: a CEO takes an ethical stand in the face of great temptation to do otherwise, and in so doing imbues the executive counsel with honor. A board of directors reprimands a CEO for marginal behavior and makes its point stick by means of its powerful action and intense force of presence. Such leadership performance truly can generate the heat of "a great mass of fire." As a result of the most recent round of scandals and immaturity, some governing patterns for executive counsels are beginning to emerge.

- A shift from executive perception that their primary relationship is with shareholders to a more inclusive viewpoint that includes conscientiousness of a wider circle of stakeholder relationships.
- A rethinking of the imperative of short-term profit and revenue growth as the primary measures of success.
- An appreciation of the wisdom of transparent accountability.
- After the rapid evaporation of trillions of dollars of "wealth," a renewed reliance on the concreteness of people and their work as opposed to financial abstractions.
- A disdain for guile, pretense, and deception.

When all is said and done, mature leaders attract and retain other mature workers who in turn attract and retain customers, whose combined synergy creates financial success. Leaders keep this interrelationship constantly before them in governing the workplace. Emotions are part of this leadership equation, and emotionally intelligent leaders set the tone for the entire workplace community. When a leader despairs and ceases to govern, it is only a matter of time before the despair becomes a self-fulfilling prophecy. In contrast, an inspiring, realistically optimistic leader emanates energy that ripples throughout the work community, thus giving it needed life-sustaining force.

DEGREES OF SEPARATION: THE THIRD, FOURTH, AND FIFTH GOVERNANCE ALLIANCES

Compared to the power and impact of first two governance alliances, the last three are barely actual alliances at all for today's executive counsels and their CFO participants. Alliances with board and shareholders are supposed to be integral parts of corporate governance, but instead they are often scarcely connected to the workplace itself. There are many causes for this separation, but they are explored infrequently compared to the trend in "value management," which translates directly as shareholder wealth maximization. The fifth governance alliance is recognized only by a tiny percentage of governance thinkers. That alliance is with people and their work, and by extension with community stakeholders, as well as the environment where everybody—including shareholders and board members—lives.

For the moment, this discussion concentrates on the two more conventional corporate governance bodies, shareholders and boards, because despite their isolation from cooperative activities that create valuable goods and services, their very different values currently dominate governance priorities in most corporations. The historical path of company governance is a circuitous one. Volumes describe it from various perspectives, but the facts in the Western version come down to the following trajectory:

Path of company governance = family-regulated business based on local market interests → company owner governance

= on-site management + public interest → absentee ownership and professional nonowner management minus public interest → institutional and corporate ownership (e.g., M&A), and professional management with stock-option ownership to allegedly align their interests with absentee owners

The last segment of this path is how the corporate workplace is now governed. This current state marks the conversion of governance from what Michael Useem and others call "a passage from an era of *managerial capitalism* to one of *investor capitalism.*"[41] The critical aspect of the most current shift is that investor capitalism holds only one purpose for one stakeholder: maximization of shareholder wealth. Corporate boards and executives are still reeling from the aftershocks of the initial big M&A quake over the last twenty years, and remain justifiably paranoid about unwanted suitors.

All this makes for extremely uneasy alliances between boards, shareholders, and internal executives who run the workplace day to day. Closer inspection reveals some of the developmental roots and remedies for these troubled relationships in the chronicle of social and organizational evolution. The final section in this chapter establishes the outline of the disaffected-employee situation, and then happily moves into a discussion devoted to a developmental solution. The good news is that because the majority of organizations govern hierarchically, employee relationships are on firmer ground for developmental work, and the authority of the board of directors paves the way for this revolution in governance.[42]

The Distant Affiliation: The Board

> *Swift falcons on a roost.*[43]
>
> The Blue Cliff Record

When corporate charters still demanded—and enforced—that business consider and contribute to the public good, protectors of the community interest were appointed to oversee that the enterprise did just that. Granted, some royal charters authorized the manufacture of weapons of war—never in the interest of the average community member—but even here, guardians made sure the charter grantees held up their end of the bargain.

Intriguingly, today there is a trend for boards of directors charged with a major role in corporate governance to either put distance between themselves and their companies and/or require pricey directors and officers (D&O) insurance against the risks of shareholder suits and executive malfeasance. CFO risk managers are working hard to acquire adequate D&O protection for their board members as well as their executives. The media, too, appears to be letting board members go with either a slap on the wrist or some relatively harmless name-calling. For example, try searching for information regarding where Enron's board was during the cataclysm even though they drew in the range of $300,000 in compensation for their governance role.[44] More recently, where is HealthSouth's board of directors now when governance is sorely needed? The press barely mentions them, and the SEC filing offers not even a whisper about the HealthSouth board.

Defining Directorates   Where *were* Enron's board members? Where *are* HealthSouth's board members now? Perhaps, like today's European monarchs, directorates are merely vestigial remnants of a once-powerful force in corporate governance. Perhaps other, more appropriate functionaries have taken their place. This chapter has already discussed the two most influential governance alliances currently in the workplace: the CEO-CFO partnership and the executive counsel. As it stands, corporate boards run a distant third—if they are even in the race. Occasionally the work of a particularly strong board surfaces, such as the one mentioned in the Pfizer/Shedlarz segment earlier in this chapter, and there are undoubtedly more directorates who do good work that never make the news. Still, the questions linger: Are boards a governance anachronism that should be disbanded? Can this antique form of governance be restored to working order again? The discovery is primarily up to the CEO-CFO alliance, and the time has come for this primary governance alliance to find out what is possible in board reform and to honestly disclose the results. The CEO-CFO investigation would first need to examine three largely unquestioned assumptions about corporate governance and board participation.

Assumption 1: Corporate governance as three parts: executives, board of directors, and shareholders.

Assumption 2: Corporate boards have three major responsibilities: (a) Hire the CEO, (b) Make sure the company has a plan (i.e., a strategy), and (c) Make sure everything—financially—is under control.

Assumption 3: Boards should be independent and not have conflicts of interest. This third assumption has become as good as law (see the Sarbanes Oxley sidebar in Chapter 2).

Consider a few provocative retorts to these assumptions:

- Does governance not assume a working understanding, if not relationship? Please show the working relationship between boards and shareholders.[45]

- Are the "three major responsibilities" expected of directorates the right ones?

- Is anyone missing in the circle of governance? How about the people who make the products and provide the services?

- Is board *independence* the most important issue? Perhaps, there is something even more fundamental and more important than independence. After all, some very mature countries (e.g., Japan) think directorate independence is silly and even harmful. Maybe they know that independence isn't actually possible.

From another voice known for speaking candidly, let us hear another answer to questions about independence and the strength of board member vertebral columns.

Americans tend to operate in groups quite comfortably. And group thinking very often involves consensus. There is an overwhelming social pressure to give in to the CEO, go along with management, not raise a ruckus. Chances are, the people who join boards know the other members—they may belong to the same country clubs or have attended the same schools. Of course, one's comfort level is paramount for a person to be willing to assume the responsibility of a director's position, but that very comfort level undermines the ability of a director to exercise independent judgment—to differ, to challenge, to question.[46]

That was Arthur Levitt, the longest-serving SEC chairman, speaking to the *Harvard Business Review.*

Board Governance and CFO Leadership

The CEO-CFO team is the best governance alliance to lead the (r)evolution toward a simpler, more effective alternative to board relationships. The CEO's place is obvious, especially since it is almost certain that the board hired or at least endorsed the person filling the position. The importance of the CFO as a change agent in board governance is less evident. The CFO embraces and applies rules and roles in information creation and distribution in hierarchical governance structures. These functions support governance but in themselves are not the same as governing. In more heterarchical governance structures, the CFO sees distinct business relationships creating and using information on a case-by-case basis to demonstrate the best distribution of resources for the common good.

Just like the overseers of public good in past eras, the CFO can work with board members to articulate the public good of the workplace in alignment with the CFO's responsibility to safeguard resources/assets. The CEO participates in this paradigm but does not lead. The CFO-led plan has a sequence that works particularly well because of the passage of the Sarbanes-Oxley Act.

Use S/O as the entry point. The Sarbanes-Oxley Act offers the baseline reason to proceed with a board-related governance overhaul. The Act charges corporate boards with more responsibility and empowers them to carry out their duties, but someone needs to hold them accountable. Think about it. Whether or not your company is public, board members read the newspaper, and if they are serious about their obligations, they are going to want to change something, or at least give the current situation a thorough going-over. Good boards are used to overseeing the financial health of the company, so that is where they are going to go first. If a CFO reads this after the S/O flurry has become routine, use one or more of the following approaches.

- Base the efforts with the board on the premise that a board governance facelift makes for a good competitive image, as well as staying in government's good graces.

- Work with a small group of board members to build a case for the governance work.

- Respond with action to a more recent scandal than those cited in the *CFO Guide*.

Organize the refresh/renew efforts before the board does. This action ameliorates the risk that the board will demand a ton of information because, unless they are already a very good governance body, they may operate by the information rule that "more is better; more is safer." Organizing the efforts to change converts to a lot of work for the CFO, but by guiding the process, you narrow the range of activity focus. If the board has already taken the initiative and is in the process of evaluating governance, take the upper hand and volunteer to do some legwork for them. Either approach provides the format for the CFO to have an active hand in shaping the scope of the governance work.

Pay them what they are worth. If you want someone to do a good job, there has to be a little something for the effort. Find the best people for the job, and then pay them what they are worth. The payment part is simple if the company gets value for money. This opportunity offers a good time to work with the CEO to identify who the "them" is. This is the perfect opportunity to bring on new members, or to thank those who *will* be leaving and wish them well. In any case, board membership should have a limited term set up in rotation fashion.

Articulate clear, actionable purposes for board governance activity. The appropriate prime measure for corporate governance is company health and longevity. The current, influencing prime measure is maximization of shareholder wealth. These two measures can exist interdependently as the health and longevity of a company means, by definition, financial success. How much financial success and for whom is the sticking point. The natural logic is, if a company is healthy and long-lived, more people benefit more handsomely over time, which is the real issue. Time and success cannot be defined as some irrational return to shareholders in one quarter, or even three, or ten. Building a company takes time; sustaining it takes even more. Shareholder expectations have become unglued from reality.

As should be clear by now, the involvement of the board in heterarchical governance goes beyond hiring the CEO, checking off the strategic plan, and having a quick look at controls. As mentioned earlier, more than half the states in America are actively pursuing laws to expand the responsibility of board members to employee and community stakeholders. Standing in the way of this movement is the current primary duty of board members: maximizing shareholder wealth. Shareholders should not, of course, be abused; rather, a combination solution must emerge that brings other stakeholders—employees and the community—into equity with shareholders. Right now, just about anyone can see that shareholders are extracting wealth from firms (not contributing it) in the form of headcount reduction, offshore manufacturing, pricing pressure, and the like.

The reason so much trouble has occurred with the current corporate governance goes back to the dynamics in Exhibit 5.1. If the primary obligation of a corporation is to maximize shareholder wealth, by definition, this obligation is antagonistic to the interests of other stakeholders. Complicating matters, although big business takes the hit for crass materialism and abuse of nonshareholder constituents, anyone who has a retirement account is also a shareholder. "We have met the enemy, and he is us," as Pogo says. Institutional investors manage a huge portion of equity holdings: your pension fund, your 401(k), or your bank-managed IRA. One can't rail against shareholder greed and in the next breath curse one's 401(k) management company for poor returns on retirement monies. This acknowledgment of stakeholder interdependency is key to achieving the developmental transformation in corporate governance for which everyone is searching. But one step at a time.

Put them to work. Now the plan gets interesting. Along with paying board members what they are worth, the CEO gets to play a part now by assigning them real work to earn their pay. Nobody should get paid to eat free food and rubber-stamp executive decisions. (We'll address the "time" objection presently.) This part of the alternative is the turning point, developmentally speaking, because it paves the way for the next step in heterarchical governance: inclusion and participation of the workforce in the governance circle. The "put them to work" step is a critical precursor. Think about the synergy: Employees get the benefit of the personal attention of an expert, a mentor, an advisor. Board members gain a very concrete understanding of what makes the organization run. Just the regular exposure to different employees (versus financial statements and plant tours) increases board member awareness. You know now what that means: Organizational awareness feeds into relationships. A few concrete work items for board members include:

- Researching current issues and questions before the executive counsel and the board and reporting findings.
- Mentoring executives and managers being groomed for promotion or succession.
- Using special expertise to advise a project team (e.g., capacity management).
- Teach employees in formal educational settings—if nothing else, about governance.

The obvious objection is predictable: Board members *don't have time* for this kind of service; "We can barely get to quarterly meetings." In that case, you have some dead weight on your hands. If they can hardly get to meetings, how can they possibly govern? The profile of the entire board is the proper target of analysis. As Mr. Levitt suggests, board members and executives are often socially acquainted; that is not necessarily a bad thing. For example, an old school chum may know a CEO's weaknesses better than anyone. However, the overall diversity profile of any board should be based on divergent points of view and a range of special expertise. With one exception, boards should secondarily look at the government-mandated "protected persons" definition of diversity. The exception is gender. Any board that does not include a healthy representation of both halves of the planet's human population is hurting itself. So, that assessment in itself opens tremendous possibilities for boards that are heavy on the testosterone count.

Another category of diversity, euphemistically called "the elderly," is another vast and untapped resource for board diversity. The term "elder statesperson" comes closest. "Elder" means wise from long experience. If someone has lived long enough to tell the tale, so to speak, they know something that others do not. Similarly, the CEO-CFO team should seek elders for the governance counsel. If you aren't convinced, ask yourself, "Would I be willing to let Joseph Juran or Peter Drucker sit on our company's board?"

Regrettably, one other pool of potentially productive board members is available. Here is the profile: Lost job as a result of merger/acquisitions/downsizing or headchopping. Excellent worker; highly educated; years of experience. After considering options, started own business (or retired early) to improve balance in life. Has time to spare. Sure, one has to be careful of the eager-consultant type, but on the other hand, in what Peter Drucker called "the postcapitalist society," there is a talent pool the size of the Mall of America.

The independence thing. Earlier chapters have established that there is no such state as "independence," and if that is a bit much to digest, you might recall Arthur Levitt's take on group dynamics. Let us be realistic. Someone off the street may feel independent when he/she arrives at the boardroom table, but if that person does a good governance job, in short order, that person knows enough about the organization and its people that independence is compromised, *in the sense that Sarbanes-Oxley* means it. The notion of independence that legislators and investors speak of so righteously is incorrect. The truly valuable quality in a board member is not independence, but first and foremost *integrity*. After that come "competence and commitment." If you have read this far, you certainly know how to spot integrity. The law-and-order types who think they can legislate ethics make a serious developmental error.

The previous sequence charts the developmental path to a valuable, working board that earns its keep, and paves the way for welcoming the fifth, and arguably the most critical governance alliance. A CFO who is secure in identity and role, and who operates from a moral perspective of moral universalism, easily does better work with more lasting and positive impacts, such as working to implement this board governance solution. People in the conformist identity (the average ethical board member) know clearly what the rules are, and if it makes sense, they can adapt to new rules, even before they develop a universal perspective. This CFO hears and sees more than the conformist line of behavior, and relies on information gathered from empathic listening to diverse points of view, and then acts on all facts and advice to the benefit of most people. The key for this CFO (and organizational) identity milestone is to be crystal clear about who can best serve good governance.

Assessing the CFO Role in Governance

Leadership maturity determines the level of CFO participation in corporate governance. Internal social configuration and executive responsibility perspectives establish the context and constraints in which CFO maturity can develop/evolve. A CFO, by definition, cannot govern (a) outside the organizational form (e.g., hierarchy), or (b) outside the operative laws and codes of the development peers. Just as with the maturity assessments in Exhibits 5.4 and 5.5, the degree of CFO participation in corporate governance parallels the governance maturity of the entire organization. The CFO can use Exhibit 5.6 to determine current governance participation levels and the professional developmental work needed to progress to the next level.

The CFO role currently serves as an information resource for governance participation in most organizations. In a heterarchical system of corporate governance, the CFO proactively creates and uses information on a case-by-case basis to demonstrate the best ways to distribute resources for the common good. Because resource allocation generates most internal conflicts, the CFO emerges in the new role of arbiter. The first step in this process is represented in the assessment at the top of Exhibit 5.6, which ascertains the CFO's degree of participation in company governance. The second step assesses the relevant leadership competencies. Interestingly, the four relevant EI competencies come from each of the four EI competency sets:

Competency Set	Competency
Self-awareness	Self-confidence
Social awareness	Service
Self-management	Transparency
Relationship management	Teamwork and collaboration

The Divided House: Active, Activist, and Absent Shareholders

Reclining dragons always fear the blue pool's clarity.[47]

The Blue Cliff Record

If the purpose of the board of directors is to oversee the health and longevity of the workplace, what is the purpose of shareholders? The twentieth-century-text-

www.

EXHIBIT 5.6   CFO GOVERNANCE ROLES DIAGNOSTIC

<u>Context</u>: **CFO governance participation**

<u>Assessment</u>: **Governance activities**

Choose a place on the scale from 0 to 5 that best represents the CFO's activities in company governance.

Hierarchy 0   1   2   3   4   **5 Heterarchy**

Embraces and applies rules and roles for information creation and distribution	Sees distinct interrelationships. Creates and uses information on a case-by-case basis to demonstrate resource distribution for the common good.

<u>**EI Relevant Competencies:**</u>

One from each EI quadrant:

self-confidence, service, transparency, teamwork/collaboration

For each of these four EI competencies, choose a place on the scale to indicate how the CFO exercises the leadership competency in terms of governance expectations and participation boundaries established by the organization's governance structure.

Self-Confidence

Hierarchy 0   1   2   3   4   **5 Heterarchy**

Holds professional ground in regulator/administrator role	Functions as arbiter and holds ground in resource distribution for common good

Service

Hierarchy 0   1   2   3   4   **5 Heterarchy**

To company in abstract terms; executives always top priority	Most important focus: broad, inclusive attention to people, resources, information

Transparency

Hierarchy 0   1   2   3   4   **5 Heterarchy**

Only to peers/authority	To everyone according to need

Teamwork/Collaboration

Hierarchy 0   1   2   3   4   **5 Heterarchy**

CFO/AFF work within the functional boundaries of accounting/finance	CFO/AFF an integral part of everyone's work and accepts the identity of new work-centered partnerships

book answer is to provide capital to the firm for its use, and to receive a return on their investment. There is a big problem with this reciprocal arrangement: Except for initial public offerings (risky), and secondary offerings of new shares by an established company (rare), there are no inflows of capital to the firm from the shareholders. However, shareholders expect a stream of capital out of the company as long as they hold the stock. Depending on the year in question, a tiny fraction (in one calculation less then one per cent) of the value of all shares purchased goes to companies; the rest goes to other speculative investors who wish to buy the shares.[48] This figure has serious implications for the validity of shareholders as owners, and for CFO guidance on the capital structure of the firm. Perhaps the definition of "investment" needs rethinking.

The title of this section refers to three classes of shareholders. Whether they earned, bought, or were gifted with the shares does not matter. Shareholders come in many forms and hold several types of shares, and a CFO gets to deal with most of them; in fact, the CFO often *is* one of them—most commonly as the beneficiary of a retirement account, and sometimes as a direct owner of stock and stock options. For purposes of simplicity, the three classes are defined as follows:

Active: A shareholder who is on the company payroll
Activist: A person who may or may not own shares, but who is committed to better corporate governance through participation in it
Absentee: Where absentee means a speculative shareholder whose interest is confined to profit, and whose concern with people and the work they do is restricted to how their productivity impacts ROI.

The first category is easy to see: founder/owners, executives with stock and stock options, and so forth. The second category is relatively new and is examined shortly; it has tremendous potential impact for CFOs and their companies. The third category is most of the rest of us in the form of retirement monies or other investment holdings. These three groups of shareholders rarely meet, yet they are all considered company owners. Each has an interest in the success of the workplace, but their motivations are quite dissimilar. The active shareholder has a keen interest in the health and longevity of the company as a workplace providing a steady income stream in the form of salary and benefits. The active shareholder is also interested in the longer-term health of the share price because, in the average case, the value of the shares held determines the level of retirement comfort. This structure of course leaves out the speculative-employee shareholder-executive who swoops in, gets a boatload of stock options, exercises the options and disappears in a cloud of dust.

The third category, absent shareholders, is the one that receives all the flack from the press and shareholder activists. The worst offenders in this category are corporate raiders and some analysts. A new twist to an old adage holds true for all absentee shareholder groups: Absence makes the heart grow absent. Fund managers of all stripes are supposed to act in the interest of any person who has an investment account of any kind. But this presumption is problematic when, as a composite, the retirement account owners are also employees of the firms they work for. What CFOs have known as a fact of the marketplace is becoming well known by the general population, which is the source of the development push in shareholder governance.

Conditions   As this book is written, certain socioeconomic conditions are present:

- The star CEO has become the chump CEO. Public mistrust in top corporate leaders has drastically deteriorated.

- Investors are demanding that executive pay be tied to long-term performance.

- Lots of people have put into action supposed remedies for the problem, making it the eleventh hour for irrational executive pay and benefits, inflated commissions, laddering in IPOs (underwriter/fund manager shenanigans), and cozy investment banking cadres.

- Every person on the street is now edgy about their retirement portfolio, and many are blaming the disgraced CEOs for the lackluster, or outright horrifying, condition of their nest eggs.

- These same people, or people very much like them, couldn't have cared less about what was going on in the corporate halls in the mid-1990s because their retirement funds performed well then.

- This same retirement money is invested in the companies for which these people work. Most people don't make this connection.

- These same people are directly encouraging (even enabling) corporations to persist in short-term thinking in the interest of returns. They do so by pressuring their companies and benefits executives, who in turn pressure the fund managers, who in turn pressure the companies. It's the interdependent butterfly wings once again.

Who is responsible for this state of affairs? All of the above and none of the above. Everyone and no one. As social thinker and shareholder activist Robert A. G. Monks succinctly says, "A corporation with a million shareholders has no owners."[49] Firing a CEO has the cathartic effect of a public hanging. It is satisfying to blame the fallen CEOs, and granted, some are to blame for specific situations in particular places. It also feels good to vent about the decline in retirement portfolio value, and condemn "them" for not managing things better—as if a retirement account was some sort of entitlement that someone else was supposed to handle. None of these move us any closer to a better way. The actual problem lies in the various definitions of corporate ownership.

"I began thinking of ownership in very human terms," Robert A. G. Monk said, reflecting on his epiphany when two separate incidents became interdependent in his mind. The first incident occurred along the Penobscot River where Monk observed "big, slick white bubbles of industrial foam, damaging vegetation along the bank." The second incident occurred as Monk performed his duties as chairman and trustee of a firm's multibillion-dollar equity assets. He was about to rubber stamp a proxy statement, when he noticed that the proxy was from the "same company that was floating the foam."[50] At that point, he became firmly committed to the straightforward idea that shareholders should attend to the health and longevity of the companies they own, and that *then* they have a right to expect a reasonable return on their money.

You Can't Govern a Company You Don't Own

Everybody wants the same thing for different reasons that end up being the same reason because they are interdependent: success of the enterprise. How to bring the fragmented alliances together with their respective views is the challenge. What are shareholders to do when executive stock options do not work to consistently align management performance with shareholder interests? The hostile takeover option is very unsightly. That leaves firing somebody: *Aha!* That arrogant, good-for-nothing CEO and his "little dog, too," the CFO. What is a CFO to do under conditions where everyone is just trying to survive the next change of management? Small-company CFOs aren't off the hook, because if their firms are healthy, they emerge as delectable morsels for the big M&A fish. If the firm underperforms but has some juicy assets, owners often get out while the getting is good, and sell at a loss. What is a CFO to do, indeed? One thing is certain: Something must be done, and it must be done proactively. Several routes to the same end might be employed, some of them distinctly more mature than others. They may be considered alone or in combination.

Go *private*. Going private is perhaps one of the most mature moves a CFO can orchestrate, and with a deflated market many CFOs are doing just that. Reasons include: depressed market so repurchase is within reach, cranky shareholders, burdensome new regulations for public companies, and for the weariest, just being able to concentrate on products and services again. Some standard ways of restructuring include management buyout and merger with a nonpublic firm. *CFO Magazine* cites other restructuring methods: leveraged recapitalization merger, reverse stock split, and asset disposition.[51] *CFO Magazine* also reports that one of the most prominent companies to go private is Dole Food Co., whose executives cited short-term pressures as one major reason for the exit. Other departures include companies of all sizes and types: Coast Dental Services in Tampa, Landair Transport (of Tennessee, with 2001 revenues of $106 million), and National Golf Properties in a deal worth $1.1 billion, to name a few. The going-private trend appears to be steadily increasing.[52]

Year	2000	2001	2002	2003
Number of Deals	197	282	316	372★

★ projection based on first 3 months of 2003

Employee ownership is clearly a highly mature option. This could take the "going private" forms mentioned above. Some cooperative-based companies, like the high-end sporting goods company REI, already are fully into employee ownership. Imagination, again, is the limit to how employee ownership may be accomplished. Some "company" towns operate in partnership for the long-term interest of their shared communities, like Hershey, Pennsylvania, and number two on the *Business Ethics* "Best Corporate Citizens" list, Columbus, Indiana, home to Cummins Engine.

Forge stronger links between board and shareholders. This move includes making your board members "active" actual shareholders, if they are not already. This action offers a way to get the board interested in company well-being. Another version related to the developmental transformation of the board discussed in the previous section is to set board members the task of building, repairing, and renewing relationships with absentee shareholders.

Court mature shareholder-partners. These owner-partners, of course, have the long term in mind as well, and have the fund power to help consolidate the fragmented shareholder base. For example, there are socially and environmentally conscientious mutual funds. Periodically, *Business Ethics* and other corporate governance reform publications rate socially responsible mutual funds in several categories. For example, the Spring 2003 issue of *Business Ethics* listed—with phone numbers—dozens of funds, including Walden Socially Balanced Fund, and Parnassus in three categories: bond and equity, large and small cap funds. A few public pension funds (Calpers in California) take shareholder governance seriously. Of course, a big owner wants a big say, but if you are partnered with others of your kind, this design is almost always a good thing.

Organize long-term institutional investors. Efforts toward such organization in the interest of improved shareholder governance are already taking place, which should be of interest to millions of people because this is where the retirement monies of the nation reside. John Bogle, founder of Vanguard and now a retired elder, is active in this movement. In 2002, he said, "We have very, very few corrupt people in the financial world, . . . but I believe we have a corrupt system."[53] As this chapter suggests, perhaps the issue is more one of developing immature governance systems than of mass ethical corruption.

Shift capital structure. Consciously and steadily move out of equity and into debt markets. This strategy, of course, is the stock in trade of the leveraged buyout, which brings us to the most mature alternative, although a course of action that is not for everyone.

■   ■   ■

Sooner or later, everybody has to wise up because the short-term thinking is unsustainable, and the delicate interdependency structures are becoming visible. Sooner or later, the actual purpose of the workplace will reemerge, even if it takes a complete and utter implosion to do it. Hopefully, everyone is smart enough to avoid that one. Shareholders, especially institutional investors because of their longer-term perspective, as the greatest force in the equity market, are moving toward taking greater responsibility commensurate with their greater ownership position. Boards will either disappear as a governance force or will rise to the occasion like the swift falcons of the epigraph at the beginning of this section. Government, as always, serves as the legislative stopgap until developmental forces take over. Eliot Spitzer, New York attorney general, a sort of one-man SEC, embodies this part of the development push.

But the most important shareholder influences are the first two governance alliances. The CEO-CFO and executive counsel, one workplace at a time, must shape the new governance structures through focusing on people serving people, by attending to relationships among all stakeholders. You don't want to be the followers in this developmental transformation; you want to be out front—way out front—leading the way.

The Discontented Collective: People at Work

Only those on the same path know.[54]

The Blue Cliff Record

The CEO, the CFO, and the executive counsel shape the pathways and conduits that connect the internal world of the workplace with the larger network of industry, the marketplace, government, community, and ecosystem. The CEO-CFO leadership role is to understand and deal with each of the individuals in this complex of relationships. Each individual functional executive represents a much larger number of people inside and outside the organization. The sales and marketing executive is a customer advocate first and foremost, and also if mature, a good leader for the people working in this function. Every time any of us turn to face a different person, a new condition, or an unexpected change, everything and everyone reorients itself to the new circumstances and players. Yet, so far, things keep working, and people solve what needs solving.

In the workplace, however, a glaring dilemma persists that is relegated to the realm of the impossible, or to those crazy cooperatives, or to those foolish executives who gave the company away. We are talking about the answer to the core question of this dilemma: *Who owns the fruits of work?* Case law says shareholders. Common sense says those who work and contribute. In a survival situation, after the essentials are addressed (warmth, water, food, shelter), the first order of business is dividing up the tasks it will take to stay alive. Anyone who chooses not to participate, not to contribute, risks ostracism and eventually death. There is no such thing as independence.

Experimentation has taught humanity that tyrants get overthrown, communist states devolve, and socialist communities have a hard time getting any work done. What does this leave? *Democracy*—not so much in the political or patriotic sense, but rather in the participative sense. In a democracy, one person alone sometimes makes all the difference because of the immense freedom within this form of governance. A president can go against dozens of nations and their people's opinion, and attack a distant country. A small group of people can change laws: consider Mothers Against Drunk Drivers. When a crisis descends, people self-organize to help in any way they can: New York City, September 11, 2001. So far, democracy has worked better than anything else, but it hasn't been introduced to the workplace. The democratic workplace is the next developmental step.

NOTES

1. Alvaro Mutis, "The Snow of the Admiral," in *Maqroll: Three Novellas,* trans. Edith Grossman (New York: HarperCollins, 1992), 7, 25.
2. Jeffry L. Seglin, "The Myopia of Bad Behavior," *MIT Sloan Management Review,* Spring 2003, 96.
3. Michael Moore, *Stupid White Men: . . . and Other Sorry Excuses for the State of the Nation!* (New York: Regan Books, 2002).
4. The political-economic side of government (i.e., government representatives working too closely with corporations and both parties benefiting from those relationships) remains a growing conflict of interest. The halls of government increasingly house appointees from the ranks of business professionals. An even more questionable alliance exists between corporations and the American legal system. In the first twenty-five years of the twentieth century, courts began to set legal precedents by deciding more and more for the interests of the corporation and its profit-oriented investors and against workers, corporate managers, and society as a whole. The establishment of the Securities and Exchange Commission (SEC) was a predictable extension of the shifting focus toward the interests of shareholders. Financial and strategic analysis got a jump-start during and after World War II as military thinking and approaches began to infiltrate company thinking and econometric models came into wide use. See Chapter 2 in H. Thomas Johnson and Anders Bröms, *Profit Beyond Measure: Extraordinary Results though Attention to People* (New York: The Free Press, 2000).
5. William H. Whyte, *The Organization Man* (Philadelphia: University of Pennsylvania Press, 1955).

6. John Micklethwait and Adrian Wooldridge, *The Company: A Short History of a Revolutionary Idea* (New York: The Modern Library, 2003), 128–32. We acknowledge the splendid work of these two authors and recommend this history of the corporation to anyone who works in one; for executives and managers, it's mandatory reading.

7. Ibid., 186.

8. As a more tried and true historical influence on the human condition in its various organizational forms, Aristotle discussed the ethics of virtuous living more than two thousand years ago in Book 10, Sections 6, 7, 8, 9, and 10 of his *Nicomachean Ethics.*

9. For more background on such studies, see, for example, H. Bruch and S. Ghoshal, "Beware the Busy Manager," *Harvard Business Review,* February 2002, 62–69, and Sumantra Ghoshal and Heike Burch, "Going Beyond Motivation to the Power of Volition," *MIT Sloan Management Review,* Spring 2003, 51–57.

10. Herb Greenberg, "Enron Never Happened," *Fortune,* April 28, 2003, 128.

11. The following adages come from *The Blue Cliff Record*, Thomas Cleary and J. C. Cleary, trans. (Boston: Shambhala, 1992), 130, 95, 83, and 165.

12. "Just say no."

13. *The Blue Cliff Record*, 68.

14. Ibid., 176.

15. Ibid., 130.

16. Ibid., 264.

17. http://news.findlaw.com/hdocs/docs/hsouth/sechsouth31903cmp.pdf is a copy of Civil Action number CV-03-J-1516-S, an injunction brought before United States District Court, Northern District of Alabama by the Security and Exchange Commission against HealthSouth Corporation and its CEO, Richard M. Scrushy.

18. Geoffrey Colvin, "History Repeats Itself at HealthSouth," *Fortune,* May 12, 2003, 40.

19. Ibid.

20. http://news.findlaw.com/hdocs/docs/hsouth/sechsouth31903cmp.pdf is a copy of Civil Action number CV-03-J-1516-S, an injunction brought before United States District Court, Northern District of Alabama by the Security and Exchange Commission against HealthSouth Corporation and its CEO, Richard M. Scrushy.

21. Peter Asmus wrote the 2003 report published in *Business Ethics* 17, no. 1 (Winter 2003): 6–10.

22. Stories about great executives often reveal many of their leadership competencies in the emotional intelligence sense, but it sometimes takes a bit to ferret them out. In this governance alliance profile, we have inserted parenthetical notes to call attention to the qualities we've been talking about in the previous chapters. We suggest that as you encounter executives personally or in the media, you may want to regularly make your own mental parenthetical assessments. In this way you can hone your discernment of other people's maturity and leadership competencies.

23. Stephen Barr, "Pfizer Defiant: How David Shedlarz Challenges The Analysts," *CFO Magazine,* July 1, 1999. www.cfo.com.

24. Jerry Useem, "In Corporate America It's Cleanup Time," *Fortune,* September 16, 2002, 64–65.

25. Barr, "Pfizer Defiant," www.cfo.com.

26. Ibid.

27. Ibid.

28. Ibid.

29. Bruce Fogle, "Social Behaviour—Pack, Sex and Maternal Activity," in *The Dog's Mind: Understanding Your Dog's Behavior* (New York: Howell Book House, 1990), 163.

30. Katie Murray, "The Jamie Dimon Show," *Fortune,* July 22, 2002, 88, 90. Mr. Dimon has lead an amazing financial turnaround for Bank One in a very short time period. He is also a stellar leader in the hierarchical form, from all reports.

31. Robin Cooper and Regine Slagmulder, *Supply Chain Development for the Lean Enterprise: Interorganizational Cost Management* (Portland, Ore.: Productivity, Inc. 1999).

32. For an actual story of how the hierarchy has been tamed, see, Robin Cooper, "The Taiyo Group: The Bunsha Philosophy," Harvard Business Press case (9-195-080), August 24, 1994.

33. Thomas A. Stewart, "Dear Shareholders," *Harvard Business Review*, May 2003, 10. For another excellent *HBR* piece related to the "I don't know" wisdom, see John M. Mezias and WIlliam H. Starbuck, in *HBR's* "Forethought" column, "What Do Managers Know Anyway? A Lot Less Than They Think. Now the Good News," *Harvard Business Review*, May 2003, 16–17.

34. Stewart, "Dear Shareholders," 10.

35. See n. 17 this chapter.

36. Again, refer to Cooper, "The Taiyo Group."

37. For a brief, yet thorough, explication of the role Japan played in the evolution of business, see John Micklethwait and Adrian Wooldridge, *The Company: A Short History of a Revolutionary Idea* (New York: The Modern Library, 2003), 132–36.

38. Ibid., 134.

39. Johnson and Bröms, *Profit Beyond Measure,* 135.

40. *The Blue Cliff Record,* 108.

41. Michael Useem, *Investor Capitalism: How Money Managers Are Changing the Face of Corporate America* (New York: Basic Books, 1996), 55.

42. Authors' Note: For private and smaller companies, that may have inactive or nonexistent boards, the exploration of the role a board can play in organizational development can take two forms: (1) Activate or create a board to fill the roles outlined in the discussion, or if ready, (2) make the developmental quantum leap to employee governance (see Chapter 6).

43. *The Blue Cliff Record,* 165.

44. Andrew Osterland, "Board Games," *CFO Magazine,* November 2002, 39. Osterland also reports that, according to the Senate subcommittee investigation, Enron's board "failed to raise even the smallest red flag. Not once did it voice an objection to any of management's accounting practices. . . ."

45. For an outstanding discussion of this "missing link," see Cynthia A. Montgomery and Rhonda Kaufman, "The Board's Missing Link," *Harvard Business Review,* March 2003, 84–93.

46. Ben Gerson, "Conversation: Levitt on the Street," *Harvard Business Review,* April 2003, 22–23.

47. *The Blue Cliff Record,* 122.

48. Marjorie Kelly, *The Divine Right of Capital* (San Francisco: Berrett-Kohler Publishers, 2001), 192, calculated from Federal Reserve data in *Statistical Abstract of the United States, 2000*; [per M. Kelly] from the Securities Industry Association; from SEC documents; and a phone interview.

49. Marc Gunther, "Shareholders of the World Unite!" *Fortune,* June 24, 2002, 84.

50. Ibid., 80.

51. Tim Reason, "Off the Street," *CFO Magazine,* May 2003, 57.

52. Ibid., 54–58, with statistical credit to Mergerstat, and Scott Larson National-Louis University.

53. Gunther, "Shareholders of the World Unite!" 86.

54. *The Blue Cliff Record,* 155.

Working

The view from my yew tree stretches eastwards along a range of downland hills along which our first direct ancestors made their way inland. Ten or more thousand years ago, smoke would have risen from their fires as they made camp. They were venturing into vast empty tracts of land where no human footprint had been left since before the last Ice Age. As they travelled, they had to adapt to the conditions they encountered without the machines and gadgets we consider essential today. Yet these people were fully equipped. In their heads was the accumulated knowledge of our species, in their hands the skill of translating thought into action with great refinement. Their most powerful tool was the ability to reason, for our early ancestors laid the foundations for what we now call science.[1]

Raymond Mears

To design a complex mechanism, one must first understand the whole system and then have the patience to make it work, one part at a time. Learning the bears' life system was the opposite, but analogous: All I saw at first were the individual parts as the cubs demonstrated them—the seemingly disconnected behaviors that I knew had to fit somehow into a very complex behavioral mechanism. But I knew that for a part to work it had to fit into the system; and for a system to function, it needed all of its working parts. . . . But I was optimistic. I knew that everything required to make a full-grown adult bear had come in those little four-pound packages when LB and LG had been delivered into my care. All I had to do was to sort it all out.[2]

Benjamin Kilham and Ed Gray

T he first five chapters of the *CFO Survival Guide* stayed within the boundaries of business experiences as currently conducted. The chapters have built and progressed in a pattern from the specific to the general. The discussion began with a look at the status of the profession and then carefully characterized the individual chief financial officer's technical skills, experiential knowledge, and leadership competencies. With the profile of a great CFO in hand, the *Guide* followed the finance chief at work, moving into the larger organizational community—first within the accounting and finance function with AFF staff members, and then in governance roles with executives, the board of directors, and shareholders. The progress of the path so far looks like this:

Profession → CFO maturity: technical skills, experiential knowledge, leadership competencies → applied within AFF → functional and leadership service to → executives, board, shareholders →

Because development is never complete, a next step always exists. Succeeding steps are almost never easy to see. What follows the final arrow? The answer: *Work.* While financial professionals work very, very hard, they continue to work within the predominant belief system whose mantra is "maximize shareholder wealth." Often a qualifier follows the invocation: "at any cost." Corporations continue to operate, stagnant in this narrow range of service to shareholders or to owners in private companies. Everywhere one cares to look, employees are missing from the wealth and governance picture. This business-as-usual mode is no longer viable for reasons of resource depredation, the wealth-extraction mandates that burden executives, and just plain weariness from the steady increase in work hours and multiple jobs for everyone.

The recent failures in governance, too, strongly indicate admonishment for the board-as-usual practices. How can structures as sporadically effective as many boards appear to be lead and govern? As this is written, Donald H. Rumsfeld, U.S. Secretary of Defense, lives with the embarrassing implications of serving on the board of a manufacturer that has sold nuclear reactors to North Korea. Rumsfeld reports that he had no knowledge of the sale while he served on the board. Maybe he didn't. The point is, he should have because repercussions from this lack of governance could be considerably more serious than dollars lost from retirement accounts. Did he make a mistake? Yes. Is he "only human"? Of course. Is Rumsfeld one of many who are missing critical pieces of information to do their jobs? Yes, but that is no excuse. Everyone from Arthur Levitt to anticorporate radical protestors acknowledge that the governance quality of the vast number of board directorates is poor to nonexistent. Perhaps a new era of corporate board governance will emerge, but don't count on it. With the current state of board governance and the risk of its continuation, conditions are ripe for *some-*

thing more: an evolution in the way we work and the principles on which we run our workplaces.

This final chapter departs from the current business habits and customs to explain the "something more" and to endorse an evolutionary and sustainable way of "doing business." The developmental evolution comes in the form of a declaration, the Declaration of *Inter*dependence. The conditions surrounding this Declaration may follow the pattern of the Declaration of Independence that launched the United States. A revolution may occur before the evolution takes root, but no matter the developmental entry point—radical upheaval or guided transformation—the result will be the same. Because the current Western socioeconomic system is not sustainable by any definition of that term, it will be replaced by a stronger system. The final pages of the *Guide* describe the logic behind these statements, and how a developmental transformation that has already started can be guided to retain the good in what has developed so far, while paring away the pathological, unbalanced aspects of the current conditions. Just enough time remains to mobilize and lead the pack, rather than scramble behind as an also-ran follower.

THE CFO AT LARGE

> *How can you measure progress if you don't know what it costs and who has paid for it? How can the "market" put a price on things—food, clothes, electricity, running water—when it doesn't take into account the real cost of production?*[3]
>
> Arundhati Roy

The person best positioned to lead this evolutionary work inside the organization is the great CFO, in partnership with an equally mature CEO. Together the CEO-CFO leadership team patterns a vigorous and potent force. The influential, inspirational CFO brings to bear intimate knowledge of current financial beliefs and structures combined with the ability to see the trajectory of the necessary evolution in work organization. Consider that the end of the pep talk. If you expected the *Guide* to end with a cheerleading, go-out-and-get-'em pitch, better go out and purchase a warmer, fuzzier book on leadership. In the Lewis and Clark *Discovery* tradition, the next steps are rough and uncertain. No reliable maps are available, but we can rely on some time-tested principles. Risk pervades this evolutionary work because it is comprehensive and turns inside out current assumptions about work and wealth. People and the work they do rise as the top leadership priority.

The expedition into this unknown territory begins with the crucial question from Chapter 5: *Who owns the fruit of work?* The answer unfolds by first establishing the conditions compelling the evolution, drafted as a Declaration of *Inter*dependence (see Sidebar) that sets forth the principles of workplace governance and who has rights to the wealth created there.

Workplace organization and governance also have a developmental sequence. Parallel with personal and professional development, this sequence is important, as is the "no skipping steps" developmental parameter. At each step, the CFO has a critical role to play, as depicted in Exhibit 6.1. The CFO role is discussed throughout the rest of the chapter. The steps in the exhibit correlate with the order of the *Declaration*.

SUSTAINABILITY IN NATURAL SYSTEMS

What do an elitist governance system and undemocratic work practices have in common? The answer: Unsustainability. These actual conditions, and worse, exist in workplaces today. Democracy in government has succeeded better than any predecessor form, but the workplace remains in a sovereign hierarchy or totalitarian context. If this discussion pertained to countries not yet on the political-economic map, some leeway for absolution would be allowed, but the discussion does not pertain to such places. The reference is to countries with a wealth of natural resources at their disposal, sophisticated technology, and some of the best consumer markets on the planet. Why do unacceptable-to-horrid working conditions persist in such places? The answer comes from a wrong turn that business took in the early part of the twentieth century when the ship of industry began to steadily tack with

---

EXHIBIT 6.1 **CFO ROLES IN CREATING AN INTERDEPENDENT WORKPLACE**

Steps to the Democratic Workplace	Enabling Role of the CFO
1. Recognize inherent equality	Accountability system supports equality
2. Acknowledge just cause	Identify and arbitrate ethical issues
3. Practice equal justice before the law	Facilitate counsel of equals
4. Adhere to primacy of the public good	Gatekeeper of corporate action
5. Practice democratic workplace governance	Design/administer democratic processes
6. Recognize shared economic rights	Make economic workrights visible
7. Distribute wealth according to work	Design wealth distribution routes and monitor distribution equity
8. Right to abolish	Work with leadership counsel to prevent the need to exercise the right to abolish

www.

Inherent Equality

As humanity matures in the course of its evolution and development, conditions arise and converge that make it necessary to reassert the original, intrinsic interdependence as manifest in all natural systems. Actual conditions are self-evident. Each individual person is born equal to all others with inalienable rights to life, liberty, and the pursuit of happiness within the constraints and balances of a natural system.

Just Cause

The patience and hope of people who look for an equitable distribution of wealth based on the productivity of their work has been exhausted by unequal treatment before the law wherein wealthy persons who have not participated in the productive work claim and are granted the right to extract wealth from workplaces, and wherein corporations claim and are granted the rights of persons that may detract from what is wholesome and necessary for the public good.

Law unjustly permits those people who administer the expectations of the corporate owners to invade the physical and emotional privacy of workers, often under conditions of forced consent and under pain of job loss or monetary demotion.[5, 6]

Primacy of Public Good

Based on the circumstances of natural interdependence, individuals voluntarily band together to form socioeconomic work groups to produce goods and services that meet the needs of the community. For the survival and health of everyone, diverse work groups use their abilities according to their capacities to fulfill their responsibility to contribute to the public good without violating or damaging the health of the common environmental systems on which they depend.

The Democratic Workplace

Although individual workers and work groups are the natural source of all wealth in the form of goods and services—and capital—most are not permitted a voice or participation in organizational governance. The corporation is permitted to mandate and govern how people work in "unusual, uncomfortable, and distant places,"[7] for the sole purpose of complying with financial measures and maximizing stockholders' wealth.

Economic Rights to Wealth

Every person within these diverse work groups shares an interdependent right to economic resources, and that right is violated when methods of wealth distribution exclude any worker from access to representation in workplace governance.

Right to Abolish

Whenever any force becomes destructive to these ends, the people have the right to alter or abolish it, and to institute a new organization form, shaping the organization on work and governance principles that seem most likely to effect their safety and survival needs in the context of a sustainable global community.

Common sense and discretion should guide the dismantling or transformation of established work structures and governance principles, but familiarity, fear, and apathy should likewise not pose impediments to necessary modifications, reformations, or extirpation. When elite groups engage in long-term practice of discriminatory abuses and usurpations and exhibit clear intent to continue to do so, the responsibility of workers and community members is to reject such structures and to provide new configurations to serve the needs of people and planet.

the wind of shareholder wealth maximization as the prime directive of all corporations. This turn has been chronicled for almost one hundred years, but its cultural hold remains stronger than ever. In *The Modern Corporation*, Berle and Means observed that by the end of the 1920s two-thirds of industrial wealth had left the hands of individual owners and transferred to publicly traded corporations. At this point in economic history, ownership and control parted ways.[8] Over the next three-quarters of a century, a combination of legal, government, and capital market power grew so strong that it now seems impossible to veer away from the singular influences of a gale-force shareholder wind.

Tacking is not enough; the maneuver requires a hard jibe away from the wind on our nose, and a downwind run of magnificent proportions. This risky maneuver has precedent in the disposition of many despot kings and cruel rulers in past centuries. Recently, the trajectory has been clearly charted with facts, figures, and history from people with widely diverse perspectives including Johnson and Bröms[9] (*Profit Beyond Measure*), Micklethwait and Wooldridge[10] (*The Company*), Kelly[11] (*The Divine Right of Capital*), Estes[12] (*Tyranny of the Bottom Line*), Roy[13] (*The Cost of Living*), and Berenson[14] (*The Number: How the Drive for Quarterly Earnings Corrupted Wall Street and Corporate America*), to name a few. So many voices call for governance reform and workplace ethics. Still, though, financial and profitability measures prevail, as if the business of doing business were caught in a *Groundhog Day* time loop in which the same script must be repeated endlessly.

The reason for the developmental arrest is that everyone is in search of workplace patterns and principles that can backtrack to that fork in the road where socioeconomics and governance took the wrong turn. The search is on to replace the system that everyone —consciously or unconsciously— knows cannot last. As emphasized throughout the *Guide*, the reason the current socioeconomic pattern cannot last is because it does not operate according to the relevant, governing conditions pertinent to natural systems. The current, temporary paradigm that mandates maximization of shareholder wealth teeters on the edge of col-lapse. Clinging to the financial abstractions that support the mandate, those peo-ple who profit from it struggle to keep the illusion running. The wrong turn can get a lot steeper.

The *Wall Street Journal* reports: "Temps reward shareholders, a study concludes." The "study" says that when 10 percent of the workforce of a company becomes part-time or temporary, stock price and financial measures improve.[15] Good busi-ness or unethical practice? Arthur Levitt, longtime SEC chairman, in answer to what advice he would give to the 2003 SEC chairman, William Donaldson, says, "The advice I would give is to restore the morale of the agency as his top priority and manifest in every possible way the primacy of investors among the many con-stituents he is responsible for. Investors' interests should be placed above corporate, political, and all other interests. By doing that he can't go wrong."[16] Sage wisdom or myopia? Well, when you go to see a proctologist, you know where he is going to look. Was the passage of the Sarbanes/Oxley Act of 2002 an effective deterrent or a grand gesture?[17] Jeffrey Immelt, CEO of General Electric, said to GE employ-ees in 2002 global videoconferences, "Don't let anyone confuse who you are and how you work" and "Getting investors and employees on the same page is what this company is all about."[18] An attempt at better governance, or publicity hype? A 1996 study surprises a researcher who discovers in survey results that "47% of about 400 executives were willing to commit fraud by understating write-offs that cut into their companies' profits." Justified for the corporate good or immature moral ethics?[19]

People who are born and bred to see things only from a financial perspective exist in an abstract world far removed from actual people and real work; they travel the wrong-turn fork in the road without even seeing the alternate branch. Almost all MBA programs breed, clone, and grow wealth extraction officers, acolytes at the altar of shareholder wealth. Internal MBA philosophy translates: People are a means to an end—so many expenses on the income statement related to productivity. Work is something that other people do to serve the corporation and its owners, the shareholders. Emotions are for sissies and momma's boys. Relationships are in-ferior to the hoped-for profits of joint ventures and limited liability partnerships. This educated business breed deserves compassion because they have undergone a life of rigorous training in financial strategies and ratios, refined accounting moves, and savvy investments.

The reason the business breeds eschew the emotional, the concrete material world, and the actual people in it is because they have been taught to leave these things alone. Emotions make one weak. Relationships make one vulnerable. The work other people do is too hard and messy to get involved with; anyway, if they worked as hard as the business breed to get where they are, they would be rich, too.

Everybody deserves his/her chosen lot in life. Nothing is stopping anyone from getting rich in this free country, but it is a jungle out there—survival of the fittest, you know. Oh, really?

Wealth Extraction

Recall Assumption 1 from Chapter 5: *Corporate governance has three parts: executives, board of directors, and shareholders.* Anyone missing here? How about the people who make the products and provide the services? Let us conduct the promised examination. The largest embodiment of real wealth that a CFO encounters is the list of names on the payroll—human resources, company assets, corporate property, employees—the people who produce all the wealth there is in the form of goods and services. Out of the many relationships a CFO has, this one is most likely to be routinely ignored. Good-accountant CFOs attend to shareholders, prepare well for board meetings, and participate with executive decision making. These tasks are standard CFO fare. But what about the massive, energetic activity flowing from people into products and services day after day, night after night? To be blunt, the CFO usually facilitates and supports the extraction of wealth from coworkers (and self, if an equity holder) in the interest of serving up value to shareholders who are considered the actual owners of the corporation, even though they have never seen the place, do not know the name of a single employee, and may hold their equity position for less than one day. Take a long, hard look at the prevailing logic, and answer *true* or *false* to each of these six statements.

1. Shareholders are the owners of the company.
2. Shareholders are owners by right of the capital they have invested in the company.
3. Shareholders as owners have the right to control and govern the companies they own.
4. Employees are company owners by virtue of the work they do.
5. A board of directors is the actual corporate governance body.
6. The board of directors can make relevant strategy and policy decisions.

Answers:
1. False, but confusingly (by case law) True—a "legal fiction,"[20] because today, shareholders are transient speculators, not owners.
2. True, if the investment purchases shares of either an initial public offering or a secondary offering by an established company. Otherwise, False because the money paid for stock purchases after these two events goes to other speculators.

3. False, by reason of abdication: Despite the fact that case law favors a "True" answer, the fact of the matter is that speculative shareholders are absent and do not participate in the life of the company in any way.

4. True, ethically; False, legally, in the majority of cases.

5. False, legally; directors must represent the interests of the stockholders because stockholders elect the board.

6. Don't answer that. Ask Donald Rumsfeld.

So, to sum up, have another look at the actual conditions of the workplace today. Reverse the arrows and equal signs if you like; the result is the same.

Calculation #1: The immortal, boundary-less, legal-person corporation → governed by directors → represent stockholders = 100 percent of legal governance power

Calculation #2: Now add zero for employees who have no vote.

Let us take a more quantitative look at this representation. No matter which numbers are cited, the pattern is clear. Depending on how the calculations are done, and what elements are included in them, one finds estimates of wealth such that in 1998, 78 percent of the total value of stocks were owned by 10 percent of "households" and 10 percent of households own 90 percent of the wealth in bonds, trusts, and business equity.[21] In 1976 the wealthiest 1 percent of the people held approximately 20 percent of all household wealth; the figure rose to approximately 40 percent in 1997. No matter the calculation, the trend is clear.

On the not-wealthy side of life, the pattern is equally transparent. In 1979, 24 percent of Americans drew wages below the poverty level; in 1995, the number was up to 30 percent.[22] From 1987 to 1997, private-sector inflation-adjusted wages dropped 7.2 percent.[23] From the mid-1980s to the mid-1990s, American productivity rose at a 1.5 percent annual rate. Workers have retained 0.5 percent of that gain in inflation-adjusted wages.[24] In the twenty years from 1977 to 1997, workers weekly clocking fifty hours or more increased from 24 to 37 percent.[25] Revenue streams flowing to corporations compose the majority of the GDP. In the decade of the 1990s, corporate profits grew by 10 percent annually. GDP grew by about 3 percent every year.[26] Do the math. As wealth flows to wealth, someone else's pie is being eaten for lunch.

Wealth extraction is a very real and present phenomenon. Just as surely and measurably as forests and wildlife succumb to corporate hunger for land and natural resources, wealth is silently and steadily disappearing from the lower echelons of wage-earning people into the accounts and holdings of the already-wealthy. Wealth in and of itself is neutral. Wealthy people probably have a similar moral bell curve as the rest of the population. Many among the rich are probably unaware of these wealth extraction dynamics, and here lies the crux of the wealth extraction:

For actual, new wealth to appear (dot–com–type fantasy wealth does *not* count), actual people must work with physical materials and other real people to create valuable goods and services. But as the productivity statistics in the previous paragraph clearly indicate, gains in wealth from productivity (0.5 percent = one-third of gain) by any calculation is not an equitable distribution of wealth based on who actually created the new value through real work; such inequity is unsustainable.

Corporate executives dutifully adhering to the shareholder wealth maximization directive are the primary instruments of this funds flow. When improved productivity yields more profit, most of that profit goes either to shareholders in the form of dividends and price appreciation, or back into the corporation to be invested in more organizational resources to make more profit. The good-accountant CFO does his/her part by making visible the flow of real value. Well-intentioned executive groups cheer when the cost of labor and benefits are held in check; employees cheer when the company makes a profit, especially when incentives such as profit sharing are active. Speculative shareholders witness none of this, and everyone continues down that wrong-turn path, many wondering why something doesn't seem quite right. The sense of being out of balance is directionally correct.

Just as sexual maturity can become arrested at a Peeping-Tom stage of isolated voyeurism, corporate governance and ownership were captured by a powerful fancy in the earliest stages of development: the power of concentrated wealth with its well-practiced cultural rules, and refined legal protections. Only brute force engenders more universal attention as a means of human influence. Consequently, the evolution of human work is on hold until we figure out how to rationalize the power currently held by a privileged class of people who do not directly contribute to the substantive work that sustains wealth, and introduce into the workplace the democratic governance principles of wealth creation and distribution. Two potential scenarios are possible. On the one hand, judging from the more or less steadily increasing maturity of human social relationship, one could expect a scenario like the Civil Rights movement marked by bloodshed and misery certainly, but an upheaval that also brought the rapid, steady transformation of a pattern of racial discrimination. On the other hand, history has plenty of bloody scenarios when the powers-that-be resisted development to their last: Rome, British colonialism, the French monarchy. Can we learn from history? Gandhi would suggest that we can. Can we do so in a fashion consistent with natural sustainable systems? Same answer.

(Un)Sustainable Conditions

> [S]hort-term mentality and metrics are being applied to a complex, systemic problem. Ethical behavior is not a stand-alone issue and should not be addressed as

*such if a true shift is expected. Behavior can't be changed unless the motivation
for any behavior is rethought. Trying to apply cosmetic metrics to ethics initiatives
only adds to the systemic short-term mind-set that can cripple the integrity of
those working in corporations.*[27]

Jeffry L. Seglin

The reason people hang on to what no longer works well is because the tactic, belief, or approach once *did* work, and had meaning, purpose, and functionality. Behaviors can be learned, repeated on command, and become habit without a person perceiving any meaning in the activity. As psychologist Jonathan Lear observes, humans commonly "act repeatedly before understanding." When you find yourself asking, *What am I doing here? Or why did I do/say such a thing?* you can be sure you have been unconsciously acting out routines and habits that are so integral to your being that they go largely unnoticed—until something happens to bring them to light. When these habits and routines become unwelcome, embarrassing, or even frightening, the time has arrived for intentional development work. This pattern is equally valid for socioeconomic configurations. So, if people find themselves working harder and harder but losing market position, an environmental scan and a ruthless assessment of routines and habits can help reveal ingrained processes and procedures that do not validly address new conditions.

As in all events in development, once a person sees through current conventional constraints, the fog lifts and new insights cannot be reversed. The wrong turn down the mythical road of shareholder supremacy seems ludicrous once the facts are laid out. Consider here a very important caveat: Unlike some radical activist proposals, the transformation proposed in this chapter does not call for destruction or removal of any class of persons or organizations (i.e., abolishing the corporate form and the shareholders with it). Such a heedless emotional call flies in the face of development and is not morally conscientious. In the development of people as well as of socioeconomic organizations, nothing is ever lost. Rather, development works through a process of integration wherein anything learned and validated by direct experience becomes a permanent acquisition for seeing and interacting with the world differently.

Relevant Developmental Principles

Developmental integration almost never occurs instantaneously and is always influenced by the many different subsystems that are coevolving. For that reason, developmental milestones are achieved only with the deliberate, repetitive practice of various approaches to a recurrent problem or learning task—known in the vernacular as trial-and-error. Because development drives are inborn, people have an innate urge to try out actions over and over again attempting to approximate a better result. In this sense, better does not always mean more; in fact, it usually means something new. Successes lead to uncompromisable ways of addressing problems or tasks that are eventually performed automatically without thought. Significantly, pathological attachments and habits are just as easy—sometimes easier—to embrace as is the integration of developmentally progressive behaviors (think trust and mistrust or autonomy vs. shame/doubt). Once a person fully attains a healthy developmental milestone, that person literally cannot unconsciously backslide into less mature modes of behavior. If one does return to former unhealthy habits, the integration was incomplete. Think of the things that children promise to do or not to do in the face of reward or punishment. Saying the words of promises is easy, as is listing practices that with deliberate effort lead to developmental integration:

- Practice consciously and consistently a new set of behaviors based on a desire for something better.

- At a certain point when repetitious activities are not successful, previous experiences are remembered and a new approach is added to the repertoire, and another, and so on until an activity yields iterative success. Based on the initial internal discipline required when initiating a new practice, one might observe that older behaviors must "think" they are being killed or abandoned for a newer model, as the entrenched speech and actions reassert again and again, struggling to survive. This stems from the fundamental imperatives of any living system: survive, reproduce. Understanding old behavior flare-ups in this context can lend patience to the process.

- Frequent slipping back into less mature behaviors, of course, undermines and delays development.

- The development process includes learning a cumulative set of all trial-and-error experiences, which together become integrated into the new operative behavior.

- When trying something that goes against cultural norms and beliefs, expect ambient public clamor for you to de-evolve; for example, suggestions to act as "you should," demands to give up the foolishness, and so on.

These developmental principles apply directly to evolution in the workplace and to the relative immaturity of corporate governance. To extend the royal metaphor from *The Divine Right of Capital*, the corporation is the socioeconomic equivalent of a child-king ruling those who are more mature. Other aspects of human relationship—race, class, sex, and treatment of the mentally ill—have continued to mature, exposing bias and prejudice, and correcting them. Marketplace and workplace maturation has not kept pace. In fact, because other systems of human interaction have matured, people have found themselves suddenly (in less than one century) unable to cope with a less mature corporate governance system (the child-king) that is simply dominating them.

The problem, of course, is that there seems to be no formal means to address the maturity imbalance, that is, the behavior that the child-king has over other systems. Take a simple analogy. Say you live next to the household of a young couple who has a three- to four-year-old child whose noise and activities increasingly disrupt your neighborhood. Social convention offers a number of practical mechanisms to address the situation, and the methods escalate in terms of persuasive force: (1) go to the parents, discuss the issue, and ask for relief; (2) deploy a neighborhood group to persuade by sheer numbers; (3) involve law enforcement agencies; and (4) bring in social agencies. In this basic example many avenues are open to solving a problem of isolated, unchecked immaturity. Parallels for dealing with global corporate immaturity are much harder to come by. The World Trade Organization has a corporate value system. The United States Chamber of Commerce is interested in trade, not development. The United Nations is not in the business of business, and has proven ineffective in the governance realm by failing to prevent the Bush administration from going to war in Iraq despite overwhelming world opinion.

Above All Other Interests

Investors' interests should be placed above corporate, political, and all other interests.[28]

Arthur Levitt

Hmmm. If one accepts the premise that the primacy of shareholder interests is morally, socially, and democratically shortsighted and that it has inexorably led to accelerating wealth extraction—the largely one-way distribution of productivity gains—we seem to have a problem here. The best way to end wealth extraction by people who perform no work is to redefine ownership, which begs the question: ownership of *what*? Prior chapters established the immateriality of financial abstractions, and the dot-com bust vividly proved the insubstantiality of inflated share prices. These financial assets are worth owning only as long as the fiction surrounding them holds up. Alternatively, one might consider that the only source of marketplace wealth is applied human mental-physical-emotional effort in the interest of profitably serving others—otherwise known as work. In this context, the inquiry can be refined to *who owns the work and the workers?* Where is the value (not burden) of employees summarized on the income statement and balance sheet? Hopefully, the question of ownership of workers can be briskly addressed. In a nation that calls itself "the land of the free," workers cannot be owned. Owning a worker has historically been called "slavery," and America settled that question politically and socially in the mid-nineteenth century.

So, *inherent equality,* the primary principle of the Declarations of Independence and of Interdependence stands: *Each individual person is born equal to all others with inalienable rights to life, liberty, and the pursuit of happiness within the constraints and balances of a natural system.* Progressing from the assumption of at least "life and liberty"—"happiness" being problematic from Aristotle to the current Dalai Lama—the question narrows further to *who owns the work?* The investigation can be framed under two governance systems, current and sustainable:

1. *Current:* Shareholders own the work, as defined within the construct of a financial entity called the corporation that is designed and managed for the purpose of maximizing shareholder wealth.

2. *Sustainable:* People who do the work own it, where "people" is defined as those who productively contribute to the physical or intellectual creation of marketable goods and services.

System one is examined first; system two is scrutinized in a subsequent section, *Work in Process.* Succinctly, governance system one is not a reasonable long-term investment for any CFO who understands the survival principles in this book. To put finer points on the logic, answer the following:

- Can an increasingly global economy operating within pluralistic world values support wealth and natural resource extraction by people who perform little or no work and bear no responsibility for corporate malfeasance?

- How can a mature ethical CFO support governance system one knowing that it discriminates against more than 99 percent of the people on the planet, and puts at serious risk the natural resources common to everyone— air and water as the baseline examples?

- The logical conclusion is that either a CFO *cannot* support governance system one, or must choose *for reasons of personal gain* to ignore the consequences and effects of the current system.

Note where the other large, influential governance system—the federal government—is headed. The growing demand for safeguarding the environment, however thwarted the appeals may be by shifting administrations, is one indicator. Sarbanes-Oxley is a recent second piece of evidence. Listen to U.S. Comptroller General, David M. Walker, for more clues:

> The private sector historically defines success in terms of the bottom line and shareholder value. No doubt about it, these are important. Private sector enterprises are there to make a profit and enhance shareholder value. But that's not the only reason they exist, and they are affected by the broader economic and social climates in which they operate. No individual, company, or country is an island. I think that there is a growing awareness of the need to look beyond those primary, traditional measures of success because there's a difference between being primary and being exclusive. In fact, we are going to be working with a variety of groups to develop some national performance indicators in the areas like economics, health, the environment, and construct a

dashboard of national indicators that will help people assess overall progress with a portfolio approach. It doesn't exist now.[29]

One might easily translate "affected by broader economic and social climates" as "interdependence." Likewise for the phrase, "No individual, company, or country is an island." Mr. Walker may very possibly have had shareholder interests in mind when he pointed out the "difference between being primary and being exclusive."

ENTER THE CFO: STEP ONE TO A DEMOCRATIC WORKPLACE—EQUALITY

The cultural ambience of competitiveness, upward mobility, and rugged individualism combine to give Americans tremendous advantage in the marketplace. However beneficial these attributes are, they are not necessarily a good foundation for development. Such rush to success leaves little time for integration. As in the growth of any natural system or living entity, developmental steps cannot be rushed, skipped, or foreshortened. If serious wrong turns are made, the time to correct and gain new momentum is proportionate with the length of developmental delay. So, the CFO leading the way to a democratic workplace today may expect hard work along with developmental progress. Development is a natural process and it takes time. Leaders face these actual conditions and consider them informative, not prohibitive. Leadership patience, empathy, and optimism competencies can compensate for the long timelines.

The first step to a democratic workplace is the same as in the original Declaration of Independence: *equality*. Not that the tools of the hierarchy, rank, and chain of command are discarded, rather they are often useful in organizing large human efforts. A morally mature CFO who recognizes inherent equality builds an accountability system to make visible breaches of this fundamental condition. Within most corporations at this time, the CFO does not have a great deal of reinforcement other than the good fortune to have mature peer executives, especially CEOs. Outside the corporation, more mature systems do offer help: legal protections, safety requirements (OSHA), and so on. Some of the most valuable resources for a CFO committed to organizational development are activists working on corporate social responsibility. (See the feature in this chapter: "Corporate Social Responsibility Resources.") Not so long ago, corporations heaped scorn (and worse) on environmental activists; today, most publicly visible companies try their best to have an environment-friendly image.

The relatively mature systems of the democratic government may be doing their best to prevent the child-king from running roughshod over the populace. But as you know, development cannot be legislated, mandated, or forced. Judicial punishment is a stopgap, but it is a terribly immature method for the long term.

The accountability systems devised and revised by the Financial Accounting Standards Board (FASB), Financial Executives International (FEI), American Institute of Certified Public Accountants (AICPA), and other professional associations cannot fix this developmental dilemma because they are devout wealth extraction practitioners handicapped by their business and financial educations.

Boards of directors, however worthy the individuals among them may be, are a long shot for developmental work that is truly transformative. If, somehow, boards could recognize the inequities between work and wealth, maybe they could pave the way for inclusion and participation of the workforce in the governance circle. Perhaps, but such a shift would require expanding the base of constituents for whom they work. Meanwhile, the child-king corporation views the bulk of the human community in two ways: as a commodity used to produce someone else's wealth, and as a consumer of what other workers produce. A snake eating its own tail couldn't be in a worse position.

Change from within guided by the pivotal CEO-CFO leadership team is the best way to begin the journey to a democratic workplace. Alongside the CEO, the advisor-CFO walks in two worlds and interprets the intersections of financial paradigms with the actual work of the company. He/she is an expert in the terrain and lexicon of shareholder wealth maximization and board governance, and uses this expertise to make timely and cogent points about inherent inequalities in the sources of wealth and its distribution. The CFO does so by working beyond expertise in financial and governance abstractions and making visible the sources and flow of wealth—always advocating that more people enter the governance and wealth distribution circles. Specifically, although the CFO uses financial information as a convenient and familiar point of departure, he/she rapidly disassembles the conceptual to lay open the workings of value creation and productivity, showing direct gains generated by actual work. On this foundation, the CFO advocates for inclusion of those doing the work in wealth distribution, while cautioning against wealth exclusivity for anyone.

In the beginning, whether or not the wealth distribution actually changes does not matter. The seed of seeing has been planted. For the first time, the CFO's role is concrete as he/she works toward heterarchical goals that include people and their work seen for the first time as part of the governance plurality where authority is based on knowledge and functionality. The CFO works with the only points where transformation is possible: speaking to individual minds to inform and correct their perspectives, shaping organization form to adhere to natural system requirements, and sometimes—sometimes—impacting ambient conditions like the belief in shareholder primacy. This approach requires ethical resonance. At this level of leadership, the need for ethics committees, ethics handbooks, and corporate responsibility officers drops away, and ethics becomes a way of doing business.

CORPORATE SOCIAL RESPONSIBILITY RESOURCES

From a world once dominated by monarchy and aristocracy, civilization in the twentieth century crossed a great divide into a world of democracy. But we have democratized only government—not economics. . . . [O]ur corporate worldview remains rooted in the predemocractic age, and . . . [in] wealth privilege, which is the hallmark of aristocracy. Wealth privilege means serving the wealthy few and disregarding the many.[30]

Marjorie Kelly

Though the perspective of the epigraph may grate and annoy, its sentiment is one that organizations, especially large corporations, ignore at their own peril. Voices like Marjorie Kelly's are not going away, and as Kelly herself points out, a tiny group can generate huge transformations: "The very idea of monarchy once seemed eternal and divine, until a tiny band of revolutionaries in America dared to stand up and speak of equality. They created an unlikely and visionary new form of government, which today has spread around the world. And the power of kings can now be measured in a thimble."[31] What Kelly and others are saying, in essence, is that corporations as a social and economic form garnered their immense power prematurely before they developed sufficient moral and psychosocial maturity. In the process, business in general switched its top priority from public good to the profit imperative: maximize shareholder wealth.

Thirty years ago activist voices could sometimes rightly be chalked up to unethical radicals. Today, as starkly exhibited in the Seattle demonstrations, concern about corporate social responsibility slices across social and economic boundaries. Some of the most ardent activists, such as David Korten, a Stanford University Ph.D. in business, come from long experience within the established economic structure.[32] The message of such spokespersons sweeps from the reasoned to the radical. Kelly and Korten exemplify the reasoned but divergent proposals for corporate reform. Kelly looks for reform while retaining much of the corporate structure. The more strident, like Korten, call for nothing less than the dismemberment of the corporate form of economic and social life. Some activists work to reform from within capitalism; others have lost hope of improvement within existing structures.

Emerging Conditions

The present and emerging set of conditions portrayed by activists does not lend itself to any exclusive viewpoint, simply because no single perspective is universal enough to conscientiously encompass the needs of the many diverse populations touched by business activities. The root of this disconnect is not a clash of one idea against another, but rather a cumulative network of shocked encounters between *people with differing levels of maturity*. The very diversity of perspectives surrounding corporate social responsibility argues for a developmental vantage point, which goes for procorporate, anticorporate, and pro/anti–corporate opinion holders. For instance, a proponent of obliterating corporations may act from a planetary conscientiousness but find moral solutions in the punishment/obedience stage. Conversely, an executive may privately speak the language of a universalist point of view, but because she has not acted in accord with the values of that stage in her work life, her so-called universalist posture remains just that—a posture. The interactions of the various developmental subsystems can be tricky to decipher, but one thing is certain: talk is cheap.

When consumer advocate, Ralph Nader, starts looking down his nose at the behavior of an industry, agency, or profession, stand by. In March 2003, he formed the Association for Integrity in Accounting (AIA). This new public-interest group intends to scrutinize the SEC and the accounting oversight group that Congress created in 2002. The AIA will also watchdog targeted accounting issues such as stock options. Nader's words should be melodious to the ears of every ethical CFO: "[The AIA will] . . . encourage more fearless publication of what's on the minds of accountants around the country." And, "Inside a corporation, people are subjected to a lot of pressures. It's very important for them to feel they have people outside supporting their decisions."[33]

Like it or not, voices in the circle of Kelly, Korten, and Nader herald a significant portion of the next developmental growth in corporations: integrating and retaining the valuable lessons and methods of the hierarchy while transitioning to heterarchy with its environmental conscientiousness. Any executive who discounts the intention, intelligence, perseverance, and evolving systematization of these reform movements falls short of carrying out at least half of the most basic scan of contingent environmental conditions, commonly known as a SWOT analysis—strengths, weaknesses, opportunities, and threats.

Motives for Attention

Executive leaders have multiple motives to pay attention to the formation of corporate responsibility expectations: first, because it is in the interest of their own survival not only from activists' slings and arrows, but from companies' own disregard and spoilage of irreplaceable natural resources. A more subtle cause for attention hinges on the fact that what activists have to say can be tremendously helpful in charting a more rapid and effective development path to organizational maturity, the core objective of the *CFO Survival Guide*. Corporate executives, who have the courage and wisdom to lead proactive explorations into this escalating relationship between business and activists of many stripes (including shareholder activists), are quickly compelled to take developmental stock of themselves and their organization form. They should be aware that the majority of serious, scientific developmentalists, like Ken Wilber, diagnose corporate work life at too low a maturity level to handle the immense power they possess. Imagine a mere toddler mind inside the strength of an adult sumo wrestler body.

Because of media exposure and environmentalist enterprise, unlikely as it may seem, multinationals are proving to be fertile developmental ground. Whether the result of pressure or honest intention, large companies are going out of their way to at least *appear* environment- and people-friendly. Right now, if one digs beneath the surface of this "appearance," one is likely to unearth environmental responsibility (but often only when it serves the financial interests of the firm), and people-friendly policies (as long as staff terminations are not necessitated by economic conditions, or a merger). Regardless of the depth of intention, more mature behaviors are emerging, and there is as at least as much chance that they will blossom as perish.

Alcoholics Anonymous has a maxim: "Act as if until it's real." Applied here, the maxim holds that even if multinational decision makers are "acting as if," this staged posture has its effect in time. A quirk of human psychology makes it necessary (for most people) to justify the line between their words and their actions. Ergo, if an executive who does not give a spotted owl's derriere about holistic issues must *act as if* there is nothing more important than environmental preservation, sooner or later one of two things will happen. In the first scenario, the posturing executive remains true to actual earth-*un*friendly attitudes that inevitably lead to at least one slipup revealing hypocritical speech and/or behavior that someone hears and brings to light. (Incidentally, this sample executive probably doesn't believe in interdependence or connectivity.) In the second version, the thespian executive masters slips of the tongue and makes great effort to be seen behaving in earth-friendly, humane ways. Knowing what you now know about development, how long do you think a person can act so sincerely without the act becoming real? From a more optimistic, and just as likely view, some executives (maybe many) hold holistic values and sincerely act on them. This may be especially true of people who came of age in the 1960s many of whom now live at influential levels within organizations, and only now are coming into the fullness of their organizational power.

Shareholder Activists

The ranks of corporate social responsibility activists include some exceptionally powerful and knowledgeable people who have founded companies. John Bogle, Vanguard, advocates that mutual funds become active shareholders. Robert A. G. Monks founded an entire institution devoted to shareholder activism: Institutional Shareholder Services with 300 employees and 750 institutional clients. Monks and Nell Minow[34] created their own investment fund, the Lens fund, founded in 1991, to prove that socially responsible investing can pay. It did and it has. Public-sector institutional investors like Calpers (California Public Employees Retirement System) use their invested influence to persuade corporations to "consider" social responsibility. Corporate activism in short is big business that believes shareholders should attend to the health and longevity of the companies they own, and that *then* they have a right to expect a reasonable return on their money.

WORK IN PROCESS—STEPS TWO AND THREE TOWARD A DEMOCRATIC WORKPLACE

Steps to the Democratic Workplace	*Enabling Role of the CFO*
2. Acknowledge just cause	Identify and arbitrate ethical issues
3. Practice equal justice before the law	Facilitate counsel of equals

The evolution in the workplace is already in process, albeit as unfinished goods. For all the maturity of law and order, the values of the hierarchy make exposure of "just cause" and "equality before the law" problematic. In contrast, the heterarchy encourages the innate human predisposition to make a just cause visible, and to seek justice. Similarly, people often appear to enjoy working together and attain great satisfaction from group accomplishments, and the social celebrations that coincide with success. When working together, people often form a temporary community wherein reciprocal help and support are the norm—in short, a work community.

Justice, Hope, and Productivity

> **Just Cause:** The patience and hope of people that look for an equitable distribution of wealth based on the productivity of their work has been exhausted by unequal treatment before the law wherein wealthy persons who have not participated in the productive work claim and are granted the right to extract wealth from workplaces, and wherein corporate representatives claim and are granted the rights of persons that may detract from what is wholesome and necessary for the public good.

People work in hope of reward even if that reward is just putting food on the table and a humble roof overhead. Everywhere one cares to look people are working hard at work, trying to figure out how to work faster, more productively, more profitably, more efficiently, more humanely, with more ease. Change management and leadership models are so ubiquitous that the very mention of any activity in these categories is enough to make some people wince.

Leadership has been a real hot button lately. In 2000, companies spent almost $50 billion on leadership-related education, consultants and coaches, and assessments.[35] The customer gets no end of attention in methods from Total Quality to Customer Relationship Management. Processes, too, have ownership, core competence, and statistical models, to name a few. Suppliers have value chains and interorganizational cost management. Shareholders are, of course, on the supreme pedestal with most of the customer, process, and supplier efforts focused on profitability results and subsequent shareholder wealth. In the last ten to fifteen years, a new set of methods under the value management umbrella have come to the fore. Scorecards in various shades and colors try to bring it all together with a unifying focus from value propositions to strategy to process. A sustainable corporate governance system remedies this situation.

But where do people and the work they do fit into these models? What equivalents do working people have compared to all the emphasis on the inanimate aspects of doing business? Consider the current conditions. Empowerment has been around for some time. Then there are self-managing work teams and quality circles. Most organizations do have a human resources department to oversee wage and hour laws, compensation and benefits, job descriptions, and when economics allow, training and education. While some of these methods offer valid contributions, with the possible exception of self-managing teams, none address the dynamics of human beings of various developmental levels interdependently working together. Everywhere one cares to look, people are missing or barely visible in strategic, process, and cost models.

All the conceptual models without people underscore the reasons for inequitable wealth distribution based on work contribution and productivity. Workers are virtually invisible when it comes to participation in resource allocation decisions and governance. That brings us right up against the need for a sustainable corporate governance system that practices wealth distribution (ownership of work) on the basis of *people who do the work, defined as those who productively contribute to the physical or intellectual creation of marketable goods and services.* This system is not only more reasonable in the long-term, it is the only long-term solution, because the current system, by any definition, is not sustainable.

Identify and Arbitrate

For the CFO who chooses to work for a sustainable system of corporate governance, the work is to (1) dismantle the current shareholder primacy system (2) while retaining the fundamental goodness of people and the work they do, and (3) as opportunities arise, shape a democratic workplace. In this early phase, the CFO has two specific roles. The first responsibility is to identify and arbitrate ethical issues, especially as they pertain to invasion of employee privacy, loss of constitutional rights while working, and inequitable wealth distribution. The value parameters underpinning identification of ethical issues relate directly to justice in the workplace. These parameters are discussed in a subsequent section, *Conditions for Justice.*

Facilitate Counsel of Peers

Second, the CFO oversees and facilitates the processes for addressing ethical issues by *practicing equal justice before the law.* Specifically, this step entails assuring clear and just corporate policies that are widely and regularly disseminated and personally explained (i.e., communication). The step also includes guaranteeing due process as in any democratic system of justice. Perhaps most importantly, this step means being judged by a counsel of one's peers. In practice this "counsel" would be a random rotating assembly instructed in due process and appropriate parameters, and facilitated—not judged—by the CFO arbitrator. Any person of any station employed by the company may come to the counsel at any time to request guidance, to expose a grievance, and to air suggestions for improvement. Executives should be on the lookout for opportunities to send people to the counsel with good ideas to give them a wider hearing, even if the executive intends to use the suggestion as well.

Obviously, this part of a sustainable governance system depends heavily on integrity and trustworthiness, as well as on information quality, accessibility, timeliness, and visibility. The CFO in this setting continually strives to create information and interpretation that make functional and external interdependencies visible. This information is critical to the counsel of peers so they can guide, recommend, sanction, or implement improvements with the most complete information possible.

When it comes to development in the corporate form, the good news for the second and third steps to a more democratic workplace is the considerable support for and information about socially and environmentally responsible corporate behavior. A little-known secret about multinational companies with their tremendous resources and influence is that, like it or not, they are developing too. Once multinational executives comprehend that the power of their companies is interdependent with everyone and everything else, they just may take on the energy and profile of a religious conversion. It is possible. Marjorie Kelly notes that German companies have started to practice "codetermination" manifested as employee board seats.[36] Signs closer to home include the development of employee ownership in its many forms, as well as "going private"—management and sometimes employees so tired of short-term thinking and investor primacy that they take themselves out of the investor market. Speaking of markets, another bright spot is the emergence of socially aware employee retirement and pension funds, and the legal voice they potentially have in corporate governance. So far, most of these are in the public sector; corporate funds are behind in this regard.

Conditions for Justice

> In a society that almost demands life at double time, speed and addictions numb us to our own experience . . . it is almost impossible to settle into our bodies or stay connected with our hearts, let alone connect with one another or the earth where we live. Instead, we find ourselves increasingly isolated and lonely, cut off from one another and the natural web of life. One person in a car, big houses, cellular phones, Walkman radios clamped to our ears, and a deep loneliness and sense of inner poverty. That is the most pervasive sorrow in our modern society.[37]
>
> Jack Kornfield

Although much can be done internally, the CFO and peer executives should use organizational awareness and environmental scanning competencies to inform themselves. Ignorance can be costly. Rather than describe current corporate conditions, a description of conditions necessary for the livelihood of a democratic workplace provides marks to shoot for, circumstances to encourage or not, and more rapid shaping of organizational form—as rapid as developmental shaping can be. Importantly, a company can immediately begin conscious, internal practice of all five conditions for workplace justice. No external conditions prevent it. Also, the five conditions for justice in the democratic workplace can serve as a value system for the CFO's arbitration and counsel of peers' responsibilities (see Exhibit 6.2).

Condition 1: Acknowledgment. A person can't be respected if he/she is nameless, faceless, or worthless. The antidotes to these states in a practical sense become relationship practices, especially for managers and executives. First, know as many coworker names as possible and use them liberally. Second, regularly eschew email and voicemail in favor of face-to-face discussion, or at least voice-to-voice. Ignore rank and hierarchical position; if the CEO wants to know why the cost of waste is up, don't ask the CFO; ask the shop supervisors. Third, people should be compensated based on their worth. This third aspect can be implemented alongside wealth distribution changes. Another way to acknowledge people's worth is to bring them into the business discussion. Look for opportunities for junior staff to accompany, observe, and eventually participate in management-level meetings, especially staff members who have prepared work for an executive to present. Partnering with the staff member in delivering the presentation gives credit where it is due, shows "developing others" in action, and contributes to building AFF back-up. When the portion of the meeting that concerns the junior person is over, excuse them to go back to work. Inclusion and participation do not necessarily mean full, all-the-time, in-everything.

Condition 2: Respect. Democratic justice flows from the assumption of inherent equality; it manifests as consistent respect. Neither respect nor equality are strong points of most current corporate cultures. Such attitudes usually must first be called to awareness. Years ago, Motorola developed a concept called "integrity entitlement." The purpose of the initiative was to cultivate respect in the workplace. Re-

EXHIBIT 6.2   FIVE CONDITIONS FOR JUSTICE IN A DEMOCRATIC WORKPLACE

1. Acknowledgment
2. Respect
3. Attention to people and work before numbers
4. Owner/investor distinctions
5. Diverse governance representation

spect has a long history at Motorola. Bob Galvin, modern CEO of the company said, recalling his father's values, "Dad once looked down an assembly line of women employees and thought, 'These are all like my own mom—they have kids, homes to take care of, people who need them.' It motivated him to work hard to give them a better life because he saw his mom in all of them. That's how it all begins—with fundamental respect."[38]

Whether the respectful image is of a parent, a close friend, or an especially good boss, the beginning of the practice of respect begins with awareness of respect for at least one person. Combined with a commitment to inherent equality of all persons, conscious practice extends respect actually felt for a particular person to *each* person encountered.

Condition 3: Attention to people and work before numbers. A conventional monthly or quarterly review is attended by executives and selected managers. The CFO plays a key role because the focus is on "the numbers." Where the CFO runs a conventional accounting shop, one can add the adjective *historical* to "the numbers." The fact that the CFO and the numbers are the traditional center of attention provides a perfect opportunity for the CFO to single-handedly (with CEO agreement) change the format of these meetings. Instead of focusing on manufacturing variances, for instance, quickly show the unfavorable materials usage variance, and then call on a prepared, small group of manufacturing and purchasing representatives to explain the situation and the solution they have already put in place. This is simplistic, but you get the general idea.

Condition 4: Shift from shareholder as owner to workers as owners and employees as investors. Unless shareholders have actually paid money directly to the corporation, they are speculative investors, not owners. Even when purchasing IPO or secondary offering shares, if the investor is not active, he/she remains a speculator. Nothing wrong with this, but sorting out the actual roles of all those interested in the company's success is important. The partnership form of business may also be a viable alternative in smaller companies.

Condition 5: Diverse representation in governance circles. When ownership and investing are understood, governance alterations are easy. Owners have a say in governance. Investors have a right to expect some return, but not the lion's share. The governance counsel is actually a nested series of circles. Peers at the local level hear local concerns. Executive peers hear executive matters and so on. However, when decisions about resources, markets, customers, and the like are addressed, whoever has the knowledge and experience to contribute sits in governance. Steadily, governance comes down from its lofty perch—where it sees little and does less—and becomes widely participative with groups shifting with the focus of attention. Soon, governance becomes an archaic word because it has morphed into management: that thing leaders are supposed to do all along. In parallel, with shareholders balanced with other contributing constituents, the focus between work and financial results naturally equalizes as well. In this way, the actual (versus conceptual) economics of business activities emerges clearly.

The concepts are elegantly simple. At this point, three troubling thoughts usually arise. (1) *Can the company change that much?* (2) *Are people ready for these changes?* (3) *Am I ready for these changes?* As CFO (or a peer executive) you will have time to watch the unfolding process, make corrections, and learn from experience. Because working toward a democratic workplace is directionally correct, barriers to progress prove easier to remove than, say, continuous extraction of wealth from the company for shareholder benefit.

Yes, the company has the *potential* to change that much. Whether it will or not is largely up to you and your fellow executive leaders. But the potential for transformation is already there because the people in the company make it a living entity, and living entities, especially human ones, have innate adaptive abilities and genetic development mandates. Workforce readiness is case by case when it comes to sophisticated mechanical models. Underlying requisite skills sometimes need to be learned first. But when it comes to being ready for a democratic workplace, you can bet that employees are ready for acknowledgment, respect, a just distribution of wealth, and certainly a voice in governance. Those factors are what the original American Experiment was based on. If Americans were ready for that experience, they can certainly handle workplace democratization. The biggest barrier for managers is letting go of the need to control and the hierarchy's training in doing so. Again, control is appropriate in some circumstances but is neither desirable nor possible when dealing with human beings. The next section speaks pointedly about other workforce readiness factors.

WORKFORCE READINESS

A democratic workplace functions under assumptions and conditions inclusive of, but beyond, other organizational forms such as the hierarchy or loose confederation. After the Enron round of scandals, much talk has taken place about "getting back to the business basics." Yet, the definition of the basics is always mushy. What well-intentioned, back-to-basics types are trying to say is, "Get back to work!"

Work is exactly what most people have been doing while a few dallied in financial abstractions. Now that those abstractions have come undone, the people who dallied are looking for a comfort blanket—something tangible and warm. Well, that comfort would be found in the workforce. When work goes well, discussion of it is not puffed up and vaporous; it is concrete, visible, and substantive, whether the work is making physical products or servicing customer and stakeholder relationships. The concreteness of actual work is mesmerizing. Most everyone has experienced it—even if they have a desk job—in gardening, remodeling, or other hands-on activities. While truly working, no time remains for mind games or psychobabble. Being able to make something with your hands is innately satisfying; equally satisfying are customer encounters where the relationship is served well. Building products and serving relationships both generate self-confidence. Work holds our attention because it is always different, especially in relationship work. A house painter adapts to changing weather, types of paint, and shape of house. A customer service worker adapts to the tone of voice on the line, to the nature of the request or complaint, and to the options available for meeting the customer's needs.

Workforces are ready for a democratic workplace: concrete mind-set, practical approach, knowledge of how things work, experience of working with others, definable skills. The very nature of work prepares people for democratic action. In addition to these fitness qualifications, others include the following:

- Workers have a vested interest in company success; it is their livelihood. This contrasts with the unvested interests of absentee shareholders.

- Workers almost always live in the community where they work. They have intimate knowledge of community needs and, again, a personal interest in addressing those needs. Speculators do not have these qualities in general.

- Workers are already citizens of a democracy. Whether or not they exercise their rights, they are graced with the conditions of democratic freedoms.

One wonders if the lack of democratic freedoms and values within corporations may not be a chief source of worker discontent. In functional communities (i.e., towns, cities) hierarchical relationships are less important than knowing the right connections to get work done. Likewise, community resources of all kinds are precious, so because resource use directly benefits community members, time and materials are used carefully. Corporate leaders are often active community members. They would do well to study community functions and transfer best practices and lessons learned to the workplace. Corporate resources, too, are precious; therefore, leaders must make sure that just the right people are working together on just the right things. Simple as the concept is, this path leads to reduction in waste resources and elimination of waste before it starts.

CFO, GATEKEEPER OF THE PUBLIC GOOD: THE FOURTH STEP TO A DEMOCRATIC WORKPLACE

Steps to the Democratic Workplace	*Enabling Role of the CFO*
4. Adhere to primacy of the public good	Gatekeeper of corporate action

Primacy of Public Good: Based on the circumstances of natural interdependence, individuals voluntarily band together to form socioeconomic work groups to produce goods and services that meet the needs of the community. For the survival and health of everyone, diverse work groups use their abilities according to their capacities to fulfill their responsibility to contribute to the public good without violating or damaging the health of the common environmental systems on which they depend.

The large-scale corporate return to the tradition of acting in the interest of the public good may be some ways down the road. Before one can ask about the public good, however, one must ask what potential good the company can do in the community. Some communities are literally built around and for the company. Hershey, Pennsylvania, retains the community spirit of its founder. Cummins Engine of Columbus, Indiana, is a civic giant, not to mention in the top ten of "best corporate citizens," according to *Business Ethics* magazine's annual ranking. Smaller towns sometimes live and die according to the success of one major employer, like the century-old Marvin Windows and Doors in Warroad, Minnesota, and its neighboring town, Roseau, home of the Polaris snowmobile.

Attention to the public good extends well beyond philanthropic gifts. A corporation that is a good citizen offers not only well-compensated jobs and a stable employment future, but also contributes to public works including scholarships, community centers, libraries, and the like. The good-citizen corporate leaders conscientiously and closely monitor the environmental impact the company has on its local and global communities. It does not poison their water, pollute their air, or defile the native soil. In contrast, a detrimental corporate citizen does commit some or all of these crimes, and further takes from the community in the form of substandard wages, discounted property and income tax rates, and other unreciprocated use of community resources. Reciprocity is not in this citizen's vocabulary.

A company needs public trust and community goodwill to survive in the long term. It also needs the best workers from the community and their continued regard. In towns of all sizes, word travels quickly about employers' attributes, what they pay, and how they treat their employees. Planetary environment concerns reap a great deal of attention, as they should, but in addition to global stewardship, a company has a job to do at home.

CFO as Gatekeeper

In this context, the CFO is corporate gatekeeper and guardian of the company's *reputation* locally and globally. The finance chief is best suited for this role for two obvious reasons. First, the CFO is the chief *accountability* officer and guardian of corporate assets. Worker, community, and state government favor are priceless assets. Once a constituency decides a corporation is a bad citizen, it is usually only a matter of time until the business incurs an expensive relocation. This action could be viewed as a community hostile takeover, not with share bids, but with stock in reputation. A gatekeeper usually lets people into and out of a walled community. In the corporate context, the CFO monitors more heavily what goes out from the corporation to the community. The criteria for what goes out are identical with the characteristics of a good corporate citizen: source of livelihood, healthy working conditions, care for the common environment, and participation in the life of the community. These elements are, in fact, the very purpose of the company's presence in the community.

Service orientation is the second reason that the CFO is suited for the community gatekeeper role. The combination of service orientation and skill with the tools of accountability provides for an effective gatekeeper function. Obvious concerns of the CFO-gatekeeper are company activities that generate pollution and destruction of natural resources. Not so obvious is clarity and communication of corporate purpose in the community and a consistent awareness of their interdependence. For example, is the company a mediocre provider of jobs or an engine for wealth creation throughout the community? Does the corporation funnel the bulk of any profits to distant shareholders, or are significant funds channeled to community aims. A multinational corporation belongs to everyone and no one. Here CFOs must make certain that wherever the company has facilities, good corporate citizenship is practiced. Such CFOs view residence in a community as a condition requiring responsible, involved relationship.

A CFO makes a tremendous contribution to community relations and the public good when he/she develops and advocates accountability statements that quantitatively reflect the depth of the interdependencies between company, workers, and community. Marjorie Kelly suggests Employee and Community Income Statements.[39] Such statements depict the flows of time and funds and their reciprocal impacts. These statements are the essence of transparency and full disclosure. These social responsibility statements need not be complex; in fact, the more accessible they are, the wider audience they will have. Reporting categories include worker time spent on community efforts sponsored by the company, progress updates on any environmental issues, and compensation comparisons to industry and geographic region.

An excellent source of information and ideas on such reporting is the Global Reporting Initiative (GRI), whose members initially focused on environmental concerns but quickly enlarged their perspective to include community service measures and compensation studies. GRI's Web site (www.globalreporting.org) reports that more than one-third of the largest global companies—predominantly European—now issue annual environmental disclosures aligned with GRI standards. The GRI site also reports that the GRI guidelines for areas such as philanthropy, diversity, and compensation are used in whole or in part by companies such as AT&T and GM in the United States, Electrolux in Sweden, and Shell in the United Kingdom.

Conditions Preventing a Return to Serving the Public Good

Make no mistake, the role of good corporate citizen is not easy where shareholder primacy dominates. The singular focus on investors does not make it easy for executives to opt in favor of serving the public good. Fortunately, antidotes are available for each of the symptoms of this malaise. Exhibit 6.3 gives a few examples.

The Ultimate Governance Alliance

Most of the recent discussion surrounding corporate governance centers on serving the shareholder primacy mandate and, therefore, focuses on board and SEC activities. Such thinking falls prey to two traps characteristic of hierarchical thinking: (1) working inside the box of existing structures, and (2) either-or approaches. As previously stated, reconfiguring board governance is a long shot. The SEC does a commendable job in protecting investor interests, but so far has not expanded beyond that. So, including the best of current board and SEC structures, the ultimate corporate governance model is a widened alliance with workers and their

EXHIBIT 6.3   ANTIDOTES FOR SUSTAINABLE CORPORATE CITIZENSHIP

Symptom	Antidote
Shareholder primacy	Equitable wealth distribution
Growth mandate	Balance growth and investment (Pfizer model)
Profit imperative	Balance short-term success with long-term profit (Hewlett Packard, Shell)
Market competition	Strategic alliance and an era of coopetition
Lack of home base	Commitment to multiple local communities, and in the case of multinationals, to multiple nations
New community citizen	Build bonds and relationships
General distrust of corporations	Transparency and integrity to foster trust
Corporations seen as "takers"	Reciprocity by way of philanthropy, job creation, and care of environment

communities. For a firm that operates within conventional structures, three logical phases frame the transformation as leadership and governance maturity extends outside the walls of the company to build relationships, cultivate patterns of connection, and assure a healthy environment. Usually, the company must initiate partnership talks. The three-phase progression is *inclusion, participation,* and finally *integration.* Inclusion begins with a company's invitation to community members to discuss common goals and concerns. Some cities, like Jacksonville, Florida, are eminently prepared for such talks. For example, Jacksonville City government operates by quality-of-life criteria and measures.

From these conversations, specific joint action is identified, and that leads to two-way participation. Community members sit on the company board or special committees; some company meetings are open to the community at large, especially whenever there is even a hint of unacceptable corporate behavior. Likewise, the corporation actively promotes productive involvement with the community through philanthropy, but more importantly, through ongoing connections to community interests. For example, a firm can visibly reward good citizenship in the workforce. The legal profession's pro bono tradition is a good model. The input and cross-pollination of this kind of interaction between diverse constituents in and of itself accelerates corporate maturity. The CFO as gatekeeper of corporate actions raises internal awareness of what passes out of the company and into the community. Importantly, serving the public good and social responsibility are not isolated programs and contributions; they are long-term relationships based on trust. Integration arises naturally as a result of all these associations. So does corporate social responsibility to the public good.

THE REPRESENTATIVE CFO IN THE DEMOCRATIC WORKPLACE—STEP FIVE

Steps to the Democratic Workplace	Enabling Role of the CFO
5. Practice democratic workplace governance	Design/administer democratic processes

> **The Democratic Workplace:** Although individual workers and work groups are the source that produces all wealth in the form of goods and services—and capital—most are not permitted a voice or participation in organizational governance. The corporation is permitted to mandate and govern how people work in "unusual, uncomfortable, and distant places," for the sole purpose of complying with financial measures and maximizing stockholders' wealth.

Consider these terms: industrial revolution, financial capital, scientific management, information age, process improvement, strategic objectives. Compare those terms with this list: trust, leadership, participation, broad constituency, freedom, integrity, community awareness. Just for a moment, get the comparative *feel* of the two lists. Notice the difference. If you are open to this exploration, as a businessperson you may experience something like the following when reading the first set of terms: hard, tangible, businesslike, no-nonsense, actionable, most suitable to a laboratory or military campaign. As a human being, you may react to the second list in the following sequence: (1) too touchy-feely to be practical—that is the business part of you is still skeptical; (2) well, maybe there is something to this—that is your heart responding. At this point, most businesspeople pull back and say, "Ah well, wouldn't it be nice, but not in this world. And anyway, where would I find the time?" And that is that. Work life goes on as usual. What if, instead of backing off, the response was something like, "Yes, that's what we need! Yes, how do we do that? What *if* we did that?"

The first list covers some of the sterling accomplishments of hierarchical governance. The second list depicts work life as it is emerging in the heterarchy. It also characterizes democratic governance, which has proved to be a more mature way to govern human communities over the long term. Democracy should work just as well in the workplace. Truth be known, workplace democracy should be a fairly easy transition given that it has already been done in government. The limiting conditions in the previous section present penetrable barriers that drop away as governance perspectives widen and mature. The dropping away is hardly a swift fall; rather, as in all development, sooner or later—barring any radical assaults such as more wars or revolutionary upheaval—enough learning accrues from trial and error and enough unsatisfactory results teach their lessons that people are bound to become curious about alternatives. This process is very natural.

The Representative CFO

> *What is your greatest source of happiness?. . . What is the contribution you could make to the world that would give you the most satisfaction? . . . What would you have to do in your life today to begin this service, this contribution? Why not begin?*[40]
>
> Jack Kornfield

The process for guiding a workforce into democratic governance form follows the same path as reengaging the public good: inclusion, participation, and integration. Inclusion is already off to a good start as a result of the practice of justice in steps two and three, including the CFO responsibilities to identify and arbitrate ethical issues and to facilitate a counsel of peers. Once people trust that the company is serious about steps one through three and the company has demonstrated community commitment, the foundations are solid for moving into representative—or participative—governance. The CFO, working with the CEO and executive peers, provides the focal point for gathering and representing the interests of various stakeholder groups. In this context, governance means running the business—the actual work of planning and executing intentions. So, the primary stakeholder is logically the workforce itself.

The CFO's leadership and advocacy role for the internal work community is appropriate because the finance role has always been one of monitoring resources and their allocation. That role does not change in a more mature context; it just expands to include the most important embodiment of corporate resources, its workforce. The EI-mature CFO uses the social awareness competencies—organizational awareness, service orientation, and empathy—to gather information about people, work, and resources; to assess their needs in the context of all stakeholder needs; and to design resource distribution to fit overall company intentions. The CFO obviously does not sit alone designing and deciding all this. A major mechanism that enables such bold thinking is the formation of representative/participative governance by and for the workforce. The first task of the CFO, the CEO, and other executives who are ready is the performance of an intense internal environmental scan to assess and configure the governance units, representatives and/or participants, and community principles.

Units of Governance   Governance *of* the people: Now that the corporation values inherent equality, consistently adheres to equality before "the law," and has a very good sense of the ambient community, executives can make an informed decision about the appropriate units of governance. In small companies (up to about one hundred people), this group may be all employees. In medium-size companies with fewer than ten physical locations, the unit level is best, but with communities of work-related interest as the organizing principle. Using management hierarchies as a convenient way to organize is all too easy. Although this step is not bad for the interim, as soon as possible the units represented should be cross-functional, cross-unit, and unbiased to rank or position, all centered around a specifically identified work or job function.

Representation and/or Participation   Governance *by* the people: Whenever possible and practical, create a means to include as many people as possible. In small firms, it is possible to call a company meeting for 100 percent of the workforce. In medium and large companies, Web conferencing makes this feasible (and far less expensive than travel costs) for everyone to at least observe governance. In the example of the ten-location company, the diversity includes direct-contact service staff (people in sales, customer service, human resources), fabrication (people dealing with production from raw material to finished goods), design (process and product engineers), management (unit heads and functional managers), infrastructure service (people from accounting, IT, facilities management), and so on.

Staggered rotation through each of these representative groups allows for ongoing fresh input and more opportunities for total participation. This assembly of sub-groups is responsible for

- Informing leadership during direction setting. Picture leadership presenting a strategic plan draft and looking for feedback.
- Working out interfunctional process and product/service issues. Imagine an oversight group of rotating membership that is continually aware of continuous improvement discoveries across locations—perhaps one of the responsibilities of this subgroup is to work with information technology (IT) to create a knowledge system that actually works!
- Gathering data for decision making. Picture an accountant, an engineer, and a marketing professional all heading up ad hoc groups to "test" product/service ideas. Companies who practice even this small aspect are amazed at the wealth of insight it generates.
- Communicating often and in detail with constituents.

In short, all these functions are what one might expect in a representative democracy. Now imagine the possibilities for participative democracy and informed corporate citizens. Suppose a new product design meeting, a strategic planning session, and a committee exploring compensation and benefit structures all gathered to work on the same day at different physical locations. No big deal, right? But now add the capability for any employee to call up the day's meeting schedule by laptop while traveling, by desktop if an office worker, and at computer kiosks if computers aren't a normal piece of work equipment. (The FedEx in-house communication system, for instance, serves as a good prototype model. The theory that appears to work for FedEx and others is that the more information that people can access, the better and faster they make decisions.) Now, on with the show: Work meetings are posted well ahead of time whenever possible, especially for lengthy improvement projects. Any individual or group of employees can "sit in" on these meetings at any time without announcement to meeting participants, but with appropriate notice to coworkers. Naturally, because this work is real, coworkers expect to hear back about better process practices, the new product in design, and what changes are being considered in compensation and benefits. Imagine what could potentially happen:

- Rapid dissemination of process and service-excellence practices.
- Education on the work of other functions that are upstream or downstream customers or suppliers.
- Demonstration of any number of skills, including new and better accounting systems

- Information on what is in the pipeline from products and services to a new large customer, to economic forecasts, to new FASB rules.

Now that is a knowledge system! Sort of like an in-house education channel, one designed on living system principles such as self-referencing, free flow of information, and transparency. And if you are in a small- to medium-size company and are breathing a sigh of envy, this same model works for a consortium of improvement/development-minded companies. Industry-based and interest-based "communities of interest" emerge anywhere people identify a common cause. Of course, until strategic alliances mean what they imply and until coopetition is a reality, security procedures, passwords, blackouts, and the like are in order. But by the time such use of already-available technology emerges, the business context is likely to align with such openness as well.

Now imagine yourself, as CFO, deliberately pacing and leading the design and implementation of such a system and the cultural values that go with it. Here is another one you can take to the bank: Who knows? Such good governance may even rekindle the embers of a national democracy. Wouldn't that be a corporate coup?

Governance Principles   Governance *for* the people. This third aspect follows the Japanese idea of business purpose: People serving people. At this stage of corporate governance development, shareholder primacy is an embarrassing piece of history. If shareholding is still practiced, this constituency takes its place in equal relationship to all other stakeholders. The climate has now rendered unthinkable the concept of taking corporate action that pollutes, poisons, or just plain deeply annoys the surrounding community. Equally unthinkable is to value financial instruments and targets above the human work community. Importantly, however, the effective command-and-control competencies of the hierarchy form are still practiced when necessary. Some circumstances cannot tolerate democratic debate, and leaders must be capable of quickly identifying these times. Some draft principles for the democratic workplace include the following:

- Always ask who else should know about this, and who else should participate in this.
- Test business intentions and actions with all stakeholder communities.
- Information is free in all the meanings of that word.
- Go to the source of the knowledge wherever that person(s) lives in the company.
- Always link leading nonfinancial process measures with financial results measures, and work on the business in that order.
- Keep debate, discussions, work groups, and meetings focused on actual work; part of leadership's job is to privately develop, mentor, and advise people and groups on self-awareness and self-management competencies.

These points begin to show the possibilities for transformation. Governance is an important set of interlocking dynamics within the triple helix. Governance, too, develops and transforms. Developmental transformations in corporate governance require certain structuring conditions, thus it is critical to identify and work with the structuring conditions that enable transformation.[41]

WEALTH DISTRIBUTION: STEPS SIX AND SEVEN IN THE DEMOCRATIC WORKPLACE

Steps to the Democratic Workplace	*Enabling Role of the CFO*
6. Recognize shared economic rights	Make economic workrights visible
7. Distribute wealth according to work	Design wealth distribution routes; monitor distribution equity

> **Economic rights to wealth**: Every person within these diverse work groups shares an interdependent right to economic resources, and that right is violated when methods of wealth distribution exclude any worker from access to representation in workplace governance.

When financial measures are the only measure of value, life is bound to become abstract and unbalanced. When actual owners and speculative investors are the only ones served, there is bound to be misery in the workplace. The corporate world generally operates under both these assumptions. So, to enter the space of the democratic workplace, these assumptions are the first that have to go. Of course, financial means are still necessary except for people who live off the land and off the power grid. (And you'll still catch a fair number of those sneaking into town for beer and a burger.) If you have stayed with the logic of the democratic workplace so far, it is obvious that the economic rights to wealth are not working as currently practiced. If they were working, conditions would look quite different now.

First, equity investing would resemble both parenting and gambling. Parenting, because well-intentioned investors would risk time and money to raise up a nascent, budding, or blossoming business to its full potential. The risk? Ask any parent. Gambling, because other investors would engage the practice for fun and speculative adventure, with the same range of risk appetite as the crowd at Las Vegas. Investors might receive a bank rate of return for the courtesy of using their money, and investment would begin to look a lot like a loan. The investor is still free to sell the debt instrument to a willing buyer, but for both parties the focus on the long-term income stream from a healthy business would be the criterion of instrument worth. Such investors would be valuable interested parties, but not shareholders. Curiosity begs the question whether equity and debt instruments might not merge into a single, but diverse, opportunity pool with corporate assets and income streams serving as collateral for both.

As for workers, they would be much less panicked about retirement funding because they would have had the opportunity to take home far more in actual wages than their entire retirement account worth; wealth distribution is done on the basis of the value of *goods and services that actual work produces.* In short, wealth distribution would be *work equitable.* Their workplace conditions would be quite comfortable, and the equipment they work with would be first rate, because along with better pay for workers the corporation also reinvests in the business for the longer term. Primary objectives are employee retention, and research and development. Environmental conditions improve steadily as well because of the long-term commitment of leadership to the communities that are their homes. People generally recognize that common community wealth—natural and constructed—belongs to everyone. There are still plenty of opportunities to make money, and even become wealthy, but not without working for it. Appropriate changes in inheritance tax law have been made, and multinational corporations that profit from globalization pay taxes commensurate with their unfavorable impact on people, social conditions, and the environment.

These speculations reflect on conditions as they may look if and when the economic rights to wealth for people in the workplace catch up with other democratic practices. The particulars of the conditions are unpredictable because when wealth is no longer the dominating cultural value, anything could happen. More than half a century ago, FDR put forth "The Four Freedoms." America has done exceptionally well—so far—on the first two freedoms: speech and worship. The last two freedoms are within our grasp if we have the will to work for them.

Freedom from Want; Freedom from Fear

> *To act in the world most effectively, our action cannot come from our small sense of self, our limited identity, our hopes and our fears. Rather we must listen to a greater possibility and cultivate actions connected with our highest intentions . . . There is a deep current of truth that we can hear. When we listen and act in accordance with this truth, no matter what happens, our actions will be right.*[42]
>
> Jack Kornfield

Equitable wealth distribution based on equal governance opportunity and on work contributions is the key to realizing both freedom from want and freedom from fear. So far, some good experiments in better distribution practices have occurred, but as in all development, they have been learning experiences, trial and error. Many other coevolving systems must continue their development paths if we are to improve on recognition of inherent equality as manifest in equal justice before the law, and the public good raised to preeminence. Nobel laureate in economics Amartya Sen[43] urges nations to move away from measures of well-being like income per capita, trade balances, and commodity consumption, and to move with all due speed toward more informative measures that direct resources effectively for the public good. He also strongly recommends changes in property law where wealth is a measured as "functional opportunity." Sen's book, *Development as Freedom,* examines "five instrumental freedoms: (1) political freedoms, (2) economic facilities, (3) social opportunities, (4) transparency guarantees, and (5) protective security."[44] Sen defines poverty as "capability deprivation." Listen to just two of his, and others, research findings that exemplify why Sen is a Nobel laureate.

When nations or districts invest in education (especially for women) and in healthcare, relatively rapid and not-so-surprising changes occur. Birth rates decline and, of course, income per capita goes up (e.g., Indian district of Kerala). In fact, Sen cites an analysis by Murthi, Guio and Dreze concluding that ". . . the *only* [variables] that have a statistically significant effect on fertility are female literacy and female labor force participation."[45]

Long life is not the result of economic well-being. "For example, in the United States, African Americans as a group have no higher—indeed have a lower—chance of reaching advanced ages than do people born in the immensely poorer economies of China . . . Sri Lanka, Jamaica or Costa Rica."[46]

Development as Freedom overflows with thorough research exploding the distributive conventional economic assumptions that underlie both government programs and economic paradigms. The book is required reading for anyone even mildly interested in the democratic workplace. The biggest hurdle to making it into Sen's world is to drop the assumption that wealth is about individuals (e.g., the one hundred richest, income per capita, and so on) and see more accurately that *wealth is communal, and is most effective when used in the interest of the public good.* So, wealth distribution is not a leveling to the mediocre, or to vast class differences such as in the Russian experiment. Wealth distribution is about the longevity and health of all of us. It is about freedom from want, and freedom from fear.

The Paradox of Equal Rights to Wealth

The practice of equal rights to wealth operates in a number of paradoxes. These rights are both process and result; they are the first and last concerns in a democratic society; where these rights are exercised, less is more. Every democratic CFO's responsibility is to make these paradoxes visible.

First and Last Concerns   Although the endpoint objectives of wealth distribution are freedom from want and freedom from fear, the process of wealth distribution is what moves a people to those freedoms, or not. The paradox reveals its workings if one sees equal rights to wealth running parallel to all the other steps starting with the first one, inherent equality. As everyone knows, when the self-evident truth was first penned—"all men are created equal"—equality meant something quite different than it does today. Humanity has made great strides since 1776, but validated models such as the one explicated in *Development as Freedom* give further pause for thought about the meaning of the word. Using Sen's definition of poverty as "capability deprivation," only a short leap is necessary to begin to see the role of resources in equality. Not equality as in just about everybody has nothing, but rather a wise and precise application of resources that improves the whole of the public good. To the point, right alongside of step one—recognition of inherent equality—place equal rights to wealth. Also, in addition to the economic definition of wealth (number two in Sen's model), add Sen's other four "freedoms," which can be interpreted in this context as (using Sen's numbering) the wealth of

1. Political freedoms
2. Freedom to associate—social opportunities
3. Free information—transparency guarantees
4. Freedom from fear—protective security

Together these five forms of wealth, or freedom, generate freedom from want.

Process and Result   Likewise, as the process of shaping the democratic workplace proceeds, equal rights to wealth become a guiding principle, especially when the definition of wealth is expanded as above. For example, the workplace practice of equal justice before the law imparts the wealth of political freedoms. Adherence to the public good yields the wealth and freedom of social opportunities, and representative/participative workplace governance produces the wealth of free information and transparency guarantees. So, at each step along the way, wealth distribution is a direct consideration. At this point, it is fair to say that these forms of wealth coevolve, rather than follow one another in strict sequence.

Less Is More   The determination to transform workplace governance may at first be fueled by economic hopes: "If people are happier, they will be more productive." This type of thinking is ends-means-based, instrumental, and hedonistic. The next stage is a child of the industrial and scientific revolution: "If we just find the right rules and governing laws, we can make everybody more efficient." Not until the territory of moral universalism do interdependency and practice of equality emerge. Then we begin to see the actual—the natural—connections in a living world. No, accounting rules do not equal more profit. Wise application of human and material resources equals profit. When the actual, operating conditions are understood, resources can be precisely applied. The paradox here is that the more one truly sees interdependency and life as it is, the less important profit becomes, and the more the value of humans rises.

One of the main causal factors in corporate governance developmental arrest is the general failure of business methods and customs to integrate scientific principles and disciplines. Clearly, as currently practiced, neither business nor economics are true sciences—although both work hard to look as though they are, at least in academic circles. Economics is largely a theoretical game of mathematical models that, as the old saying goes, never reach a conclusion when laid end-to-end. Current business practices are, for the most part, a blend of mechanical/technical expertise and financially driven behavior patterns, with a token nod to the human dimension. The combination of the science of becoming (development), the research-validated emotional intelligence leadership competencies, and the proven way of democratic governance based on inherent quality can change all that.

SURVIVAL PATTERNS

Steps to the Democratic Workplace	*Enabling Role of the CFO*
Right to abolish	Work with leadership counsel to prevent the need to exercise the right to abolish.

Right to abolish: Whenever any force becomes destructive to these ends, it is the right of the people to alter or abolish it, and to institute a new organization form, shaping the organization on work and governance principles that seem most likely to effect their safety and survival needs in the context of a sustainable global community.

Common sense and discretion should guide the dismantling or transformation of established work structures and governance principles, but familiarity, fear, and apathy should likewise not pose impediments to necessary modifications, reformations, or extirpation. When elite groups engage in a long practice of discriminatory abuses and usurpations and exhibit clear intent to continue to do so, the responsibility of workers and community members is to reject such structures and to provide new configurations to serve the needs of people and planet.

To "abolish" means to "cause not to survive." The *CFO Survival Guide* intends to disclose and foster principles of workplace governance that will stand the test of time—that will survive. The answers that emerge from exploring one question will determine that survival: *Who has rights to the wealth created in the workplace?* The weight is not all on corporate shoulders. Many hands support the work that is to be done: a more mature democratic government, corporate responsibility activists, and executive leaders, but most of all, we the people, with all our hearts, are ready to work for the democratic work community.

Hopefully, the *Guide* has traveled well beyond mere survival for the CFO. If it has met its goal, the book has provided glimpses of an entirely new way of seeing organizations, the people in them, and the work they do. This approach contrasts to running a business strictly by the numbers, by the whims of the market, or by the unscrupulous plans of a few greedy executives.

Survival. Survival is a concern that goes well beyond the office of the chief financial officer. It isn't hard to find people who, when asked about their hopes for the future, say, "To have one." Just listing the possible causes of harm and death could be cause for despair. Put in perspective, however, despair may recede and a certain optimism emerge. Survival is *the* strongest urge running through all life, and the urge is never stronger than when life is threatened. Threats and severe discomfort cause living beings to listen more deeply, pay more attention, see more clearly, and use available resources more wisely. Life is fragile, easily snuffed out, hard to sustain. We know this in our bones.

Wilderness survival experts speak of the essential order of survival activities, in reference to the tasks necessary to maintain life. In priority sequence, the tasks are shelter, water, fire, and food. Some people are forced into survival events. Others seek them out. What is the difference between a recreational skier and an experienced mountain climber, both caught in a sudden snowstorm on the same mountain? The natural conditions of the storm do not distinguish between the two. The distinction comes down to two things: *Intention and preparation.* The skier came to the mountain prepared and expecting to ski and have fun. The mountain climber came for adventure, but prepared and expecting to survive. The leadership parallels are obvious.

A similar sacred order of survival exists in organizational life. The consequences of defying the order are eventually just as catastrophic as carelessness with the laws of nature. To keep the life glowing inside the workplace, shelter, water, fire, and food are also needed; however, they come in specific forms. The organization, itself, is the shelter, the place people come to earn their keep, to feed and shelter themselves and their families. The flow of work and resources is the nourishing water within the organization. No work, and survival is threatened.

With shelter and water (i.e., a place to work, work to do, and resources to do it with), human beings can survive for relatively long periods. But at some developmental point, mere survival is not enough. To thrive, humans need warmth and food. In the organization, the fire comes from warm, sustaining relationships, and meaningful collaborative work for the good of the whole. Naturally, to continue into long life, energy must be replenished. In the organization this energy comes in the form of ever more skillful acquisition and deployment of resources: time, material, space, equipment, coworkers. In any survival scenario, nothing is wasted.

Chief financial officers have the opportunity to be heroes under the current conditions of professional crisis and organizational efforts to survive. Responding to the emergency requires courage, risk taking, and stepping into the unknown, one day, one person at a time. Heroes usually don't set out to be heroes. They just set out to do what they see needs doing. Heroes don't typically have a strategic plan to achieve hero status. More often than not, the ones who count, the ones we eventually call "heroes," were guessing about what to do most of the time. The difference is their willingness to take the risk of guessing.

We have managed to unchain children through child labor laws, to unchain women from a one-option work world, and unchained millions of workers from cruel working conditions through unions and legal means. This time, let us unchain everyone, all together. Annihilation is not good for business. You can not make a deal if you are dead.

NOTES

1. Raymond Mears, *The Outdoor Survival Handbook* (New York: St. Martin's Press, 1992), 9.
2. Benjamin Kilham and Ed Gray, *Among the Bears: Raising Orphan Cubs in the Wild* (New York: A John Macrae Book, Henry Holt and Company, 2002), 88, 90.
3. Arundhati Roy, *The Cost of Living* (New York: Modern Library, 1999), 16.
4. The authors wish to acknowledge the influence of Marjorie Kelly's "Six Principles of Economic Democracy" from her book, *The Divine Right of Capital* (San Francisco: Berrett-Kohler Publishers, 2001), 15. Kelly's work inspired the *Declaration of Interdependence*. Although, the authors agree with Kelly's "principles," developmentally they are not in proper sequence. Development always follows a sequenced learning pattern—e.g., arithmetic then algebra then calculus. Here, understanding the sequence of how rights and responsibilities coevolve into a sustainable system is crucial to the success of any deliberate transformative efforts, because rights flow from responsibilities based on equality before the law. Kelly's original "Six Principles" are presented here:

   Enlightenment: Because all persons are created equal, the economic rights of employees and the community are equal to those of capital owners.

   Equality: Under market principles, wealth does not legitimately belong only to stockholders. Corporate wealth belongs to those who create it, and community wealth belongs to all.

   Public Good: As semipublic governments, public corporations are more than pieces of property or private contracts. They have a responsibility to the public good.

   Democracy: The corporation is a human community, and like the larger community of which it is a part, it is best governed democratically.

   Justice: In keeping with equal treatment of persons before the law, the wealthy may not claim greater rights than others, and corporations may not claim the rights of persons.

   (R)Evolution: As it is the right of the people to alter or abolish government, it is the right of the people to alter or abolish the corporations that now govern the world.

5. No laws prohibit companies from monitoring employee mail and email. Many customer service centers greet the caller with an automated message announcing that the "call may be recorded," usually on the premise of better quality and customer service, but nothing stops

companies from using the recordings for other purposes. Surveillance cameras are common—to catch intruders—but again, nothing prevents other uses of the tapes. Offices, lockers, and any other workspaces may be searched at any time. An American Management Association survey reports nearly 75 percent of large companies engage in some or many kinds of employee surveillance. See Sarah Boehle, "They're Watching You," *Training*, August 2000, 51.

6. Another particularly disturbing practice of privacy invasion occurred in California where a Nabisco plant would not permit female employees to personally decide when they would go to the bathroom. Some women reported they were obliged to wear diapers to work. The women filed suit in 1995; Nabisco settled on "undisclosed terms" in 1996. See "Ending Nabisco's Bathroom Brawl," *Business Week*, April 29, 1996, 50.

7. Quote from the U.S. Declaration of Independence. Examples from the authors' own eyewitness experience include:

- A large consulting firm did not permit a male manager to return home from a distant client site to be with his wife while she delivered their first child. The consultant was told that he would be fired if he disobeyed. He did disobey, and voluntarily left the company soon after.

- A woman in her thirties who worked for a large accounting firm had a car accident and suffered lacerations and a concussion. At the time, she was completing a report on the assignment; it was due the day after the accident. Her employer would not allow her to take vested sick time to recover and demanded she come into the office to finish the report. She did so while suffering pain and nausea.

- A South Chicago manufacturing plant had a welding "shed" at the back of its large facility. Welders worked there year-round under these conditions: open-sided structure (not unusual in welding), a tin roof that leaked in many places and absorbed heat in the summer. The large, heavy pieces they worked on were laid across multiple two-by-four boards strapped together about ten inches from the gravel floor of the "shed." The workers therefore had to kneel in ice and in deep puddles and bend 90 degrees or more in precise and steady positions to produce the welds.

8. Adolf Berle and Gardiner Means, *The Modern Corporation and Private Property* (London: Transaction Publishers, 1991), xxxviii, li.

9. H. Thomas Johnson and Anders Bröms, *Profit Beyond Measure: Extraordinary Results through Attention to People* (New York: The Free Press, 2000).

10. John Micklethwait and Adrian Wooldridge, *The Company: A Brief History of a Revolutionary Idea* (New York: Modern Library, 2003).

11. See n. 4, this chapter.

12. Ralph W. Estes, *The Tyranny of the Bottom Line: Why Corporations Make Good People Do Bad Things* (San Francisco: Berrett-Kohler Publishers, 1996).

13. See n. 3, this chapter.

14. Alex Berenson, *The Number: How the Drive for Quarterly Earnings Corrupted Wall Street and Corporate America* (New York: Random House, 2003).

15. Nandu Nayar and G. Lee Willinger, "Good for Business?" *Wall Street Journal*, March 26, 2002, 1. The study covered the years 1978–1991, with data from approximately 370 companies. The authors of the study are affiliated with Lehigh University and University of Oklahoma, respectively.

16. Julia Homer and Lori Calabro, "You Are the Guardians," *CFO Magazine*, May 2003, 66.

17. Ibid., 68. The article reports that Arthur Levitt, in a speech at a "CFO Rising" Conference, cited research by Deloitte & Touche/*Business Week* that found approximately ". . . one-third

of CFOs in the research did not believe that the Sarbanes-Oxley Act would make another Enron 'less likely.'

18. Carol Hymowitz, "Managers Must Work to Counter Growing Distrust from Employees," *Wall Street Journal,* February 19, 2002. The same column says that GE's employee stock ownership plan comprises "more than 70% of such assets in its own stock," and that Mr. Immelt opposes legislative caps on 401(k)-type assets. GE was also one of the first public companies to announce it would expense stock options before a legal decision was made on this controversial practice.

19. Sarah Boehle, "They're Watching You," page 50.

20. Kelly, "The Divine Right of Capital," 87.

21. Ibid., 201.

22. Lawrence Mishel, Jared Bernstein, and John Schmitt, *The State of Working America: 1996–97* (Washington, D.C.: Economic Policy Institute, 1996), 147–48.

23. Lawrence Mishel, Jared Bernstein, and John Schmitt, *The State of Working America: 1998–99* (Washington, D.C.: Economic Policy Institute, 1998), 126.

24. Stephen Roach, "The Hollow Ring of the Productivity Revival," *Harvard Business Review,* November 1996, 86.

25. James Lardner and James T. Bond, "World-Class Workaholics," *U.S. News & World Report,* December 20, 1999, 42.

26. Richard Waters, "10,001: A Stock Odyssey," *Financial Times* (London), March 17, 1999, 12.

27. Jeffry L. Seglin, "The Myopia of Bad Behavior," *MIT Sloan Management Review,* Spring 2003, 96.

28. Julia Homer and Lori Calabro, "You Are the Guardians," 66.

29. Catherine Stenzel and Joe Stenzel, "A Conversation with David M. Walker, Comptroller General of the United States", in dialogue with the authors. *Journal of Cost Management* 17, No. 1 (Jan.-Feb. 2003) 19.

30. Kelly, "The Divine Right of Capital," xi.

31. Ibid., xiii.

32. David Korton, *When Corporations Rule the World* (San Francisco: Berrett-Koehler Publishing, 2001).

33. David Campbell, "Newswatch: Ralph Rides Again," *CFO,* May 2003, 23.

34. Writings of Monks and Minow on corporate power and accountability can be downloaded free from www.ragm.com (Monks) or www.thecorporatelibrary.com (Minow). Such authors may well be among the most important "recommended reading."

35. R. M. Fulmer and M. Goldsmith. *The Leadership Investment: How the World's Best Organizations Gain Strategic Advantage through Leadership Development* (New York: AMACOM, 2000).

36. Kelly, "The Divine Right of Capital," 91–92.

37. Jack Kornfield, *A Path with Heart* (New York: Bantam Books, 1993), 24.

38. Gay Hendricks and Kate Ludeman, *The Corporate Mystic* (New York: Bantam Books, 1996), xix.

39. Kelly, "The Divine Right of Capital," 95–106.

40. Kornfield, *A Path with Heart,* 202.

41. Structuring conditions set the boundaries of what is developmentally perceived as certain, likely, probable, possible, difficult, unlikely, impossible. Given that many nations have followed the American transition to democratic governance, we know that democracy is neither impossible nor unlikely. These seven stages of perceived confidence provide a condensed map to the terrain of all development, including the development of the democratic workplace. The sequence begins with an awareness that there is an alternative. Once the alternative becomes conscious, it typically runs headlong into *impossible*, where many times the innova-

tion is stopped in its tracks and languishes or dies. That's where the second structuring condition plays its part.

Consciously engage curiosity and imagination. All development begins in the mind and is fueled by curiosity: what if, what's that, who am I, how can I/we, and so on. Lucidity enables productive curiosity. Human attention does not rest, but it takes many forms: daydreaming, focus on physical or emotional pain, environmental scanning, and so on. Practicing lucidity means training attention—a higher-brain, neocortex function. Once one becomes aware of a perception, nuance, difference, or any other draws on awareness, discipline attention to follow the thread, learn what it is about, what it has to say. This is the natural pattern of inventors and explorers who have these functions in abundance.

Reflection is the third structuring condition for developmental transformation—reflection on self and other—in this context, my role as CFO, within the corporate community that is within the larger local and global communities. To narrow it down, attend to this discussion of the democratic workplace and explore its attractions, barriers to it (self and other), and so on. The EI-intelligent CFO should be well equipped for this work.

The rest of the sequence is *openness, receptivity, responsiveness, adaptation,* and *agility.* Living consciously like this is an integrated experience that takes practice, but greatly amplifies and enables the EI competencies. Naturally, as with developmental subsystems, these structural conditions operate and evolve simultaneously and iteratively. Although some people consciously practice such competencies, much determination is needed to do so in the midst of current business conditions. One can still make attempts as the opportunity arises, or more actively cultivate these practices if they are already familiar. Next, steps six and seven on the journey to the democratic workplace actually run parallel throughout all steps. New perceptions of wealth are the beginning and the result of working in the democratic structure.

42. Kornfield, *A Path with Heart,* 300.
43. Amartya Sen, *Development as Freedom* (New York: Alfred A. Knopf, 1999).
44. Ibid., 10.
45. Ibid., 198.
46. Ibid., 21.

Index